Sport Management: Principles and applications

Now available in a fully revised and updated third edition, *Sport Management: Principles and applications* examines the nature of the sport industry and the role of the state, nonprofit and professional sectors in sport. It also focuses on core management principles and their application in a sporting context, highlighting the unique challenges faced in a career in sport management.

Written in a highly accessible style, each chapter has a coherent structure designed to make key information and concepts simple to find and to utilize. Chapters contain a conceptual overview, references, further reading, relevant websites, study questions and up-to-date case studies from around the world to show how the theory works in the professional world. Topics covered include:

- strategic planning
- organizational culture
- organizational structures
- human resource management
- leadership
- governance
- financial management
- marketing
- performance management.

This book provides a comprehensive introduction to the practical application of management principles within sport organizations. It is ideal for first and second year students studying sport management related courses, as well as those studying business focused and human movement/physical education courses who are seeking an overview of sport management principles.

Russell Hoye is Professor of Sport Management and Director, Centre for Sport and Social Impact at La Trobe University, Australia. His most recent books include *Participation in Sport* (2011), *Sport and Policy: Issues and Analysis* (2010), *Sport and Social Capital* (2008) and *Sport Governance* (2007).

Aaron C.T. Smith is Professor and Deputy Pro-Vice Chancellor at Royal Melbourne Institute of Technology (RMIT) University. His research interests include psychological, organizational and policy change management in business, and sport and health.

Matthew Nicholson is an Associate Professor in the Centre for Sport and Social Impact at La Trobe University, Australia. His research interests focus on sport policy and development, the contribution of sport to social capital and the relationship between sport and the media.

Bob Stewart is Associate Professor in Sport Studies in the School of Sport and Exercise Science at Victoria University, Melbourne, Australia. Bob teaches and researches in the fields of professional team sport regulation, drug-use cultures in sport and body project practices in gyms and fitness centres.

Hans Westerbeek is Professor of Sport Business and Director of the Institute of Sport, Exercise and Active Living (ISEAL) at Victoria University in Melbourne, Australia. He also holds an appointment as Professor of Sport Management at the Free University of Brussels. His main research interests relate to international sport business.

"The third edition of *Sport Management: Principles and applications* is a welcome edition with its exciting new cases studies and contemporary updates. The authors' have produced a textbook which will engage both students and teachers – they provide a straightforward and powerful overview of sport management theory and sport industry analysis and great examples that illustrate the breadth of sport management from its global manifestations through to the local grass roots contexts."

Professor Tracy Taylor, Deputy Dean of the UTS Business School,
University of Technology, Australia

"An excellent critical introduction to sport management. It maps out the environmental context of sport management and the application of management principles in a structured and accessible fashion, striking an excellent balance between theory and practice with key case study materials. The book has quickly and deservedly established itself as a core text for sport management programmes."

Professor Ian Henry, Director of the Centre for Olympic Studies and Research,
Loughborough University, UK

Sport Management

Principles and applications

Third edition

Russell Hoye
Aaron C.T. Smith
Matthew Nicholson
Bob Stewart
Hans Westerbeek

Routledge
Taylor & Francis Group

LONDON AND NEW YORK

First published 2005 by Butterworth-Heinenmann, an imprint of Elsevier

This edition published 2012
by Routledge
2 Park Square, Milton Park, Abingdon, Oxon OX14 4RN

Simultaneously published in the USA and Canada
by Routledge
711 Third Avenue, New York, NY 10017

Routledge is an imprint of the Taylor & Francis Group, an informa business

British Library Cataloguing in Publication Data
A catalogue record for this book is available from the British Library

Library of Congress Cataloging in Publication Data
Sport management : principles and applications / Russell Hoye... [et al.]. -- 3rd ed.
p. cm.
1. Sports administration. I. Hoye, Russell, 1966-
GV713.S6775 2012
796.06'9--dc23
2011038598

ISBN: 978-0-415-50070-8 (hbk)
ISBN: 978-1-85617-819-8 (pbk)
ISBN: 978-0-08-096432-4 (ebk)

Typeset in Sabon
by Saxon Graphics Ltd, Derby

Printed in Great Britain by Ashford Colour Press Ltd.

Contents

Contents

Contents

List of figures

List of tables

List of In Practice examples

In practice examples

List of case studies

Preface

This third edition of *Sport Management: Principles and Applications* continues to fill the gap for an introductory text in sport management that provides an appropriate balance between management theory and contextual analysis of the sport industry. The success of the first and second editions, as illustrated by its adoption in many educational institutions across Australia, Canada, New Zealand, the United Kingdom and Europe, shows that we have the balance right. Our intention with this edition remains unchanged; that is, we are not seeking to replace the many very good introductory texts on management theory, nor to ignore the increasing volume of books that examine the international sport industry. Our aim remains to provide a textbook that includes sufficient conceptual detail for students to grasp the essentials of management, while highlighting the unique aspects of sport management across the globe.

The book provides a comprehensive introduction to the principles of management and their practical application to sport organizations operating at the community, State/provincial, national and professional levels. The book is primarily written for first and second year university students studying sport management courses and students who wish to research the commercial dimensions of sport. It is especially suitable for students studying sport management within business-focused courses, as well as students seeking an overview of sport management principles within human movement, sport science or physical education courses.

As with the first two editions, the book is divided into two parts. Part one provides a concise analysis of the evolution of sport, the unique features of sport and sport management, the current drivers of change in the sport industry and the role of the state, nonprofit and professional sectors of sport. Part two covers core management principles and their application in sport, highlighting the unique features of how sport is managed compared to other industrial sectors with chapters on strategic management, organizational structure, human resource management, leadership, organizational culture, financial management, marketing, governance and performance management.

To assist lecturers and instructors, all chapters include an overview, a set of objectives, a summary of core principles, a set of review questions, suggestions for further reading, and a list of relevant websites for further information. In addition, Chapters 2 through to 13 each contain three substantial examples we have dubbed 'In Practice' that help illustrate concepts and accepted practice at the community, State/provincial, national and international levels of sport. The majority of these have been completely rewritten with new examples, and the remainder extensively revised with up-to-date information.

We have also written 12 entirely new case studies, one for each chapter, which can be used by lecturers and instructors for classroom discussion or assessment. For those academics who prescribe the book as essential reading for students, a comprehensive website is available that contains:

- an updated set of PowerPoint slides that summarize each chapter;
- teaching notes to accompany each of the new case studies to guide instructors in their use for in class activities or assessment tasks;
- updated tutorial activities to accompany each chapter; and a
- testbank of questions for use in online learning environments.

(See www.routledge.com/cw/hoye)

Hans Westerbeek would like to acknowledge the great support he received from Jonathan Robertson in updating the chapter on leadership. Finally we would like to thank our colleagues and students for their valuable comments on the first two editions of the book. As always we acknowledge and thank our respective partners and families for understanding our need to devote our time and energy toward this third edition.

Russell Hoye
Aaron Smith
Matthew Nicholson
Bob Stewart
Hans Westerbeek

The sport management environment

In this part:

1. Sport management
2. The role of the State in sport development
3. Nonprofit sport
4. Professional sport

Chapter 1

Sport management

Overview

This chapter reviews the development of sport into a major sector of economic and social activity and outlines the importance of sport management as a field of study. It discusses the unique nature of sport and the drivers of change that affect how sport is produced and consumed. A three-sector model of public, nonprofit and professional sport is presented, along with a brief description of the salient aspects of the management context for sport organizations. The chapter serves as an introduction to the remaining sections of the book, highlighting the importance of each of the topics.

After completing this chapter the reader should be able to:

- describe the unique features of sport;
- understand the environment in which sport organizations operate;
- describe the three sectors of the sport industry; and
- explain how sport management is different from other fields of management study.

What is sport management?

Sport employs many millions of people around the globe, is played or watched by the majority of the world's population and, at the elite or professional level, has moved from being an amateur pastime to a significant industry. The growth and professionalization of sport has driven changes in the consumption, production and management of sporting events and organizations at all levels of sport.

Managing sport organizations at the start of the twenty-first century involves the application of techniques and strategies evident in the majority of modern business, government and nonprofit organizations. Sport managers engage in strategic planning, manage large numbers of human resources, deal with broadcasting contracts worth billions of dollars, manage the welfare of elite athletes who sometimes earn 100 times the average working wage, and work within highly integrated global networks of international sport federations, national sport organizations, government agencies, media corporations, sponsors and community organizations.

Students of sport management therefore need to develop an understanding of the special features of sport and its allied industries, the environment in which sport organizations operate and the types of sport organizations that operate in the public, nonprofit and professional sectors of the sport industry. The remainder of the chapter is devoted to a discussion of these points and highlights the unique aspects of sport organization management.

Unique features of sport

Smith and Stewart (2010) provide a list of ten unique features of sport which can assist us to understand why the management of sport organizations requires the application of specific management techniques. A unique feature of sport is the phenomenon of people developing irrational passions for sporting teams, competitions or athletes. Sport has a symbolic significance in relation to performance outcomes, success and celebrating achievement that does not occur in other areas of economic and social activity. Sport managers must learn to harness these passions by appealing to people's desire to buy tickets for events, become a member of a club, donate time to help run a voluntary association, or purchase sporting merchandise. They must also learn to apply clear business logic and management techniques to the maintenance of traditions and connections to the nostalgic aspects of sport consumption and engagement.

There are also marked differences between sport organizations and other businesses in how they evaluate performance. Private or publicly listed companies exist to make profits and increase wealth of shareholders or owners, whereas in sport, other imperatives such as winning premierships, providing services to stakeholders and members, or meeting community service obligations may take precedence over financial outcomes. Sport managers need to be cognizant of these multiple organizational outcomes, while at the same time being responsible financial managers.

Competitive balance is also a unique feature of the interdependent nature of relationships between sporting organizations that compete on the field but cooperate off the field to ensure the long-term viability of both clubs and their league. In most business environments the aim is to secure the largest market share, defeat all competitors and secure a monopoly. In sport, clubs and teams need the opposition to remain in business, so they must cooperate to share revenues and playing talent, and regulate themselves to ensure the uncertainty in the outcome of games between them, so that fans' interest will be maintained. In some ways such behaviour could be construed as anti-competitive.

The sport product, when it takes the form of a game or contest, is also of variable quality. While game outcomes are generally uncertain, one team might dominate, which will diminish the attractiveness of the game. The perception of those watching the game might be that the quality has also diminished as a result, particularly if it is your team that loses! The variable quality of sport therefore makes it hard to guarantee quality in the marketplace relative to providers of other consumer products.

Sport also enjoys a high degree of product or brand loyalty, with fans unlikely to switch sporting codes because of a poor match result, or the standard of officiating. Consumers of household products have a huge range to choose from and will readily switch brands for reasons of price or quality, whereas sporting competitions are hard to substitute. This advantage is also a negative, as sporting codes that wish to expand market share find it difficult to attract new fans from other codes due to their familiarity with the customs and traditions of their existing sport affiliation.

Sport engenders unique behaviours in people, such as emulating their sporting heroes in play, wearing the uniform of their favourite player, or purchasing the products that celebrity sports people endorse. This vicarious identification with the skills, abilities, and lifestyles of sports people can be used by sport managers and allied industries to influence the purchasing decisions of individuals who follow sport.

Sport fans also exhibit a high degree of optimism, at times insisting that their team, despite a string of bad losses, is only a week, game or lucky break away from winning the next championship. It could also be argued that the owners or managers of sport franchises exhibit a high degree of optimism by touting their star recruits or new coach as the path to delivering them on-field success.

Sporting organizations, argue Smith and Stewart (2010), are relatively reluctant to adopt new technologies unless they are related to sports science, where on-field performance improvements are possible. In this regard sport organizations can be considered conservative and tied to traditions and behaviours more than other organizations.

The final unique aspect of sport is its limited availability. In other industries, organizations can increase production to meet demand, but in sport, clubs are limited by season length and the number of scheduled games. This constrains their ability to maximize revenue through ticket sales and associated income. The implication for sport managers is that they must understand the nature of their business, the level of demand for their product and services (whatever form that may take) and the appropriate time to deliver them.

Sport management environment

Globalization has been a major force in driving change in the ways sport is produced and consumed. The enhanced integration of the world's economies has enabled communication to occur between producers and consumers at greater speed and in greater variety, and sport has been one sector to reap the benefits. Consumers of elite sporting events and competitions such as the Olympic Games, World Cups for rugby, cricket and football, English Premier League Football, the National Basketball Association (NBA) and Grand Slam tournaments for tennis and golf enjoy unprecedented coverage. Aside from actually attending the events live at a stadium, fans can view these events through free-to-air and pay or cable television; listen to them on radio and the internet; read about game analyses, their favourite players and teams through newspapers and magazines; receive progress scores, commentary or vision on their mobile phones; and sign up for special deals and information through online subscriptions using their email address. The global sport marketplace has become very crowded and sport managers seeking to carve out a niche need to understand the global environment in which they must operate. Thus, one of the themes of this book is the impact of globalization on the ways sport is produced, consumed and managed.

Most governments view sport as a vehicle for nationalism, economic development or social development. As such, they see it as within their purview to enact policies and legislation to support, control or regulate the activities of sport organizations. Most governments support elite training institutes to assist in developing athletes for national and international competition, provide funding to national sporting organizations, support sport organizations to bid for major events and facilitate the building of major stadiums. In return for this support, governments can influence sports to recruit more mass participants, provide services to discrete sectors of the community, or have sports enact policies on alcohol and drug use, gambling and general health promotion messages. Governments also regulate the activities of sport organizations through legislation or licensing in areas such as industrial relations, anti-discrimination, taxation and corporate governance. A further theme in the book is the impact that governments can have on the way sport is produced, consumed and managed.

The management of sport organizations has undergone a relatively rapid period of professionalization over the last 30 years. The general expansion of the global sports industry and commercialization of sport events and competitions, combined with the introduction of paid staff into voluntary governance structures and the growing number of people who now earn a living managing sport organizations or playing sport, has forced sport organizations and their managers to become more professional. This is reflected in the increased number of university sport management courses; the requirement to have business skills as well as industry-specific knowledge or experience to be successful in sport management; the growth of professional and academic associations devoted to sport management; and the variety of professionals and specialists that sport managers must deal with in the course of their careers. Sport managers will work with accountants, lawyers, taxation specialists, government policy advisors, project management personnel, architects, market researchers and media specialists, not to mention sports agents, sports scientists, coaches, officials and volunteers. The ensuing chapters of the book will highlight the ongoing professionalization of sport management as an academic discipline and a career.

The final theme of the book is the notion that changes in sport management frequently result from developments in technology. Changes in telecommunications have already been highlighted, but further changes in technology are evident in areas such as performance enhancing drugs, information technology, coaching and high performance techniques, sports venues, sport betting and wagering, and sporting equipment. These changes have forced sport managers to develop policies about their use, to protect intellectual property with a marketable value and generally adapt their operations to incorporate their use for achieving organizational objectives. Sport managers need to understand the potential of technological development but also the likely impact on future operations.

Three sectors of sport

In order to make sense of the many organizations that are involved in sport management and how these organizations may form partnerships, influence each other's operations and conduct business, it is useful to see sport as comprising three distinct sectors. The first is the State or public sector, which includes national, state/provincial, regional and local governments, and specialist agencies that develop sport policy, provide funding to other sectors and support specialist roles such as elite athlete development or drug control. The second is the nonprofit or voluntary sector, made up of community-based clubs, governing associations and international sport organizations that provide competition and participation opportunities, regulate and manage sporting codes, and organize major championship events. The third sector is professional or commercial sport organizations, comprising professional leagues and their member teams, as well as allied organizations such as sporting apparel and equipment manufacturers, media companies, major stadia operators and event managers.

These three sectors do not operate in isolation, and in many cases there is significant overlap. For example, the State is intimately involved in providing funding to nonprofit sport organizations for sport development and elite athlete programmes, and in return nonprofit sport organizations provide the general community with sporting opportunities as well as developing athletes, coaches, officials and administrators to sustain sporting participation. The State is also involved in commercial sport, supporting the building of major stadia and other sporting venues to provide spaces for professional sport to be played, providing a regulatory and legal framework for professional sport to take place and supporting manufacturing and event organizations to do business. The nonprofit sport sector supports professional sport by providing playing talent for leagues, as well as developing the coaches, officials and administrators to facilitate elite competitions. Indeed, in some cases the sport league itself will consist of member teams that are technically nonprofit entities, even though they support a pool of professional managers and players. In return, the professional sport sector markets sport for spectators and participants and in some cases provides substantial funds from TV broadcast rights revenue. Figure 1.1 illustrates the three sectors and the intersections where these relationships take place.

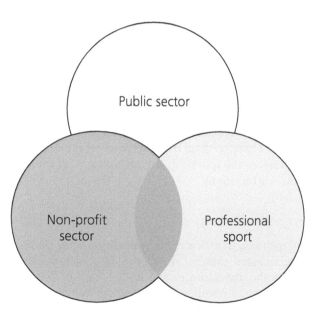

Figure 1.1: **Three-sector model of sport.**

What is different about sport management?

Sport managers utilize management techniques and theories that are similar to managers of other organizations, such as hospitals, government departments, banks, mining companies, car manufacturers and welfare agencies. However, there are some aspects of strategic management, organizational structure, human resource management, leadership, organizational culture, financial management, marketing, governance and performance management that are unique to the management of sport organizations.

Strategic management

Strategic management involves the analysis of an organization's position in the competitive environment, the determination of its direction and goals, the selection of an appropriate strategy and the leveraging of its distinctive assets. The success of any sport organization may largely depend on the quality of their strategic decisions. It could be argued that nonprofit sport organizations have been slow to embrace the concepts associated with strategic management because sport is inherently turbulent, with on-field performance and tactics tending to dominate and distract sport managers from the choices they need to make in the office and boardroom. In a competitive market, sport managers must drive their own futures by undertaking meaningful market analyses, establishing a clear direction and crafting strategy that matches opportunities. An understanding of strategic management principles and how these can be applied in the specific industry context of sport are essential for future sport managers.

Organizational structure

An organization's structure is important because it defines where staff and volunteers fit in with each other in terms of work tasks, decision-making procedures, the need for collaboration, levels of responsibility and reporting mechanisms. Finding the right structure for a sport organization involves balancing the need to formalize procedures while fostering innovation and creativity, and ensuring adequate control of employee and volunteer activities without unduly affecting people's motivation and attitudes to work. In the complex world of sport, clarifying reporting and communication lines between multiple groups of internal and external stakeholders while trying to reduce unnecessary and costly layers of management, is also an important aspect of managing an organization's structure. The relatively unique mix of paid staff and volunteers in the sport industry adds a layer of complexity to managing the structure of many sport organizations.

Human resource management

Human resource management, in mainstream business or sport organizations, is essentially about ensuring an effective and satisfied workforce. However, the sheer size of some sport organizations, as well as the difficulties in managing a mix of volunteers and paid staff in the sport industry, make human resource management a complex issue for sport managers. Successful sport leagues, clubs, associations, retailers and venues rely on good human resources, both on and off the field. Human resource management cannot be divorced from other key management tools, such as strategic planning or managing organizational culture and structure, and is a further element that students of sport management need to understand to be effective practitioners.

Leadership

Managers at the helm of sport organizations need to be able to influence others to follow their visions, empower individuals to feel part of a team working for a common goal and be adept at working with leaders of other sport organizations to forge alliances, deal with conflicts or coordinate common business or development projects. The sport industry thrives on organizations having leaders who are able to collaborate effectively with other organizations to run a professional league, work with governing bodies of sport and coordinate the efforts of government agencies, international and national sport organizations, and other groups to deliver large-scale sport events. Sport management students wishing to work in leadership roles need to understand the ways in which leadership skills can be developed and how these principles can be applied.

Organizational culture

Organizational culture consists of the assumptions, norms and values held by individuals and groups within an organization, which impact upon the activities and goals in the workplace and in many ways influences how employees work. Organizational culture is related to organizational performance, excellence, employee commitment, cooperation, efficiency, job performance and decision-making. However, how organizational culture can be defined, diagnosed and changed is subject to much debate in the business and academic world. Due to the strong traditions of sporting endeavour and behaviour, managers of sport organizations, particularly those such as professional sport franchises or traditional sports, must be cognizant of the power of organizational culture as both an inhibitor and driver of performance. Understanding how to identify, describe, analyse and ultimately influence the culture of a sport organization is an important element in the education of sport managers.

Financial management

Financial management in sport involves the application of accounting and financial decision-making processes to the relatively unique revenue streams and costs associated with sport organizations. It is important for sport managers to understand the financial management principles associated with membership income, ticketing and merchandise sales, sports betting income, sponsorship, broadcast rights fees, and government grants and subsidies. Sport managers also need to understand the history of the commercial development of sport and the ways in which sport is likely to be funded and financed in the future, in particular the move to private ownership of sport teams and leagues, sport clubs being listed on the stock exchange, greater reliance on debt finance and public-private partnerships.

Sport marketing

Sport marketing is the application of marketing concepts to sport products and services, and the marketing of non-sport products through an association with sport. Like other forms of marketing, sport marketing seeks to fulfil the needs and wants of consumers. It achieves this by providing sport services and sport-related products to consumers. However, sport marketing is unlike conventional marketing in that it also has the ability to encourage the consumption of non-sport products and services by association. It is important to understand that sport marketing means the marketing of sport as well as the use of sport as a tool to market other products and services.

Governance

Organizational governance involves the exercise of decision-making power within organizations and provides the system by which the elements of organizations are controlled and directed. Governance is a particularly important element of managing sport organizations, many of which are controlled by elected groups of volunteers, as it deals with issues of policy and direction for the enhancement of organizational performance rather than day-to-day operational management decision-making. Appropriate governance systems help ensure that elected decision-makers and paid staff seek to deliver outcomes for the benefit of the organization and its members and that the means used to attain these outcomes are effectively monitored. As many sport managers work in an environment where they must report to a governing board, it is important that they understand the principles of good governance and how these are applied in sport organizations.

Performance management

Sport organizations, over the last 30 years, have undergone an evolution to become more professionally structured and managed. Sport organizations have applied business principles to marketing their products, planning their operations, managing their human resource and other aspects of organizational activity. The unique nature of sport organizations and the variation in missions and purposes has led to the development of a variety of criteria with which to assess the performance of sport organizations. Sport management students need to understand the ways in which organizational performance can be conceptualized, analysed and reported and how these principles can be applied in the sport industry.

Summary

Sport has a number of unique features:

- people develop irrational passions;
- differences in judging performance;
- the interdependent nature of relationships between sporting organizations;
- anti-competitive behaviour;
- sport product (a game or contest) is of variable quality;
- it enjoys a high degree of product or brand loyalty;
- it engenders vicarious identification;
- sport fans exhibit a high degree of optimism;
- sport organizations are relatively reluctant to adopt new technology; and
- sport often has a limited supply.

Several environmental factors influence the way sport organizations operate, namely globalization, government policy, professionalization and technological developments.

The sport industry can be defined as comprising three distinct but interrelated industries: the State or public sector; the nonprofit or voluntary sector; and the professional or commercial sector. These sectors do not operate in isolation and often engage in a range of collaborative projects, funding arrangements, joint commercial ventures and other business relationships.

There are some aspects of strategic management, organizational structure, human resource management, leadership, organizational culture, financial management, marketing, governance and performance management that are unique to the management of sport organizations. The remainder of the book explores the three sectors of the sport industry and examines each of these core management issues in more detail.

Review questions

1   Define sport management.
2   What are the unique features of sport?
3   Describe the main elements of the environment that affect sport organizations.
4   What sort of relationships might develop between sport organizations in the public and nonprofit sectors?
5   What sort of relationships might develop between sport organizations in the public and professional sport sectors?
6   What sort of relationships might develop between sport organizations in the professional and nonprofit sectors?
7   Explain the major differences between managing a sport organization and a commercial manufacturing firm.
8   Why does the sport industry need specialist managers with tertiary sport management qualifications?
9   Identify one organization from each of the public, nonprofit and professional sport sectors. Compare how the environmental factors discussed in this chapter can affect their operation.
10 Discuss whether the special features of sport discussed in this chapter apply to all levels of sport by comparing the operation of professional sports league, an elite government sport institute and a community sport club.

Further reading

Fort, R. (2011) *Sport Economics*, 3rd edition, Upper Saddle River, NJ: Prentice Hall/Pearson.
Hoye, R., Nicholson, M. and Houlihan, B. (2010) *Sport and Policy: Issues and Analysis*, Jordon Hill: Elsevier/Butterworth Heinemann.
Hoye, R., Nicholson, M. and Smith, A. (2008) 'Unique aspects of managing sport organizations', in C. Wankel (ed.), *21st Century Management: A Reference Handbook*, Thousand Oaks, CA: Sage, pp. 499–507.
Jarvie, G. (2006) *Sport Culture and Society*, London: Routledge.
Nicholson, M. (2007) *Sport and the Media: Managing the Nexus*, Oxford: Elsevier Butterworth-Heinemann.

Parkhouse, B.L. (2005) *The Management of Sport: Its Foundation and Application*, 4th edition, New York: McGraw-Hill.

Quirk, J. and Fort, R. (1999) *Hard Ball: The Abuse of Power in Pro-team Sports*, Princeton, NJ: Princeton University Press.

Sandy, R., Sloane, P. and Rosentraub, M. (2004) *Economics of Sport: An International Perspective*, New York: Palgrave Macmillan.

Shilbury, D., Westerbeek, H., Quick, S. and Funk, D. (2009) *Strategic Sport Marketing*, 3rd edition, Sydney: Allen & Unwin.

Slack, T. and Parent, M. (2006) *Understanding Sport Organizations: The Application of Organization Theory*, 2nd edition, Champaign, IL: Human Kinetics.

Smith, A., Stewart, B. and Haimes, G. (2011) *The Performance Identity: Building High-Performance Organizational Cultures in Sport*, New York: Nova Science Publishers.

Relevant websites

The following websites are useful starting points for general information on the management of sport:

European Association for Sport Management – www.easm.net
North American Society for Sport Management – www.nassm.com
Sport Management Association of Australia and New Zealand – www.smaanz.org

Chapter 2

The role of the State in sport development

Overview

This chapter examines the different ways in which the State can influence the development of sport systems and practices. Particular attention is paid to the reasons why the State seeks to intervene in the building of sport infrastructure and its operation and the different forms such intervention can take. A distinction is made between interventions that assist and promote sport on one hand, and interventions that control and regulate sport on the other. A distinction is also made between State initiatives that aim to increase levels of community participation and those aimed at improving levels of elite athlete performance. Throughout the chapter examples, incidents and cases are used to illustrate both the concepts and theories that underpin State intervention in sport and the outcomes that arise from this intervention.

After completing this chapter the reader should be able to:

- explain the role and purpose of the State;
- explain how and why the State intervenes in the nation's economic, social and cultural landscape;

- identify the different forms the intervention can take, paying particular attention to assistance and support on one hand, and regulation and intervention on the other;
- list the different ways the State can influence the development of sport structures and practices;
- distinguish between socialist, reformist, neo-liberal and conservative ideologies, and how they influence the way the State goes about assisting and regulating sport; and
- explain how each of the above ideologies shapes the values, structure and operation of sport.

Defining the State

The State, by which we mean the structures that govern and rule societies, has always played an important role in the provision of sport experiences to people. The ancient Olympic Games and other sport festivals were funded and organized by the various city states that made up ancient Greece, and ruling monarchs in Europe during the Middle Ages organized an array of tournaments and combat games to hone the skills of their warrior classes (Mechikoff and Estes 1993). As the world became industrialized and modernized, the State expanded its provision of sport activities. In the USA, for example, many government-funded schools and colleges established sport facilities ranging from manicured playing fields and small indoor arenas to large stadia seating anywhere from 10,000 to 80,000 spectators (Fort 2010).

Today, the State, through its government institutions, provides a complex array of sport facilities and services. Many sport stadiums throughout the world were initially financed by government funds and, while subsequently controlled and operated by independent operators, are now subject to government legislation and policy guidelines (John and Sheard 1997). In most Western nations the central government has funded both the establishment of training centres for elite athletes and their ongoing operation. As a result many thousands of coaches, sport scientists and sport facility managers are now on the government payroll.

In Practice 2.1

Why should the State engage with sport?
Sport, especially in Western nations, is highly valued by the State, even though many people – and even those with significant political clout – consider it to be a frivolous use of valuable time. It is often seen to be superficial, fleeting, anti-intellectual and trivial (Stebbins 2007). Sport was summarized by the 1960s USA sport broadcaster Howard Cossell as the 'toy department of life' (Lipsky 1981: 46–47). Be that as it may, millions of people around the world use sport to satisfy a number of drives and motives. One critic argued that 'sport… is life… and the rest a shadow', 'To play sport, or watch others play,

and to read and talk about it is to uphold the nation and build its character'
(Horne 1964: 40). So, is there really a place for the State in sport, or is it there
only because it feels obliged to be?

This idea that sport can be used to build the nation is something to which
the State has a strong affinity. The State has responsibility for creating the
commercial and cultural space where people can not only build strong families,
neighbourhoods, communities and workplaces, but also healthy ones. The fact
of the matter is that nearly all modern States allocate a special space for sport,
since sport is seen to be a practice that delivers a multitude of individual and
social benefits. This is the case in Cuba, North Korea and China as much as it is
in the USA, Great Britain and Germany. This is why, from a global perspective,
the State has constructed so much infrastructure to service sport's needs, and
has given so much money to assist sport organizations deliver services to
members. So, what are these 'things' that sport delivers, and that the State
values so much? It is not all that difficult to identify the benefits and social
utility that the State believes arises from the sport experience.

First, sport is supposed to contribute to the well-being of society by providing
the context in which appropriate values, attitudes and behaviours are learnt
and perpetuated. It is claimed that sport participation allows young people
to better fit into mainstream cultural and behavioural patterns of society.
In this way it contributes to the stability, maintenance and perpetuation of
established society.

Second, sport is seen as character-building, a principle that was the
cornerstone of the British public school education system during the Victorian
and Edwardian era. The popular nineteenth century novel, Tom Brown's
Schooldays, provided the most idealized and romanticized descriptions of the
deep and culturally significant experiences that were supposed to come from
playing sports. But not only does sport build 'character', it inculcates values
that support and reinforce the central beliefs of modern industrial societies.
These beliefs and attitudes are the ones that that industrial societies hold so
dear to their hearts, and the ones that drive the progress of these societies
(Coakley et al. 2009; Rigauer 1981).

So, what exactly are these values? First and foremost, they include a strong
belief in the idea that success comes through hard work, self-discipline, and
lots of initiative. They also include a respect for authority and adherence to
rules and laws. Finally, they include all those traits and dispositions that make
for a compliant and diligent workforce, which include leadership, hierarchy,
cooperative behaviour and the desire for success and goal achievement.
These are exactly the sort of traits a twenty-first-century State wants from
its citizens, since they enable a fully functioning commercial system, and
a strong sense of civic pride, to flourish. Moreover, these are exactly the
same values that characterized the newly industrialized nineteenth century
societies and strengthened their commitment to the 'Protestant work ethic',
which is precisely what enabled them to progress out of feudalism. Sport is
seen to be the ideal practice for building these values (Rigauer 1981).

But it doesn't end there for the State in the twenty-first century. It also increasingly recognizes that sport has many other functions that can strengthen the bonds between disparate communities and build a healthier and stronger society. For instance, it is seen to be a mechanism for the dissipation and management of tension. For some, sport is seen as a socially approved outlet for otherwise unacceptable behaviour and attitudes. For example, mass audiences, with their vicarious enjoyment, serve psychologically the unintended function of channelling and releasing otherwise unpeaceable emotions. Aggression is therefore cathartically released by crowds of spectators cheering the players and jeering the umpires. Sport can also increase levels of excitement, which means participants use sport to increase tension and stress as an antidote to the routines of their work life (Coakley et al. 2009).

The State also understands that discipline and compliance are just one side of a productive collective psyche and that, in order to sustain a reasonable level of mental health, there needs to be a means of escape from the restricted and bureaucratic world of contemporary work. Recreational sport is the perfect release, and wilderness sports like bushwalking, snow skiing and bicycle touring reflect this urge to escape the automated banality of urban life. It is also a means of providing peak experiences, since sport can be a vehicle for 'realizing' oneself, and removing oneself from the safe realities of everyday life. Sport consequently becomes a 'sacred' time, full of excitement, exhilaration and peace (Stebbins 2007).

The State also recognizes the capacity of sport to deliver a sense of deep spirituality, since it emanates from a natural impulse for freedom, symbolic meaning and the pursuit for perfection. In this sense, sport is a 'natural' religion. It involves asceticism, a sense of awe and fate, a quest for community, a desire for participation in the rhythms of nature and a respect for the mystery and power of one's own being. Sport is also a religion in the liturgical aspect of sport spectacles, where the vestments, rituals and pageantry bespeak a sacred type of celebration involving a tremor of anticipation and reverence.

With the recognition that sport also delivers healthy bodies and fresh minds, the State is left with no doubt about sport's capacity to build better societies. As a result, a State that does not invest in sport is actually denying its citizens the opportunities not only to find their ideal sports space, but also to find themselves. So, when faced with the demand to explain itself, and its apparent obsession with sport, the State can, with confidence, say that it has a duty to properly resource sport, since to deny sport any assistance is to undermine the nation's capacity to grow and prosper commercially, socially and spiritually.

So, how does all of this discussion sound to you? Are you convinced that the State has a major role in sports planning, and delivering sport to all member of society?

Reasons for State intervention

The State has always intervened in the affairs of its society for the fundamental reason that it enables it to set the nation's economic and political direction. More specifically, the State believes that by its various interventions it can improve the well-being of society (Braithwaite and Drahos 2000). For example, by providing rail and road infrastructure it can improve transport systems and thereby increase the levels of overall efficiency in industry and commerce. Similarly, by funding the establishment of schools, universities and hospitals it can go a long way not only in improving the educational abilities of its citizens, but also enhancing their capacity to work more productively, and more vigorously participate in the cultural and commercial affairs of the nation. The same sort of logic underpins the State's goal of having a fit and healthy people that can defend the nation's sovereignty in times of war and generate international kudos and prestige through the success of its elite athletes.

At the same time the State may wish to more directly control the behaviour of its citizens by establishing laws that prohibit things like industry pollution and anti-competitive behaviour by businesses, and various forms of discrimination and anti-social behaviour of individuals. The aim here is to reduce the negative 'market externalities' (Braithwaite 2008: 27). In this context the State has a history of regulating sport to ensure the safety of its participants. One of the best examples is boxing, where the risk of injury is very high and rules are essential to ensure a lower chance of sustaining acute injury and long-term brain damage.

Because of sport's potential to deliver significant social benefits, there are a number of sound reasons for the State wanting to invest in it. However, government resources and taxpayer funds are always scarce, and sport is one of many institutions that wants to claim part of the government budget. As a result, sport assistance cannot always be guaranteed, and it must compete with defence, health, policing, social welfare and education. Additionally, in capitalist economies at least, sport has also traditionally been seen as outside the scope of government responsibility on the grounds that it is far removed from commerce, and more in the territory of volunteer amateurs. However, it is not that difficult to mount a case for State intervention in sport. For example, a case can be made to support the view that not only will society be better off with more sport facilities and services, but that without State support, the resources invested in sport will be far less than optimal.

Market failure and the supply of sport services

In capitalist nations like Australia, Canada, Great Britain, New Zealand and the USA, resources are in the main allocated in markets through the interaction of demand, supply and prices. However, there are often cases where markets do not operate in the best interests of the community or nation. This is known as market failure (Gratton and Taylor 2000). Market failure can occur when the full benefits of markets are not realized because of an under-supply of socially desirable products or, alternatively, an over-supply of less desirable products. Market failure and under-supply arises in situations where there are significant external or social benefits in addition to private benefits. Private benefits are the value consumers obtain from the immediate purchase of a good or service and are measured by the prices people are prepared to pay for the experience. In sport, private benefits arise from a number of activities and practices. They include attending a major sport event, working out at a gymnasium, playing indoor cricket or spending time at a snow resort. Social benefits, on the other hand, comprise the additional value communities obtain from the production of a good or service. These social benefits are over and above the private benefits. In those cases where social benefits can be identified, society would be better served by allocating additional resources into those activities. However, private investors will not usually do this because of a lack of profit incentive. Consequently, it will be left to government to fill the breach and use taxpayers' money to fund additional sporting infrastructure and services.

In other words, since sport provides significant social benefits, it deserves State support to ensure that the welfare of the whole community is maximized. According to the proponents of sport assistance, social benefits can arise from both active participation and spectatorship. In the case of active participation, the benefits include improved community health, a fall in medical costs, a reduction in the crime rate, the inculcation of discipline and character, the development of ethical standards through the emulation of sporting heroes, greater civic engagement and the building of social capital. Research into social capital building suggests that sport not only expands social networks, but also produces safer neighbourhoods and stronger communities (Productivity Commission 2003). Moreover, the social benefits linked to social capital are extended when sport groups and clubs look outward and encompass people across diverse social cleavages. This bridging or inclusive social capital can be contrasted with bonding social capital, which characterizes sport groups and clubs with a narrow ethnic, social or occupational base (Putnam 2000: 22). Either way, sport is seen to be a great builder of social capital.

In the case of elite and spectator sports, the social benefits include tribal identification with a team or club, social cohesion, a sense of civic and national pride, international recognition and prestige, economic development and the attraction of out-of-town visitors and tourist dollars (Gratton and Taylor 1991). When these social benefits are aggregated the results are quite extensive, as can be seen in Table 2.1. At the same time, they are often difficult to quantify and in some cases the evidence to support the claimed benefit is soft and flimsy.

Sport as a public good

A case can also be made for the State's involvement in sport on the grounds that sport is often a public or collective good (Li *et al.* 2001). Public goods are those where one person's consumption does not prevent another person's consumption of the same good. For example, a decision to visit a beach, or identify with a winning team or athlete, will not prevent others from doing the same. Indeed, the experience may be enhanced by others being in proximity.

Table 2.1: **Social benefits of sport development**

Arising from active participation	Arising from elite athlete successes
Improvement in community health and productivity	Tribal identification and belonging
Fall in medical costs	Social cohesion
Reduction in juvenile crime rate	Civic and national pride
Development of 'character and sense of 'fair play'	International recognition and prestige
Building of social capital, social cohesion, and civic engagement	Economic development and tourism

Adapted from Stewart *et al.* (2004)

This is the non-rival feature of the good. Public goods are also goods where, in their purest form, no one can be prevented from consuming the good. Again, a visit to the beach, and identifying with a winning team meet this criterion. This is the non-excludable feature of the good. Public goods can provide substantial benefits throughout the whole of society and are usually not rationed through high prices. However, they are not attractive to private investors since there is no assurance that all users will pay the cost of providing the benefit. As the number of so called free-riders increase there is a shrinking incentive for private operators to enter the public good market. In this instance it is argued that the State should provide for this higher demand by increasing its funding to ensure an appropriate infrastructure and level of service.

Sport equity and inclusiveness

Finally, it can be argued that the State should fund sport on equity grounds. For example, it might be argued that the whole community benefits from being fit and healthy, and therefore no one should be excluded because of low income or lack of facilities. In these cases, the optimal community benefit can only be realized if everyone has access to appropriate sport and recreation services to help them to improve their health and fitness, enhance their self-image, and build the community's social capital. In order to improve accessibility and ensure equality of opportunity, the State can establish its own low-cost sport facilities, subsidize existing sport activity providers and design targeted programmes for disadvantaged groups.

Regulation and control

There are also many situations where the State may want to regulate and control the provision of sport activities, and limit the resources devoted to some activities (Baldwin and Cave 1999). For example it may be necessary to enact laws and rules that safeguard public order when a large number of people are spectators of, or are playing in, a sporting event. In most countries there are laws that clearly define the parameters within which sport grounds are to be constructed. These laws will cover things like design specifications, the provision for seating, the number of entry and exit points, and fire prevention facilities (Frosdick and Walley 1997). There may also be rules that govern the behaviour of spectators. Most commonly these laws will relate to the consumption of alcohol, and disorderly and violent behaviour (Greenfield and Osborn 2001).

One of the most highly regulated activities is horse racing. It is not just a case of ensuring the animals are treated humanely, but also of making sure the gaming and gambling practices that surround the sport are tightly controlled so that corrupt practices are minimized. There are many cases around the world where horses have not been allowed to run on their merits. This can involve doping activities where stimulants will be given to horses to make them run quicker, or depressants administered to make them go slower. In both instances the aim is to undermine the betting market, and through the use of inside information to back the horse that has been advantaged, and avoid the horse that has been slowed. Similar incidents are now happening more frequently in a number of professional team sports around the world. Crime syndicates and bookmakers have bribed sport officials, players and even referees to provide confidential information on the game, deliberately play poorly, and make decisions that favour one team and not another. Two recent cases involved Italy's premier football competition and the Pakistan cricket team. In each instance government action was immediately taken to more strictly regulate the competitions.

Another form of regulation involves the media in general and TV in particular. In both Australia and England there are anti-siphoning rules that effectively give free-to-air television stations privileged access to major sport events at the expense of pay and cable television providers. This means that a major sport event like the Australian Football League (AFL) Grand Final must initially be offered to free-to-air stations before being offered to pay TV stations. This is done on the grounds that a sport of national significance should be made as widely available as possible. In Australia the pay TV subscriptions cover less than 50 per cent of all households, and it would therefore be inequitable to give rights to a pay TV station only.

In Practice 2.2

State regulation over sport: boxing and the martial arts

In some sports there are very few rules that govern the conduct of its activities. The relatively gentle sport of lawn bowls is a case in point. Apart from having to abide by the laws of the land, lawn bowlers are not externally regulated in any additional ways by the state. At the same time it has to be said that players in lawn bowls clubs are sometimes highly regulated internally, particularly when it comes to dress codes for the playing rink.

At the other extreme are the more combative sports of boxing and the martial arts, including judo and karate. As mentioned above, one of the most highly regulated sports is boxing, particularly at the professional level (Hoye *et al.* 2010). Many countries have legislation which effectively sets up government-controlled agencies that both issue licences to promoters and participants, and monitor the conduct of the sport.

Take the case of the state of New South Wales in Australia. Boxing and kick-boxing are the largest professional combat sports in New South Wales and the industry is regulated under the *Boxing and Wrestling Control Act of 1986*. The Act provides for the establishment of the Boxing Authority of NSW (BANSW) to control and regulate the conduct of professional boxing events in this State. According to BANSW, professional boxing is an inherently dangerous sport and as a result it is essential that some type of boxing control authority is established to regulate the industry and safeguard its participants.

The Act sets out the requirements for registration of professional boxers and industry participants, which includes promoters, matchmakers, managers, trainers, seconds, referees, judges and timekeepers. It further determines the conditions under which competitors can compete and events be staged. It effectively restricts free entry into the industry and makes participation conditional upon meeting certain safety and registration requirements. The Act also controls wrestling, amateur boxing and kick-boxing through a permit system administered by NSW Sport and Recreation under ministerial delegation.

Registration of all boxers and industry participants together with permits to conduct promotions are required under the Act and can be obtained through the NSW Department of Sport and Recreation on behalf of the Boxing Authority. The Department of Sport and Recreation maintains a register of all professional boxers and industry participants and provides general assistance to the industry. Permits are also required for the conduct of amateur boxing, kick-boxing, amateur and professional wrestling, and the Department of Sport and Recreation sets out conditions of permit to conduct such events.

A similar model operates in the USA, where there is a national Boxing Commission whose job is to regulate the professional boxing industry and ensure minimum acceptable standards of operation. Its rules are enforceable under the *Professional Boxing Safety Act of 1996*. The Act begins by identifying the key stakeholders involved in the planning and conduct of a boxing match, which include the following:

1 'boxer' meaning an individual who fights in a professional boxing match;
2 'licensee' which means an individual who serves as a trainer or second;
3 'manager' which means a person who receives compensation for service as an agent or representative of a boxer;
4 'matchmaker' meaning a person who proposes, selects and arranges the boxers to participate in a professional boxing match;
5 'physician' which means a doctor of medicine legally authorized to practice medicine by the State in which the physician performs such function or action; and
6 'promoter' meaning the person primarily responsible for organizing, promoting and producing a professional boxing match.

Under the above 1996 Act the Commission also has a responsibility to register all boxers. It requires that boxers register with the boxing commission of the State in which such boxer resides. In those instances where boxers are residents of a foreign country, or reside in a USA state where there is no boxing commission, they must register with the boxing commission of any other state. In short, all boxers who want to fight professionally must be registered somewhere in the USA.

The other crucial thing the Boxing Commission does is to uphold basic safety standards. Under its current standards, no person may arrange, promote, organize, produce or fight in a professional boxing match without meeting each of the following requirements as a means of protecting the health and safety of boxers:

1 a physical examination of each boxer must be conducted by a physician. The physician must then certify whether or not the boxer is physically fit to safely compete in the boxing match. Copies of the certification must be subsequently submitted to the Boxing Commission;
2 other than in exceptional circumstances, an ambulance or medical personnel with appropriate resuscitation equipment must be continuously present on the site of the boxing match;
3 a physician must be continuously present at ringside; and
4 health insurance must be provided for each boxer in order to ensure medical coverage for any injuries sustained in the match.

While the degree of control varies from country to country, the most severe controls are in Norway, where professional boxing is banned. Any Norwegian boxer who wants to enter the professional ranks must relocate to another country.

The basic reason why boxing and the martial arts have such problematic status is because they provide not only community benefits, but also community costs. The community benefits include an opportunity to engage in a vigorous sport that requires both extreme physical fitness and mental toughness. There is also some evidence that boxing and the martial arts are a very effective means of channelling the energies of disadvantaged youths into socially constructive activities and subjecting them to a valuable form of personal discipline. On the other hand, boxing and the martial arts are highly combative and have high injury rates. In the case of boxing there is a high risk of brain damage, which brings with it enormous personal and social costs. Therefore, in order to minimize the risk of physical damage to the participants, a high degree of regulation is required (Hoye *et al.* 2010). More generally, boxing is seen as a brutal sport that has little relevance to a civilized society where there are rules against physical assault in everyday life. There are a number of medical associations and groups whose aim is to ban competitive boxing on the grounds that it has a net social cost to the community and that as a result we would all be better off without it. However most national governments do not agree and, at the amateur level in particular, it is supported and funded and, in addition, is still an integral part of the Olympic Games schedule.

Extent and form of State intervention

As indicated above, the State can intervene in sport in all sorts of ways. The extent of the intervention, and the form it takes, is strongly influenced by the ideology, values and overall philosophy of the State and its governing institutions (Gardiner *et al.* 2009).

The first ideology is *conservatism*. A conservative ideology values tradition and customary ways of doing things. Conservative governments have a tendency to regulate the social lives of people, and therefore want to censor works of art and literature they find offensive. They also want to control the distribution of legal drugs like alcohol, and generally act to protect people from themselves. On the other hand, they believe that business should be left to its own devices, where the combination of individual self-interest, the profit motive and market forces will ensure a favourable outcome. However, because conservative governments believe a strong private sector is the key to progress, they are prepared to assist and protect industry when the need arises. While on one hand they recognize sport as an integral part of the social life of most people, they do not want to assist or protect it since it is not part of the world of business. Indeed, for many conservatives, it is another world altogether that is best kept at a distance from business. This sport-world is underpinned by the belief that sport fulfils its function best when it is done for its own sake, played by amateurs, managed by volunteers, and generally left to look after its own affairs.

The second ideology is *reformism* or, as it is also known, welfare statism or social democracy. Reformism is primarily concerned with social justice and equity. While reformists recognize the necessity of a strong private sector they believe it cannot be trusted to deliver fair and equitable outcomes. It therefore needs to be strictly managed. This could take the form of additional state-owned enterprises or tight regulation of business behaviour. Reformists share the conservative view that assistance and protection may be necessary in the public interest. Unlike conservatives, though, reformists believe primarily in social development, which not only means legislating for social freedom but also for social justice. Income redistribution to disadvantaged groups is important, and is done by ensuring that wealthy individuals and corporations are taxed most heavily. State spending is also crucial to reformists, since it is used to stimulate the economy when demand and spending are low. Reformist governments tend to be more centralist and aim to use this centralized power to engineer positive social outcomes. Reformists consequently see sport as a tool for social development and aim to make sport more accessible to the whole community. In these cases programmes are established to cater for the needs of minority groups like the indigenous, the disabled, migrants who speak another language and women. In short, reformist government policy focuses more on community and less on elite sport development.

The third ideology is *neo-liberalism*. Neo-liberals believe that society is at its most healthy when people can run their daily lives without the chronic intrusion of the State. The rule of law is important, but beyond that people should be free to choose how they organize their social lives and businesses should be free to organize their commercial lives as they see fit. Neo-liberals see little value in State-owned enterprises and argue that the privatization of government services produces greater efficiency and higher quality outcomes. Moreover, deregulated industries are seen to run better than tightly controlled ones. In short, neo-liberals believe government should not engage directly in most economic activity, but rather provide only base-level infrastructure, together with legislative guidelines within which private business can thrive. Sport is valued as an important social institution but should not be strictly controlled. However, neo-liberals also believe sport can be used as a vehicle for nation building and economic development, and should be supported in these instances. This produces a sport policy that tends to focus on elite sport at the expense of community sport.

The final ideology is *socialism*. Socialists believe that a combination of privately owned and unregulated markets will produce severe levels of inequality and alienation. As a result, capitalist modes of production and distribution need to be replaced by a strong State where resource allocation is centrally controlled. Like neo-liberals, socialists agree that sport is an important social institution, but unlike neo-liberals, go on to assert that sport should be controlled from the centre to ensure a fair spread of clubs and facilities throughout society. To this end, a socialist system of sport development will be driven by a central bureaucracy that sets the sport agenda. The State also provides most of the funds and resources by which to develop sport at both the community and elite levels.

Each ideology not only contains quite different assumptions about the proper role of the State, but also different ideas about what sport can do to improve the welfare of society. As a result each ideology will produce different sport development outcomes, and the ideology often overrides the claims of interest groups like sport scientists, coaches and officials. The four ideologies described provide a simplified typology and, in practice, the State will often take bits and pieces of each ideology when forming its position on a particular sport issue or problem. At the same time, most States will be characterized by more of one and less of another ideology. Table 2.2 outlines the different ideologies and indicates how they can shape the State's views on sport development.

Table 2.2: Links between political ideology and sport development

Ideological type	Features	Implications for sport development
Conservatism	• Private ownership of business • Regulation of social practices	Arm's-length association with sport. Sport is seen as a private activity that grows out of the community, and is managed by the volunteer sector
Reformism	• Mixed economy • Regulation of both social and economic affairs	Direct involvement in sport facility construction and community sport participation
Neo-liberalism	• Emphasis on the market • Deregulation of industry	Most resources go to the elite end of sport development and its commercial outcomes.
Socialism	• Limited scope for the market • Central planning • Bureaucratic control over resource allocation	Direct involvement in all aspects of sport development. Often tightly regulated. Both community and elite sport are resourced.

As a result there is a broad array of arrangements by which the State can fund, develop and deliver sport facilities and programmes. At one extreme, the State can distance itself from sport development by claiming that sport is a private matter for individuals and communities and is therefore best left to the market and voluntary sectors to run. This arrangement was the primary feature of Australian sport until the 1970s when the national government resolved to fund sport facilities and programmes (Stewart *et al.* 2004). In the USA the national government has also adopted an arm's-length approach to sport, and has left the funding and development of sport to the market, and the school and university sectors (Chalip *et al.* 1996). At the other extreme, the State sets the sport agenda by both establishing sport facilities across the nation and funding the management of their operations. This approach was exemplified in the sport development programmes of most communist nations during the 1970s and 1980s. In the Soviet Union (USSR) and the German Democratic Republic (GDR), a national sport programme was integrated into the school curricula, and sport schools were used to identify and nurture talented young athletes. In addition, sports that had a strong civil defence and paramilitary flavour were conducted in factory and trade union facilities. Cuba had a similar sport development model in which the State, through its government bureaucracy, managed the whole sport experience for both the sport-for-all participant and the Olympic athlete. While Cuba banned professionalism in sport, it handsomely rewarded its national sporting heroes by giving them government jobs or enrolling them in college and university courses that they could complete at their convenience. In Cuba, like the USSR and GDR, sport success was not just a sporting victory but a 'psychological, patriotic and revolutionary' one as well (Riordon 1978: 147).

State assistance to sport: the Australian experience

Australia has always seen itself as a sport-loving nation, and has used sport as a means of generating civic pride, national identity and international recognition (Stewart *et al.* 2004). Between 1945 (the end of the Second World War) and 1972 (the election of a Labour reformist government for the first time in 23 years) Australians were very successful on the world sporting stage, producing a proliferation of world champions in swimming, tennis, cricket, rughy league and cycling (Cashman 1995). However, this was achieved with a minimum of government support. While local government provided many excellent playing fields and indoor sport facilities, the national government provided nothing to most national sport governing bodies, and neither did it fund the construction of many sport venues. All it did was contribute to Olympic and Commonwealth Games teams every two years, provide small annual grants to help lifesaving clubs to patrol beaches, and provide financial assistance to State-government-run fitness councils. In short, sport was left to run its own affairs.

However, this all changed in the 1970s in response to two significant forces. First, a reformist Labour national government was elected which had a mandate to change the social conditions in Australia. It replaced the stable but conservative Menzies government that had increased the nation's prosperity, but had done next to nothing for sport. One of the first things the Whitlam government did was to establish a Ministry of Sport, and start funding a programme that both increased the number of community leisure centres around Australia, and assisted national sporting bodies to improve their operations. Second, the failure of the Olympic Games team to win a gold medal at Montreal in 1976 traumatized the nation to such an extent that the national government resolved to directly intervene in the sport development process. Although the Fraser Liberal government (which replaced the Whitlam government in 1975) was for the most part highly conservative, it decided to establish a training academy for talented young athletes in response to growing community agitation that Australia was no longer a world leader in sport. The Australian Institute of Sport (AIS) was opened for business in 1981 and quickly became internationally recognized as a successful training centre for elite athletes (Bloomfield 2003). In 1984 the Australian Sports Commission was established in order to better manage the national government's sport funding initiatives, and generally implement government sport policy in a systematic and orderly manner. The rest, as they say, is history, and in the space of 25 years the national government's annual sports budget increased from around AUS$5million to just over AUS$150 million (Stewart *et al.* 2004). These funds have been used to both increase Australia's sporting infrastructure and expand the operations of the national governing bodies for sport. At the same time, there has been a change in the values and culture of Australian sport as sport became more commercialized in response to a growing involvement from the market sector. When combined with the ever-increasing national government support for sport, the whole sport system became more professionalized, and created many career opportunities for players, administrators and coaches.

Current government sport assistance is multidimensional, but it fundamentally wants to strike the elusive balance between elite sport development and community sport participation (Stewart *et al.* 2004). It can be conveniently divided into four strategic, but interconnected outcomes. First, it aims to develop an effective national sports infrastructure by enhancing the management capabilities of national sporting bodies. Programmes are directed at improving coaching standards, the management skills of officials, the day-to-day operation of national sporting bodies and the capacity of Australian sport to export its expertise. Second, it aims to improve participation in sport activities by encouraging more people to engage in club-based sport through its junior sport activities and assisting marginalized groups in securing places in sport clubs and associations. These groups include aboriginals, people with disabilities, women, children and older adults. Third, it aims to provide for continuous improvement in the performances of Australians in international sport. In this case, programmes are directed at assisting national sporting bodies to nurture talented athletes, enhancing the Australian Institute of Sport scholarship programme, providing sport science support and assisting athletes in managing their future careers. Finally, it aims to provide a climate and culture of fair play. The focus here is not only on drug control, but also eliminating discrimination and harassment, assisting indigenous communities and dismantling barriers to disabled athlete participation. The breadth of the current government sport-assistance arrangements is revealed in Table 2.3.

All of these programmes beg the question as to whether or not Australia's sport system has been improved by State intervention, or whether Australia's sport development should have been left in the hands of the commercial and voluntary sectors. If Olympic and Commonwealth Games medal tallies are any indication, then State intervention is the best thing that has ever happened to Australian sport. Whereas Australian athletes won only nine medals at the 1980 Moscow Olympic Games, the tally increased to 14 at the 1988 Seoul Games, 27 at Barcelona in 1992 and 41 at Atlanta in 1996. Even better results were achieved at Sydney in 2000 when 58 medals were snared, while in Athens in 2004, Australia (with a population of only 21 million) placed fourth in the medal tally when its athletes collected 49 medals. While its Beijing 2008 tally was only 46, giving it fourth place overall, these successes provided the national government with further evidence that its elite sport policy was working, and as a result it substantially increased its funding arrangements to support the team 2012 London Olympic Games.

However, sport development is about much more than just winning medals at international sport events. The State also has a responsibility to provide the community with rewarding sport experiences and to make sure disadvantaged groups have open and easy access to facilities (Houlihan 1997). In the past decade the Australian government has made some good

Table 2.3: Australian national government interventions in sport: 1980–2012

Focus of intervention	Examples
High performance	Australian Institute of Sport (AIS), athlete scholarships grants, elite coach education
Management improvement	Australian Sports Commission (ASC) training programmes, grants for management improvement and staff training
Economic benefit	Government agencies to secure significant sport festivals and championships. Subsidies to ensure viability of mega-sport events
Drug education and enforcement	Australian Sports Anti-Doping Authority (ASADA), drug education programmes, testing and sanctions
Community participation	Programmes and funding to encourage greater participation at grass-roots level. Working with national sport bodies to develop modified games, and implement junior development programmes.
Social capital	Volunteer training programmes, and grants to local sport bodies to improve sport facilities and administrative systems.
Diversity and equity	Women's sport programmes, anti-harassment and anti-discrimination programmes including design of member protection policies (MPP), funding to assist indigenous and disabled sport.

Adapted from Stewart et al. (2004)

progress to increase the general level of participation, but at the moment it has plateaued. Australia is now one of the most obese nations in the world, second only to the United States. This is another challenge the Australian government will be facing over the next few years. It will be interesting to see if more State funding of sport participation will solve this serious public health problem.

Summary

The State has the capacity to significantly shape the structure and scope of sport through a number of mechanisms. First, it can construct sport facilities; second, it can fund the day-to-day operations of sporting associations and clubs; third, it can deliver sport programmes to the community directly; fourth, it can establish training facilities for elite athletes to assist their ongoing development; and finally, it can control the operation of sport by introducing various laws, regulations and rules that shape the delivery of sport events, programmes and services (Hylton *et al.* 2001). However, the scale of State support, and the form it takes, will vary between nations depending on the dominant political ideology and the overall cultural importance of sport to society. In some cases the State will directly control and manage sport, while at the other end of the political spectrum the State will step back from the sport system and encourage the commercial and volunteer sectors to take up the slack. At this point in time the evidence suggests that governments have a pivotal role to play in supporting both the community participation and elite-sport ends of the sport development continuum. Through the establishment of sport infrastructure and facilities, and the funding of sport programmes, it enables greater levels of community participation, creates all sorts of health and social benefits, improved international sport performance, and enhances a country's international status and prestige.

Review questions

1   What comprises the State, and what is its role?
2   How does the State go about shaping the political and economic landscape of a nation?
3   Apart from the State what other social forces contribute to national development?
4   Explain how the State may contribute to sport development.
5   What can the State do to increase the level of sport participation and sport club membership?
6   What can the State do to increase the level of elite sport performance?
7   Why should the State want to intervene in sport?
8   Would sport development be best left to the voluntary and commercial sectors?
9   Is there any evidence that a centralized model of elite sport development is any more effective than a market-based sport development model?
10 How might the State go about increasing the scale of sport participation at the community or 'grass-roots' level?

Further reading

For a thorough analysis of the ways in which government can go about regulating a nation's economic, social and cultural affairs, see Baldwin and Cave (1999) and Braithwaite and Drahos (2000). There are now a number of publications that examine the ways in which the State has intervened in a nation's sport development. To get a detailed picture of the Australian experience you should read Bloomfield (2003) and Stewart *et al.* (2004). The British experience is nicely reviewed in Green and Houlihan (2005), Houlihan and White (2002) and Hylton *et al.* (2001). For some comparative analysis of State involvement in sport the most comprehensive treatment is contained in Chalip *et al.* (1996). Houlihan (1997) provides an excellent comparative study of Australia, Canada, Ireland and the United Kingdom. The most definitive account of sport in socialist Cuba, although now a little dated, is Pattavino and Pye (1994).

See also Coakley and Pike (2009) *Sport in Society*; Horne (1964) *The Lucky Country*; Rigauer (1981) *Sport and Work*; and Stebbins, R. (2007) *Serious Leisure*.

Relevant websites

To find out more about the State and Australian sport go to the Australian Sports Commission site – www.ausport.gov.au

To get more details of the English experience go to the Sport England site – www.sportengland.org

For a comprehensive review of the State's involvement in New Zealand sport go to the New Zealand Government Sport and Recreation site – www.sparc.org.nz

Lifesaving clubs and lifeguard associations around the world

The lifesaving movement has a rich and long history. So long as people wanted to engage with the sea and the ocean, and enjoy the pleasures of the beach, there was always the risk that they would drown. Learning to swim was a crucial means of reducing the risk, but this valuable outdoors skill was often insufficient to deal with crashing waves, a powerful rip or even a leaky boat. As a result, even in the late nineteenth century, places where people swam, and spaces where they engaged with the sea, required professional supervision to ensure that catastrophes did not occur (Jaggard 2006). One of the first initiatives to help create an international forum for international lifesaving discussion occurred in France in 1878 when delegates from around western Europe met to examine the ways in which the whole lifesaving function could be formalized and rationalized. In 1891 in the United Kingdom, the Royal Life Saving Society (RLSA) was created, and membership soon expanded to other members of the old British Empire, including Canada and Australia. In 1910 the first official international lifesaving organization (the FIS – *Fédération Internationale de Sauvetage Aquatique*) was established, and included many European member countries, especially those, like Spain, France, Italy and Great Britain, which had extensive coastlines.

Lifesaving in the form of surf lifesaving – which centred on ocean as opposed to bay-side beaches – has an especially interesting history in Australia, which is not surprising given the warm climate and hundreds of miles of swimmable ocean beaches around most of the populated areas. Clubs were formed in Australia between 1903 and 1907 in response to a spate of drownings at local Sydney beaches. The Bronte surf lifesaving club claims to be the first 'surf' club in the world, having been established in 1903. At the same time, the Bondi surf-bathers lifesaving club also claimed to be the world's first lifesaving club, but as it turns out, it was not established until 1907. The first club to be formed outside of Sydney was the Kiama surf-bather's club, which was founded in 1908. These clubs, and others like them, became necessary following the relaxing of laws prohibiting daylight bathing on Australian beaches. As a result, thousands of swimmers took to the water, and volunteer groups of men – women were not initially invited to become members of lifesaving clubs – were subsequently trained in lifesaving methods and patrolled the beaches as lifesavers looking after public safety. There are now more than 300 surf lifesaving clubs in Australia that collectively patrol over 400 beaches. Lifesavers have undertaken so many valuable tasks, and done it with so much flair, and backed it up with so much physical skills and expertise, that they have also become one of the most iconic figures of the Australian sporting landscape (Jaggard 2006).

While the United Kingdom does not have the strong beach culture that exists in Australia, it still has a strong network of lifesavers and lifeguard services under the auspices of the RLSA. Nearly all of the United Kingdom's major tourist beaches now have lifeguards and it also provides the opportunity for children to join lifesaving clubs. Like the situation in Australia, this enables them to start from an early age, build their aquatic confidence, improve their knowledge of the sea's many turbulent features and develop the skills required to save lives in the future. A lot of the UK's smaller coastal resorts can get very busy and therefore have lifeguards on duty throughout the summer. Cardigan Bay for example, which sits along the west coast of Wales has many beaches that not only fill with tourists over the summer months, but also provides an array of professional lifesavers and life guards (www.ilsf.org).

In 1971 the World Life Saving organisation (WLS) was formed, and it brought together countries such as New Zealand, the United Kingdom, South Africa and the United States, where they proclaimed their mission of protecting the public on beaches worldwide. This organization later merged with the FIS and became the International Life Saving Federation (ILSF) in 1993 (Jaggard 2006). Its mission statement says in part that its role is to '[lead, support and collaborate] with national and international organisations engaged in drowning prevention, water safety, water rescue, lifesaving, lifeguarding and lifesaving sport' (www.ilsf.org). As a result of its global initiatives we now find that all around the world on any popular coastline there are either lifesavers or lifeguards.

The other important point to note is that lifesaving and lifeguard work is not just physically demanding, it is also costly to mount. This is because it

1 is a labour intensive practice;
2 is something that requires extensive training; and
3 has to be carried out in quite different terrains and conditions.

In Europe, for example, there are also several coastal areas that are patrolled by lifeguards, even in Belgium, which has a limited coastal area of just under 70 kilometres. In Germany work is done by the Red Cross group, while Italy is covered by the Italian Swimming Federation and the National Life Saving Society. In some European countries such as Portugal and Spain coastal areas are so long that they sometimes have to be patrolled by lifeguards on quad bikes (www.ilsf.org).

In Britain, as with Australia, there are distinctions to be made between surf-beach, bay-side beach and pool lifeguards. The Royal Life Saving Society and the Swimming Coaches and Teachers Association train individuals for their national pool lifeguard qualification, and additionally teach the National Aquatic Rescue Standard. The lifeguard course comprises around 40 hours of instructional time, and is valid for two years once qualified. If anyone wishes to continue as a lifeguard they must complete a further 20 hours of training. The Royal Lifesaving Society also has an individual qualification for beach work known as the National Beach Lifeguard Qualification (NBLQ) and involves training in several modules such as rescue boat training and VHF radio operation. This all very impressive, and ensures that the pools and beaches of Britain are properly managed and supervized.

All of these global developments are absolutely essential for the creation of safe beaches and pools, but they beg the question as to how they are funded. Well, they are funded by very heavily by government. Take, for example the recent developments that have occurred in Australia. Between 2008 and 2011 the New South Wales State government provided AUS$10 million for surf lifesaving facilities on top of the annual funding arrangements. The money went into projects that contribute to beach safety, which includes things like improved access to rescue equipment and better sight lines between clubs and swimming areas. Some of the funding was also used to assist surf lifesaving clubs in making their facilities more accessible to the broader community through improved disability access, the inclusion of young people from non-English speaking backgrounds, and female-friendly amenities. In the case of the national governing body for surf lifesaving, Surf Life Saving Australia (SLSA), nearly 30 per cent of its total annual revenue of around AUS$30 million comes from the Australian national government (SLSA 2010). This means that like most other nations around the world that provide extensive lifesaving facilities, it would not have been possible without the very generous support of government.

This begs the additional and crucially important question of why government should want to involve itself in the funding of lifesaving and lifeguard services when the community who use the services could, alternatively, pay for it. What do you think, and what arguments can you mount to confirm that communities around the world will be far better off with government assistance to surf lifesavers and lifeguards than without government assistance? So, when we consider the role of surf lifesavers beach lifeguards, and pool lifeguards, and the role that might be played by government in making things happen in these very important public spaces, seven pivotal questions need to be asked:

Case study questions

1 What is the core role of lifesaving clubs and agencies?
2 What are their likely sources of income, and why?
3 How feasible would it be to get the people being rescued to actually fund the operations of lifesaving clubs and agencies?
4 Why should governments want to assist lifesaving clubs and agencies?
5 What are lifesaving clubs and agencies expected to do with the funds that are allocated to them by government?
6 What are the benefits we expect to secure from the activities of surf lifesavers and guards?
7 Would these benefits arise if the lifesaving clubs were not funded by government?

Chapter 3

Nonprofit sport

Overview

This chapter examines the role of the nonprofit sector in the provision of sport participation and consumption opportunities. The reasons why the nonprofit sector plays such a large part in the provision of sport participation opportunities and the various ways the nonprofit sector is involved in sport are reviewed. The scope of the nonprofit sector's involvement in sport around the world is examined, with a particular emphasis on the role of volunteers in administration, officiating and coaching and the role of nonprofit sport organizations in facilitating people's enjoyment of sport as active participants, supporters or consumers. The chapter also provides a summary of the relationship between nonprofit sport organizations and the state.

After completing this chapter the reader should be able to:

- describe the scope of the nonprofit sector's involvement in sport;
- understand the differences in the roles performed by the state and nonprofit sport organizations;

- understand the ways in which nonprofit sport
  organizations provide sport participation and consumption
  opportunities around the world; and
- understand some of the challenges facing the nonprofit
  sector in delivering these opportunities.

Introduction

The model presented in Chapter 1 presents the sport industry as comprising three distinct but overlapping sectors: the State or public sector, the commercial or professional sport sector, and the nonprofit or voluntary sector. This chapter focuses on the nonprofit or voluntary sector of the model; the various sport organizations that would be classified as nonprofit. Many terms have been used to refer to nonprofit organizations that operate in a variety of industry sectors and countries around the world. These terms include voluntary, not for profit, non-government, community, club based, associations, cooperatives, friendly societies, civil society and the third sector. For the purposes of this book we have chosen to use the term nonprofit organizations to describe those organizations that are institutionally separate from the State, do not return profits to owners, are self-governing, have a significant element of voluntary contribution and are formally incorporated.

The nonprofit sector comprises organizations that are markedly different from State organizations discussed in Chapter 2, and also profit-seeking organizations that are discussed in Chapter 4. Nonprofit organizations vary in size, focus and capability and include groups as diverse as community associations, chambers of commerce, private schools, charitable trusts and foundations, welfare agencies and sporting organizations. Nonprofit organizations are a major part of many industries in health services, education, housing, welfare, culture and sport.

Nonprofit sector and society

Nonprofit organizations exist to develop communities, meet the needs of identifiable and discrete groups in those communities, and work for the benefit of public good rather than wealth creation for individuals. Nonprofit organizations have evolved to fill gaps in the provision of services such as welfare assistance that are not provided by the State or market sector, and are driven largely by the efforts of volunteers with the occasional support of paid staff.

A review of nonprofit organizations in Canada (Statistics Canada 2004) noted that these organizations were vehicles for citizen engagement – they enable individuals to contribute their talent, energy and time to engaging in group activities and causes that are not otherwise provided by the public or private sectors. Nonprofit organizations are in general governed by volunteers, run on the time and money contributed by volunteers, and enable volunteers to contribute to enhancing their local, regional, national and global communities. In Canada there are more than 161,000 nonprofit organizations, that collectively utilize more than 2 billion volunteer hours, and receive more than $CAN 8 billion in donations to deliver their services. According to Statistics Canada (2004) Canadians take out 139 million memberships in these organizations, an average of four per person. These figures show us that the nonprofit sector represents a major part of the economic activity of many nations and plays a pivotal role in encouraging people to engage in social, religious, charitable, philanthropic and sport related activities.

Nonprofit organizations usually focus on delivering services to very specific population groups or within defined geographic areas. Many of them provide services to targeted groups and only a few focus solely on providing services to members. The variety of activities carried out by nonprofit organizations is very broad ranging, from providing sporting opportunities to funding hospital and medical services. As a result, the revenue sources, cost base, numbers of paid staff and volunteers, and the sophistication of management systems also vary.

The nonprofit sector is not without its problems. The larger organizations such as independent schools, colleges and hospitals receive the majority of funding and almost half the funding for most nonprofit organizations comes from government. The resourcing of nonprofit organizations in some sectors continues to be inadequate as they struggle to keep up with demand, particularly in the welfare, housing and charitable sectors. By far the biggest problem facing nonprofit organizations is the inability to fulfil their missions due to problems securing adequate numbers of volunteers, finding board members and attracting enough sustainable funding (Cuskelly 2004). As governments around the world seek to decrease their costs and devolve responsibility for service delivery to the private and nonprofit sectors without adequately funding such delivery, nonprofit organizations will find it increasingly difficult to operate.

In Practice 3.1

The Australian nonprofit sector

According to a recent review by the Australian Productivity Commission (2010) many not-for-profit organizations (NFPs) feel they are poorly understood by government and the general public. Pressures to be more efficient have seen overhead spending reduced that, in turn, reduces effectiveness. While the Australian nonprofit sector is diverse, NFPs display some common behavioural patterns. First, in contrast to for-profit organizations, the behaviour of NFPs is driven mostly by their mission or community purpose. Second, demonstrated commitment to their community purpose underpins support for their activities, whether by members for member-serving NFPs, or by donors and government who provide funding for community-serving NFPs. Third, processes, often highly participatory, matter for NFPs because they provide value to the volunteers and members, and because of their central importance to maintaining trusting relationships that form the basis for effective service delivery. Finally, control can be a major motivating factor for the managers of NFPs. While generally motivated by altruism, NFP management also benefits personally from their role when it confers status or power, builds their skills and contacts, and where it improves the environment for their other activities.

The Productivity Commission argued that these characteristics have implications for the drivers of efficiency and effectiveness, namely:

1   Processes that appear messy and inefficient to outsiders can be essential for effective delivery of services, especially those requiring engagement with clients who face disadvantages and are wary of government and for-profit providers.

2   They can also be important to attract and retain volunteers, the involvement of whom can be valued as much for the engagement outcomes as for replacing the need for paid labour.

3   It is possible that, for some managers, 'doing' can take precedence over 'achieving'. Unless NFP boards are able to act decisively, such behaviour can undermine efficiency and effectiveness and threaten the sustainability of an NFP.

4   While greater scale and sharing of support services can improve production efficiency, NFPs can be reluctant to merge or collaborate where other interests might be eroded or where the purchase of support services adds to overheads.

Community-serving NFPs may also lack adequate feedback mechanisms on their effectiveness (or lack thereof) as clients are often grateful for the assistance. This contrasts strongly with member-serving organizations, particularly small grass roots organizations, where member satisfaction is paramount to survival.

While historically Australia fits in the 'liberal' social origin category (where government social spending is low and NFP activity is relatively large), since the 1970s government funding of the sector has grown. From the 1980s, this has increasingly been under competitive allocation arrangements, with greater use of the sector to deliver government-funded services. More recently, social enterprise is being seen as a way to harness network governance to address social issues. Along with demographic, ethnic and cultural changes (such as increasing environmental awareness), these forces are increasing demand for NFP activities. In responding to rising demand, NFPs report constraints arising from growing regulation and contract requirements, and challenges in accessing funding, finance and skilled workers. Government can assist in addressing these constraints to facilitate sector growth and development; nevertheless the sector remains responsible for its own future.

Source: Productivity Commission (2010) *Contribution of the Not-for-Profit Sector*, Canberra: Commonwealth of Australia, pp. 13–14.

Nonprofit sector and sport

The International Classification of Nonprofit Organizations (ICNPO) has a designated category for sports and recreation organizations. This category includes three broad groups: (1) sports including amateur sport, training, fitness and sport facilities, and sport competition and events; (2) recreation and social clubs such as country clubs, playground associations, touring clubs and leisure clubs; and (3) service clubs such as Lions, Rotary, Kiwanis and Apex clubs. Of particular interest are those organizations that operate on a nonprofit basis in sport including professional service organizations, industry lobby groups, sport event organizations and sport governing bodies.

Nonprofit professional service organizations operate in sport in similar ways to professional associations like accrediting medical boards, or associations for lawyers and accountants.

These organizations assist in setting standards of practice in their respective industries, provide professional accreditation for qualified members and offer professional development opportunities through conferences, seminars or training programmes. They operate in a business-like fashion but the aim is to return surpluses to members through improved service delivery rather than create wealth for owners.

In Australia, the Australian Council for Health, Physical Education and Recreation (ACHPER) is a national professional association representing people who work in the areas of health education, physical education, recreation, sport, dance, community fitness or movement sciences. The roles of ACHPER include advocating for the promotion and provision of sport opportunities, providing professional development programmes for teachers, and accrediting and training people wanting to become community fitness instructors. Similar groups operate in Canada (Canadian Association for Health, Physical Education, Recreation and Dance), the USA (American Alliance for Health, Physical Education and Dance), the UK (British Institute of Sports Administration) and New Zealand (Physical Education New Zealand).

A number of industry lobby groups, representing the interests of nonprofit sport organizations, also operate throughout the world. A leading example is the Central Council of Physical Recreation (CCPR) in the UK, the representative body for National Sports Organizations. They act as the independent umbrella organization for national governing and representative bodies of sport and recreation in the UK to promote their interests to government and other players in the sport industry. In Australia, this role is undertaken by Sport Industry Australia, a similar nonprofit organization.

Some of the largest and most influential sport event organizations in the world operate on a nonprofit basis, including the International Olympic Committee (IOC) and the Commonwealth Games Federation (CGF). The IOC was founded in 1894 by Baron Pierre de Coubertin, and is an independent nonprofit organization that serves as the umbrella organization of the Olympic Movement. The IOC's primary role is to supervise the organization of the Summer and Winter Olympic Games.

Similar to the IOC, the role of the CGF is to facilitate a major games event every four years but it also provides education assistance for sports development throughout the 53 Commonwealth countries. There are more Commonwealth Games Associations (CGA) (71) than countries (53) because some countries like the UK have seven CGAs (Scotland, England, Northern Ireland, Wales, Isle of Man, Jersey and Guernsey) that all compete in the Games as separate nations (www.commonwealthgames.com). Both the IOC and CGF fund their operations through contributions from governments that host the games, and the sale of international broadcasting rights, corporate sponsorship, ticket sales, licensing and merchandizing sales.

There is also a range of specialist nonprofit organizations that focus on discrete community groups. Foremost among these is the International Paralympic Committee (IPC) which is the international representative organization of elite sports for athletes with disabilities. The IPC organizes, supervises and coordinates the Paralympic Games and other multi-disability sports competitions at elite level (www.paralympic.org). Other similar nonprofit organizations include the Cerebral Palsy International Sports and Recreation Association and the International Blind Sport Federation which facilitate major events for athletes.

Our focus for the remainder of the chapter is on those nonprofit sport organizations that provide sporting competition or event participation opportunities for their members and other members of the public – sport governing bodies and sports clubs. In countries such as Australia, the UK, Canada, New Zealand, Hong Kong and others with club based sporting systems, almost all sporting teams and competitions are organized by nonprofit sport organizations (Lyons 2001). These organizations take many forms. They include small local clubs that may field a few teams in a local football competition; regional associations that coordinate competitions between clubs; and state or provincial organizations that not only facilitate competitions, but also manage coach development, talent identification, volunteer training, marketing and sponsorship. They also comprise national sporting organizations that regulate the rules of competition in a country, coordinate national championships between state or provincial teams, manage elite athlete programmes, employ development officers to conduct clinics, and undertake many other tasks that facilitate participation in sport. Finally, there are international sports federations that coordinate the development of sport across the globe and facilitate rule changes and liaison between countries on issues like international competitions.

The common element amongst all these sport organizations is their nonprofit focus – they exist to facilitate sporting opportunities for their members who may be individual athletes, coaches, officials or administrators, clubs, associations or other sport organizations. They are also interdependent, relying on each other to provide playing talent, information to access competitions, resources for coach, official and player development and funding to support their activities. It is important to note that volunteers are at the heart of these organizations, playing significant roles in service delivery and decision-making at all levels of nonprofit sport organizations. At the same time though, many of the larger nonprofit sport organizations contain a significant number of paid staff who support their ongoing administration and service delivery to member associations and clubs.

Governing bodies of sport

Sport clubs compete against other clubs in competition structures provided by regional or state/provincial sporting organizations. State-based teams compete in competitions facilitated by national sporting organizations, and nations compete in leagues or events provided by international federations of sport, such as the Fédération Internationale de Football Association (FIFA), or major competition organizations such as the International Olympic Committee or the Commonwealth Games Association. These organizations are known as governing bodies for sport, having the responsibility for the management, administration and development for a sport on a global, national, state/provincial level or regional level.

The structure of the International Netball Federation Limited (IFNA) typifies the relationships between these various governing bodies of sport. The members of IFNA comprise 39 national associations from five regions: Africa, Asia, Americas, Europe and Oceania. Each region elects two members to direct the activities of the world governing organization who are responsible for setting the rules for netball, running international competitions, promoting good management in the regions, striving to seek Olympic accreditation for netball and increasing participation levels around the globe.

Netball Australia, one of the 39 members of IFNA, has more than 350,000 registered players who participate through eight state/provincial associations. They in turn have a total of 541 affiliated associations. Each of the state/provincial associations has a delegate to the national board who, along with the staff of Netball Australia, are responsible for communicating rule changes from IFNA to their members, managing a national competition, promoting good management in the state/provincial organizations, increasing participation nationally and bidding to host world events.

One of the largest members of Netball Australia, Netball Victoria, has 110,000 registered players who compete in 250 affiliated associations, organized into 21 regions and six zones across the state. Netball Victoria's role differs markedly from Netball Australia and IFNA, with responsibility for coach, official and player development, managing state competitions, promoting good management in the clubs, providing insurance coverage for players, assisting in facility development, trying to increase participation in the state, bidding to host national events and managing two teams in the national competition. Finally, netball clubs field teams, find coaches and players, manage volunteers, conduct fundraising and may own and operate a facility.

It is important to remember that these sport governing organizations are volunteer based, with volunteers involved in decisions at every level from clubs to international federations. As discussed in Chapter 12, nonprofit sport organizations do not operate as top-down power hierarchies, with clubs always abiding by regional directives, or national governing bodies agreeing with international policy initiatives. Communication and agreement can be difficult between these organizations, which may have competing priorities and localized issues. A spirit of cooperation and negotiation is required to make the nonprofit sport system operate effectively. The simple exerting of authority in a traditional organizational hierarchy is not appropriate for most nonprofit sport organizations.

The sport club environment

At the centre of sport development in countries such as Canada, New Zealand, Australia and the UK is the local or community sport club. It is worth taking some time to reflect on the role of the sport club, how volunteers and staff work in the club environment and how clubs contribute to sport development.

A background report initially prepared in 2001 and updated in 2002 for Sport Scotland provides a snapshot of sport clubs in Scotland (Allison 2002). The most striking thing about local sport clubs is their diversity. Sport clubs have many functions, structures, resources, values and ideologies and they provide an enormous range of participation opportunities for people to be involved in sport. Most clubs provide activity in a single sport, and have as their focus enjoyment in sport, rather than competitive success. Sport clubs in Scotland come in various sizes, with an average membership size of 133, and most tend to cater for both junior and adult participants. They operate with minimum staffing, structures, income and expenditure, and often rely on a small group of paid or unpaid individuals to organize and administrate club activities. The majority of club income comes from membership payments, so they tend to operate fairly autonomously. The management of local sport clubs in Scotland is regarded as an 'organic and intuitive process based on trust and experience rather than formal contracts and codes of practice' (Allison 2002: 7).

The characteristics of local sport clubs in other countries are similar. The vast majority of sport clubs rely almost exclusively on volunteers to govern, administer and manage their organizations and to provide coaching, officiating and general assistance with training, match-day functions and fundraising.

Administrators

Administrators who fill roles as elected or appointed committee members have the responsibility for the overall guidance, direction and supervision of the organization. According to the Australian Sports Commission (2000: 2) the responsibility of the management committee of a sports club extends to:

- Conducting long-term planning for the future of the club.
- Developing policy and procedures for club activities.
- Managing external relations with other sport organizations, local governments or sponsors.

- Managing financial resources and legal issues on behalf of the club.
- Carrying out recommendations put forward by members.
- Communicating to members on current issues or developments.
- Evaluating the performance of officials, employees (if any) and other service providers.
- Ensuring adequate records are kept for future transfer of responsibilities to new committee members.
- Acting as role models for other club members.

While governance is covered in detail in Chapter 12, it is important to note here that the ability of clubs to carry out these tasks effectively will vary according to their resources, culture and quality of people willing to be involved. The important administrative roles within local sports club are the chairperson or president, secretary, treasurer and volunteer coordinator. Other committee roles might involve responsibility for coaching, officiating, representative teams, match-day arrangements, fundraising or marketing.

The chairperson or president should be the one to set the agenda for how a committee operates, work to develop the strategic direction of the club, chair committee meetings, and coordinate the work of other members of the committee. Club secretaries are the administrative link between members, the committee and other organizations and have responsibility for managing correspondence, records and information about club activities. The treasurer has responsibility for preparing the annual budget, monitoring expenditure and revenue, planning for future financial needs and managing operational issues such as petty cash, payments and banking. The position of volunteer coordinator involves the development of systems and procedures to manage volunteers such as planning, recruitment, training and recognition.

Coaches

Coaches working in the sport club system may be unpaid or paid, depending on the nature of the sport and the resources of individual clubs. The role of the coach is central to developing athletes' skills and knowledge, in helping them learn tactics for success and enjoying their sport. Coaches also act as important role models for players and athletes.

Most sports provide a structured training and accreditation scheme for coaches to develop their skills and experience to coach at local, state/provincial, national or international levels. In Australia, for example, the National Coaching Council established a three tier National Coaching Accreditation Scheme (NCAS) in 1978. Coaches can undertake a Level 1 introductory course, Level 2 intermediate course and Level 3 advanced course in coaching. NCAS training programmes comprise three elements: (1) coaching principles that cover fundamentals of coaching and athletic performance, (2) sport-specific coaching that covers the skills, techniques, strategies and scientific approaches to a particular sport, and (3) coaching practice where coaches engage in practical coaching and application of coaching principles.

Officials

Sports officials include those people who act as referees, umpires, judges, scorers or timekeepers to officiate over games or events. The majority of officials are unpaid, but some sports such as Australian Rules Football, basketball and some other football codes pay officials at all levels, enabling some to earn a substantial salary from full-time officiating. Other sports such as netball, softball or tennis rarely pay officials unless they are at state or national championship level. Sports officials are critical to facilitating people's involvement in sport but are the hardest positions to fill within the nonprofit sport system since they absorb a lot of time and often have low status.

All sports provide a structured training and accreditation scheme for officials, in much the same way as coaches, to develop their skills and experience at local, state/provincial, national or international levels. The Australian National Officiating Accreditation Scheme (NOAS) was established in 1994, modelled on the NCAS, but does not prescribe formal levels of officiating as these vary greatly between sporting codes. The NOAS aims to develop and implement programmes that improve the quality, quantity, leadership and status of sports officiating in Australia through training programmes that comprise of three elements: (1) general principles of officiating and event management, (2) sport-specific technical rules, interpretations, reporting and specific roles, and (3) practice at officiating and applying the officiating principles.

General volunteers

Sport clubs also depend on people to perform roles in fundraising, managing representative teams, helping with match-day arrangements such as car parking or stewarding, or helping to market the club. The majority of general volunteers have an existing link to a sport club through being a parent of a child who plays at the club, having some other family connection, or through friends and work colleagues involved in the club.

The Volunteering Australia 2004 publication, *Snapshot 2004: Volunteering Report Card*, provided a detailed picture of volunteer involvement in a range of activities. In the 12 months prior to April 2004, an estimated 4.3 million persons over the age of 15 in Australia were involved in organized sport and physical activity – 27 per cent of the total population. Of those, 1.5 million persons were involved in non-playing roles such as coach, official, administrator, scorer, medical support or other role, and about one-third of them had more than one non-playing role. Only about 12 per cent of these people received payment for their role, which means that 88 per cent of these 1.5 million people involved in non-playing roles were volunteers. Of these 1.5 million people, 60 per cent also played sport. The majority of non-playing involvement was associated with junior sport. While making comparisons between data sets is difficult due to differences in sampling methods and instruments, the data between 1993 and 2004 indicated that while the numbers of people coaching remains constant, the numbers of people involved in officiating and administration has declined. The majority of these would be volunteers, highlighting the potential fragility of a sport system dependent on volunteers to facilitate involvement.

Figures on voluntary participation in New Zealand show that just under 20 per cent of the adult population was involved as a volunteer in the physical leisure sector in 1998 (Hillary Commission 2000). These roles included 11.1 per cent as coaches, 8.7 per cent as officials, and 8.8 per cent as administrators, with people donating an average of 2.7 hours week volunteering. This voluntary contribution was estimated to be more than 77 per cent of the equivalent full-time workforce, and worth nearly $NZ1,900 million a year. These figures clearly illustrate the enormous contribution volunteers make in roles such as coaches, officials and administrators in order to facilitate people's involvement in sport. However, there are some worrying signs that such voluntary involvement may be on the wane and that in order to sustain current levels of involvement in sport, the management of sport volunteers needs to improve.

Government intervention

The substantial funds allocated to nonprofit sport organizations by governments to support their activities in areas of mass participation or elite performance has meant that governments are increasingly trying to influence the way in which the nonprofit sector of sport operates.

Examples of these attempts include the Australian Sports Commission Volunteer Management Program and the policy of Sport England to have national organizations develop 'whole of sport' plans. These are briefly reviewed below to highlight the increasingly interdependent nature of government and sport organizations in seeking improvements in nonprofit sport.

The Australian Sports Commission (ASC) developed the Volunteer Involvement Program in 1994 in partnership with the Australian Society of Sports Administrators, the Confederation of Australian Sport and state departments of sport and recreation. The programme aimed to improve the operation of nonprofit sport clubs and associations by providing a series of publications on sport club administration. In 2000, the Volunteer Management Program (VMP) and the Club and Association Management Program (CAMP) resources were published, and the ASC encouraged all clubs to join a Club Development Network and engage in strategic planning and other management techniques.

Another example is the policy developed by Sport England to require national sport organizations to develop 'whole of sport plans'. In 2003 Sport England identified 30 priority sports, based on their capability to contribute to Sport England's vision of an active and successful sporting nation and is now working with the national sport organizations to develop and implement these plans. The plans are designed to outline how a sport from grass roots right to the elite level will attract and keep participants and improve their sporting experiences. The plans will drive decisions by Sport England to provide funding to national organizations based on clearly articulated ideas of the resources they need to drive their sport. The plans will also provide for measurable performance results and assist Sport England evaluate the benefits that accrue from funding nonprofit sport organizations.

The Clubmark programme developed by Sport England is indicative of the approach many governments have taken towards trying to enhance the capacity of the nonprofit sport sector at the community club level. Because approximately 60 per cent of young people in England belong to a sports club outside of school (where government can influence delivery standards via the education system), the government sought to improve the standard of service delivery that young people receive from community sport clubs by creating Clubmark, a cross-sport quality accreditation for clubs with junior sections run by Sport England. The main purpose of Clubmark was to encourage sport clubs to seek accreditation as a Clubmark club. National governing bodies of sport (NGBs) and county sport partnerships (CSPs) award Clubmark to proven high quality clubs. The national scheme has been in place since 2002 and midway through 2011 there were more than 10,750 accredited clubs in the Clubmark scheme.

Clubmark accreditation is awarded to clubs that comply with minimum operating standards in four areas: the playing programme; duty of care and child protection; sports equity and ethics; and club management. Clubs working towards accreditation can receive support and advice from their NGB and other partners such as county sports partnerships (CSPs). Circumstances vary between clubs and sports but the process of accreditation is the same. The benefits of implementing a single, national standard for sport club operations gives sports clubs of all types structure and direction, specifically in areas such as:

- Club development – The foundation for any club is its youth structure. By encouraging and attracting young members, it is building a strong future.
- Increased membership – Addressing issues like equity and child protection gives parents confidence when choosing a club for their children.
- Developing coaches and volunteers – As part of Clubmark, clubs receive help in developing the skills of those involved in their organization.
- Raised profile – Once Clubmark accredited, clubs are listed on a national database and in other directories, to help them attract new members and grow.

The Clubmark programme provides sport clubs with a framework for volunteer management as well as a series of templates that they can adapt for their specific circumstances. Clubmark is managed by Knight, Kavanagh & Page (KKP) on behalf of Sport England. It is responsible for validation of NGBs and CSPs, for moderation of its impact on clubs and for the marketing and promotion of the programme throughout England (Sport England 2011a).

In Practice 3.2

Sport England Sport Makers

One of the more ambitious government intervention programmes aimed at influencing the direction and capacity of the nonprofit sport sector is the Sport Makers programme, an initiative tied to the London 2012 Olympic Games. According to the Sport England website, the Sport Makers programme will recruit, train and deploy 50,000 new sports volunteers aged 16 years and over to organize and lead community sporting activities across England. The programme is based on volunteers:

> [having] a positive and inspiring introduction to the world of sport volunteering via a series of workshops delivered locally through a training provider and in conjunction with a county sports partnership. We anticipate that many volunteers will continue to give of their time, further increasing sport participation long after the 2012 Games are held in the UK. These Sport Makers will organize and support hundreds of thousands of new hours of grassroots sport, creating new opportunities across the country. While doing so, they will bring the Olympic and Paralympic values to life in every community. Sport Makers will be fully inclusive and target participants including people who have a disability, both males and females and participants from BME groups
>
> (Sport England 2011b)

The Sport Makers programme is scheduled to run from April 2011 until September 2013 with a budget of £4 million drawn from National Lottery Funding, with approximately half delivered via county sport partnerships. The outcomes are planned to include (Sport England 2011b):

- 50,000 new Sport Makers recruited and invited to an orientation workshop delivered locally through a CSP and by an inspirational trainer.
- 40,000 Sport Makers provided with deployment opportunities to increase participation for a minimum of ten hours each by their CSP. Of those deployed, it is anticipated 20,000 will continue to volunteer in sport beyond these 10 hours.
- The Olympic and Paralympic values are brought to life for the Sport Makers through their orientation workshop so that they feel part of the Olympic movement and role model these values in raising participation.
- As a result of their deployment, thousands of new opportunities for people aged 16 and over to participate will be created.

It remains to be seen if this programme involving the British Olympic Association, London Organizing Committee of the Olympic Games, National Governing Bodies, County Sports Partnerships, local authority sports development teams, local governments, and range of national and county/sub-regional voluntary partners will make any substantive difference to the operation of England's nonprofit sport sector.

Source: Sport England (2011b) *Sport Makers Fact Sheet*. London: Sport England.

Issues for the nonprofit sport sector

A range of challenges exist for the nonprofit sport sector around the globe. Foremost among these is the dependence on volunteers to sustain the sports system in areas such as coaching, administrating and officiating. As highlighted earlier in this chapter there is evidence to suggest that the rate of volunteerism is declining for roles such as officiating and administration in sport. Governments and nonprofit sport organizations will need to address this issue if their mutually dependent goals of increasing participation in organized sport are to be achieved.

The increasingly litigious nature of society and the associated increase in costs of insurance for nonprofit sport organizations directly affects the cost of participation. In Australia fewer insurers are providing insurance cover for sporting organizations and insurance premium prices have risen significantly in recent years. For example, the public liability insurance premium for the Australian Parachute Federation increased from $127,000 to $1.1million in two years. Public liability insurance is vital to run sport events and programmes and these costs are passed onto participants for no additional benefits, which raises the question of whether people can afford to keep playing sport in traditional nonprofit systems.

A further issue for nonprofit sport organizations is the trend away from participating in traditional sports, organized through clubs and associations, to a more informal pattern of participation. Some people are unwilling to commit to a season of sporting involvement, and are seeking ways to engage in sport and physical activity on a more casual basis, either through short-term commercial providers or with friends in spontaneous or pick up sports (Stewart *et al.* 2004). The increase in options available to young people to spend their discretionary leisure dollars, euros or pounds has also presented challenges for nonprofit sport organizations to market themselves as an attractive option.

As highlighted earlier, nonprofit organizations, including nonprofit sport organizations, face significant capacity problems. They are often constrained by the size of their facilities or venues, and may struggle to attract enough quality people to manage the operations of their organization. They are also constrained by the interdependent nature of sport – they require other clubs, teams and organizations to provide competition – so they need to work cooperatively with other nonprofit sport organizations to expand their 'product'.

The very nature of nonprofit sport organizations requires adherence to frequently cumbersome consultative decision-making processes, often across large geographic areas and with widely dispersed and disparate groups of stakeholders. The additional complexity of the governance and management requirements of these organizations present their own set of challenges in terms of making timely decisions, reacting to market trends, being innovative, or seeking agreement on significant organizational changes.

Lyons (2001) also suggests that nonprofit organizations are unique because they have difficulty in judging performance relative to their commercial counterparts, have to be accountable to a wide range of stakeholders, and must deal with tension and possible conflict between paid staff and volunteers. These tensions are due to a lack of clarity about paid staff and volunteer roles, and are exacerbated by the lack of clear performance measures. Nonprofit sport organizations are particularly susceptible to these problems, especially where there is a coterie of paid staff in senior administrative positions. In Practice 3.3 explores the challenges facing the nonprofit sport sector in the area of recruiting and retaining volunteers.

In Practice 3.3

Volunteer retention and capacity issues

A report from the UK-based Institute for Volunteering Research (2008) concluded that sport and recreation organizations were most likely to report difficulties with recruiting enough volunteers compared to other categories of nonprofit organizations. They also found that these organizations were more likely to say that they experienced difficulties with the retention of volunteers in the last year and that they were most likely to say that they wanted to involve more volunteers. Crucially the report concluded that organizations in the sports (and arts and culture) fields were less likely to have structured volunteer management practices in place or to have funding to support volunteers. Unsurprisingly, it was also more common for sport and recreation organizations to report difficulties in recruiting sufficient numbers of volunteers compared to other fields of activity. Another report from the same year identified three main problems faced by sports clubs in England: a shortage of volunteers, difficulty in recruiting new volunteers and the fact that work is increasingly left to fewer people. These are common problems in most westernized countries of the world where sport is primarily delivered through nonprofit sport organizations.

The reasons why this may be the case can be found in an earlier report commissioned by the peak government agency responsible for sports development in England, Sport England, that (in part) identified the challenges faced by volunteers and volunteer managers in the English sports industry (Leisure Industries Research Centre 2003). Sport volunteering in England has many of the same problems facing the sports industries of Australia, New Zealand and Canada. The 2003 report concluded that the sport system and its volunteers were subject to a variety of often competing pressures, driven by changes in government policy, technological change and market competition for leisure expenditure. Core sport volunteers, those people who work, have children, and participate in sport, were most affected. As national government and sport organizations pursue policies that attempt to increase participation at the grass roots as well as drive improvements in elite performance, volunteers are being asked to deal with an ever-increasing complexity and required level of professionalism in organizational procedures and systems. Government funding is increasingly tied to the ability of a sports organization to deliver measurable outcomes and be more accountable for their activities.

Improvements in technology and subsequent demands from end users for sport organizations to use the latest technology have placed increased demands on sport volunteers. An example of this is the shift to artificial playing surfaces for field hockey. These surfaces undoubtedly improve the playing and spectator experience but require volunteers at club level to fundraise continuously to meet significantly increased financial obligations.

The increasingly competitive leisure market has also meant volunteers at the club level have to manage their organizations to meet the demands of diverse 'customers' rather than the traditional member. People who are new to a sport may find it hard to differentiate between community club providers and commercial facilities and expect volunteers to meet their demands without becoming engaged in the life of the club. An example is the parent who treats the nonprofit sporting club as a cheap child-minding option by dropping off and picking up their child without donating any time, energy or skills to the running of the club.

The capacity of nonprofit sport organizations and their volunteers to deal with these pressures varies enormously. Some have well-established systems and resources, others flounder from one crisis to the next, continuously playing catch up. The organizations and volunteers at the community level are the ones most affected. The 2003 report recommended the use of a range of flexible and practical solutions to assist nonprofit sport organizations deal with these pressures. These included the provision of better education and training resources, simplified government funding requirements, reducing the compliance burden of reporting for sports organizations and talking to nonprofit sports organizations in language more attuned to their core values of individual volunteer motivations and commitment than overly sophisticated business and management language.

Sources: Leisure Industries Research Centre (2003) *Sports Volunteering in England 2002: A Report for Sport England*, Sheffield: Leisure Industries Research Centre; Institute for Volunteering Research (2008) *Management Matters: A National Survey of Volunteer Management Capacity*, London: Institute for Volunteering Research; and Institute for Volunteering Research and Volunteering England (2008) *A Winning Team? The Impacts of Volunteers in Sport*, London: Institute for Volunteering Research.

Summary

Nonprofit organizations were defined as those organizations that are institutionally separate from the State, do not return profits to owners, are self-governing, have a significant element of voluntary contribution and are formally incorporated. Nonprofit organizations exist to develop communities, meet the needs of identifiable and discrete groups in those communities, and work for the benefit of public good rather than wealth creation for individuals. The majority of nonprofit organizations are driven largely by the efforts of volunteers rather than paid staff.

Sport organizations that operate on a nonprofit basis include professional service organizations, industry lobby groups, sport event organizations and sport governing bodies. By far the greatest number of nonprofit sport organizations are those that provide sporting competition or event participation opportunities for their members and other members of the public – sport governing bodies and sports clubs. The common element amongst all these sport organizations is their nonprofit focus – they exist to facilitate sporting opportunities for their members who may be individual athletes, coaches, officials or administrators, clubs, associations or other sport organizations. They are also interdependent, relying on each other to provide playing talent, information to access competitions, resources for coach, official and player development and funding to support their activities.

Sport governing bodies and clubs rely almost exclusively on volunteers to govern, administer and manage their organizations and to provide coaching, officiating and general assistance with training, events and fundraising. The substantial funds allocated to nonprofit sport organizations by governments to support their activities in areas of mass participation or elite performance has meant that governments are increasingly trying to influence the way in which the nonprofit sector of sport operates. Finally, a number of challenges exist for the nonprofit sport sector including the dependence on volunteers to sustain the sports system, the increasingly litigious nature of society and the associated increase in costs of insurance for nonprofit sport organizations, the trend away from participating in traditional sports, significant capacity problems and the additional complexity of the governance and management requirements of these organizations.

Review questions

1   What is the role of the nonprofit sector in relation to sport?
2   What are the unique aspects of nonprofit sport organizations that set them apart from profit oriented or privately owned sport organizations?
3   Describe the role of a local sport association.
4   Explain how the State and the nonprofit sector may contribute to sport development.
5   In what ways are volunteers important to the delivery of sport?
6   What are the important management roles in nonprofit sporting clubs?
7   Explain the role of a club president.
8   Why does the government attempt to intervene in the management of nonprofit sport organizations? Explain how governments do this in your own country.
9   How can nonprofit sport organizations reduce the costs to participants?
10 Explain how nonprofit sport organizations have to work cooperatively with each other but still compete on the playing field.

Further reading

Cuskelly, G., Hoye, R. and Auld, C. (2006) *Working with Volunteers in Sport: Theory and Practice*, London: Routledge.

Green, M. (2006) 'From "sport for all" to not about "sport" at all: Interrogating sport policy interventions in the United Kingdom', *European Sport Management Quarterly*, 6(3): 217–238.

Houlihan, B. and Green, M. (2007) *Comparative Elite Sport Development: Systems, Structures and Public Policy*, London: Elsevier.

Houlihan, B. and White, A. (2002) *The Politics of Sports Development: Development of Sport or Development through Sport?* London: Routledge.

Hylton, K. and Bramham, P. (eds) (2008) *Sports Development: Policy, Process and Practice*, 2nd edition, London: Routledge.

Productivity Commission (2010) *Contribution of the Not-for-Profit Sector*, Canberra: Commonwealth of Australia.

Sport England (2011a) *Clubmark Factsheet*, London: Sport England.

Sport England (2011b) *Sport Makers Fact Sheet*, London: Sport England.

Relevant websites

The following websites are useful starting points for further information on nonprofit sport organizations:

Association for Research in Nonprofit Organizations and Voluntary Action – www.arnova.org
Australian Sports Commission – www.ausport.gov.au
Clubmark website – www.clubmark.org.uk/about/about-clubmark
Sport and Recreation New Zealand – www.sparc.org.nz
Sport Canada – www.pch.gc.ca/progs/sc/index_e.cfm
Sport England – www.sportengland.org
Sport Scotland – www.sportscotland.org.uk
Volunteering Australia – www.volunteeringaustralia.org

England Hockey Board

This case study explores the difficulties faced by nonprofit sport organizations in delivering sport through a network of volunteer-controlled, community-based organizations. As the chapter has highlighted, the capacity of nonprofit sport organizations varies enormously according to the local environment in which it operates, the degree of support it receives from its local government authority, its asset base, the competitiveness of the local market (i.e. how many other sports can people choose to play) and, crucially, the management system used by its volunteers and their individual abilities, skills and experience in managing a sport organization.

The England Hockey Board is the National Governing Body (NGB) for field hockey in England. The EHB was established in 2002, taking over from its predecessor, the English Hockey Association (EHA) which, in turn, was formed in 1996 to unite the then separate men's, women's and mixed associations. The England Hockey Board employs 70 full-time staff who work with volunteers at club, county, regional and national level to coach, officiate and administer the sport. The EHB is affiliated to the European Hockey Federation (EHF) and International Hockey Federation (FIH). The FIH is responsible for the production of the 'Rules of Hockey', which are the rules that are followed worldwide by all players and umpires participating in the game. The role of the EHB is to govern hockey in England from grass roots to the elite end of the sport.

Governance of the game is devolved at a regional and local level to Regional and County Associations. There are six Regional Associations – East, Midlands, North, South, West and the Combined Services who represent the three single service Associations. Counties affiliate to their respective Region. These bodies bring clubs together at a local level and ensure that information is cascaded up and down through the game. They are also responsible for implementing the Disciplinary Code of England Hockey.

The Regional Associations are represented on the Regional Consultative Committee (RCC) which supports the work of the Board to ensure it is operating in line with the agreed Memorandum and Articles of England Hockey and follows best practice in terms of the financial management of the company's affairs. England Hockey has more than 1,050 affiliated clubs. These clubs also affiliate to their County and Regional Associations. The EHB website states that 'the bedrock of club activity is league hockey played mostly on Saturdays almost exclusively on artificial turf pitches'. This is organized through Regional and County Leagues with the top Men's and Women's clubs playing nationally in the English Hockey League of which the men's game is played on Sunday. Parallel umpiring associations and committees ensure that the games are controlled, where possible, by suitably qualified officials and just as there is a progression through leagues for teams so umpires will progress from the grass roots of the game through to national and international level.

Clubs consist of up to 20 teams who usually have a regular booking at a local hockey pitch or field, either at a school or a leisure centre and will use a pub (hotel) for post-match social activity. Other clubs will own their own clubhouse and pitch(es). Other club activity will include midweek training and an increasing number of clubs undertake youth development work on weekdays after school, in the evenings and on Sundays. Hockey is a very popular sport with young people and is played in schools as well as junior sections of clubs. Regions and Counties play an important role in the promotion of the game through the work they undertake with development schemes and initiatives and organizing age group representative sides – often in partnership with other local agencies.

A key aspect of the delivery of hockey throughout the country is Hockey's Single System, the development pathway for players, coaches and officials. It is based on a set of principles that puts the participant at the centre and is based on scientific research that has been widely accepted by the majority of other major sports within England. The system delivers opportunities for people of most ages to participate in hockey and is based on a complex system of service providers, clubs, schools and associations working together to coach and support players.

A cornerstone of the EHB (and many other sports) are the affiliation fees charged to members which enable the EHB to deliver the strategy to develop hockey. Affiliating to the EHB provides clubs access to:

- ClubsFirst, an industry-wide and hockey-specific kite mark scheme linked to Sport England's Clubmark accreditation, which means your club can be recognized as *effective, safe and child-friendly.*
- Over 40 different organized and managed competitions for clubs and teams to compete in.
- Grow Your Own resources and support.
- Industry-approved coaching qualification courses.
- Regional support offices – staff with local knowledge to help support your club on issues relevant to you.
- Safeguarding guidance and templates to make it easier for clubs to provide a safe environment for children, helping you to protect young people and your club.
- The provision of coaches, umpires, tutors and assessors for clubs, counties and regions who help raise the standards of hockey and ensure a more enjoyable playing experience.
- Easy to understand, fair and transparent player pathways, from picking up a stick for the first time through to representing your country in hockey.
- Discounted and exclusive insurance for your club, to cover liability and personal accident insurance for your members.
- Awards in officiating, safeguarding young people and leadership, to support individuals and club development.
- A quarterly copy of *Hockey News* magazine keeping you up-to-date with club and national hockey news.
- Benefits from funding and sponsorship such as reduced fees in junior and adult competitions.
- Access to capital funding.
- Individual guidance and support on how to develop your club, or how you as an individual can develop your skills on or off the pitch.
- Information, resources and website downloads so you can get the latest hockey news and information relevant to you.
- Criminal Records Bureau (CRB) checking at a low cost, designed to help clubs meet government requirements of working with young people, and including all the follow-up required when a CRB reveals detrimental information.

Source: Much of the material for this case study is based on the contents of the EHB website that can be found at: www.englandhockey.co.uk.

Case study questions

1 Visit the EHB website and document all the roles where volunteers are involved in the governance, management and operations of hockey in England.

2 Explain how the Single System for hockey operates across England. What are the roles of volunteers versus paid staff in this system?

3 Identify the strengths and weaknesses of the voluntary system used by the EHB to deliver hockey throughout England.

4 What alternative structures or systems could replace the nonprofit sector for hockey in England?

Chapter 4

Professional sport

Overview

This chapter examines the key features of professional sport organizations and provides examples of the unique features of professional sport leagues and clubs. The chapter does not examine community, state or national sport organizations, but does comment on the relationship between these organizations and professional sport, as well as the impact professional sport has on the sport industry in general.

After completing this chapter the reader should be able to:

- identify the ways in which professional sport dominates the global sport industry;
- understand and explain the ways in which the media, sponsors and professional sport organizations engage in corporate synergies to market and sell their products and services; and
- understand and explain the roles of players, agents, sponsors, leagues, clubs and the media in professional sport.

What is professional sport?

Professional sport, wherever it is played, is the most expensive, most visible and most watched sporting activity. It captures the lion's share of media coverage, as well as almost all sponsorship revenue and corporate support that is on offer. Professional sport is played in cities all over the world, from Kolkata, India to Rio de Janeiro, Brazil to Melbourne, Australia, in the very best stadiums (Eden Gardens, Maracana Stadium, Melbourne Cricket Ground), by athletes who often earn, depending on the size of the market, millions of dollars. Professional sport, and the industry that surrounds it, dominates world sport and those who play it are cultural celebrities on a global scale. Local, regional, state and national sport organizations are often geared around feeding professional sport leagues by developing player talent or spectator interest. These same organizations are also often forced, somewhat ironically, to compete in vain with professional sport for media coverage, sponsorship and general support (from fans, governments and communities). At its best, professional sport is the peak of the sports industry that supports those organizations below it by generating financial resources and cultural cachet. At its worst, it is a rapacious commercial animal with an insatiable appetite for financial, cultural and social resources.

Professional sport leagues, such as the National Football League in the United States of America, dominate weekly media and social interests within the cities in which they are popular, with fans attracted to plots and subplots each week in the form of winners and losers, injuries and scandals, sackings, transfers and crisis events (financial, human and organizational). In the late nineteenth century American college football games were played on an ad hoc basis, largely special events that captured the attention of some football followers and some media outlets. College football only became a part of the national psyche and identity when games were organized around seasons, when media outlets and fans alike could plan their sport production and consumption around a weekly routine. The constancy and consistency of professional sport leagues has been the foundation upon which their popularity has been built. In many cities around the world, professional sport leagues have become an ingrained part of what it means to belong to a cultural or social group. In other words, professional sport leagues and their clubs have become, for many fans, an essential way of understanding and defining who they are.

Professional sport events, such as the Rugby Union or Cricket World Cups have also become part of our cultural and commercial consumption. They are held periodically (usually every four years) and capture audience attention because they provide out-of-the-ordinary sport action and are typically fuelled by nationalism. At a lower level, we are also exposed to annual events, such as world championships, and to circuits, such as the world rally championship, which hosts rounds in countries such as Japan, Cyprus and New Zealand. Each day of our lives we are bombarded by saturation media coverage of these events through television, radio, magazines, newspapers and the internet. There is no escaping the reach of professional sport.

Professional sport is now big business. It is not simply about what happens on the field of play, like it once was (in broad terms prior to the commercialization of sport in the 1970s), but is also about what happens in the boardroom and on the stock exchange. Table 4.1 lists *Forbes* magazine's estimation of the football/soccer teams with the highest value in the world in 2010. Although some of the estimations are arguable, the list demonstrates that many of these teams are significant corporate entities – seven of the top ten also have estimated annual revenues in excess of US$300 million.

In the first chapter of this book you were introduced to the three sector model of sport: public, nonprofit and private. In Chapters 2 and 3 the public and nonprofit sectors were examined, while this fourth chapter examines professional sport. It would be a mistake,

Table 4.1: Highest value football/soccer teams 2010

Team	Country	Value (US$)
Manchester United	England	1,835,000,000
Real Madrid	Spain	1,323,000,000
Arsenal	England	1,181,000,000
Barcelona	Spain	1,000,000,000
Bayern Munich	Germany	990,000,000
Liverpool	England	882,000,000
AC Milan	Italy	800,000,000
Juventus	Italy	656,000,000
Chelsea	England	646,000,000
Inter Milan	Italy	413,000,000

Source: www.forbes.com

however, to assume that the terms private and professional are synonymous in the context of sport organizations and their operations. Rather, in this chapter we are examining those sport organizations in which competitive commercial revenue is used to sustain their operations, as opposed to organizations that are funded by the State or almost exclusively through membership fees or subscriptions. It is important to recognize that many of the organizations featured in this chapter are actually nonprofit, and are not privately owned. Professional sport organizations have two important features that define them. First, they share a scale of operations (particularly commercial and financial) that means they exist at the apex of the sport industry, and second, all the players or athletes are 'professionals' – sport is their job and they are paid to train and play full-time. Sports in which the players or athletes are required to find additional employment to supplement their income cannot be considered professional.

The example of the Australian professional football landscape is useful for illustrating and understanding the distinction between private and nonprofit organizations within professional sport, as well as the differences that exist between sports. In the Australian Football League (AFL) all the clubs are essentially member-based organizations (in which supporters who buy memberships are entitled to attend games, as well as vote in a Board of Directors). AFL clubs have annual revenues of up to AUS$50 million, but they are nonprofit organizations – all the money is used on club operations (e.g. to pay players and staff, maintain facilities or promote the club) and none of the money earned by the clubs is returned to an owner or to shareholders. Although it is essentially a collection of nonprofit organizations, the AFL is the wealthiest and most popular professional sport organization in Australia, which captures the greatest share of sponsorship and broadcast rights revenue. Like the AFL, Australia's National Rugby League (NRL) consists of many member-based clubs, but there are also some that are privately owned. In the instances where a club is privately owned, the annual profit or loss is either returned to or borne by the private owner. For example, if the Melbourne Storm, one of the NRL's most successful and controversial clubs in the first decade of the twenty-first century, secures a profit, it is returned to its owner, multinational media conglomerate News Corporation. In contrast to the AFL and NRL, all eight clubs in the Australian A-League (soccer) are privately owned, but the governing body, Football Federation Australia, is a nonprofit organization. In this case the responsibility for ensuring a healthy and viable professional league is shared between private and nonprofit organizations. Throughout this chapter, and the remaining chapters of the book, it is important to keep in mind that both nonprofit and private organizations compete in professional sport leagues.

In Practice 4.1

Manchester United

Formed in 1878 under the name of Newtown Heath LYR (Lancashire and Yorkshire Railway), Manchester United now claims to be the most popular football team in the world. Since it took the name Manchester United in 1902, the club has become one of the most successful in the English Premier League, having won 18 League premierships by 2010, including three in a row in 2007, 2008 and 2009, 11 FA Cups and three European Cup/UEFA Champions League titles.

Manchester United has also become a powerhouse off the field. According to its 2010 bond prospectus and research conducted by TNS Sport, the club claims to have 139 million core fans and 333 million followers worldwide. This fan base means that the club is able to maximize its match-day, sponsorship, merchandise and media revenues. According to the 2010 bond prospectus, Manchester United's football stadium has a capacity of 75,797 seats, of which approximately 54,000 are sold to general admission season tickets holders, 7,500 to executive members, 10,000 to general admission fans of the club and 3,000 to away fans. The club reports that the average attendance has been 99 per cent for more than a decade and that in 2008–2009 match-day revenues of £108.8 million accounted for 39.1 per cent of total revenue.

Manchester United is also a prominent brand in traditional and new media. In July 2010 Manchester United launched a page on the influential social networking site Facebook. By early 2011 the club's page had more than 11 million fans. One fan site analyser (fangager.com) lists the Manchester United page as the third highest of all fan sites in terms of the number of active fans. According to fangager.com, Manchester United has more than 255,000 active fans, which represent 2.6 per cent of its overall fans, the highest percentage of the top 100 fan sites. According to its 2010 bond prospectus, Manchester United estimates that an average of 45 million people watch each of its matches. This large number of committed fans means that the club has been able to spread itself across a range of different media platforms, of which its internet site and content delivery via mobile phones are prominent. In 2008–2009, the club captured almost £100 million from media revenues, equivalent to 35.8 per cent of total revenue.

Manchester United's fan base and media exposure allows it to capture additional sponsorship and merchandizing revenues that fall outside match-day and media revenues. In 2008–2009 commercial revenues accounted for £69.9 million, equivalent to 25.1 per cent of total revenue. Manchester United's shirt sponsor is the Aon Corporation, an international insurance and risk management company. The sponsorship is estimated to be worth £20 million per year. The other significant commercial partner is Nike, the global sporting goods manufacturer. The Manchester United-Nike contract runs until 2015 and covers the club's global merchandizing, licensing and retail operations. Manchester United also has a diverse stable of sponsors that illustrates both the complexity of contemporary professional sport as well as the ways in which the commercial landscape can be segmented: Audi is the official car supplier; Singha is the official beer; Thomas Cook is the official travel partner; Hublot is the official timekeeper; Turkish Airlines is the official airline partner; Epson is the official office equipment partner; Betfair is the official betting partner; Concha Y Toro is the official wine partner; Smirnoff is the official responsible drinking partner; and DHL is the official logistics partner.

Source: Manchester United website (www.manutd.com)

Circuits of promotion

In order to describe and explain the interconnections between professional sport, the media, advertisers and business, Whitson (1998) used the concept of 'circuits of promotion'. The key premise that underpins the circuit of promotion concept is that the boundaries between the promotion of sports and the use of sport events and athletes to promote products, which were previously separate, are now being dissolved. In other words, it is becoming increasingly more difficult to see where the sport organization ends and where the sponsor or media or advertiser begins. They are becoming (or have become) one, where one part of the professional sport machine serves to promote the other, for the good of itself and all the other constituent parts.

The relationship between Nike and former Chicago Bulls and Washington Wizards player Michael Jordan is a perfect example of a circuit of promotion at work. The Nike advertising campaigns that featured Jordan contributed to building the profile of both the company and the athlete, while Jordan's success in winning six NBA championships with the Bulls enhanced the corporate synergy between the two 'brands' and helped to increase the return on Nike's investment. Furthermore, the success of Jordan and the global advertising campaigns developed by Nike increased the cultural, social and commercial profile of the National Basketball Association (NBA) in America. In turn, the global promotion and advertising by the NBA, that either did or did not feature Jordan, helped to promote both Jordan, as the League's most visible and recognizable player, and Nike, as a major manufacturer of basketball footwear and apparel, either by direct or indirect association. Lastly, any advertising undertaken by Jordan's other sponsors, such as Gatorade, served to promote Jordan, but also the NBA and Nike through their association with Jordan. At its best, a sporting circuit of promotion is one of continuous commercial benefit and endless leveraging opportunities for the athletes and organizations involved.

Sport circuits

Sport circuits involve a league or structured competition. NASCAR has been one of the most popular sports in the United States of America for over 50 years. It is broadcast on the FOX, SPEED, ABC, ESPN and TNT television networks and stations. Like some other professional sports such as the National Hockey League in America, the Bundesliga in Germany and the National Rugby League in Australia, NASCAR operates to a seasonal calendar, with races in different American cities and towns each week, from February through to November at race tracks such as the Phoenix International Raceway, Daytona International Speedway and the Talladega Superspeedway. Scheduling races at different venues ensures good live attendances, but also enables NASCAR and its competing teams and drivers to capitalize on an array of sponsorship opportunities.

The European Champions League is an example of a global sport circuit that is based around a league model, whereby teams play in different cities depending on who qualifies for the tournament and teams are progressively knocked out until a winner is determined. The men's and women's professional tennis tours are examples of a global circuit in which a series of events represent the structured competition. Each event or tournament on the tour may be entered by ranked players (who may have qualified through a lesser 'satellite circuit'), who compete for prize money, as well as points that go towards an overall ranking to determine the world's best player. In both the above cases, the circuit is managed or overseen by a governing body, although in the case of tennis the responsibility for managing and running individual tournaments is devolved to the host organization. For example, the Australian Open, the Grand Slam of the Asia-Pacific region, is managed and run by Tennis Australia, the sport's governing body in Australia.

The locations of events or tournaments that are part of national and global sport circuits are often flexible and cities or countries are able to bid for the right to host the event. In the case of the European Champions League the teams that qualify for the tournament are entitled to host their home games (a performance based flexibility), while in tennis the grand slam tournaments of the Australian Open, the US Open, the French Open and Wimbledon are the only marquee events (no flexibility). In Formula One racing, however, cities can compete for the rights to host rounds of the championship. The Formula One season is based around Europe, but events are also held in Asia and North and South America. The races are broadcast to more than 160 countries and cities are often encouraged to bid for rights to host an event by the promise of economic benefits that might accrue as a result of securing a long-term contract. For example, China was added to the circuit in 2004, with racing held at the purpose built Shanghai International Circuit.

The biggest global sport circuits are the Olympic Games and the FIFA World Cup, which are also the biggest events of any type staged in the world. Both events are held every four years and have a complex arrangement whereby countries and cities can bid to host the event. For a city to win the right to host the Summer or Winter Olympic Games it must go through a stringent, two-phase selection process. In the first phase – the 'candidature acceptance procedure' – national Olympic committees may nominate a city, which is then evaluated during a ten-month process in which an International Olympic Committee (IOC) administrative committee examines each city based on technical criteria such as venue quality, general city infrastructure, public transport, security and government support. The cities accepted as applicants for the 2016 Summer Olympic Games were Chicago (USA), Prague (Czech Republic), Tokyo (Japan), Rio de Janeiro (Brazil), Madrid (Spain), Baku (Azerbaijan) and Doha (Qatar). The selected 'candidate' cities move through to the second and final 'candidature phase'. Chicago, Tokyo, Rio de Janeiro and Madrid were selected as candidates for the 2016 Games. In this phase the cities must submit a comprehensive candidature file to the IOC and are visited by the IOC's evaluation commission. The evaluation commission's report on the candidate cities is made available to all IOC members, who subsequently elect a host for the Games at a full session of the IOC (for the election of the 2016 Games the IOC session was held in Copenhagen in October 2009, at which it was announced that the Rio de Janeiro bid had been successful).

There are also global sport circuits in which participation in the event is dependent almost entirely on money, which situates them at the apex of the professional sport pyramid. Like the Olympic Games, the America's Cup is held every four years, but unlike the Olympic Games, a team can only enter if it has enough financial support to mount a challenge. For example, BMW Oracle Racing, the team which won the thirty-third America's Cup, was supported Oracle, one of the largest software companies, with annual revenues of in excess of US$10 billion, while BMW is one of the world's leading prestige automotive manufacturers. It is estimated that each of the teams that challenge for the America's Cup need to allocate in excess of US$100 million to the task, with research and development costing US$20 million, yacht hulls US$1.5 million each and skippers paid in excess of US$500,000 per year.

Media

Media organizations have become essential partners for professional and nonprofit sport organizations alike. The breadth and depth of coverage that media organizations provide their professional sporting partners is of such significance that it has the capacity to influence the social and commercial practices of millions, if not billions of people. The scale and scope of the financial relationship they enjoy is also important, so much so that sport and the media are often regarded as interdependent (Bellamy 1998; Nicholson 2007). The impact of sport news on the popularity and profitability of new media forms has only been equalled by the transformation that sport has undergone, as a result of its interplay with the media. It might have been possible in the 1890s to think about sport and its social and commercial relevance without reference to the media, but by the 1990s the task was impossible. It is now as if 'one is literally unthinkable without the other' (Rowe 1999: 13).

The media is often considered to provide three broad functions in a society: information, education and entertainment. However, in terms of the sport-media relationship, it has become increasingly clear that media organizations and consumers are interested in professional sport because of its entertainment value. The exploits of leagues, teams and athletes are reported throughout the world, across a wide range of print (e.g. newspapers and magazines) and broadcast (e.g. radio, television and the internet) media. Some of this media coverage is provided as 'news', which essentially means that media organizations report on what is happening in sport in much the same way they report on politics or world events. However, a significant component of broadcast coverage is provided through exclusive arrangements in which media organizations purchase the rights to broadcast an event or season(s).

Figure 4.1 provides a graphic representation of the relationships that exist between sport organizations, media organizations, advertisers and consumers. Sport organizations supply media organizations with content. In some instances the sport organization receives a fee, usually from television or radio broadcasters, while in others they provide media outlets, such as newspapers and magazines, with access to games or players. This is done in the hope that the additional promotion and exposure will attract more fans or commercial support. Both the broadcasters and other media represented in Figure 4.1 secure a return on their investment (staff and infrastructure, as well as money) by selling their product to consumers or by selling advertising time and space. The amount of money they are able to charge for selling their product is dependent on its popularity. Professional sport is typically very popular with consumers, particularly football leagues, international sport circuits and major events, which in turn makes it very attractive to media organizations and advertisers.

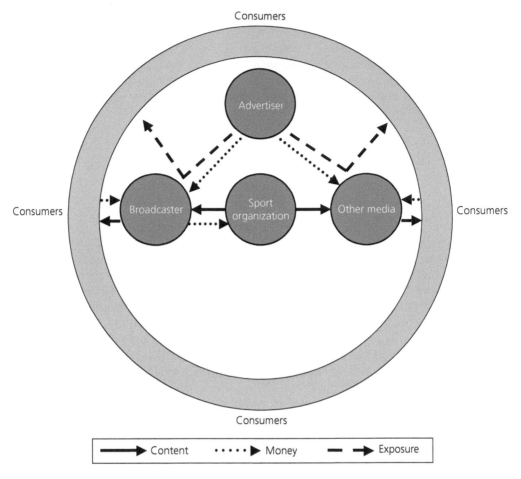

Source: adapted from Nicholson (2007)

Figure 4.1: Sport and media relationships.

Whereas sport organizations once relied on ticket sales as their primary source of income, they now rely on the sale of broadcast rights (and, to a lesser extent, sponsorship revenue). For example, in 1930, 85 per cent of FIFA's income was derived from ticket sales and subscriptions from its member associations, yet by 2002 these revenue sources accounted for only 1 per cent. During the period 1999–2002, the sale of broadcast rights accounted for an average of 61 per cent of FIFA's annual income. The Olympics is also an outstanding example of the growth in broadcast rights fees paid by broadcasting networks across the globe, as well as the actual and perceived popularity of sports. Figure 4.2 illustrates the magnitude of broadcast rights for the Olympics over the previous quarter of a century. Clearly, sport is effective in attracting both audiences and advertisers. Importantly, the relationship between professional sport and the media has reached a point where professional sport would not survive in its current form without the media.

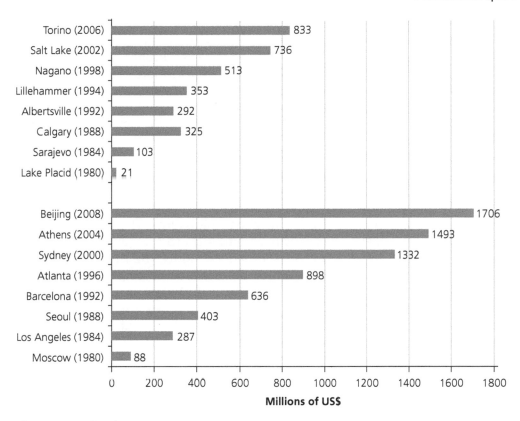

Source: www.olympic.org

Figure 4.2: Olympic broadcast rights 1980–2008 for Summer and Winter Olympic Games.

In Practice 4.2

Paying to watch
Sporting leagues throughout the world are increasingly dependent on broadcast rights fees to sustain their operations. Each league has a different model for maximizing the value of these rights, while in some instances governments seek to intervene via regulation in order to protect consumers. In most cases the rights to broadcast games or matches in a professional league are shared between free-to-air (or terrestrial broadcasters) and pay television (or cable broadcasters). Free-to-air and pay television broadcasters have different revenue models; in short, free-to-air broadcasters rely on selling advertising space in the form of advertisements or commercial breaks, while pay television broadcasters rely on selling subscriptions and to a lesser extent advertising. Sport content is often considered an important driver in the penetration or take-up of pay television.

The National Football League (NFL) in the USA secures the greatest broadcast rights revenue of any sport league in the world. The current rights deal, which runs until 2013, ensures that the NFL is paid slightly more than US$3 billion per year from its arrangements with broadcasters CBS, NBC, Fox and ESPN. Cable television provider ESPN pays US$1.1 billion per season (2006–2013) for the exclusive rights to broadcast Monday night football. Viewers are able to view games for free through free-to-air broadcasters such as NBC, but must subscribe to ESPN in order to view the premium Monday night football games.

In the UK the English Premier League (EPL) rights are shared between Sky Sports, ESPN and the BBC. Pay television provider Sky Sports has the rights to the majority of the EPL, while by contrast the BBC, the only free-to-air broadcaster with rights, only has access to highlights. This means that in order to view live EPL action fans must either go to the game or subscribe to pay television. In addition to UK broadcast rights, the rights to the EPL are also sold internationally via a bidding process. For example, the rights to broadcast the EPL in Singapore for the 2010–2013 were secured by SingTel for an estimated £200 million. The previous rights were held by StarHub, a pay television operator, and SingTel paid more than double the previous deal, indicative of the trend among pay television broadcasters to compete to secure premium sport content in order to increase subscription sales.

In Australia, the rights to broadcast the 2012–2016 seasons of the Australian Football League (AFL) have been shared by pay television provider Foxtel and free-to-air broadcaster Channel 7, for in excess of AUS$1.2 billion. Prior to the 2012–2016 round of bidding, government regulation meant that free-to-air broadcasters has first access to the rights, but changes to the regulation allowed pay television provider Foxtel to secure the rights to televise all nine games per round live, with free-to-air broadcaster Channel 7 securing the rights to broadcast premium games on Friday and Saturday nights, as well as two other games. This arrangement is an unusual one, in that it sets up a direct competition between a free-to-air and pay television provider for four games per week. As the leading pay television provider in Australia, securing the rights to broadcast all games of the most popular sporting league live may allow Foxtel to substantially increase its number of subscribers.

Source: National Football League (www.nfl.com); English Premier League (www.premierleague.com); Australian Football League (www.afl.com.au)

Sponsorship

The amount of money available to professional sport organizations through sponsorship arrangements or deals is directly related to the return on investment that the sponsor is able to achieve. In broad terms, the return on investment is dependent on an increase in sales or business, which a sponsor achieves through increased awareness or direct marketing. Sport organizations with large supporter bases, such as Manchester United, are able to secure significant sponsorship deals because the sponsor is able to market its product directly to a large number of Manchester United supporters, as well as increase its awareness through media coverage of the club and the English Premier League. Sport organizations with global, regional or strong national profiles have a distinct advantage in the sponsorship market.

Sponsors want to be involved with a club or league that has very good network television coverage, which reaches a broad audience. This is most often achieved through exclusive broadcast rights arrangements. However, the general news media coverage that a club or league receives in a variety of media forms and outlets, including television, radio, newspapers, magazines and the internet, can also influence its attractiveness to sponsors. This media coverage promotes the club or league and generally encourages fans to consume the sport, either by attending the game live or by accessing a mediated version. The club or league that is able to attract a greater amount of this news media coverage is more likely to be embedded in the commercial consciousness of audiences and consumers. Thus, the amount of media coverage received is a measure of the audiences that can be reached by advertisers (or sponsors) through a commercial association with a professional sporting club or league and is directly proportional to the worth of the sponsorship.

The value of sponsorships differ between sports, between leagues, between clubs and across countries. At the highest level the IOC created 'The Olympic Partner Programme' (TOP) in 1985, in order to provide companies with exclusive worldwide marketing rights to the Games. The Top VII partnership programme, which included the 2010 Winter Olympic Games in Vancouver and the 2012 Olympic Games in London, comprised the following companies: Coca-Cola, Acer, Atos Energy, GE, McDonalds, Omega, Samsung, Visa and Panasonic; BMW, BP, British Airways and Adidas were among the official partners of 2012 London Olympic Games. At other levels of professional sport the sponsorship or marketing arrangements may go further, as clubs and leagues are willing to enter into sponsorship arrangements whereby commercial organizations are able to acquire naming rights or enter into arrangements that give them either exclusive or increased access to fans. The development of the internet and online marketing has been particularly instrumental in this respect.

The English Premier League provides an example of the proliferation of sponsors within professional sport leagues and clubs. The competition is known as the Barclays Premiership, sponsored by a United Kingdom-based financial services group engaged in banking, investment banking and investment management. The English Premier League also has a range of secondary or associate sponsors. For example, EA Sports and Nike are 'official partners', while pharmaceutical company GlaxoSmithKline is an 'official supplier' through its Lucozade sport drink. Furthermore, the clubs that play in the Barclays Premiership have significant sponsorship deals. The primary sponsor of each club is entitled to place its brand prominently on the front of the playing strip. Manchester United's primary sponsor is AON, an international insurance and risk management company, a deal which is worth an estimated £80 million over four years. Arsenal is sponsored by Emirates, one of the world's leading airlines (previous sponsors of Chelsea), Chelsea is sponsored by Samsung, an electronic goods manufacturer, Liverpool is sponsored by Standard Chartered, a bank, Everton has been sponsored by Chang, a Thai beer, since 2004 and Tottenham Hotspur is sponsored by Investec, a specialist bank and asset manager, a subtle change from its previous sponsor Mansion.com, an online casino.

Like broadcast rights revenue, sponsorship revenue within professional sport has grown exponentially. In the early 1960s, NASCAR driver Fred Lorenzen's sponsorship, from a Ford dealership, was US$6,000 for an entire season. By the late 1980s, it was estimated that approximately US$3 million in sponsorship was required for a team to break even over the course of the season. In 2000, UPS announced its sponsorship of the Robert Yates No. 88 team driven by Dale Jarrett, which was estimated to be worth US$15 million per year.

Professional sport

The sponsorship of professional sport goes further than commercial agreements between clubs and leagues. Individual athletes also have sponsorship agreements that provide them with additional income to supplement their playing contracts (for team sports) or prize money (for individuals). Well-chosen brands with a global profile can enhance an athlete's overall image and in the case of more popular athletes a sponsor can establish the athlete as a brand in their own right. Sponsorship of professional athletes is not restricted to superstar athletes like David Beckham of the Los Angeles Galaxy (football/soccer), Tiger Woods (golf) or Yao Ming of the Houston Rockets (basketball). Rather, sponsorship of professional athletes exists wherever there is a market, whether it a mass market in the case of global athletes or a niche market in the case of small or cult sports.

In Practice 4.3

Sponsoring Serena

Serena Williams is one of the most recognizable athletes in the world. Williams turned professional in 1995 and has become one of the most successful tennis players of all time. Williams has won 13 Grand Slam titles, comprising five Australian Open titles, four Wimbledon titles, three US Open titles and one French Open title; Williams has also won 12 Grand Slam doubles titles with her sister Venus and has won Olympic Games gold medals in the doubles in 2000 and 2008. As of 2011, Williams' on-court prize money was US$33 million, the highest of any female athlete in history. Williams' on court successes have been mirrored off-court by her commercial endorsements and media profile. According to Forbes, Williams' income in 2010 was $20 million, much of which was earned off-court. In 2011 she was sponsored by a wide range of companies and products, including the following:

- Nike: one of the world's largest manufacturers and distributors of athletic apparel and equipment.
- Wilson: one of the world's leading manufacturers of ball sports equipment, including for tennis, baseball, American football, golf, basketball, softball, badminton and squash.
- HP: a technology company operating in more than 170 countries, specializing in computers and computing.
- Mission Skincare: a company producing 'athlete-engineered' skincare products.
- Kraft: a food and confectionery company, which includes the Nabisco stable of biscuits such as Oreo.
- EA Sports: an interactive entertainment software company that produces software for Internet, PC and video game systems.
- HSN: a television, online and catalogue retailer.
- Gatorade: the leading brand of sport drink in America.

Many of Williams' sponsorships are sport- or tennis-related, such as Nike, Wilson, EA Sports and Gatorade, where there are obvious commercial benefits for Williams and the sponsor. For example, through the Nike website consumers can purchase items from the 'Serena Williams Collection', which allows tennis fans and players to look like Williams on the court. In many team sports the clothing and apparel are relatively generic, with fans able to customize products by adding their favourite player's name and number. By contrast, individual athletes such as Williams allow companies such as Nike to manufacture and market a diverse range of themed products, such as skirts, dresses, caps, jackets and shoes. Williams has been a particularly good investment for Nike in this respect, as she has become known as a tennis fashion icon. Williams is also sponsored by a range of companies that are not sport-related, such as HP, Kraft and HSN, indicative that her appeal extends well beyond tennis fans.

In the 2010 edition of *Sports Illustrated*'s list of the top 50 American athletes by earnings, Tiger Woods ranked number 1 with US$20 million in winnings and US$70 million in endorsements, despite off-field scandals that reduced his sponsorship value. Williams did not make the top 50, an indication of the power and popularity of male-dominated sports such as football, basketball, baseball in the US market. Of the international contenders, Roger Federer topped the list with overall earnings of US$61.8 million.

Source: Serena Williams official website (www.serenawilliams.com); *Sports Illustrated* website (www.sportsillustrated.com); Forbes website (www.forbes.com).

Player management

As sport has become increasingly professional and the amount of money secured through broadcast rights and sponsorship deals has increased, the salaries of players and athletes have also increased. The growth in player and athlete income has been mirrored by a concurrent rise in the expectations of clubs and leagues, an increase in the complexity of contract negotiations and greater off-field commercial opportunities for prominent 'sport stars'. These developments in the world of professional sport have led to the evolution of an industry focused on player and athlete management, which is essentially geared towards providing players and athletes with services in return for a share of their income.

One of the most prominent player and athlete management companies is the International Management Group (IMG), which was formed in the 1960s and employs in excess of 2,000 staff in 70 offices in 30 countries. What began exclusively as a player management business has evolved into a complex commercial operation that includes television and publishing divisions. Golfer Arnold Palmer, winner of the US Masters golf tournament in 1958, 1960, 1962 and 1964, the US Open in 1960 and the British Open in 1961 and 1962, was the first athlete in the world to be branded by Mark McCormack, the creator and head of IMG. Back in the 1960s the 'brand-name' principle by which Palmer and McCormack approached sport was the first attempt to transform the business activities of leading athletes. Sport and business were previously related, but the scale of their operation was unique. The level of vertical and horizontal integration was essential to what became known as 'Sportsbiz' (Boyle and Haynes 2000). McCormack took the relationship of the agent further than before, and began to handle contract negotiations, proactively sought business opportunities and planned the sale of the Palmer brand on a long-term basis, rather than previous attempts that might be characterized as ad hoc. McCormack set an important precedent by selling people as marketable commodities.

Professional sport

Octagon is a global sport marketing company and competitor to IMG. It represents and promotes more than 800 athletes in 35 different sports across the world. Its clients include some of the most prominent sportsmen and women, such as tennis players Amelie Mauresmo and Jelena Jankovic. Octagon provides a broad range of services for the athletes it manages, including the following:

- Contract negotiations
- Marketing initiatives and endorsements
- Public relations and charity involvement
- Financial planning
- Media management
- Property development
- Speaking engagements

Octagon claims that it generates annual marketing revenues of in excess of US$300 million, by maximizing its athletes' off-field corporate relationships. The company states that it does this by developing a unique and individual marketing plan for each of its athletes. Octagon represents American swimmer Michael Phelps, winner of eight gold medals at the 2008 Beijing Olympic Games. The company claims Phelps is a perfect case study in what successful sport marketing and management can provide for an athlete in the contemporary hyper-commercial sport environment. Octagon suggests that Phelps laid the foundation with his performances in the pool, but that Octagon enhanced the Phelps story with a targeted publicity campaign, which included appearances in *Time*, *People*, the *Wall Street Journal* and *USA Today*. The result was what Octagon claims to be the creation of a connection between Phelps and corporate America, including the largest ever endorsement deal in swimming with Speedo and subsidiary deals with VISA, Omega and AT&T Wireless.

In many respects, athletes competing in individual sports are logical targets for both agents and sponsors, however athletes in team sports are often as valuable, if not more so. In the United States the term 'multiples' is used to refer to an athlete that has the ability to attract multiple media and endorsements. The multiples' play on the field is at the highest level, they help to bring fans to the game, help the team to secure broadcast contracts or sponsorships deals, help the team in merchandizing and licensing and in the extreme cases have the potential to increase the net financial worth of the organization. Thus, the athlete's commercial potential can be calculated in individual earnings (through the team or an agent), but also in terms of the growth of the club or league of which they are a part. In 2002 Yao Ming led the Shanghai Sharks to the championship in the Chinese Basketball Association, averaging 32.4 points, 19.0 rebounds and 4.8 blocked shots. A member of the Chinese national team since he was 18 years old, 229 cm Ming was selected as the first pick in the 2002 NBA draft by the Houston Rockets. In his first season in the NBA Ming was voted rookie of the year and the Rockets improved their winning percentage from 34 per cent to 52 per cent. The Houston Rockets website is available in English or Chinese, in order to cater for Ming's enormous popularity in China (www.nba.com/rockets). Ming's success with the Rockets means that merchandizing and broadcast possibilities are significant, for both the team and the league. 'The Year of the Yao', a movie about Ming's first year in the NBA and his transition from China to America was released in cinemas in 2005, further evidence of Ming's popularity and commercial value.

Professional sport stars are well paid by any measures. Importantly, their salaries are relative to revenue of the clubs, leagues, tournaments and events of which they are a part. In fact, in some professional sports with strong player unions, the level of remuneration for players is set as a percentage of league revenue. Table 4.2 is an estimate of the highest paid football/soccer players in the world in 2009. Their annual earnings are indicative of their

Table 4.2: Highest value football/soccer players 2009

Player	Team	Annual Earnings (US$)
David Beckham	AC Milan; Los Angeles Galaxy	40,000,000
Cristiano Ronaldo	Real Madrid	30,000,000
Ricardo Kaka	Real Madrid	25,000,000
Ronaldinho	AC Milan	25,000,000
Thierry Henry	Barcelona	21,000,000
Lionel Messi	Barcelona	20,000,000
Frank Lampard	Chelsea	17,000,000
John Terry	Chelsea	16,000,000
Zlatan Ibrahimovic	Barcelona	16,000,000
Steven Gerrard	Liverpool	15,000,000
Wayne Rooney	Manchester United	15,000,000
Samuel Eto'o	Internazionale	13,000,000
Fabio Cannavaro	Juventus	12,000,000
Rio Ferdinand	Manchester United	11,000,000
Francesco Totti	AS Roma	11,000,000

Source: www.forbes.com

on-field worth and the significant investment made by their respective teams, as well as their commercial worth off the field. That David Beckham is by far the world's highest paid soccer player, but is nearing the end of his career, is indicative of the importance placed on individual celebrity athletes by teams and leagues. Beckham was recruited by the LA Galaxy for his global profile and marketing appeal as much as his on-field abilities.

Ownership and outcomes

Professional sports utilize different ownership and governance models in order to regulate and manage their businesses effectively. Some of the models have strong historical traditions, while others have been selected or adapted for their utility. One of the key distinctions is between professional sport teams and leagues that can be considered 'profit maximizers' and those that are 'win maximizers'. There is some debate as to whether these terms accurately reflect the practice of professional sport teams and franchises, but they are useful for broadly categorizing operational and financial priorities. Profit-maximizing teams, such as those in the major American professional sport leagues, are typically owned by individuals or businesses who seek to maximize the financial return on investment. In some sports, however, such as English, Scottish and Australian football and cricket (Quirk and Fort 1992), the need to win is a greater priority than the need to make a profit. In fact, in some instances win-maximizing teams will place the club in financial jeopardy, particularly by purchasing players it cannot afford.

In some cases, the ownership model has adapted to meet specific conditions brought about by commercial change. In the J-League, Japan's professional football (soccer) competition, teams like the Kashiwa Reysol are privately owned. The Reysol is owned by the Hitachi corporation that specializes in the manufacturing of electrical goods and equipment. Originally established as an amateur team of the Hitachi corporation, the Reysol was professionalized in order to participate in the inaugural J-League season in 1993.

Whether teams are win maximizing or profit maximizing, they must cooperate with each other at some level to ensure that fans, sponsors and the media remain interested and involved with the sport. Sport leagues that are dominated by one or two teams are often perceived to be less attractive to fans than leagues in which the result of games is uncertain. There is, however, a long history of leagues in which strong rivalries have maintained interest in the game (Los Angeles Lakers versus Boston Celtics in the NBA and Rangers versus Celtic in the Scottish Premier League for example), although often the teams that are part of the rivalry benefit at the expense of teams that perform poorly. A league that is not dominated by only a couple of teams and in which there is an uncertainty of outcome (of a game or season) is said to have 'competitive balance' (Quirk and Fort 1992). Leagues across the world have instituted a range of measures to try to achieve competitive balance, which is often elusive. Perhaps the most obvious and publicized measure is the draft system that operates in football leagues such as the National Football League in America or the Australian Football League. The draft allows the league to allocate higher draft preferences (the best athletes on offer) to poorer performed teams, in order to equalize the playing talent across the league and create more competitive games.

Summary

This chapter has presented an overview of professional sport and some of the central relationships that are essential to its ongoing prosperity and survival. The media, sponsors, agents, owners, advertisers, leagues, clubs and athletes are part of a self-sustaining commercial alliance, in which each of the partners promotes and supports the activities and interests of the others. Commercial networks are the binding forces that are holding professional sport together in the twenty-first century. Since the middle of the twentieth century, professional sport leagues and clubs have increasingly become willing partners in the promotion of their activities (sports and events), as well as the promotion of subsidiary products and services, and in the process have become major players in a multibillion dollar industry.

Review questions

1   Use the circuit of promotion concept to explain the role of sponsors and the media in the professional sport industry.
2   Explain the rationale behind a company sponsoring a professional sport club, league or athlete.
3   Is the media important to the survival of professional sport? Why?
4   Identify an international and a domestic professional circuit and examine its operation. What are the special features that attract fans and media?
5   Choose a professional sport league and identify the fees paid by television broadcasters over the previous 20 years for the broadcast rights. Has it increased or decreased over the period? Explain why.

6   Choose a sport in which the location of events or tournaments is not fixed. Imagine that the city you live in is going to bid for the right to host the event and create a list of potential benefits – consider such features as the economy, environment, transport, public services and housing.

7   Choose a high profile athlete and identify what companies or products sponsor the athlete. Is the athlete represented by an agent or did they secure the sponsorships or endorsements themselves?

8   Choose a sporting league of the world and identify whether it should be classified as 'win maximizing' or 'profit maximizing'. Provide a rationale for your answer that includes a commentary on the ownership of teams in the league.

9   Create a list of the top five paid sportspeople in the world. What does the list tell you about the size of the commercial markets that the sports are played in and the popularity of the sports?

10 Create a fictional international sport circuit. What cities of the world would host your events and why?

Further reading

Bellamy, R. (1998) 'The evolving television sports marketplace', in L. Wenner (ed.) *MediaSport*. Routledge, London, pp. 73–87.

Boyle, R. and Haynes, R. (2000) *Power Play: Sport, the Media and Popular Culture*. Longman, London.

Cousens, L. and Slack, T. (2005) 'Field-level change: The case of North American major league professional sport', *Journal of Sport Management*, 19(1): 13–42.

Euchner, C. (1993) *Playing the Field: Why Sports Teams Move and Cities Fight to Keep Them*. John Hopkins University Press, Baltimore, MD.

Fielding, L., Miller, L. and Brown, J. (1999) 'Harlem Globetrotters International, Inc.', *Journal of Sport Management*, 13(1): 45–77.

Nicholson, M. (2007) *Sport and the Media: Managing the Nexus*. Elsevier Butterworth-Heinemann, London.

O'Brien, D. and Slack, T. (2003) 'An analysis of change in an organizational field: The professionalization of English Rugby Union', *Journal of Sport Management*, 17(4): 417–448.

Shropshire, K. (1995) *The Sports Franchise Game*. University of Pennsylvania Press, Philadelphia, PA.

Stewart, B. (ed.) (2007) *The Games are Not the Same: The Political Economy of Australian Football*. Melbourne University Press, Melbourne.

Relevant websites

Americas

National Football League – www.nfl.com
National Basketball League – www.nba.com
Major League Baseball – www.mlb.com
National Hockey League – www.nhl.com
Nascar – www.nascar.com
Professional Golfers' Association – www.pga.com
Ladies Professional Golf Association – www.lpga.com

Professional sport

Australia and New Zealand

Australian Football League – www.afl.com.au
Cricket Australia – www.baggygreen.com.au
National Rugby League – www.nrl.com
Super 12 Rugby Union – www.rugby.com.au
New Zealand Rugby – www.nzrugby.com

Great Britain

English Premier League – www.premierleague.com
British Rugby League – www.therfl.co.uk

Asia

J-League – www.j-league.or.jp/eng
Japanese Sumo Association – www.sumo.or.jp/eng/index.html

Europe

European Champions League – www.uefa.com
Serie A (Italy) – www.lega-calcio.it
Real Madrid – www.realmadrid.com/portada_eng.htm
Bundesliga (Germany) – www.bundesliga.de
European Professional Golfers' Association Tour – www.europeantour.com

Global

Olympics – www.olympic.org
World Cup – www.fifa.com
America's Cup – www.americascup.com
Tour de France – www.letour.fr
Formula One – www.formula1.com
Association of Surfing Professionals – www.aspworldtour.com
Association of Tennis Professionals (men) – www.atptennis.com
Women's Tennis Association – www.wtatour.com
World Rally Championship – www.wrc.com

National Basketball Association

This case explores the organization and operations of the National Basketball Association (NBA). The National Basketball Association is a professional sport league in the United States of America and competes with the National Football League (NFL), Major League Baseball (MLB), the National Hockey League (NHL) and NASCAR for public support, media coverage, media revenue and sponsorship revenue, as well as the ability to retain and promote its players as brand icons.

The National Basketball Association began in 1949 after a merger between the Basketball Association of America (which began in 1946) and the rival National Basketball League. Throughout the 1940s, 1950s and 1960s the league expanded and contracted as teams attempted to establish basketball in various towns and cities throughout America. Teams also moved from city to city in search of financial sustainability. The rival American Basketball Association formed in the late 1960s, but despite a period of limited success was merged with the NBA in the mid-1970s; the NBA has remained unchallenged as the premier professional basketball competition in America ever since. The NBA consists of 30 teams, 29 of which are located in the United States of America and one of which is located in Canada. There are also two leagues that operate in their own right, but are affiliated with and promoted by the NBA: the Women's National Basketball Association (WNBA), the premier professional basketball competition for women in America and the NBA Development League (D League), which acts as a minor league for the NBA, in a similar way to the established minor league system in baseball. The WNBA, which celebrated its fifteenth anniversary in 2011, consists of 12 teams, some of which are in established basketball markets such as Los Angeles, New York and Chicago, whereas others are located in lesser markets that do not have significant competition from other professional sports such as Tulsa and Connecticut. The D League consists of 16 teams, each of which is affiliated to at least one team in the NBA. D League teams are located throughout America, typically in small markets.

The NBA is split into the Eastern and Western conferences and each conference is split further into three divisions (Atlantic, Central and Southeast in the Eastern conference and Northwest, Pacific and Southwest in the Western conference). The divisions are geographically based, in order to minimize travel as much as possible within the confines of the scheduling rules. Teams play an 82-game season in which each team plays their division opponents four times (16 games), teams in the other two conference divisions three or four times (36 games) and teams from the opposing conference twice (30 games). In order to qualify for the playoffs, teams must finish in one of the top eight places in either conference. The playoffs consist of a series of in-conference elimination rounds (1 versus 8, 2 versus 7, 3 versus 6 and 4 versus 5 in the first round), until the Eastern and Western conference champions play each other for the NBA Championship.

As noted previously, the NBA consists of 30 teams. Although teams have been added to the league during the last 25 years and some teams have relocated, the league has remained relatively stable. Teams such as the Los Angeles Lakers and the Boston Celtics are well known in America and throughout the world because of their recent successes and high profile, as well as their past rivalries and the exploits of former players such as Magic Johnson (Lakers) and Larry Bird (Celtics). The Chicago Bulls became equally well known in the late 1980s and 1990s as a result of the exploits of Michael Jordan, who won six NBA championships, including three in a row twice. Like the WNBA, the teams in the NBA are spread throughout America and Canada. Table 4.3 lists all 30 NBA team in order of the size of the population of the city in which they are located. It is clear from the table that some teams such as the New York Knicks, Los Angeles Lakers, Chicago Bulls and the Houston Rockets are located in large urban centres of America, while other teams such as the Utah Jazz, Orlando Magic, New Jersey Nets and the New Orleans Hornets are located in relatively small cities. The Toronto Raptors have the advantage of not only being located in a large city, but the only Canadian city with an NBA franchise. The Los Angeles Clippers, by contrast, are located in a large city, but compete with perhaps the most famous basketball team in the world, the Lakers, which essentially makes them Los Angeles' second team. Table 4.3 list the NBA teams by their estimated worth and estimated annual revenue.

The financial success of NBA teams is built in large part on the revenue secured through the sale of broadcast rights. In 2003 the NBA entered into agreements with broadcasters ABC, ESPN and TNT, agreements that were subsequently extended in 2007. Both ABC and ESPN are owned by the Walt Disney Company, which declared in 2007 that contractual commitments relating to broadcast rights for the NFL, NBA, NASCAR, MLB and college football were worth US$19,200 million, spread over eight years. It is estimated that the NBA receives approximately US$930 million annually from the broadcast agreement extended to the 2015–2016 season. Through ESPN primarily, the NBA is broadcast in more than 200 countries worldwide, capitalizing on the global popularity of the game.

The NBA's media profile extends beyond television, although television coverage remains the most important way in which the league ensures its financial sustainability and maintains its fan base. The NBA's games are broadcast on both national and local television. Many of the games are broadcast into specific markets, so that the fans in the home city are able to watch their favourite team. Games that are considered out of market are now able to be accessed through the purchase of an 'NBA League Pass', which entitles the user to access out of market games. These games are available to the consumer through cable television, but are also available through a high speed internet connection to a computer or a mobile device. NBA fans outside America are able to purchase an international league pass, which enables them to watch games via the internet. The ability to watch out of market games for American consumers is a relatively recent phenomenon, while the ability to watch NBA games on demand is a revolution for international NBA fans, who were previously restricted to watching a small number of games purchased by local free-to-air or pay television providers.

The media coverage that the NBA receives is enhanced by the profile of its players. As with all professional sports, the organization, its players and importantly its sponsors play a major role in promoting basketball. The company most often associated with the sport of basketball is Nike, the global footwear and apparel company. Nike has long been associated with the game of basketball, particularly through its association with Michael Jordan. Nike is currently confirming its relationship with basketball and the NBA through its association with contemporary players such as Kobe Bryant, LeBron James, Kevin Durant and Blake Griffin. Nike's promotion of basketball is heavily focused on personalities and individual athletes, an acknowledgement that personalities such as Kobe Bryant, and his Nike alter ego, The Black Mamba, are essential in driving the sales of basketball footwear in particular.

Table 4.3: NBA team by city population size

Team	City Population	Metropolitan Area Population
New York Knicks	8,175,133	22,085,649
Los Angeles Lakers	3,792,621	17,877,006
Los Angeles Clippers	3,792,621	17,877,006
Chicago Bulls	2,695,590	9,080,021
Toronto Raptors	2,631,725	5,113,149
Houston Rockets	2,099,451	6,051,363
Philadelphia 76ers	1,526,006	6,533,683
Phoenix Suns	1,445,632	4,192,887
San Antonio Spurs	1,327,407	2,142,508
Dallas Mavericks	1,197,816	6,731,317
Indiana Pacers	820,445	2,080,782
Charlotte Bobcats	731,424	2,402,623
Detroit Pistons	713,777	5,218,852
Memphis Grizzlies	646,889	1,316,100
Boston Celtics	617,594	7,559,060
Washington Wizards	601,723	8,572,971
Denver Nuggets	600,158	3,090,874
Milwaukee Bucks	594,833	1,751,316
Portland Trail Blazers	583,776	2,226,009
Oklahoma City Thunder	579,999	1,322,429
Sacramento Kings	466,488	2,461,780
Atlanta Hawks	420,003	5,618,431
Miami Heat	399,457	5,564,635
Cleveland Cavaliers	396,815	2,881,937
Golden State Warriors	390,724	7,468,390
Minnesota Timberwolves	382,578	3,615,902
New Orleans Hornets	343,829	1,214,932
New Jersey Nets	277,140	8,791,894
Orlando Magic	238,300	2,818,120
Utah Jazz	186,440	1,744,886

Source: US Census 2010 website at www.2010.census.gov/2010census; Statistics Canada website at www.statcan.gc.ca

Table 4.4: NBA team values

Team	Estimated worth (US$ million)	Estimated annual revenue (US$ million)
New York Knicks	655	226
Los Angeles Lakers	643	214
Chicago Bulls	511	169
Boston Celtics	452	151
Houston Rockets	443	153
Dallas Mavericks	438	146
Miami Heat	425	124
Phoenix Suns	411	147
San Antonio Spurs	404	135
Toronto Raptors	399	138
Orlando Magic	385	108
Golden State Warriors	363	119
Detroit Pistons	360	147
Portland Trail Blazers	356	127
Cleveland Cavaliers	355	161
Utah Jazz	343	121
Philadelphia 76ers	330	110
Oklahoma City Thunder	329	118
Washington Wizards	322	107
Denver Nuggets	316	113
New Jersey Nets	312	89
Los Angeles Clippers	305	102
Atlanta Hawks	295	105
Sacramento Kings	293	103
Charlotte Bobcats	281	98
New Orleans Hornets	280	100
Indiana Pacers	269	95
Memphis Grizzlies	266	92
Minnesota Timberwolves	264	95
Milwaukee Bucks	258	92

Source: Forbes (www.forbes.com)

Case study questions

1 Is there a correlation between where an NBA team is located and its estimated revenue or total worth? Why might this be the case?
2 The NBA offers access to out of market games via its NBA League Pass system. Why would it not offer fans the opportunity to see all games via this system?
3 As noted in the case, the NBA is responsible for the management and promotion of the WNBA and the D League. Do these leagues operate as competition or a complementary product to the NBA?
4 Visit the Nike basketball website and investigate the ways in which NBA players are featured, particularly the use of social media and the creation of alter egos such as Kobe Bryant's 'The Black Mamba'. Does the NBA benefit from this promotion, and if so, how?

Source: National Basketball Association website at www.nba.com; Walt Disney Company website at http://corporate.disney.go.com/index.html; US Census 2010 website at www.2010.census.gov/2010census; Nike website at www.nike.com

Part 2

Sport management principles

In this part:

- **5** Strategic sport management
- **6** Organizational structure
- **7** Human resource management
- **8** Leadership
- **9** Organizational culture
- **10** Financial management
- **11** Sport marketing
- **12** Sport governance
- **13** Performance management

Chapter 5

Strategic sport management

Overview

This chapter reveals the processes and techniques of strategic management. Specifically, it focuses on the analysis of an organization's position in the competitive environment, the determination of its direction and goals, the selection of an appropriate strategy, the leveraging of its distinctive assets, and the evaluation of its chosen activities. These processes are reviewed within the context of a documented plan.

After completing this chapter the reader should be able to:

- understand the difference between strategy and planning;
- appreciate why strategic management should be undertaken;
- differentiate the steps of the strategic management process;
- identify the tools and techniques of strategic management;
- specify the steps involved in the documentation of a strategic plan; and
- explain how the nature of sport affects the strategic management process.

Strategic management principles

In the simplest terms possible, strategy is the match or interface between an organization and its external environment. Looking at strategy in this way is a helpful start because it reinforces the importance of both the organization itself and the circumstances in which it operates. At the heart of strategy is the assumption that these two elements are of equal importance. Furthermore, strategy concerns the entirety of the organization and its operations as well as the entirety of the environment. Such a holistic approach differentiates the strategy management process from other dimensions of management.

One troublesome aspect of strategic management relates to its complex, multifaceted nature. Johnson *et al.* (2008), for example, noted several important features associated with strategic decision-making:

1   Strategy affects the direction and scope of an organization's activities.
2   Strategy involves matching an organization's activities with the environment.
3   Strategy requires the matching of an organization's activities with its resource capabilities.
4   The substance of strategy is influenced by the views and expectations of key stakeholders.
5   Strategic decisions influence the long-term direction of the organization.

With Johnson *et al.*'s points in mind, it is easily concluded that the management of strategy requires a keen understanding of the organization and its environment, as well as the consequences of decisions. But these points miss one vital outcome in the strategy process. The central purpose of strategy is to become different from the competition. From this viewpoint, strategy should help explain how one football club is different from the next, or why a customer should choose to use a recreation facility over another in the same area. The match between an organization and its environment should result in a clear competitive advantage that no other organization can easily copy.

Before we proceed, it is necessary to make several important distinctions in definition and terminology. First, strategy and planning are not the same. Strategy can be defined as the process of determining the direction and scope of activities of a sport organization in light of its capabilities and the environment in which it operates. Planning is the process of documenting these decisions in a step-by-step manner indicating what has to be done, by whom, with what resources, and when. In short, strategy reflects a combination of analysis and innovation; of science and craft. Planning identifies in a systematic and deductive way the steps and activities that need to be taken toward the implementation of a strategy. Strategic management marries strategy and planning into a process.

Second, the term strategy can legitimately be used to explain three levels of decision-making. At the first level, a sport organization is faced with the task of establishing clarity about what business it engages in. For example, is the core business providing sport competitions, managing facilities, developing players, winning medals, championships and tournaments, selling merchandise, making a profit or improving shareholder wealth? At the second level, the term strategy is commonly used to identify how the organization will compete successfully against others. Strategy offers an explanation of how competitive advantage is going to be created and sustained. Third and finally, strategy can also be used at an operational level to identify how regular activities are to be undertaken and how resources are to be deployed to support them. For example, a broader strategy to improve player scouting methods might be supported by an operational strategy specifying the purchase of some computer software. Keep in mind that strategic management forms both a process and way of thinking that can be applied to multiple levels of a sport organization.

Why undertake strategic management?

Surprisingly, the need for management of the strategy process is not always considered necessary. Some managers believe that the fast-paced nature of the sport industry precludes the use of a systematic strategic management process. Strategy for these managers is developed 'on the run' and in response to emerging circumstances and events. However, this approach contradicts the principles of strategic management, which emphasize the importance of actively shaping the future of one's own sport organization rather than waiting for circumstances to prompt action. Proactivity drives good strategy because it helps to reduce the uncertainty that accompanies chaotic and changeable industries like sport, where on-field performance can have such a radical effect on an organization's success.

Those versed in the concepts of strategic management would argue that with more uncertainty comes the need for greater strategic activity. Thus, a sport club that can generate a sizable surplus with a performance at the top of the ladder, but a dangerous deficit with a performance at the bottom of the ladder, should engage in the strategy process in order to seek new ways of managing its financial obligations. In addition, those who favour reactive approaches to strategy assume that opportunities are always overt and transparent. This is seldom true. Identifying new opportunities that have not already been leveraged by competition rarely proves easy and requires thorough analysis and innovative thinking. Neither of these can be achieved easily without the investment of time and energy on strategy development.

Allied to the notion of proactivity is the importance of coordination. Without a broad approach to the strategy process, different parts of the organization are likely to pursue their own agendas. Scarce resources need to be deployed in a coordinated and integrated manner consistent with an overarching strategy. Such a coordinated approach to strategy ensures that new strategy represents change. In many sport organizations for which change is a necessary condition for survival, strategy represents the intellectual part of management that can be planned. The result of this process should be a coordinated attempt to achieve goals that have been agreed upon by organizational stakeholders taking into account resource requirements. Efficiency arrives as an important benefit from sound strategic management.

Strategic sport management

One of the biggest issues in sport strategy comes in finding the balance between two or more divergent obligations. For example, sport organizations commonly seek both elite success as well as improved participation levels. Deploying resources to both of these commitments may be troublesome from a strategic viewpoint because they are not necessarily compatible. International success for a particular sport can motivate people to participate. However, the retention of new participants in sport tends to be poor in the medium term and negligible in the longer term. To make matters more complex, the choices of direction inherent in sport can be distracting, from the necessity to develop players or increase participation, to the pressure to make more money or win at all costs.

Strategy with Arsenal Football Club
Arsenal Football Club is undoubtedly one of the most well-known football clubs in the world. Like all great clubs it has a need for a large income to support the development, purchase and salaries of new players together with the salary of its executives, coaches and support staff. To gain additional income Arsenal has trodden both recognized and innovative pathways.

In a major attempt to increase income the club set about building a new stadium taking capacity from around 34,500 to a little over 60,000. This allowed for additional season ticket holders who previously had been unable to obtain such tickets, a greater number of hospitality boxes and improved conditions for supporters. To pay the £430 million for the new stadium, and in the absence of any public subsidy, Arsenal initially borrowed most of the money from a banking consortium. Realizing that repayment for this was unsustainable, Arsenal replaced most of the bank debt with bonds. It was the first publically marketed, asset-backed bond issue by a European football club.

The club then secured a £100 million sponsorship deal with Emirates Airline for 15 years of naming rights to the new stadium. A further £15 million came from a catering company in exchange for exclusive catering rights. In an innovative act, the club then set up a subsidiary company and obtained a £260 million loan facility to pay for the development of apartments and other public facilities on surplus land around the old stadium. These homes have now been completed and almost all are sold. In the 2009–2010 financial year the club announced that it had made a £56 million profit, nearly 25 per cent more than the year before. They added that the debt on their housing development, which totalled £130 million at one point, has been paid off in full and income from the property has boosted finances.

Arsenal's concern was for the future of the club. It identified an opportunity, developed an innovative financial strategy and sold the idea to its shareholders. The results have been spectacularly successful.

The strategic management process

Strategic management is a process designed to find the intersection of preparation and opportunity. This way of thinking has emerged from the first uses of the strategy concept, which came from the military. On the battlefield, the importance of imposing conditions that disadvantage the enemy in combat is paramount. For example, one of the key principles of military strategy is to manoeuvre an adversary into a position where they are outnumbered at the point of conflict. Variables like terrain and the opportunity to outflank, or attack the enemy from both the front and side simultaneously, make strategic decisions more complicated. These principles are also applied in the strategic sport management process, which is illustrated in Figure 5.1.

Like an army general, the sport manager must first make an assessment of the 'battle' conditions. They do this by studying the capacities and deficiencies of their own organization, competing organizations, stakeholder groups and the business environment or 'battlefield'. This first stage in the strategic management process is known as *strategy analysis*.

Strategy analysis	**Internal analysis** (capabilities, deficiencies and stakeholders)	Strengths Weaknesses
	External analysis (environment, competitors and customers)	Opportunities Threats
Strategy direction	**Mission Vision Objectives**	Performance measures
Strategy formulation	**Strategic options**	Generic strategies Cost leadership Differentiation Focus
Strategy implementation	**Deployment of strategy**	Products Services Systems Structure Culture
Strategy evaluation	**Performance measurement**	Corrective action

Figure 5.1: **The strategic management process.**

Next, and in light of the information obtained from the first stage, the sport manager must make some decisions about the future. These are typically concentrated into a 'mission' statement recording the purpose of the organization, a 'vision' statement of the organization's long-term ambitions and a set of objectives with measures to identify the essential achievements along the way to the vision. This second stage of the strategic management process is called *strategy direction*.

Setting a direction only determines what an organization wants to achieve. In the next step, the sport manager must consider how the direction can be realized. This is the most creative part of the strategic management process. Here, the sport manager, and his or her team, must work together to imagine the best methods or strategies for the organization. At this time, sport managers attempt to match the unique circumstances of the organization to its unique environmental conditions. When undertaken well, opportunities are found. This stage is called *strategy development*.

With a clear direction and a sharp idea of how that direction can be achieved, the task of the sport manager becomes one of implementation. At this point the range of products, services and activities that the organization engages with, and the systems that support them, are adjusted in line with the overarching strategy that was developed in the previous step. This is known as the *strategy implementation* stage.

Finally, strategy is rarely perfect the first time around. Modifications are always essential. Mostly this means a minor adjustment to the way in which the strategy has been implemented. However, sometimes it does require a rethink about the suitability of the strategy itself. Neither of these can be successfully undertaken without some feedback in the first place about the success of what has been done. That is why the final stage in the strategic management process, *strategy evaluation*, is necessary. In this stage, the organization reviews whether objectives have been achieved. Most of the time, some corrective action will need to be taken. Typically, the catalysts for these changes are unexpected events that affect the environment in which the sport organization operates, necessitating a return to strategy analysis. In this sense, the strategic management process never stops. In fact, moving back and forth between the stages in order to develop the best outcomes is normal. The strategy process works best when management takes the view that it is not linear or discrete but rather a circular and continuing activity.

Stage 1: Strategy analysis

One of the biggest challenges facing sport managers lies with combating the desire to set strategy immediately and to take action without delay. While a call to action is a natural inclination for motivated managers, many strategies can fail because the preliminary work has not been done properly. This preliminary work entails a comprehensive review of the internal and external environments. The tools for doing this include: (1) SWOT analysis; (2) stakeholder and customer needs analysis; (3) competitor analysis; and (4) the five forces analysis.

SWOT analysis

One of the basic tools in the environmental analysis is called the SWOT analysis. This form of analysis helps to examine an organization's strategic position, from the inside to the outside. The SWOT technique considers the strengths, weaknesses, opportunities and threats that an organization possesses or faces.

There are two parts to the SWOT analysis. The first part represents the internal analysis of an organization, which can be summarized by its *strengths* and *weaknesses*. It covers everything that an organization has control over, some of which are performed well and can be viewed as capabilities (strengths), while others are more difficult to do well and can be seen as deficiencies (weaknesses). The second part of the SWOT technique is concerned with external factors; those which the organization has no direct control over. These are divided into *opportunities* and *threats*. In other words, issues and environmental circumstances arise that can either be exploited, or need to be neutralized.

The SWOT technique helps sport managers to find the major factors likely to play a role in the appropriateness of the organization's direction or the success of its strategy. With this in mind, the sport manager should be looking for overarching issues. A good rule of thumb is to look for no more than five factors under each of the four headings. This way the most important issues receive the highest priority.

Given that the strengths and weaknesses part of the analysis concerns what goes on inside the organization, it has a time-orientation in the present; what the organization does right now. Strengths can be defined as resources or capabilities that the organization can use to achieve its strategic direction. Common strengths may include committed coaching staff, a sound membership base or a good junior development programme. Weaknesses should be seen as limitations or inadequacies that will prevent or hinder the strategic direction from being achieved. Common weaknesses may include poor training facilities, inadequate sponsorship or a diminishing volunteer workforce.

In contrast, the opportunity and threats analysis also has a future-thinking dimension, because of the need to consider what is about to happen. Opportunities are favourable situations or events that can be exploited by the organization to enhance its circumstances or capabilities. Common opportunities tend to include new government grants, the identification of a new market or potential product, or the chance to appoint a new staff member with unique skills. Threats are unfavourable situations which could make it more difficult for the organization to achieve its strategic direction. Common threats include inflating player salaries, new competitors or unfavourable trends in the consumption of leisure such as the increased popularity of gaming consoles with young people over playing traditional sports.

Stakeholder and customer needs analysis

Before an analysis of the environment is complete, an assessment of the organization's stakeholders and customers remains essential. Stakeholders are all the people and groups that have an interest in an organization, including its employees, players, members, league or affiliated governing body, government, community, facility owners, sponsors, broadcasters and fans. The constant question that a sport manager has to answer is concerned with whom they are trying to make happy. Either deliberately or inadvertently serving the interests of some stakeholders in preference to others has serious implications for the setting of strategic direction and for the distribution of limited resources. For example, some professional sport clubs tend to focus on winning to the exclusion of all other priorities, including sensible financial management. While this may make members and fans happy in the short term, it does not reflect the interests of governing bodies, leagues and employees, for whom a sustainable enterprise is fundamental.

Sponsors and government sport funding departments sometimes withdraw funding if their needs are not met. A careful analysis of the intentions and objectives of each stakeholder in their affiliation with the sport organization must therefore be completed before a strategic direction can be set. The substance of strategy is influenced by the beliefs, values and expectations of the most powerful stakeholders.

Competitor analysis

Opportunities and threats can encompass anything in the external environment, including the presence and activities of competitors. Because the actions of competitors can greatly affect the success of a strategic approach, *competitor analysis* ensures that an investigation is conducted systematically.

There are many forms of competitor analysis, and they can range in detail considerably. However, most competitor analyses consider the following dimensions, as summarized in Table 5.1. For each competitor, these eight dimensions should be considered. Time and care should be taken in assessing competitors' strategies, their strengths, vulnerabilities and resources, and as well as their next likely actions.

Five forces analysis

An extension of the competitive environment analysis is the *five forces analysis,* which was developed by Michael Porter. It is the most commonly used tool for describing the competitive environment. The technique does this by focusing upon five competitive forces (Porter 1980).

Table 5.1: Competitor analysis dimensions

Dimension	Description
Geographic scope	Location and overlap
Vision and intent	Ranges from survival to attempts at dominance
Objective	Short- to medium-term intentions
Market share and position	From small player to virtual monopolist
Strategy	Methods of gaining a competitive advantage
Resources	Volume and availability
Target market	To whom the products and services are directed
Marketing approach	The products and services, and the promotions, pricing and distribution behind them

---

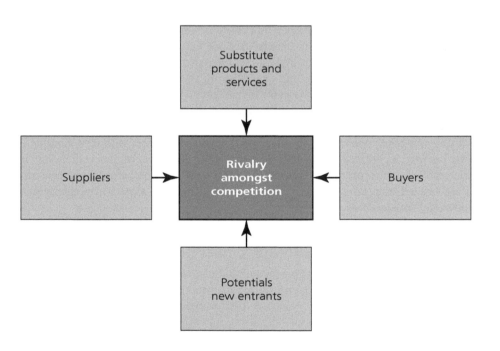

Figure 5.2: Five forces competitive analysis.

The threat of new entrants: Every organization is faced with the possibility that new competitors could enter their industry at any time. In some forms of professional sport, this is unlikely as the barriers preventing entry are very high. For example, it would be extremely difficult for a private independent league to enter the market against any of the professional football leagues in Europe. On the other hand, new sport facilities, events, sport apparel companies and new equipment manufacturers are regular entrants in the sport industry.

The bargaining power of buyers: Buyers are those individuals, groups and companies that purchase the products and services that sport organizations offer. The nature of the competitive environment is affected by the strength, or bargaining power, of buyers. For example, most football fans in the UK hold little power, if the price of football tickets is any indication. When there is buying power, prices are lower. Despite some extravagant sums paid by broadcasters for the media rights of certain sports, the bargaining power of media buyers should be relatively strong. For most sport organizations, however, the chief buyers – fans – do not work together to leverage their power and therefore the bargaining power of buyers is limited.

The bargaining power of suppliers: When suppliers of raw materials essential to sporting organizations threaten to raise prices or withdraw their products or services, they are attempting to improve their bargaining power. This may come from suppliers of the materials necessary in the building of a new facility or from sporting equipment suppliers. The most important supplier issue in sport has come about with the unionization of professional players in an attempt to increase their salaries and the salary caps of clubs. Where player groups have been well organized, their bargaining power has proven significant.

The threat of substitute products and services: Increasingly, the traditional sport industry sectors are expanding, and it is more common for different sports to compete against each other. When this threat is high, a sport organization is faced with the problem of being out-competed by other kinds of sports, or worse, by other forms of leisure activity.

The intensity of rivalry among competitors in an industry: The more sport organizations offering virtually identical products and services, the higher the intensity of rivalry. For example, in the sport shoe marketplace, the rivalry between Nike and Adidas is extremely intense. Rivalry is more ambiguous between sport clubs in the same league that share a general geographical region. London football clubs, Melbourne Australian football clubs and colleges in the same state in the United States, are examples. In these cases, it is unlikely that one club would be able to 'steal' supporters from another local club. Nor is the alumnus of one college likely to start attending home games of another college team. However, these clubs do intensely compete for media exposure, corporate sponsorship, players, coaches, managers and management staff. Of course, they also compete with the most intense rivalry imaginable for the championship.

Stage 2: Strategy direction

Once the strategy analysis has been completed, the strategic direction can be set. There are four conventional tools used to clarify and document this direction: (1) mission statement; (2) vision statement; (3) organizational objectives; and (4) performance measures.

Mission statements

A *mission statement* identifies the purpose of an organization. While it may seem strange to need to put this in writing, such a statement reduces the risk of strategic confusion. For example, players, members, spectators, staff, coaches, media, sponsors and government representatives may all hold different interpretations of the purpose of a sport organization. The mission statement should define why an organization was set up, what services and products it provides, and for whom it provides them. When reduced to a single statement, this mission is a powerful statement of intention and responsibility. It usually does not exceed one paragraph.

Vision statements

It goes without saying that behind the idea of setting a strategic direction is the need to be visionary: to look into the future and form a clear mental image of what an organization could be like. Thinking in this manner means being able to interpret the information collected during the analysis stage and find the opportunities they present. A *vision statement* represents the culmination of this kind of thinking. It is a statement that declares the medium- to long-range ambitions of an organization. The statement is an expression of what the organization wants to achieve within a period of around three to five years. The statement is normally no longer than a sentence.

Organizational objectives

Given that the vision statement is a reflection of the medium- to long-term ambitions of an organization, *organizational objectives* serve as markers on the way to this destination. Objectives reflect the achievements that must be made in order to realize the vision. For example, if a club is situated at the bottom of the championship ladder, their vision might be to finish in the top three. However, achieving this vision inside a single season is unrealistic, so an objective might indicate the ambition to improve by three places by next season, as a progression toward the overarching vision. Objectives are normally set in each of the major operational areas of an organization, such as on-field performance, youth development, finances, facilities, marketing and human resources. However, it is essential that objectives stay measurable.

Performance measures

Key performance indicators (KPIs) are used in combination with organizational objectives in order to establish success or failure. KPIs are therefore inseparable from objectives and should be created at the same time. Each time a performance measure is used, care should be taken to ensure that it can indeed be measured in a concrete way. For example, a marketing objective of 'improving the public image' of an organization is meaningless unless it is accompanied by something quantifiable. It is worth noting that measures do not have to focus exclusively on outputs like volumes, rankings and trophies. They can also be used to measure efficiency; that is, doing the same with less or doing more with the same resources.

Stage 3: Strategy formulation

Strategic analysis reveals the competitive position of a sport organization and setting the strategic direction plots a course for the future. The next question is how to get there. In the strategy formulation stage of the strategic management process, the sport manager and his or her team face the task of positioning their organization in the competitive environment. This necessitates a combination of imagination and scenario thinking. In other words, they must consider the implications of each potential strategic approach. To help matters, however, from a strategic positioning viewpoint there are a finite number of strategies available to the sport manager. These are called *generic competitive strategies*.

In Practice 5.2

Strategy and opportunity in Russian tennis

As mentioned, one of the basic tools in the environmental analysis is the SWOT analysis. Often, an external factor can arise, which if seized, may provide a lever to move an industry or a sport forward. Such a situation arose in Russia in the early 1990s when a seemingly innocuous picture of President Boris Yeltsin playing tennis appeared in the Russian press. Almost overnight copies of the photo started appearing in much of the world's media. The result was that tennis was immediately seen in Russia as a popular and fun sport.

The opportunity was initially seized upon by both industry and entrepreneurs who realized that investment in the sport, in the building of infrastructure and in the underwriting of competitions, was a way to make money. Professional tennis in Russia took off, led by industry and pursued by the sport itself.

In 1990, the old USSR had less than 200 courts. Now it has close to 3,000. In 1990 only around 120 tournaments were played but currently the country hosts over 1,000 tournaments. Registered players under the age of 18 years number in excess of 20,000.

Although an initial follower in the expansion of the sport, the Russian Tennis Federation (RTF) has not been slow to capitalize on the popularity of the sport. By sponsoring tournaments and funding junior development, the RTF has turned the opportunity provided by others into a strength for itself. International sport management agencies now have to vie with Russian sport management agencies for the right to control the ever-increasing number of professional tennis players produced by Russia. The growth potential for tennis in Russia appears to be as good, if not better, than anywhere else in the world.

In the case of Russian tennis, the initial opportunity was exploited by those external to the sport. Very quickly, however, the sport administrators recognized the opportunity and turned it into a strength; one that has been exploited and has seen the rise of Russian tennis to a dominant place in the sport.

Generic competitive strategies

Porter (1985) contended that there are only three fundamental or generic strategies that can be applied in any organization, irrespective of their industry, products and services, environmental circumstance and resources. Generic competitive strategies answer the most basic question facing a sport manager while forming a strategic choice: what is going to be our source of *competitive advantage*? To put it another way, every sport organization must take a position somewhere in the marketplace. The challenge is to find a position that is both opportune *and* advantageous. As a result, some sport organizations try to out-compete their adversaries because they can provide their products and services cheaper; others compete on the basis of a unique product or service that is hard for others to replicate; others still attempt to position themselves as the exclusive supplier to a small but loyal niche in the marketplace. These three strategic positions are described below:

- Cost leadership
  To become a cost leader by supplying products and services at the lowest possible cost to as many customers as possible. The logic of this strategic approach is driven by volume and market share where more sales than any other competitors lead to greater profitability. Essential to this generic competitive strategy is efficiency and the ability to keep costs to a minimum. While this approach is common in consumer products like shampoo, it is less common in sport. However, some equipment and sport apparel manufacturers do provide their products at the cheap end of the market in the hope that they can significantly outsell their more expensive competitors. Similarly, many leisure facilities try to attract customers on the basis of their lower prices.

- Differentiation
  To provide a differentiated set of products and services that is difficult for competitors to replicate. The logic of this strategic approach is underpinned by an assumption that consumers will place a high value on products and service that are unique. Typically, this approach is supported by an attempt to build a strong brand image and incorporate regular innovations and new features, as well as responsive customer service. Many sport organizations are thrown into this position almost by default because of the nature of their offerings. A tennis club, for example, offers a range of services that are by definition differentiated, at least when compared to other sports or leisure activities. However, when two tennis clubs compete in a similar area, it may become necessary for one to take a new strategic position. One option is to further differentiate their services, perhaps by offering something new or innovative like a creche for mid-week players or a gym for conditioning the more seriously competitive players.

- Focus
  To provide a set of products and services to a niche in the market with the intention of dominating market share. The logic guiding this strategic approach is that being dominant in a small section of a larger market allows an organization to have early success, without having to compete with much larger and better resourced organizations. To succeed with this strategic approach it is necessary to choose the market segment very carefully, aware that the products and services provided must fill particular needs in customers very well. Many sport organizations take this approach. Examples include specialist sport equipment, and less mainstream sport clubs and associations like rock climbing and table tennis.

The key to making a decision between these three alternatives returns to the analysis and direction stages of the strategic management process. A strategy-savvy sport manager is always looking for a way to position the organization in a cluttered market. Part of the choice is in determining what the sport organization is likely to be able to do better than others; their competitive advantage (like keeping costs low or delivering great customer service). The other part is in finding the opportunity in the environment that is worth exploring. Where there is a match between these factors consistent with strategic direction, strategic formulation is born. It is worth remembering that the worst place to be is 'stuck in the middle' between strategies, but that combining strategic options can be advantageous if managed effectively.

Stage 4: Strategy implementation

Strategy implementation represents the introduction of the organization's choice of competitive strategy. For example, if a differentiation strategy has been selected, the implementation stage considers how it can be brought about across the organization's products, services and activities. There is an important distinction to be made here between the strategic level of decision-making and the implementation level. To return to the military analogy, strategy concerns how an entire army is deployed. At the implementation level, tactical and operational decisions are made as well. These are like the choices of what each battalion, unit or platoon does. Always the overarching goal is a reflection of the army's objectives, but each smaller part of the army works towards bite-sized achievements that will eventually bring about success in the battle.

Once decisions have been finalized concerning the strategy that will be employed to achieve organizational objectives, the task of converting them into action begins. This means that representatives from each major area or department of the organization must become involved in deciding how they can contribute towards the generic strategy. For example, if one objective in a club is concerned with on-field performance, it is likely that the leaders of the developmental programmes will play a role in planning. Equally, an objective associated with financial performance will require marketing staff responsible for sponsorship to become involved. As a result, the strategy implementation process should permeate the organization including junior development, community liaison, coaching, facilities, governance, marketing, finance and human resources, for example. In each of these areas a plan should be developed that illustrates the set of activities that will be performed at the tactical and operational levels to support the generic strategy. Like objectives, each of these actions requires a measure or KPI of some sort. Often the implementation process also requires changes to resource allocation, organizational structure, systems for delivering products and services, organizational culture and leadership. These areas are considered in subsequent chapters.

In Practice 5.3

Competitive advantage at Barcelona Football Club

Several of the more successful and larger football clubs in the world have thriving youth academies. FC Barcelona, Ajax, Manchester United and Real Madrid immediately spring to mind. Almost without exception most youth academies recruit both nationally and internationally. For FC Barcelona, however, the emphasis is on local youth. Players are recruited at age six and may stay at the club until they are 18 years old. While some players do come from South America and Africa, the bulk of the 300 youth players in Barcelona's Academy are from Catalonia.

The life of the youth academy centres on an old eighteenth century farmhouse known as La Masia. Here, the cream of the young players live and train together. Since 1979, when La Masia was remodelled to house the youth facility, over 500 of these aspiring players have lived at La Masia.

From the very beginning all Academy players are taught a similar style of play to that used by the Barcelona first team. But, in addition, their lifestyles, attitudes and education reflect the values held by the parent club, even to the extent that all lessons are in Catalan. As a consequence, the unique bonding that comes with shared life generates within the youngsters a true belief in FC Barcelona. The end result is that ex-Academy players make up the bulk of the Barcelona team.

Is the emphasis on developing local youth, by having them live, train and be educated in a similar value system successful? In 2010 La Masia achieved the distinction of producing all three finalists for the Ballon d'Or in Lionel Messi, Andrés Iniesta and Xavier Hernández, while in July 2010, Spain won the World Cup with eight players from Barcelona, seven of whom had graduated from La Masia.

In setting up a top-class Academy for youth players, FC Barcelona sought a competitive advantage over many of its rivals, and by concentrating much of its resources on one region only, that of Catalonia, Barcelona extended that advantage. The concept of a full-time residential centre for its elite youth players added yet greater advantage. These actions provided, however, only the foundation for Barcelona's most astute competitive advantage. The immersion of the youth players in the traditions of FC Barcelona, in its values, beliefs and even in its Catalan language, inculcated within that youth a total belief in the righteousness of the brand that is FC Barcelona, which is why so many of the graduates of La Masia have sought to remain with the club throughout their careers.

Stage 5: Strategy evaluation

One of the more difficult aspects of strategic management is the control or evaluation of what has been done. In sport there are numerous issues that make this process more complicated including the obvious one that on-field performance can have a tendency to overwhelm the other elements of strategy. Chapter 13, 'Performance management', considers these important issues in detail.

The *strategic evaluation* stage requires an assessment of two related aspects of the strategy. First, the KPIs associated with each organizational objective need to be compared with actual results and, second, the success of the implementation actions needs to be ascertained.

Strategy as practice

An emerging issue in strategy emphasizes the blurred line between strategy and the practice of management, particularly where organizing forms are considered an integral part of the strategizing process. This position is reflective of the wider strategy-as-practice trend in strategic management, which is concerned with how managers 'do strategy', or strategize. The view that organizing forms within structures remain subservient to strategy may be considered old-fashioned, as it demands a sharp distinction between the two as different properties and processes. However, strategy and organization are not necessarily distinct states. Organization does not follow strategy. Instead, the more contemporary view holds that organization *is* the strategy. For example, investment in sophisticated IT infrastructure may be instrumental in enabling a sport organization to enter new markets and reach more fans. The assumption here is that a change to organizing forms is a strategic change. In addition, the use of the terms organizing and strategizing lies central to this proposition. As verbs, the terms impart the importance of continuous rather than static change processes. Organization and strategy therefore become organizing and strategizing.

From the standpoint of a sport manager, success is not so much a function of getting strategy and structure right in the first place, but rather is about having the capability to adjust them continuously alongside shifts in competitive and market forces. A sport organization's knowledge – its know-how – relies on managers' abilities to think about strategy and organizing decisions at the same time. Like a sport team without designated playing positions, strategizing without organizing is limited in scope. The strategizing-organizing way of thinking also suggests that middle- and lower-level managers need to engage in the strategy-making process.

Summary

This chapter is concerned with the process of strategic management. This process is founded on the principle that opportunity is discovered by analysis rather than luck. Strategic management, we have argued, is therefore at the heart of the success of a sport organization.

Five stages in the strategic management process have been identified. The first stage is strategy analysis, which demands the assessment of both internal organizational capacities as well as external environmental conditions. The second stage is strategy direction, which sets the vision and objectives of an organization. The third stage is strategy formulation, where a definitive strategic position is selected for an organization. The fourth stage is strategy implementation, where the strategy is directed to action across organizational areas. The final stage, strategy evaluation, involves the control and measurement of the process so that improvements can be made.

Strategic management in sport organizations requires preparation, research and analysis, imagination, decision-making and critical-thinking. It demands an equal balance of systematization and innovation. This chapter is weighted heavily toward the system side, but that is simply a necessity to convey the principles and techniques of strategic management. It is up to the reader to provide the imagination in their own strategic management activities.

Review questions

1   Why is strategic management important in the turbulent world of sport?
2   What is the basic principle that underpins strategic management?
3   Name the five stages of strategic management.
4   What is the relationship between a SWOT analysis and competitor analysis?
5   How do stakeholders influence the setting of strategic direction?
6   Explain the differences between the three generic strategies.
7   What is the relationship between KPIs and strategy evaluation?
8   Select a sport organization that has a strategic plan on its website. Conduct an analysis of this plan, and comment on its approach to each of the five steps of strategic management explained in this chapter.
9   Select a sport organization that you know well and that does not have a strategic plan available. Based on your background knowledge, make point form comments under the headings of the five steps in strategic management to illustrate your approach to forming a plan.

10   Provide an example where a new kind of organizing method in a sport organization could impart a strategic effect.

Further reading

Ferkins, L., Shilbury, D. and McDonald, G. (2009) 'Board involvement in strategy: Advancing the governance of sport organizations', *Journal of Sport Management*, 23(3): 245–277.

Jarzabkowski, P. and Spee, P.A. (2009) 'Strategy-as-practice: A review and future directions for the field', *International Journal of Management Reviews*, 11(1): 69–95.

Johnson, G., Langley, A., Melin, L. and Whittington, R. (2007) *Strategy as Practice: Research Directions and Resources*, New York: Cambridge University Press.

Johnson, G., Scholes, K. and Whittington, R. (2008) *Exploring Corporate Strategy*, 8th edition, London: Prentice-Hall.

MacLean, J. (2009) 'Auditing performance management practices: A comparison of Canadian sport organisations', *International Journal of Sport Management and Marketing*, 5(3): 295–309.

Porter, M. (1980) *Competitive Strategy*, New York: The Free Press.

Porter, M. (1985) *Competitive Strategy: Creating and Sustaining Superior Performance*, New York: Simon & Schuster.

Soares, J. and Correia, A. (2009) 'Factors and focuses in the strategic decisions of sporting organisations: Empirical evidence in sports associations', *International Journal of Sport Management and Marketing*, 5(3): 338–354.

Relevant websites

Arsenal Football Club – www.arsenal.com
England Cricket Board – www.ecb.co.uk
FC Barcelona – www.fcbarcelona.com/web/english
Russian Tennis Federation – www.tennis-russia.ru

Strategic planning with the England Cricket Board

On 1 January 1997, the England Cricket Council, Test and County Cricket Board, and the National Cricket Association merged to form the England and Wales Cricket Board (ECB). In its first meeting the new Board recognized that it was essential to stop the fragmentation of the sport and to seek common, clear objectives. This need for strategic direction was highlighted two years later when, in 1999, the World Cricket Cup was hosted by and predominantly played in England. The results for the host country were crushing with South Africa, India and even lowly Zimbabwe achieving better results in the Group Stage of the competition. England, for so long a major force in world cricket, was excluded from the play-offs.

Following on from the World Cricket Cup, the ECB took its first major step in formulating its strategic intent. After reviewing its current position and having undertaken a basic Strengths, Weaknesses, Opportunities and Threats (SWOT) analysis, the ECB set out in 1999, in an 'informal' strategic plan, its National Strategy for Cricket (2000–2004). Among other things, the plan set out to increase the number of participants in the sport, increase interest in the sport at school level, and to improve performance at all levels. The vision was to ultimately place the England cricket teams, both men and women, on top of the world rankings. Although receiving a significant financial boost from the National Lottery Sports Fund and other funding bodies, including some serious investment from local authorities, the ECB determined that strategic implementation might best be usefully undertaken in stages.

In 2000 the National Facilities Strategy (NFS) was unveiled. Based upon an extensive survey of existing facilities throughout England and Wales, its aim was to ensure that appropriate facilities of the right standard were available for the realization of the National Strategy for Cricket. The NFS set out a vision of first-class facilities being available for all county teams. Of priority was the need to improve the range and quality of grass pitches for all first class teams and to provide England and Wales with a National Academy for the most talented eligible cricketers aged between 18 and 23 years. While reasonably successful in its approach, particularly in its development of the Loughborough Cricket Centre of Excellence, the NFS had several major failings. In particular, it did not represent an implementation plan, and it lacked the ability for any success to be accurately measured.

By 2005 England had achieved marked cricketing progress. While still not dominating world cricket, record-breaking success had been achieved with both men's and women's teams. Indeed, the achievements of the ECB in terms of inserting elements of cricket into several subjects allied to the national curriculum of schools were in many ways quite revolutionary. Students might, for example, consider forces at work in batting and bowling when undertaking science, or they may be required to write an essay in an English class on how a cricket captain might motivate his/her team.

Innovations like twenty20 cricket had brought renewed enthusiasm for the game and importantly, sponsorship and television deals brought additional financial security. With this background, the ECB introduced its first formal strategic plan – 'Building Partnerships' – which covered the period up to 2009. Its aim was to pursue cricketing success through the development of the sport at all levels and to ensure England's return to cricket dominance. The plan was fundamentally structured around the development of four key planks:

- effective leadership and governance;
- a vibrant domestic game;
- enthusing a strong participation and following especially among young people; and
- the development of successful England teams.

David Collier, the Chief Executive of the ECB, acknowledged upon the introduction of 'Building Partnerships' that 'For the first time, the ECB is laying out a strategic plan based upon clear and measurable goals' and that 'For the first time we are setting ourselves targets by which we and our stakeholders will track our progress'. As Collier stated, the goals were clearly spelled out and objectives aimed at achieving them were specified in the strategic plan. Of equal importance, 'Building Partnerships' did contain an effective implementation plan. Although the plan failed to secure all of its goals, the majority of them achieved high levels of success.

The current ECB Strategic Plan 2010–2013, 'Grounds to Play', was built upon the foundation of the earlier strategic plan in conjunction with the various County Strategic Plans. It was developed only after KPMG had completed an investigation into the state of club and county finances and a comprehensive SWOT analysis had been undertaken. This analysis showed that at the county and club level finances were limited and capital for investment was in short supply. Significant threats to emerge included the knowledge that the global economy was less resilient than in previous years and the fact that as England was to host the 2012 Olympic Games, the likelihood of less emphasis on cricket combined with greater competition for sponsorship was highly probable. Nonetheless, the vision that underlay 'Grounds to Play' was clear and transparent. While investing generally in cricket, the overarching aim was to provide English cricket with world-leading facilities, coaching, participation and volunteering.

In 2005 the ECB had no financial reserves. One major effect of 'Building Partnerships' was to develop those reserves. By 2010 the ECB had financial resources of over £23 million, a secure basis for its proposed building developments. Some of that money had already been lent to clubs and counties to help develop facilities but much remained to be done. The first major objective of the new strategic plan was, therefore, to propose greater financial support for coaches and facilities in all four of the pillars of 'Building Partnerships'. Other objectives building upon the four pillars, together with how those objectives were to be achieved, were detailed. In a similar manner to the earlier strategic plan, clear and measurable goals were specified. While the results of 'Grounds to Play' are still unknown, there are strong indications that objectives are quietly being pursued and fulfilled.

It is clear that the English Cricket Board has utilized many of the elements of strategic planning as proposed and used by both academics and industry. The combination has yielded two significant strategic plans designed not simply for the contemporary sporting environment but for the further development and enervation of a traditional sport. The second and current strategic plan builds upon the first and in so doing acknowledges the reality that development of a strategic plan is not in itself the end product but rather the foundation stone for that end product. Rarely does a strategic plan get fulfilled in totality and even more rarely is it a one-off entity. Strategic Plans are by their very nature designed to be constantly evolving, a point the ECB appears to understand quite clearly.

There are inbuilt gambles in any strategic plan and they are equally in the plans of the ECB. Some of these – the uncertain global economy, the clash with the 2012 Olympics, and possible financial and sponsorship challenges – have both been acknowledged and considered. Others such as the effect of poor Test, twenty20 and one-day results on the way in which the sport is viewed by participants, public and sponsors are difficult to determine and may have an effect on the plan.

The two strategic plans set out by the ECB provide an acceptance of cricket's current situation in the country and a vision of where it seeks to go, and what is to be achieved. Its strategic direction is appropriately focused. Objectives are well stated and implementation is aligned with the use of obtainable measures. None of this will of course guarantee success but it does provide a sound foundation upon which success may be built.

See: David Collier, 'Building Partnerships – Foreword' at www.ecb.co.uk/ecb/publications/building-partnerships/building-partnerships-foreword,530,BP.html.

Case study questions

1 England's predominant sport is soccer. The media and broadcasting rights combined with sponsorship, gate receipts and in-venue advertising continue to bring in vast amounts of money. This is the arena in which cricket must compete. Should the emphasis in the ECB's strategic plans relate more to the financial underpinnings of the sport than to its development at the youth level?
2 Consider the way in which the ECB has chosen to develop English cricket. What are their chances of success?

Chapter 6

Organizational structure

Overview

Organizational structure is a phenomenon that has spawned a large number of textbooks and research articles designed to explain the finer points of organizational structure, as well as its impact on organizational performance, employee behaviour, culture and the drivers of change in relation to organizational structure. Rather than replicate some already excellent existing material on this topic, this chapter highlights the unique aspects of the structure of sports organizations. Consequently, this chapter reviews the key concepts of organizational structure, provides examples of the unique features of sport organization structures and summarizes the key research findings on the structure of sport organizations. The chapter also provides a summary of principles for managing organizational structures within community, state, national and professional sport organizations.

After completing this chapter the reader should be able to:

- describe the key dimensions of organizational structure;
- understand the unique features of the structure of sport organizations;

- understand the various models of organization structure that can be used for sports organizations;
- identify the factors that influence the structure of sport organizations; and
- understand some of the challenges facing managers and volunteers involved in managing the structure of sport organizations.

What is organizational structure?

An organizational structure is the framework that outlines how tasks are divided, grouped and coordinated within an organization (Robbins *et al.* 2004). Every sport organization has a structure that outlines the tasks to be performed by individuals and teams. Finding the right structure for an organization involves juggling requirements to formalize procedures whilst fostering innovation and creativity. The 'right' structure means one in which owners and managers can exert adequate control over employee activities without unduly affecting people's motivation and attitudes to work. It also provides clear reporting and communication lines while trying to reduce unnecessary and costly layers of management.

An organization's structure is important because it defines where staff and volunteers fit in with each other in terms of work tasks, decision-making procedures, the need for collaboration, levels of responsibility and reporting mechanisms. In other words, the structure of an organization provides a roadmap for how positions within an organization are related and what tasks are performed by individuals and work teams within an organization.

Dimensions of organizational structure

When designing any organization's structure, managers need to consider six elements: work specialization; departmentalization; chain of command; span of control; centralization and formalization (Robbins *et al.* 2004). Netball Victoria (NV), the State sporting organization responsible for the management and development of netball across Victoria, one of the major states of Australia, uses a typical nonprofit sport organizational structure. Netball is the largest female participation sport in Australia and has more than 110,000 registered participants in Victoria. NV provides a range of programmes and services for netball players, coaches, umpires, administrators, associations and clubs with the aim of increasing and enhancing participation experiences. In addition to facilitating participation opportunities, NV holds the license for the Melbourne Vixens, the Victorian team that competes in the transnational netball competition, the ANZ Championships. NV is responsible for the management and marketing of the team, and staging the ANZ Championship games in liaison with Netball Australia.

More than 250 associations or groups affiliate with Netball Victoria, which provides access to netball events, programmes and services as well as a pathway to State, national and international representation. These associations are geographically grouped into one of 21 Regions, and then Regions are grouped into one of six Zones. A team of 30 staff work with a board of management and an extensive network of volunteers to deliver these programmes, services and events across Victoria. The organizational structure for the State office staff developed by NV to enable this to happen is based around the key functional departments of marketing, development, association services, high performance and finances and administration. The structure allows individuals to be appointed to carry out specialized tasks and for the establishment of clear communication between the lower levels of the organization and the Chief Executive (see Figure 6.1). The six dimensions of organizational structure help us understand why an organization such as NV is structured a certain way.

Work specialization

Creating roles for individuals that enable them to specialize in performing a limited number of tasks is known as work specialization. This concept can easily be applied in organizations that manufacture things such as sporting goods, or need to process a large volume of resources such as distributing uniforms and information to volunteers for a large sporting event. The advantage of breaking jobs down to a set of routine repetitive tasks is an increase in employee productivity and reduced costs through the use of a lower-skilled labour force. This advantage must be balanced against the risks of making work too boring or stressful for individuals, which can lead to accidents, poor quality, lower productivity, absenteeism and high job turnover.

The majority of sports organizations employ small numbers of staff who are often required to perform a diverse range of tasks over a day, week or year. In these cases, the structure of the organization will require a low level of work specialization. For example a sport development officer within a state or provincial sporting organization would be involved in activities such

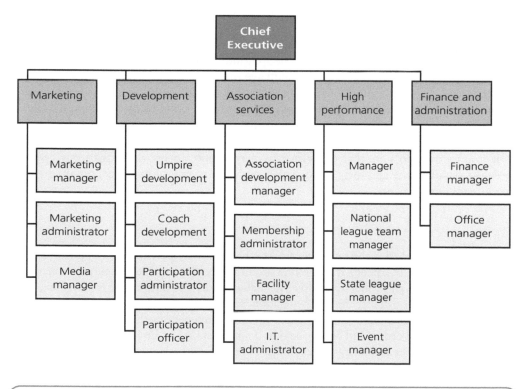

Figure 6.1: Netball Victoria structure.

as conducting skills clinics with junior athletes, designing coach education courses, managing a database of casual staff or representing the organization to sponsors or funding agencies over the course of a season. These roles require very different skill sets and in such an organization the structure would benefit from a low level of work specialization.

Departmentalization

Departmentalization is the bringing together of individuals into groups so that common or related tasks can be coordinated. In essence, people are assigned to departments in order to achieve organizational goals. Organizations can departmentalize on the basis of functions, products or services, processes, geography or customer type.

The most common form of departmentalizing is based on assigning people or positions to various departments according to the function a person may perform. For example, a state or provincial sporting organization might group their staff according to athlete development, competition management, special events and corporate affairs departments, with each department having a very specific function to perform.

Alternatively, a sport organization that manufactures cricket equipment may group their staff according to the product line they produce, with groups of people handling the manufacturing, sales and service for cricket apparel, cricket bats and training aids. In this case, the functions of marketing, human resource management, financial management and production are all replicated in each department. These criteria can also be applied to service-based sport organizations. For example, an athlete management firm may offer a range of services under financial planning, career development, life skills and public relations training. Again, each department would manage their own marketing, human resource management and financial management systems.

Sport organizations can also design departments on the basis of geography. For example, the operations for a sports law firm may be split into departments for capital city offices or regions. Each of the offices or regions would have responsibility in regard to their operations in a designated geographical region. Finally, sport organizations can arrange their departments on the basis of their various customer types. This approach could be used by an organization like the Australian Institute of Sport, which might create departments that support individual athletes or team sports.

It is important to note that organizations may choose to use more than one criterion to devise departments and their choice will depend on organizational size, capabilities and operational requirements.

Chain of command

The chain of command is the reporting trail that exists between the upper and lower levels of an organization. In essence it is the line of authority that connects each position within an organization to the Chief Executive. It encompasses the notions of establishing clear authority and responsibility for each position within the organization. Authority refers to the rights managers have to give orders to other members in the organization and the expectation that the orders will be carried out. If managers at certain levels of an organization are provided with the authority to get things done, they are also assigned a corresponding level of responsibility. Having a single person to whom an employee is responsible is known as the unity of command. Having a single 'boss' avoids employees having to deal with potential conflict when juggling the demands of two or more managers and it helps achieve clear decision-making.

Robbins *et al.* (2004) argue that the basic tenets of the chain of command are less relevant today due to the increase in the use of information technology, and the corresponding ease with which most employees can communicate with each other at all levels of the organization and access information that was previously restricted to top level managers. Nevertheless, managers of sports organizations should be cognizant of the basic principle of the chain of command when designing their organizational structure.

Span of control

Span of control refers to the number of staff which any manager can directly supervise without becoming inefficient or ineffective. The exact number which any manager can effectively control is determined by the level of expertise or experience of the staff – the logic being that more experienced and skilled staff require less supervision. The complexity of tasks, the location of staff, the reporting mechanisms in place, the degree to which tasks are standardized, the style of managers and the culture of an organization also play a role in determining what the ideal span of control might be for an individual manager in an organization. The span of control impacts on how many levels of management are required in any given organization. The wider the span of control, the more employees can be supervised by one manager which leads to lower management costs. However, this reduced cost is a trade-off with effectiveness, as this single manager must devote more of his or her time to liaison and communication with a large number of staff.

The trend over the past ten years has been for organizations to introduce wider spans of control and a subsequent flattening of organizational structures. This must be done in conjunction with the provision of more employee training, a commitment to building strong work cultures and assistance to ensure staff are more self-sufficient in their roles.

Centralization and decentralization

Centralization refers to the degree to which decision-making is located at the top of an organization. An organization is deemed to be highly centralized when the majority of decisions are made by senior managers with little input from employees at lower levels. Alternatively, an organization is decentralized when decisions are able to be made by employees and lower-level managers who have been empowered to do so. It is important to understand that the concepts of centralization and decentralization are relative, in the sense that an organization is never exclusively one or the other. Organizations could not function if all decisions were made by a small group of top managers or if all decisions were delegated to lower-level staff.

Nonprofit sport organizations tend to be more centralized than decentralized due to the influence of their traditional structures. Decision-making is often concentrated at the board level, where volunteers make decisions related to strategy for paid staff to implement at an operational level. This can lead to problems (see Chapter 12) of slow decision-making or politics. On the other hand, the nature of nonprofit sport organizations that are often made up of disparate groups and spread over a wide geographical area, requires local-level decision-making for clubs, events and sporting competitions to operate effectively.

Formalization

Formalization refers to the extent jobs are standardized and the degree to which employee behaviour is guided by rules and procedures. These rules and procedures might cover selection of new staff, training, general policies on how work is done, procedures for routine tasks, and the amount of detail that is provided in job descriptions. Formalizing an organization increases the control managers have over staff and the amount of decision-making discretion individual staff may have. An organization such as a local sport club may have very few procedures or rules for how things are done, but the tribunal for a professional sports league will have a very detailed set of procedures and policies in regard to how cases are reported, heard and prosecuted.

In Practice 6.1

Melbourne Cricket Club

The Melbourne Cricket Club (MCC) is a private club, incorporated under the Melbourne Cricket Club Act 1974, boasting by far the biggest membership of any sporting club in Australia. It also has the public responsibility of managing the iconic sporting arena, the Melbourne Cricket Ground (MCG), home of many an Ashes defeat by Australia over the old enemy England, and home to one of the world's great sporting events, the Australian Football League Grand Final each year.

The MCG is built on crown land and is a significant asset of the Victorian people. The Melbourne Cricket Ground Trust, established by the Melbourne Cricket Ground Act 1933, is responsible for the ground management of the MCG. Section 7(1) of the Act states 'the function of the Trust is to manage and control and make improvements to the Ground at its discretion'. In 2003, following the signing of the Management and Indemnity Deed between the Melbourne Cricket Club, the Melbourne Cricket Ground Trust and the Treasurer of Victoria, the MCC is contracted to manage the MCG until 2042. Under the terms of the Deed the MCC has the exclusive rights to manage the MCG in accordance with the terms of the Management and Indemnity Deed.

The business and affairs of the MCC are overseen and controlled by a Committee. The Committee comprises members of the club elected to honorary office-bearer positions, namely, a president, three vice-presidents and a treasurer, and nine other club members elected to the Committee. To assist in the execution of its responsibilities, the Committee has established a number of sub-committees to which the president appoints committee members. Committee members are also involved in the following additional sub-committees and related funds or corporate bodies: MCC Sporting Sections, Cricket, Legal, AFL, MCC Foundation and MCC Nominees.

Additionally, the Committee reviews the performance of the club's management team in consultation with the Chief Executive Officer (CEO), measuring results against the business plan objectives, ensuring compliance with legal requirements and monitoring the strategic and operational risk management plan. The MCC manages the ground through eight departments responsible to the CEO: Member and Customer Services, Events, Executive, Facilities, Finance and Information Systems, Commercial Operations, Heritage and Tourism (including MCG Tours), and Human Resources. There are about 140 permanent club employees and event staff are drawn from a pool of 900-plus for match-day duties at the ground.

Source: MCC website at www.mcc.org.au.

Structural models

The types of structure adopted by sports organizations can be categorized into four common types: the simple structure, the bureaucracy, the matrix structure and the team structure. Let's examine each of these briefly and explore their relevance for sport organizations.

The simple structure has a low degree of departmentalization and formalization, wide spans of control and would most probably have decisions centralized to few people. Such a structure would be used by a small sporting goods retail store that might have ten casual and permanent staff and an owner/manager. There would be no need for departments, as most decisions and administrative tasks would be performed by the owner/manager and all other staff on the sales floor. The majority of procedures would be executed according to a simple set of rules and the owner/manager would have all staff reporting directly to him or her. The advantages of the structure in this case are obvious: decisions can be made quickly, it ensures a flexible workforce to cater for seasonal needs and busy periods, and accountability clearly rests with the owner/manager.

If the owner/manager wanted to expand the operation and open other stores in other locations, he or she would require a different structure to cope with the added demands of controlling staff in multiple locations, making decisions across a wider number of operational areas, and ensuring quality products and services are provided in each store or location. The owner/manager might consider adopting a bureaucratic structure.

The bureaucratic structure attempts to standardize the operation of an organization in order to maximize coordination and control of staff and activities. It relies on high levels of formalization, the use of departments to group people into discrete work teams that deal with specific functions or tasks, highly centralized decision-making and a clear chain of command. An organization such as Sport England, the Australian Sports Commission, or a state or provincial government department of sport would be structured along these lines. Obviously, as an organization expands in size, increases the number of locations it delivers services, or diversifies its range of activities, the more likely it is to reflect some elements of bureaucratization.

The matrix organization structure reflects the organization of groups of people into departments according to functions and products. For example, an elite institute for sport might group specialists such as sports psychologists, biomechanists, skill acquisition coaches and exercise physiologists into discrete teams. At the same time, individuals in these teams might be involved in providing services to a range of different sporting groups or athletes, effectively creating two bosses for them. This breaks the unity of command principle, but allows an organization to group specialists together to maximize sharing of expertise while

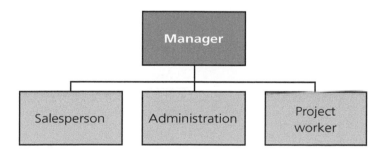

Figure 6.2: **Simple structure.**

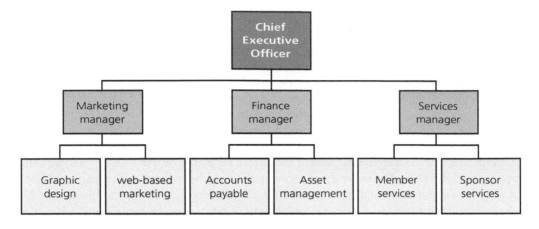

Figure 6.3: **The bureaucratic structure.**

facilitating their involvement in a number of projects or service delivery areas. The argument for this arrangement is that it is better to have the specialists work as a team than to appoint individuals to work in isolation to provide their services. While this allows the organization to provide a range of services, it does increase the potential for confusion in regard to managing the demands from two bosses, which in turn may lead to an increase in stress.

A relatively new structural design option is the team structure. The team structure requires decision-making to be decentralized to work teams that are made up of people with skills to perform a variety of tasks. A football club franchise might employ such a structure with teams formed for club events or marketing campaigns as it will allow quick decision-making in regard to finance, staffing or impacts on players.

While these generic structures can be applied to all types of organizations, there has been some research that has attempted to categorize the various structures that exist within nonprofit sport organizations. Kikulis *et al.* (1989) developed a structural taxonomy for provincial (state) Canadian amateur sport organizations based on the organizational dimensions of specialization, standardization and centralization. The evolution of Canadian sport organizations in the 1980s to a more professional and bureaucratized form prompted the researchers to attempt to establish exactly what form this evolution had taken. Kikulis *et al.* (1989) identified eight structural designs for voluntary sport organizations, ranging in scale of complexity for the three structural

	Football operations division	Corporate services division	Marketing division
Team 1	Manager 1	Project worker 1	Worker 1
Team 2	Manager 2	Project worker 2	Worker 2
Team 3	Manager 3	Project worker 3	Worker 3

Figure 6.4: **The matrix structure.**

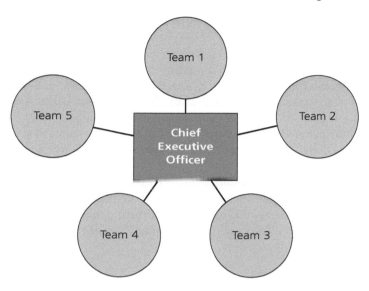

Figure 6.5: **Team structure.**

dimensions. Theodoraki and Henry (1994), in a similar study defined a typology of structures for British sport governing bodies. They too utilized the structural elements of specialization, standardization and centralization to distinguish between various structural designs.

Identifying design types for national level sport organizations was the focus of a study by Kikulis *et al.* (1992) in which organizational values and organizational structure dimensions were used to identify three distinct designs – kitchen table, boardroom and executive office. Each design represents a distinct mix of organizational values comprising their orientation toward private or public interests; the domain of activities conducted (ranging from broad participation based to a focus on high performance results); the degree of professional involvement in decision-making; and the criteria used to evaluate effectiveness.

Now that we have explored the elements of structure and the various ways they can be used, we can examine the factors that influence the structure adopted by a sport organization.

What influences the structure of a sport organization?

There are generally four factors that influence the structure of an organization: strategy, size, technology and environmental uncertainty. Each of these is briefly reviewed.

Strategy

In a perfect world, an organization's structure would be designed purely around the requirement to maximize the chances of an organization's strategic goals being achieved. This is rarely possible, but strategy does play an important part in determining the structure adopted by a sport organization. Whether an organization is pursuing an overall strategy of innovation, cost minimization or imitation will necessitate the design of a specific organizational structure.

An important trend to note in the development of structure for nonprofit sport organizations has been the impact of the introduction of paid professional staff, a very deliberate strategy in response to increases in government funding in sport in most club-based sporting systems around the world. The impact of such a strategy on the structure of Canadian provincial voluntary sport organizations (VSOs) was explored by Thibault *et al.* (1991). They found that specialization and formalization increased after the introduction of professional staff, but that centralization, after initially increasing, actually decreased over time. It was suggested that centralization increased because volunteer board members sought to retain control over decisions, and then decreased as the relationship between board members and staff stabilized. Such resistance to changes in structure were noted by Kikulis *et al.* (1995), who studied the changes in specialization, standardization and centralization of Canadian national sport organizations (NSOs) over a four year period. They found that incumbent volunteers resisted change across all three elements of organizational structure, highlighting the role of human agents and personal choice in determining organizational change outcomes.

Size

The size of an organization also plays an important part in the determination of what will be its best possible structure. Larger organizations tend to be more formalized, with more specialist roles and departments and more levels of management than smaller organizations. This makes sense as managers need to implement greater control measures to manage the volume and communication of information in a large organization. Amis and Slack (1996) state that much of the research into the relationship between organizational size and degree of centralization suggest that as 'organizations become larger, decision-making becomes more decentralised' (p. 83). In terms of nonprofit sport organizations they also found that with an increase in size of the organization, control over organizational decision-making remains at the voluntary board level, and concluded that a 'central role of decision-making as a means of control and the desire for volunteers to retain this control' (ibid.: 84) meant that the boards of many sport organizations were reluctant to relinquish control to professional staff.

Technology

Technology does have an impact on organizational structure. Robbins *et al.* (2004) argue that if organizations predominantly undertake routine tasks then there is a high degree of departmentalization, and a high level of centralized decision-making. This appears logical because non-routine tasks require decisions to be made at the level of organization where they actually happen. In regard to a sport organization such as a professional sport club, the increased use of information and communication technology means that it requires additional specialist staff such as video technicians, statisticians and network programmers who may have replaced staff that used to perform tasks manually. The net effect is a higher level of departmentalization and specialization amongst the workforce.

Environmental uncertainty

Environmental uncertainty for sport organizations can be influenced by the actions of suppliers, service providers, customers, sponsors, athletes, volunteers, staff, stakeholder groups and government regulatory agencies, as well as general changes in economic or market conditions. For example, if a group of professional athletes behave inappropriately, their actions can affect the ability of their club or team to maintain or develop sponsorships, which in turn may affect their ability to retain staff and hence require a structural adjustment. Similarly, a downturn in the economy can directly affect sales of sporting merchandise, and organizations may have to adjust their structure accordingly to reduce costs or change product lines.

There are some additional drivers of structural change in sport organizations that are worth noting. These include poor on-field performance, changes in personnel due to politics, competition and market forces, government policy changes and forced change via mergers and amalgamations. Poor on-field performance by professional sporting teams or clubs can lead to an end-of-season purge of playing or coaching personnel, and may entail a review of how the group of staff involved in coaching, athlete support or allied health services is organized. The political nature of some sport organizations that elect individuals to govern their activities can lead to structural change being implemented due to personal preferences of elected leaders or a mandate for change. Competition and market forces affect all organizations, but the interdependent nature of clubs operating within a league or competition necessitates them sharing information. Consequently, these organizations tend to be structured in similar ways, making structural change difficult. Governments may also change the way they fund high performance programmes or tie funding levels to the performances of international teams or individuals. Poor international performances may consequently reduce funding and therefore the capability of an organization to sustain their organizational structure. Finally, structural change may be forced upon sports organizations, either by economic conditions (such as population loss in rural areas forcing clubs to merge) or government policy (such as forcing single gender sport organizations to merge).

The example of Sport Scotland highlights how the four generic factors of strategy, size, technology and environmental uncertainty can influence the structure of a sports organization.

In Practice 6.2

Sport Scotland

Sport Scotland is the lead agency tasked with developing sports in Scotland, both in terms of developing participation in sport and increasing elite sport performances. The website for Sport Scotland states that they work with partners to develop the Scottish sporting system, investing in and joining up the people, places, partnerships and planning that make sport happen, specifically:

- advising the Scottish government and supporting delivery of its policies;
- leading, supporting and coordinating key organizations involved in sport;
- investing National Lottery and Scottish government funding;
- delivering quality products and services in targeted areas;
- promoting the power of sport and the contribution it makes to life in Scotland;
- collaborating with UK and international sporting systems to ensure Scottish sport is well represented and integrated; and
- adding value to major sporting events and additional investment.

Sport Scotland's organizational structure is directly linked to their strategy. As their website proclaims,

> as the national agency for sport, we are a non-departmental public body, responsible through ministers to the Scottish Parliament. We are also

a National Lottery Fund distributor and we are governed by National Lottery distribution rules. We invest Scottish Government and National Lottery resources to support people in Scotland to participate, develop and achieve in sport. We continually strive to ensure these resources are invested wisely so as to achieve best value and maximum impact.

Sport Scotland incorporates a head office in Glasgow and a high performance arm, the Sport Scotland Institute of Sport (SSIS), in Stirling. The Sport Scotland Trust Company also operates three national training centres, Glenmore Lodge, Inverclyde and Cumbrae. These centres provide quality, affordable and appropriate residential and sporting facilities for people to develop in sport.

The entire organization is based on a simple structure, with the CEO having three direct reports (or a span of control of three): a Director of High Performance who works with the SSIS, a Director of Sports Development who has four direct reports (heads of coaching and volunteering, sporting pathways, school and community sport, and facilities), and a Director of Corporate Services who has five direct reports (office support, strategic planning, finance, communications and human resources).

It is clear that each of the four contingency factors noted earlier in the chapter have impacted on the structure of the organization. Sport Scotland has a very clear mandate to deliver professional services and support for elite athletes and to increase the number of people involved in sport in Scotland. Accordingly the structure reflects these core functions or strategic foci. Any increase in the number of elite sports or athletes supported by Sport Scotland would not necessarily lead to a change in structure, rather each of the existing teams would simply expand to cater for the increased service requirements. As a government-owned enterprise, its structure is in part determined by its mandate to deliver services to the Scottish sport industry, and is unlikely to be unduly affected by environmental uncertainty. The drivers of change in structure would include any significant shifts in strategy or government policy, such as a move to focus on selected number of priority sports, which would perhaps require a redesign in organizational structure.

Source: Sports Scotland website at www.sportscotland.org.uk.

Challenges for sport managers

An ongoing challenge facing sport managers is the need to strike a balance between lowering costs by using fewer staff and increasing productivity. This can be achieved through a greater use of technology for communication, data management and analysis, the appointment of skilled staff able to use technology, and the development of semi-autonomous work teams that are able to make operational decisions quickly. This requires the use of a more flexible organizational structure than perhaps is the norm for the majority of contemporary sport organizations.

A further challenge for sport managers is to ensure that their organizations are flexible enough to quickly react to opportunities in the market or to the demands of their stakeholders, while at the same time maintaining adequate forms of control and accountability. Sport managers will need to establish clear guidelines for decision-making and acceptable levels of formalization for standard procedures, without unduly constraining the flexibility to modify those guidelines and formal procedures.

An aspect of managing organizational structures that is relatively unique to sport is the presence of both paid staff and volunteers, often with volunteers directing the work of paid staff. Sport managers will need to be cognizant of the need to maintain close links between these two significant parts of their workforce and maintain a suitable structure that allows these groups to communicate effectively and work to achieve organizational outcomes.

Sport managers also need to ensure the structure can enable strategy to be realized. If strategic plans are devised, new markets identified or new product and service offerings developed in the absence of concomitant changes to the organizational structure, then the ability of the organization to deliver such planned changes is questionable. It is imperative that sport managers pay attention to designing their structure to enable specific strategic directions to be achieved.

As illustrated in the previous chapters, organizations that work within the sport industry must work within a myriad of other organizations from the public, private and nonprofit sectors. Often, sport organizations have many stakeholders involved in setting the strategic direction of the organization. The organizational structure should therefore facilitate decision-making processes that engage all relevant stakeholders.

Finally, the interdependent relationships that exist between sports organizations that may be involved in a league, a collection of associations, a joint venture or a funding agreement with multiple partners and sponsors, necessitate organizational structures that reflect these connections. This may extend to establishing designated roles for external liaison within the structure or incorporating representation from members of external organizations on internal decision-making committees.

The structure adopted by Hockey Canada represents an attempt to deal with many of these challenges.

In Practice 6.3

Hockey Canada

Hockey Canada is the sole governing body for amateur hockey in Canada. More than 4.5 million Canadians are associated with Hockey Canada as players, coaches, officials, trainers, administrators or volunteers. More than 550,000 registered players and another 1.5 million casual or unregistered participants play hockey at more than 3,000 arenas throughout Canada. Hockey Canada employs over 75 staff and has offices in most Canadian provinces. The organizations that affiliate with Hockey Canada include 13 Branch associations, the Canadian Hockey League and Canadian Inter-University Sport. In conjunction with these member organizations, Hockey Canada facilitates participation in amateur hockey leagues, teams and games through player, coach and referee development, grading of competitions and establishing appropriate rules and regulations for amateur hockey across Canada.

Hockey Canada exists to:

- foster and encourage the sport of amateur hockey throughout Canada;
- foster and encourage leadership programmes in all areas related to the development of hockey in Canada;

- recognize and sanction the establishment of governing bodies in Canada in accordance with the principles, philosophy and practices of the Association;
- support and encourage Branches and other members in the development of amateur hockey within their jurisdictions and areas of responsibility;
- establish and maintain uniform playing rules for amateur hockey;
- maintain national insurance programmes;
- affiliate with and cooperate with other national or international amateur hockey organizations;
- conduct Inter-Branch and international contests of amateur hockey; and
- provide representation for international open hockey competition.

An important element of the structure of Hockey Canada is the large size of the Board of Directors which comprises Officers (eight), Branch Presidents (13), Council Representatives and Directors (eight) and Special Advisory Council Members (five). Each of these positions represents a specific constituent group within Hockey Canada. In addition, the Board of Directors receives reports from a Hockey Development Council of 24 members, again made up of individuals representing the specific interests of regional affiliates or membership types (i.e. coaches, officials). The Board of Directors has five policy sub-committees that deal with areas such as elite competitions, women's programmes, policy development, programmes of excellence and junior development. Finally, there are ten standing sub-committees that report to the Board on issues such as insurance, marketing, finance, management and other areas of activity. This appears to be a very cumbersome way to manage the affairs of a relatively simple activity like facilitating games of ice hockey, but the sheer scale and geographic spread of its constituents requires Hockey Canada to maintain a comprehensive governance structure that facilitates decision-making and communication amongst its 4.5 million participants.

Sources: Hockey Canada website at www.hockeycanada.ca and Hockey Canada (2010) *Annual Report 2010*. Calgary: Hockey Canada.

Summary

Organizational structure was defined as the framework that outlines how tasks are divided, grouped and coordinated within an organization. An organization's structure is important because it defines where staff and volunteers fit in with each other in terms of work tasks, decision-making procedures, the need for collaboration, levels of responsibility and reporting mechanisms.

Six key elements of organizational structure were reviewed: work specialization, departmentalization, chain of command, the span of control, centralization and formalization. In addition, four basic models for how an organization may use these six elements to design an appropriate structure were reviewed: the simple structure, the bureaucracy, the matrix structure and the team structure.

The generic contingency factors that influence organizational structure – size, strategy, technology and environmental uncertainty – were reviewed as well as some unique drivers of change to the structure of sport organizations. Finally, a number of unique challenges for sport managers in dealing with structure were presented. Sport managers should be aware of these factors that drive structural change and the specific structural elements they can influence that are likely to deliver improved organizational outcomes and performance.

Review questions

1   Define organizational structure in your own words.
2   If you were to manipulate any of the six elements of structure, which do you think could have the most impact on the day-to-day role of the chief executive of a sports organization?
3   Do staff in small sports organizations have a low degree of work specialization? Why or why not?
4   Which structural model would suit a large sports event such as the Commonwealth or Olympic Games? Why?
5   How are organizational strategy and structure related?
6   How does a change in size affect the structure of a sports organization?
7   Compare the organizational structure of a sport manufacturing organization and a local community sports facility? How do each of the six elements of organizational structure differ? Which elements are similar?
8   Explain how environmental uncertainty can force change to the structure of a sports organization.
9   Interview the CEO of a medium-sized sports organization. What is their most significant challenge in managing their organizational structure?
10 Explore the structure of a small community sport club. Are the principles of organizational structure outlined in this chapter directly applicable? Why or why not?

Further reading

The use of organizational theory in the analysis of structures for nonprofit sport organizations is well established. Three broad questions have been addressed in these studies. These are: first, investigating the relationship between organizational structure and organizational effectiveness; second, attempting to categorize organizational types; and third, exploring the impact of professionalization on various elements of organizational structure. Students interested in reading further should consult the following journal articles.

Amis, J. and Slack, T. (1996) 'The size-structure relationship in voluntary sport organizations', *Journal of Sport Management*, 10(1): 76–86.
Frisby, W. (1986) 'The organizational structure and effectiveness of voluntary organizations: The case of Canadian national sport governing bodies', *Journal of Park and Recreation Administration*, 4(3): 61–74.

Organizational structure

Kikulis, L.M., Slack, T. and Hinings, B. (1992) 'Institutionally specific design archetypes: A framework for understanding change in national sport organizations', *International Review for the Sociology of Sport*, 27(4): 343–368.

Kikulis, L.M., Slack, T. and Hinings, B. (1995) 'Toward an understanding of the role of agency and choice in the changing structure of Canada's national sport organizations', *Journal of Sport Management*, 9(2): 135–154.

Kikulis, L.M., Slack, T., Hinings, B. and Zimmermann, A. (1989) 'A structural taxonomy of amateur sport organizations', *Journal of Sport Management*, 3(2): 129–150.

Stevens, J. (2006) 'The Canadian Hockey Association merger and the emergence of the Amateur Sport Enterprise', *Journal of Sport Management*, 20(1): 74–101.

Theodoraki, E.I. and Henry, I.P. (1994) 'Organizational structures and contexts in British national governing bodies of sport', *International Review for the Sociology of Sport*, 29(3): 243–263.

Thibault, L., Slack, T. and Hinings, B. (1991) 'Professionalism, structures and systems: The impact of professional staff on voluntary sport organizations', *International Review for the Sociology of Sport*, 26(2): 83–98.

Relevant websites

The following websites are useful starting points for further information on the structure of sport organizations:

Australian Sports Commission – www.ausport.gov.au
Netball Victoria – www.netballvic.com.au
Sport and Recreation New Zealand – www.sparc.org.nz
Sport Canada – www.pch.gc.ca/progs/sc/index_e.cfm
Sport England – www.sportengland.org
Sport Scotland – www.sportscotland.org.uk

Racing Victoria Limited

Thoroughbred horse racing in the State of Victoria, Australia is governed by Racing Victoria Limited. RVL's vision is 'to enhance the Victorian thoroughbred racing industry's position as a leading world-class sporting industry, delivering integrity, quality and entertainment'. On 17 December 2001, Racing Victoria Limited was registered as a public company limited by guarantee under the federal Corporations Act. On 19 December 2001, RVL assumed the functions and responsibilities as the new Principal Club (now known as the Principal Racing Authority) governing thoroughbred racing in Victoria. This coincided with the commencement of the Racing (Racing Victoria Ltd) Act 2001.

Prior to RVL's establishment, the Victoria Racing Club, the race club that hosts the famous Melbourne Cup at their Flemington race track each November, had responsibility as the Principal Club in Victoria. RVL was established with the support of the racing clubs, racing industry bodies and the State government to provide independent governance of thoroughbred racing in Victoria.

RVL's Member Shareholders consist of Country Racing Victoria Inc. (CRV), Melbourne Racing Club Inc. (Melb RC), Moonee Valley Racing Club Inc. (MVRC) and Victoria Racing Club (VRC), along with the Thoroughbred Racehorse Owners Association (TROA), Thoroughbred Breeders Vic. (TBV), Australian Trainers Association (Victorian Branch) (ATA), Victorian Jockeys Association (VJA), Australian Jumps Racing Association (AJRA), Victorian Bookmakers Association (VBA) and unions representing the Australian Liquor Hospitality and Miscellaneous Workers' Union (Victorian Branch) (LHMU), Australian Services Union (Victorian Branch) (ASU), Australian Workers' Union (Victorian Branch) (AWU) and the Media, Arts and Entertainment Alliance (MEAA).

RVL's constitutional objectives are to develop, encourage, promote and manage the conduct of the racing of thoroughbred horses in Victoria by ensuring:

- *excellence*: Victorian thoroughbred racing is, and is recognized throughout Australia and worldwide as, a centre of racing excellence;
- *service of customers*: Victorian thoroughbred racing competes effectively in the leisure and entertainment markets by providing excellent customer service to patrons, punters and other customers; and a source of exciting entertainment for a wide audience;
- *integrity*: Victorian thoroughbred racing generally, and race meetings in particular, are managed and conducted to ensure the highest integrity, building continuously on the reputation and integrity of Victorian thoroughbred racing;
- *efficiency*: Victorian thoroughbred racing is managed with optimal efficiency in order to best enable the meeting of the objectives;
- *participation*: Victorian thoroughbred racing is managed to encourage the fullest participation by the widest range of people, particularly women and young people;
- *economic benefits*: the management of RVL's and Victorian thoroughbred racing clubs' revenues, costs, assets and liabilities optimizes the economic benefits delivered by Victorian thoroughbred racing to all of its stakeholders and participants, including in particular the owners and breeders of thoroughbred racehorses, other participants and stakeholders in Victorian thoroughbred racing, the communities in which Victorian thoroughbred racing operates; and the Victorian economy generally;

- *social obligations*: Victorian thoroughbred racing is conducted to ensure that it meets its social obligations to Victoria and the communities in which it operates, including but not only, by promoting Victorian country thoroughbred racing, encouraging responsible wagering and gaming; and optimizing employment in the Victorian thoroughbred racing industry; and
- *independence*: RVL conducts its operations and exercises its powers and functions in a manner that ensures public confidence in RVL's integrity and independence from any improper external influence.

RVL's organizational structure comprises of three board portfolios (or mega-departments): Integrity, Racing Operations, and Marketing and Development. The RVL Integrity Department is broken into the two key areas of Integrity Services and Veterinary Services. Integrity Services manages all Officials including Stewards, Starters, Judges, Clerks of Scales and Barrier Attendants at race meetings and race trials. Integrity Services comprises the following functions: Integrity Management, Betting Services, Chair Meetings, Form Analysis, Stewards' Operations, Investigations, and Raceday Administration and Licensing. Veterinary Services is responsible for such things as Raceday Vets, Drug Control Programme, research and development, quarantine services and other activities dealing with the care and regulation of horses.

The Racing Operations group is responsible for the management and development of the racing programme and optimizing opportunities for owners, trainers, jockeys and breeders. The Racing Operations department undertakes regular analysis, monitoring and review of the programme and consults regularly with clients and stakeholder groups. It performs important tasks such as handicapping of courses, developing the racing programme and rating tracks on race days.

The Marketing and Development group is principally aimed at growing and developing the level of participation, interest in and awareness of thoroughbred racing in Victoria. Marketing and Development comprises of the following functions: Media and Public Relations; Publishing, Design and Website Management; the Call Centre; Sponsorship and Marketing of RVL and the Australian Racing Museum; and working with Owners and Breeders for promotional efforts.

The most recent strategy document 'Racing to 2020' stated:

> The Victorian thoroughbred racing industry is a major player in the global sports, entertainment and wagering market. It is also a key employer and contributor to the state's economy. Racing To 2020 has been developed to address Victorian thoroughbred racing's future and to ensure its continued vitality, growth and sustainability. This exciting new strategic vision provides the platform and framework for industry development over the next twelve years. It is a clear statement of our current and future objectives. Over the past decade, the landscape has changed dramatically for racing. Wagering on racing and sports is no longer the sole domain of the TABs and on-course bookmakers. Mobile telephones, the internet and competition policy have changed the racing environment forever. RVL perceives this as an opportunity to expand racing's popularity and to enhance its position as a mainstream sport and entertainment experience of choice. A sustainable future will be achieved by maintaining customer focus, maximizing revenue, renovating and renewing racing's infrastructure and increasing the returns to participants.

Source: RVL website at www.racingvictoria.net.au and Racing Victoria (2009).

Case study questions

1 Access the RVL website at www.racingvictioria.net.au and read about the history of racing in Victoria. Why do you think racing in Victoria is now governed by an independent company?
2 How is the strategy for RVL toward 2020 aligned to its organizational structure?
3 What are the barriers or constraints that might limit the effectiveness of the structure adopted by RVL?
4 What are some of the economic and market forces that RVL needs to be mindful of in order to ensure its structure meets its needs?

Chapter 7

Human resource management

Overview

This chapter reviews the core concepts of human resource management, provides examples of the unique features of human resource management within sport organizations, such as volunteer and paid staff management, and summarizes the key phases in the human resource management process. The chapter examines human resource management within community, state, national and professional sport organizations, in order to illustrate core concepts and principles.

After completing this chapter the reader should be able to:

- identify the key concepts that underpin human resource management within sport organizations;
- explain why human resource management in sport organizations can be different from non-sport organizations;
- identify each of the phases within the human resource management process; and
- explain the ways in which each of the human resource management phases would be implemented in different sport organization contexts.

What is human resource management?

Human resource management, in business or sport organizations, is essentially about, first, finding the right person for the right job at the right time and, second, ensuring an appropriately trained and satisfied workforce. The concepts that underpin effective human resource management are not particularly complex. However, the sheer size of some organizations, as well as the difficulties in managing unusual organizations in the sport industry, make human resource management a complex issue to deal with in practice. Successful sport leagues, clubs, associations, retailers and venues all rely on good human resources, both on and off the field, to ensure they achieve their objectives. Conversely, organizations with staff that lack motivation, are ill-suited to their work, underpaid or undervalued will struggle to perform.

Human resource management is a central feature of an organization's planning system. It cannot be divorced from other key management tools, such as strategic planning, financial planning, or managing organizational culture and structure. Human resource management can both drive organizational success and is a consequence of good management and planning. Importantly, human resource management is a process of continual planning and evaluation and is best viewed as part of a cycle in which an organization aims to meet its strategic goals. Human resource management, therefore, is a holistic management function in that it can be 'both person-centred and goal-directed' (Smith and Stewart 1999).

Human resource management can mean different things to different organizations, depending on their context and outlook. For professional sport organizations that are profit driven, such as the American National Basketball Association (NBA), Major League Baseball (MBL) or National Hockey League (NHL), successful human resource management is equated with profitability, long-term growth and success (on and off the court, diamond and rink). This is not to suggest that these things are pursued at the expense of employees, but rather that the success of the employees is measured by dispassionate business indicators and human resource management is a tool for driving the business towards its goals. For example, some player welfare and development programmes within professional sport organizations are designed to produce socially, morally and ethically responsible citizens. This is viewed as a good human resource strategy, not only because of the intrinsic value to the athletes, but for the extrinsic value that comes from better public relations and sponsor servicing. In other words, better behaved athletes mean greater profitability and overall success for professional sport teams and franchises.

For nonprofit sport organizations, successful human resource management is not always about bottom-line financial performance. Rather, it can encompass a range of strategies and outcomes depending on the organizational context. A local sporting club that has had a problem with alcohol consumption among its junior players may develop a range of programmes to educate its players, coaches and administrators (who may be paid or volunteer staff), in order to encourage a more responsible club culture. This player welfare programme may actually be part of a human resource management strategy, as the inappropriate club culture may have been making it difficult to attract and retain volunteers with expertise and commitment. In the case of the professional team context the player welfare programme can be used to manage image and maintain brand credibility. In the case of the local community sport club the player welfare programme can be used to retain volunteers who were being driven away from the club by poor behaviour and a dysfunctional culture. From these two examples it is clear that human resource management can be both person-centred and goal-directed at the same time.

As illustrated by the above examples, one of the significant challenges of implementing effective human resource management within sport organizations is that not all sport organizations are alike. As Taylor *et al.* (2008) have illustrated, different types of sport organizations have different staffing profiles. These staffing profiles are dependent on an organization's type, as well as its purpose or reason for being. For example, a professional sport organization, such as a club in the Spanish La Liga, will have an extensive staff of full-time paid professionals engaged in marketing, coaching, sport science and general administration, whereas a voluntary organization, such as local cricket or rugby club, is likely to have no paid staff. Other sport organizations might have a mixture of paid and voluntary staff, which work together in the day-to-day operations of the organization, or work together in their capacities as staff and members of a committee of management or board of directors. We will investigate the governance of sport organizations later in the book, but at this point it is sufficient to note that in many sport organizations paid staff are answerable to a voluntary board of directors. This relationship can be a challenge, for the overall management of the organization and the practice of human resource management more specifically.

Many of the functions of professional and voluntary sport organizations are similar, such as event management, promotion, fundraising, membership services and financial management, however, the scale of the organizations is different. While it is true that the scale and type of organization has an impact on the human resource management practices that can and need to be put in place, in many respects sport organizations are increasingly adopting human resource management practices that are underpinned by the notion of professional and standard practice. Indeed, the implementation of specific human resource management practices has been viewed as an important catalyst in the professionalization of voluntary or community sporting organizations. For example, in the early 1990s the Australian Sports Commission, in conjunction with the Australian Society of Sports Administrators, the Confederation of Australian Sport and State departments of sport and recreation, developed the 'Volunteer Involvement Program'. The original programme was designed to encourage sport organizations to adopt professional volunteer management practices, which was viewed as essential given the large numbers of volunteers involved in sport organizations and the increasing professionalization of the industry.

The programme has since been revised and improved to provide sporting clubs and associations with resources and training modules for volunteer management ('recruiting volunteers', 'retaining volunteers', 'volunteer management: a guide to good practice', 'managing event volunteers', 'volunteer management policy' and 'the volunteer coordinator'). These modules encourage Australian sporting clubs and associations to develop systematic processes and practices, although it should be acknowledged that the diversity of club-based sporting system, such as that which is in operation in Australia, means that the capacity to professionalize varies considerably.

Is human resource management in sport special?

Many of the core concepts that underpin human resource management apply to all organizations, whether they are situated in the world of business, such as soft drink manufacturer Coca-Cola or mining company BHP Billiton, or in the world of sport, such as the South African Rugby Football Union or the Canadian Curling Association. This is not surprising, given that all these organizations employ staff who are expected to execute a range of designated tasks at an appropriate level of performance. These staff will manage finances, undertake strategic planning and produce products like Fanta, iron ore, coaching clinics and national championships. There are, however, significant differences between business and sport organizations, which result in modifications to generic human resource management practices.

In particular, professional sport organizations have special features, which present a unique human resource management challenge. Sport organizations, such as the Cincinnati Bengals in America's National Football League, revolve around three distinct types of employees. First, the Bengals employ people in what they call 'the front office', such as the business development manager or the director of corporate sales and marketing. Second, the Bengals employ people in what can be referred to as the 'football operations department', such as the coaches, trainers and scouts. Finally, the Bengals employ people that comprise 'the team', the players, who are the most visible people within any professional sport organization. It could be argued that non-sport businesses operate in the same way, with different levels of management, from the chief executive officer all the way through to the employee on the factory floor. The obvious difference in the sporting context is that the human resources at the bottom of the staffing pyramid are the highest paid employees in the entire organization. The difference between sport and non-sport organizations is illustrated in Figure 7.1. It should be noted that sport organizations have employees that could be considered 'the lowest paid', but relative to non-sport organizations they are not equivalent, and as such a light blue arrow has not been included for the sport organization pyramid (sport organizations are not completely unique in this respect, however, for in many forms of entertainment, such as film or television drama, the actors are the highest paid).

In non-sport organizations, chief executive officers, general managers and other senior executives often receive performance bonuses and have access to share options that allow them to share in the wealth and profitability of the company. The workers producing the

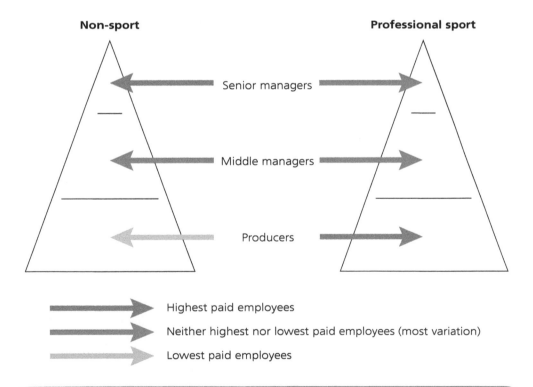

Figure 7.1: Pay and organization levels in professional sport and non-sport organizations.

product (at the Fanta bottling plant or the iron ore mine for example) do not have access to performance schemes and bonuses that might be worth millions of dollars. In professional sport organizations the situation is reversed and the performance bonuses are typically available to those who produce the product, the players. It is important to keep this special feature of sport in mind when considering the human resource management needs of professional sport organizations specifically and sport organizations more generally.

Additionally, a significant proportion of staff in semi-professional and nonprofit sport organizations are volunteers. The distinction between volunteers and paid staff in the effective management of these groups is a challenge for human resource management in sport organizations. Because sport is often played in a community environment (at a State, regional or local level), it necessarily requires the support of volunteers to maintain services, facilities and events. Some national sport organizations, like the South Africa Rugby Football Union or the Canadian Curling Association mentioned earlier, have paid staff at the national level, whose job it is to coordinate and develop programmes, events, championships and national teams. Equivalent state or regional associations for sports like these might, depending on the size, popularity and government funding afforded the sport, also have paid staff in key management, development and coaching positions. In some instances these State or regional associations will have more staff than the national body because of the requirement to deliver programmes and services, as well as manage and provide strategic direction for the sport. Local associations, again depending on the size and popularity of the sport, might also have some paid staff; however, at this level sports are supported by a significant core of volunteers. In Australia it has been estimated that sporting activities are supported by 1.5 million volunteers who collectively contribute in excess of 150 million volunteer hours per year, while in the United Kingdom it has been estimated that volunteers contribute in excess of 1 billion hours of labour (www.sportengland.org).

A significant proportion of sport is played on a weekly basis within leagues and associations across the world. Depending on whether the sport is played indoors or outdoors, the sport might have a winter season (football or ice hockey), a summer season (baseball) or might be played all year (basketball). The regularity of the season and the competition, whether at the elite or community level, means that the staffing requirements of sport organizations are predictable and remain relatively stable. There are, however, a range of sporting events and championship for which staff planning is difficult and staffing levels fluctuate greatly. These events are either irregular (a city might get to host the Olympics once in 100 years) or big enough that they require a large workforce for an intense period of time (the annual Monaco Grand Prix). The staffing for major annual sport events can be referred to as 'pulsating' (Hanlon and Cuskelly 2002), as illustrated in Figure 7.2.

In essence, major events need a large workforce, often composed primarily of volunteers or casual workers, for a short period of time prior to the event, during the event and directly following the event, and a small workforce of primarily paid staff for the rest of the year (events such as the Olympic Games or world championships will require a permanent paid staff for many years prior to the event, but most staffing appointments will conclude within six months of the event finishing). The rapid increase and decline in staffing within a one- or two-week period is a complex and significant human resource management problem. It requires systematic recruitment, selection and orientation programmes in order to attract the staff, and simple yet effective evaluation and reward schemes in order to retain them.

Large organizations with a large workforce have both the capacity and responsibility to engage in sophisticated human resource management. Often there is a dedicated team or department that manages human resources, led by a senior member of staff. In small- to medium-sized organizations, however, there is not always the human or financial capacity to devote to human

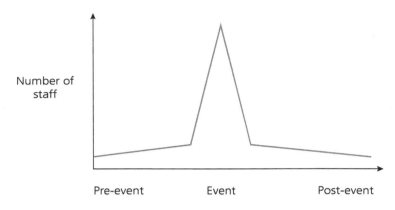

Figure 7.2: 'Pulsating' sport event staffing.

resource management practices in a formal system. Human resource management in small- to medium-sized organizations is often the responsibility of the most senior staff member, such as the chief executive or general manager or is combined with roles performed by another senior manager responsible for finances, planning or marketing, for example.

Sport leagues, clubs, associations and venues rarely have enough staff to warrant employing someone to be responsible solely for human resource management. Often the other key management roles, such as marketing, events or sponsorship are considered essential and human resource management is considered either as a luxury or peripheral to the core management functions. Furthermore, human resource management can be confused with personnel management, which encompasses more mechanistic functions such as payroll and record keeping (leave, sick pay etc.).

In Practice 7.1

twenty20 Big Bash recruitment

In 2011–2012 Cricket Australia launched the KFC twenty20 Big Bash League (BBL), an attempt to build on the success of twenty20 cricket worldwide and re-energize Australian domestic cricket. Prior to the introduction of the BBL, Australian cricket competitions were State-based within the test, one-day and twenty20 formats. The BBL was designed to introduce a city-based rivalry to the Australian domestic twenty20 competition, with teams representing the major cities, and two teams based in Australia's two largest cities of Sydney and Melbourne. As Chief Executive Officer James Sutherland noted in his media conference at the end of 2010 to announce the new league, Cricket Australia views the BBL 'as a fantastic opportunity for the game to grow off the back of the incredible popularity of Twenty20 cricket and to bring new fans to the game of cricket'.

In Australia, one of the leading internet job advertising agencies in the area of sport is a company called Sportspeople ('bringing job seekers and employers together since 1996'). The Sportspeople website contains a wide variety of job advertisements within the sport, recreation and leisure industries and is used by major and minor sport organizations in the recruitment phase of their human resource management operations. The development and implementation of a new twenty20 League required new staff, particularly in the major markets of Sydney and Melbourne. On the Sportspeople website the BBL advertised for several positions within its organization. One of these positions was the 'Big Bash League Manager', based in Melbourne. The following is an excerpt from the advertisement that appeared on the Sportspeople website:

> Cricket Australia (CA) is one of the nation's premier sporting bodies, with a vision for Cricket to be Australia's favourite sport. Operating within the sports and entertainment industry, CA offers an exciting and dynamic working environment, and is responsible for overseeing and developing cricket on a national level.
>
> The Big Bash League (BBL) is a key strategic initiative of CA and will be launched in December 2011. Contested by eight new teams with new and unique identities, the BBL provides Australian Cricket with the opportunity to build a new generation of passionate cricket fans.
>
> The BBL Manager is a pivotal leadership role, responsible for the central management of the league. You will ensure a high level of service is delivered to key BBL stakeholders including Teams, State Associations and media and sponsor rights holders. Collaborating with other members of the CA Management team, the BBL Manager will implement strategies to grow the value of the League.
>
> Specific areas of responsibility will include:
>
> - Development of industry networks;
> - Operational planning and execution;
> - Sponsorship sales support;
> - Policy development and compliance; and
> - Management of the central BBL organization including the management of budgets and leadership of the BBL team.
>
> The ideal candidate will be tertiary qualified, with extensive management experience ideally gained in a professional sports organization. Strong commercial exposure and experience in marketing and business development is essential.
>
> Key to your success is your ability to influence others, your strong stakeholder engagement skills and your commitment to ensuring a commercially successful BBL.

As detailed in the chapter, a job description is a document that covers the job content and context, while a job specification is a document that covers the job requirements, especially skills and knowledge base. It is clear that the above job advertisement was in part a job description and in part a job specification. Some of the job's content and context are dealt with in the first three paragraphs that discuss Cricket Australia, the BBL and the role of the BBL Manager. The job advertisement also covers the job requirements by articulating the 'specific areas of responsibility'. In terms of skills and knowledge base, the advertisement clearly identifies that potential candidates need to be 'tertiary qualified with extensive management experience'.

See announcement at: http://cricket.com.au/news-display/Big-Bash-League-gets-green-light/22401.

The essentials of human resource management

Human resource management in sport organizations aims to provide an effective, productive and satisfied workforce. Human resource management refers to the design, development, implementation, management and evaluation of systems and practices used by employers use to recruit, select, develop, reward, retain and evaluate their workforce. The core elements of the human resource management process are represented in Figure 7.3. The following phases are considered the core functions of human resource management, although it is important to keep in mind that these functions will differ significantly depending on the size, orientation and context of the sport organization in which they are implemented.

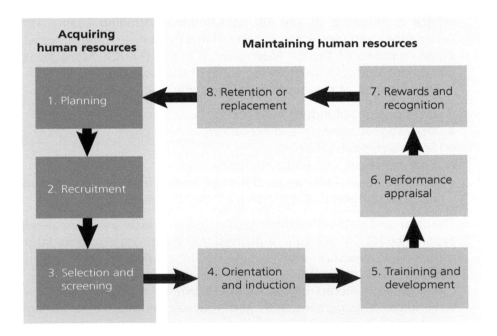

Figure 7.3: The traditional human resource management process.

Phase 1: Human resource planning

Human resource management planning is essentially about assessing and forecasting the staffing needs of the organization and is often referred to as the most important phase for effective human resource (Smith and Stewart 1999). The planning phase of human resource management is short and fairly static for organizations in which the staffing levels remain fairly constant and the types of jobs performed by staff members vary little. For organizations that are dynamic or in a state of flux (as a result of economic pressures or opportunities for example), human resource planning is a cycle of ongoing development.

In the planning phase an organization must assess whether current staffing needs will be adequate to meet future demand (or alternatively, whether fewer staff will be required), whether staff turnover is predictable and can be accommodated, whether the ratios of paid, full-time, part-time, casual and volunteer staff are appropriate or adequate, whether there are annual or cyclical fluctuations in staffing that need to be met and managed, and whether specific capabilities will be required in the future that the organization is currently lacking.

Once an organization decides that a new staff member is required or a new position is to be created, the organization must undertake a job analysis, in order to determine the job content (primary and implied tasks), requirements (skills, competencies, qualifications and experience) and context (reporting relationships and job characteristics). Once the job analysis has been completed in as much detail as possible, the organization is ready to develop a job description (a document that covers the job content and context) and a job specification (a document that covers the job requirements, especially skills and knowledge base).

There are four management principles that can be applied to job design. They are most useful for considering how a job might be positioned within an organization, as well as for identifying different types of organizations. These themes are job simplification, job rotation, job enlargement and job enrichment (Chelladurai 2006). *Job simplification* refers to the process in which a job (and the organization) is broken down into a series of simplified and specialized tasks. This simplification is intended to increase the specialization of employees, thereby increasing efficiency and productivity. Job simplification can be viewed as a positive management tool, particularly when it comes to evaluating the performance of an individual employee, however, job specialization, depending on the context, can lead to workers becoming bored and subsequently dissatisfied with their work.

The second principle, *job rotation*, is partly a remedy to the boredom and dissatisfaction that can result from simplification. Job rotation involves workers swapping jobs on a periodic basis, in order to keep fresh and stimulated, although clearly a sport organization will only have a finite range of jobs through which employees can rotate.

Job enlargement refers to a process in which employees are encouraged to enlarge the scope of their work and add tasks, even if they are simplified and specialized. The benefit of this approach is a happier workforce, but the downside is the perception of overwork.

Finally, *job enrichment* refers to the structuring of the job so that it maximizes employee motivation and involvement. This process relies on being able to design jobs that are flexible and have the capacity for growth and change, as well as the employment of people that can work autonomously. According to Chelladurai (2006), the greater levels of responsibility and challenging work that are available through job enrichment means that it is a superior method of job design.

Phase 2: Recruitment

Recruitment refers to the process by which an organization tries to find the person most suited to the job that has been designed. The greater the pool of applicants, the greater the chance the organization will find a suitable candidate. Generating a pool of applicants is not always simple, however, particularly if the job requires specific skills, knowledge, qualifications or experience that are in demand or short supply. Thus, for the chief executive position in a major professional club with responsibility for a multi-million dollar operation, the search might be extensive and costly. However, recruiting an attendant to check membership tickets at home games of the professional club might only require a small advertisement in a local newspaper. Finally, recruiting 10,000 people to act as volunteers for a major hallmark event might require a nationwide or international advertising campaign across various media forms. Increasingly, recruitment processes are becoming more sophisticated as organizations take advantage of rapidly developing communication technologies.

Phase 3: Selection

Selection and screening is the process of condensing the candidates that applied for the position during the recruitment phase to a short-list. The selection phase will usually include at least one interview of the short-listed candidates, which will supplement the application forms and curriculum vitae submitted by the applicants. These selection tools will be used to determine whether the applicant is appropriate in light of the job analysis and which of the applicants is the best person for the job. Depending on the geographic location of the applicants, the interview might be conducted in person, via telephone, via video conferencing or via the internet. Industrial relations legislation covers a range of organizational and employment issues in most countries. It is important to comply with these laws and regulations throughout the human resource management processes, such the recruitment and selection phase, so that the organization is not exposed to claims of discrimination or bias (on the basis of race, colour, country of birth, ethnicity, disability, religion, sex, age, marital status, pregnancy or sexual preference). In this respect Smith and Stewart (1999) refer to the types of questions *not* to ask in an interview:

- How old are you?
- Do you have a problem working with younger people?
- Are you married?
- Do you have any children?
- How will you care for your children when at work?
- How long have you been a single parent?
- Do you intend to have any more children?
- Where do you attend church?
- Do you have a Christian background?
- What are your views on taking prohibited drugs?
- Please send a recent photo with your application form.
- What are you going to do about your weight problem?
- Do you have a communicable disease?
- What clubs do you belong to?
- Do you belong to a trade union or professional association?
- Tell us about your political affiliations?
- Have you undertaken any military service?

An interview is the most common way of determining whether a prospective employee will be best suited to the organization and the position. However, other techniques, such as sophisticated personality and intelligence tests, are increasingly being used to determine whether the applicant has the job requirements identified in the planning phase (skills, competencies, qualifications and experience). For example, the Myers-Briggs Type Indicator (MBTI) is a personality test which, based on questions about psychological processes such as the way people like to interpret information or make decisions, categorizes people into one of 16 personality types. Based on the psychological theories of Carl Jung, the MBTI can be used by sport organizations to determine whether an applicant not only has the appropriate skills and educational qualifications for the job, but also whether their personality, attitudes and values will be a good fit for the organization.

In Practice 7.2

The NFL combine

The National Football League (NFL) is the most popular sporting League in America. The NFL consists of 32 teams throughout America in cities such as Miami (the Dolphins), Pittsburgh (the Steelers), Denver (the Broncos), Dallas (the Cowboys), Chicago (the Bears) and San Francisco (the 49ers). The NFL is one of the richest sporting leagues in the world, the foundation of which are multi-year, multi-billion dollar media rights and sponsorship deals; Monday Night Football and the Superbowl in particular are American institutions. Teams in the NFL spend in excess of US$100 million each on player salaries alone, which means that high school and college athletes throughout America compete to gain a lucrative contract in the NFL, while the NFL teams scout the nation looking for promising football talent.

In April each year the NFL conducts a draft, through which each NFL team has the opportunity to add players to its roster, typically secured through the well-developed college system. As with many sporting leagues around the world, in order to introduce a measure of competitive balance, the poorer performing teams each year are allocated higher 'picks' in the draft than the better performing teams, meaning that these poorer performed teams have priority access to the best players in that year's graduating college class (including those that nominate early for the draft). Because the NFL is such a competitive business, teams will go to great lengths to establish whether particular college players will be ready for the demands of the NFL, as well as determine whether the player will be a good fit in their organization. Like many other organizations, NFL teams must go through the 'planning' phase of the human resource management process, whereby they assess their current playing talent and attempt to determine what future talent they will require. Like a standard business that has a marketing division, a finance division, a sales division and so on, with staff in each division, so too do NFL teams, with players in specific positions – quarter backs, defensive backs, running backs, offensive lineman, wide receivers etc. In each of these 'divisions' an NFL team must assess its future requirements and attempt through the draft (as well as through trades) to secure players that fulfil their needs.

The choice of college players through the draft is not left to chance. In February each year the best college prospects for the forthcoming draft are invited to participate in the annual NFL 'combine'. During the combine the draft prospects are put through a series of rigorous physical tests. These tests are standard from year to year, so that teams and coaches can assess the performance of one year's combine prospects relative to previous years. The following is the way in which the NFL describes each of the tests:

40-yard dash

The 40-yard dash is the marquee event at the combine. It's kind of like the 100-meters at the Olympics: It's all about speed, explosion and watching skilled athletes run great times. These athletes are timed at 10, 20 and 40-yard intervals. What the scouts are looking for is an explosion from a static start.

Bench press

The bench press is a test of strength—225 pounds, as many reps as the athlete can get. What the NFL scouts are also looking for is endurance. Anybody can do a max one time, but what the bench press tells the pro scouts is how often the athlete frequented his college weight room for the last 3–5 years.

Vertical jump

The vertical jump is all about lower-body explosion and power. The athlete stands flat-footed and they measure his reach. It is important to accurately measure the reach, because the differential between the reach and the flag the athlete touches is his vertical jump measurement.

Broad jump

The broad jump is like being in gym class back in junior high school. Basically, it is testing an athlete's lower-body explosion and lower-body strength. The athlete starts out with a stance balanced and then he explodes out as far as he can. It tests explosion and balance, because he has to land without moving.

3 cone drill

The 3 cone drill tests an athlete's ability to change directions at a high speed. Three cones in an L-shape. He starts from the starting line, goes 5 yards to the first cone and back. Then, he turns, runs around the second cone, runs a weave around the third cone, which is the high point of the L, changes directions, comes back around that second cone and finishes.

Shuttle run

The short shuttle is the first of the cone drills. It is known as the 5–10–5. What it tests is the athlete's lateral quickness and explosion in short areas. The athlete starts in the three-point stance, explodes out 5 yards to his right, touches the line, goes back 10 yards to his left, left hand touches the line, pivot, and he turns 5 more yards and finishes.

Sometimes the results in these tests, like a job application in a standard organization, are a good indication of whether a player will be a high selection in the NFL draft, however, this is not always the case as prospective players are also observed throughout the previous season by coaches and talent scouts, who will assess them on game sense and performance under pressure, amongst other things. Thus, the tests provide a valuable complementary selection tool for NFL teams. At the 2011 NFL combine corner back Patrick Peterson recorded the second best time in the 40 yard dash (4.34 seconds) and was selected at pick number five in the 2011 draft by the Arizona Cardinals. By contrast, defensive back Demarcus Van Dyke recorded the best time in the 40 yard dash (4.28 seconds), but was only taken at pick number 81 in the draft by the Oakland Raiders.

Source: NFL website at: www.nfl.com.

Phase 4: Orientation

Once the employee has successfully navigated the recruitment and selection processes, they are ready to begin work in their new job within the sport organization. Before they start, however, they need to be orientated and inducted. This phase of human resource management is important, as a good quality orientation and induction programme can make an employee feel both welcome and empowered, but a poor programme, or none, can make a new employee feel as if they have travelled to a foreign country, in which they can't speak the language, don't know where to go and can't read any of the signs. In short, being in a new organization can be a daunting and frightening experience. The implementation of successful orientation and induction programmes can ameliorate some of the difficulties, concerns and anxieties. Potential problems are compounded if the employee is a volunteer and can be exacerbated further if the volunteer does not have any direct supervision from a paid employee of the organization. This is a recipe for disaster, both for the organization and the employee. Table 7.1 outlines some of the orientation and induction steps that the Australian Sports Commission recommended as part of a series of volunteer management modules.

Once an athlete has been selected to play for a team in a major professional sport league (passed the recruitment and selection processes), they are invariably faced with the completely new world of professional sport and all the demands that accompany it. The National Basketball Association (NBA) in the USA recognized that this was a difficult time for many young athletes and developed a comprehensive orientation and induction programme. Since 1986, the rookie players of the forthcoming season have been required to participate in a week-long training and development camp in the month prior to the season's start. The rookie transition programme is designed so that these young athletes can develop better life skills, which in turn will hopefully prepare them for the particular and peculiar stresses of a professional athletic career. Through the transition programme, which includes a diverse range of topics such as sexual health, nutrition and anger management, the NBA hopes that its young players will be able to make better decisions.

Successful orientation and induction programmes revolve around forthright and effective communication of information about the organization and its operations. This information might include a general overview, policies and procedures, occupational health and safety regulations, industrial relations issues, a physical tour of the organization's facilities, an overview of the training and development programmes available to employees or an explanation of the performance appraisal process (Slack 1997). The focus on orientation and induction is usually magnified when a large number of volunteers are required by the organization, such as at an Olympic Games. A total of 60,422 volunteers participated in running the Atlanta Olympics

Table 7.1: Australian Sports Commission volunteer orientation

Orientation Program Checklist

- ☑ Provide an orientation guidebook or kit
- ☑ Provide copies of current newsletter, annual report and recent marketing/promotional material
- ☑ Provide a copy of the constitution
- ☑ Enter the name, address and contact details of each volunteer into database
- ☑ Gather and file copies of qualifications and accreditation certificates from each volunteer
- ☑ Introduce the organization's culture, history, aims, funding, clients/members and decision-making processes
- ☑ Introduce key volunteers and/or staff (and organization chart)
- ☑ Outline the roles and responsibilities of key volunteers and staff
- ☑ Detail the roles and responsibilities and accountabilities of the volunteer in their new position
- ☑ Familiarise volunteers with facilities, equipment and resources
- ☑ Explain and 'walk through' emergency and evacuation procedures
- ☑ Familiarise volunteers with the organization's day-to-day operations (safety and risk management, telephone, photocopier, keys, filing system, tea/coffee making, office processes and procedures, authorising expenditure)

Source: Australian Sports Commission website at: www.ausport.gov.au.

in 1996, 47,000 volunteers participated in Sydney in 2000, while the 2004 Athens Olympics received in excess of 160,000 volunteer applications from all over the world. At the 2008 Beijing Games, 74,615 volunteers provided services at Games venues, while another 400,000 volunteers provided information, translation services and emergency aid at 550 street stalls throughout the city.

Phase 5: Training and development

Training and development is at the heart of an organization that seeks continual growth and improvement. Sport organizations that do not engage in systematic training and development programmes are destined to operate far below their optimum, not only because they will fall behind in current trends, practices and skills, but because they will not see themselves as learning organizations (Senge 1990). At its most basic, training and development is a process through which new and existing employees learn the skills required for them to be effective in their jobs. At one end of the spectrum these skills could be associated with learning how to operate automated turnstiles at a professional sport arena (training for the novice employee), or learning how to creatively brand the organization in order to compete in a hostile marketplace (training for the experienced existing employee). Where training was once a fairly mechanistic activity, it now includes more generic organizational skills that require development and implementation, such as when a major league sport franchise ensures product or service quality, or when a national sport organization develops an organizational culture that encourages compliance from State or regional sport organizations.

Dressler (2003) outlines a five-step training and development process that is useful for sport organizations. Step one is to complete a 'needs analysis', in which the organization identifies the necessary skills for its employees, analyses the current skills base and develops specific training objectives. Step two involves developing the actual training programme, which may be done internally or externally. Most sport organizations, as previously noted, are too small to have sophisticated human resource management departments that have the skill and experience to design, develop and implement comprehensive training programmes. Sport organizations will most often use external training providers, such as universities or consultancy firms, to provide tailored or standard programmes, depending on the needs analysis. Step three, validation, is an optional step in which the organization is able to validate that the training programme that has been developed or contracted satisfies the needs analysis. Step four is the implementation of the programme, during which the staff are trained (this could be anything from a one-day short course, through to a two year master's programme). In the fifth and final step the training programme is evaluated. The successful programme might be expanded to include more employees or more skills, while the unsuccessful programme needs to be discontinued or reworked, which requires the organization to re-assess the needs analysis. Like the entire human resource management process, the training and development process is best viewed as cyclical.

Phase 6: Performance appraisal

This phase of the human resource management process is potentially the most dangerous, as it has the inherent ability to pit 'management' against 'employees' at the macro level, and at the micro level cause managers to feel uncomfortable in judging others or cause employees to feel unworthy, as part of a negative appraisal. The performance appraisal process must be approached carefully by sport organizations and human resource managers within an organization must seek to develop a collaborative process in which the employee, as well as the manager, feels empowered. As Chelladurai (2006) has noted, it is useful to think of performance appraisal in terms of its administrative and developmental purposes. The administrative purpose refers to the need within organizations to make judgements about performance that are directly related to rewards and recognition, such as promotions and salary increases. The administrative purpose often requires quantitative measures, so that employees can be appraised based on similar criteria. The developmental purpose refers to developing and enhancing the capabilities of an employee, which often requires a mix of quantitative and qualitative measures, and can be a catalyst for further training and development. The administrative and developmental purposes of performance appraisal demonstrate that the human resource management process is not always a neat cycle. Rather, there is a constant to and fro between the phases.

During the performance appraisal process, managers and leaders need the ability to review performance and suggest improvement, as a way of developing overall organizational capacity. On the other hand, employees need a forum in which they feel comfortable identifying the things they did well and the things they could have done better, as part of a process of ongoing professional and career development. In this respect the performance appraisal process within any sport organization, whatever its size or type, must be seen within the simple, but effective 'plan, do, review, improve' scheme, which is usually associated with the quality assurance agenda (Deming 1993: 134–136).

In professional sports organizations in particular, the performance appraisal process is often very public, if at times convoluted. Athletes and coaches are constantly rated on their performance. In basketball the number of points, rebounds, assists, turnovers, steals, fouls and blocked shots are recorded meticulously. From year to year, goals are set for athletes and their ability to meet targets in key performance indicators can result in an extended contract with improved conditions. On the other hand, not meeting the targets can mean a player in a sport like baseball has to return to the minor leagues, to return to form or to see out their playing days. For coaches, performance appraisal is often based on one statistic alone, the win-loss record. The fact that the coach is adept at making the players feel good about themselves or has a great working relationship with the administrative staff, will count for very little when it comes to negotiating a new contract if he or she has posted a losing record.

Phases 7 and 8: Rewards and retention

Once a sport organization has planned for, recruited, selected, orientated, trained and appraised its staff, it makes good sense that it would try to retain them. Retaining good quality staff, whether they are in a paid or volunteer capacity, means that the organization will be better off financially and strategically. Organizational knowledge and intellectual property is lost when a sport organization fails to retain its staff. Constantly losing staff will mean that the organization may have the opportunity to encourage and develop new ways of thinking, but the more likely scenario is that it will lead to wasted resources, unnecessarily diverted to rudimentary induction programmes.

The first six phases of the human resource management process all contribute to retaining staff. Poor orientation, training and performance appraisal programmes in particular can all have a negative impact on staff retention. On the other side of the retention equation, rewards and compensation can encourage employees to remain with an organization. At a professional sport organization this may mean that, rather than attempting to keep wage costs low, the senior managers will be prepared to pay the 'market rate' (Smith and Stewart 1999). In a primarily voluntary organization, the reward may take the form of a letter of appreciation for being part of a successful event and an invitation to participate next year. In other words, the reward and retention strategy will depend greatly on the context in which it is being implemented and the existing level of job satisfaction.

In Practice 7.3

The Games Makers of the 2012 London Olympics
The London Olympics in 2012, like many of the recent Summer and Winter Olympic Games, required a significant volunteer labour force. In order to manage this labour force effectively and efficiently, the London Organizing Committee for the Olympic Games (LOCOG) had to develop extensive policies and procedures for each of the human resource management stages examined within this chapter. In the 'planning' phase of the human resource management cycle, an organization must assess its current and future staffing needs. For an organization such as an Olympic Games organizing committee, the 'current' staffing profile is relatively small for many of the years leading up to the Games; in the main the staff are full-time and paid. By contrast, the future staffing needs are massive, with a mix of full-time, part-time, casual and volunteer staff required; Games organizers need to use the experience of previous Olympic Games, as well as an assessment of their own specific needs, to plan for the event.

LOCOG established the 'Games Maker' volunteer programme in order to attract the number of volunteers required by the 2012 London Olympics. An examination of the variety of roles available for volunteers through the Games Maker programme reveals the extent of the planning phase of the human resource management process, and in particular the extent of the workforce forecasting by LOCOG. The volunteer roles were divided into ten departments, with 32 teams or functional areas across these ten departments:

1   Commercial, sales and brand protection
2   Competition venues and Olympic villages
3   Media, editorial and press operations
4   Olympic and Paralympic Games operations
5   Olympic and Paralympic Games services
6   Protocol and international relations
7   Sport, medical and anti-doping
8   Technology
9   Torch relays and ceremonies
10 Transport

As an example, the 'Media, editorial and press operations' department was divided into the four teams of 'editorial services', 'media and public relations', 'press operations' and 'website and new media'. Within the 'editorial services' team, up to 50 generalist volunteers were required, who would contribute to the production of a daily 'Village newspaper' to 'engage, inform and inspire athletes and team officials'. The responsibilities and tasks of a 'Village newspaper reporter' included 'working to a brief; developing content for the newspaper; researching, interviewing, writing and editing content to strict deadlines and word counts; and providing a summary of content in French if skills permit'. The key skills of this position were writing and editing, as well as French language where available.

The Games Maker programme received more than 240,000 applications for approximately 100,000 positions, all of which had the roles, responsibilities and key skills developed, as per the 'Village newspaper reporter' example above. With more applicants than available positions, LOCOG developed a process whereby all of the applicants were interviewed at locations throughout England by trained staff. These interviews were used to match prospective volunteers with available positions, enabling LOCOG to choose the best people, but to also ensure that prospective volunteers were suited to the role they had applied for. Effective recruitment and selection processes also assist an organization with the retention phase of the human resource management process. It is clear that LOCOG had this in mind when they articulated what the 'highs' and 'possible lows' of the Games Maker roles within the 'editorial services' team might be:

The highs...

The Village newspaper will be produced from an office within the Village, ensuring a unique working environment at the very heart of the Games. You may have access to athletes in order to research stories and conduct interviews, and your work on the London 2012 website will be seen by millions of people around the world.

...and possible lows

You won't set foot outside your designated work venues and will only see the sporting action on TV. The pressure to turn around multi-page newspapers to rigid deadlines and develop online content at speed mean these are not roles for anyone seeking to bask in the glamour of the Games.

Source: London 2012 website at: www.london2012.com.

Summary

Effective human resource management in sport organizations relies on the implementation of an interdependent set of processes. At one level this can be viewed as quite mechanistic, yet on another more positive level it can be viewed as a blueprint for the successful management of people through a clearly delineated set of stages. Human resource management planning, recruitment, selection, orientation, training, performance appraisal, rewards and retention strategies are essential for an organization to operate successfully in State, nonprofit or commercial sport environments, because good people management is at the core of every successful sport organization, irrespective of the context. Good human resource management allows sport organizations to deal with some of its unique and particular challenges, such as the place of athletes in professional sport organizations, the large casual and semi-permanent workforces required by major events (annual or periodic) and the large volunteer workforce within club-based sporting systems. On the other hand, poor human resource management can result in a workforce that is not only uncommitted, but also subject to low levels of morale and job satisfaction. In short, effective and systematic human resource management should be seen as an important management tool in any sport organization, whatever the size or type.

Review questions

1 Which is the most important phase of the human resource management process? Why? Refer in your answer to organizations with primarily paid staff and organizations with primarily volunteer staff.

2 Is human resource management important for the effective management of sport organizations? Why?

3   Examine the human resource management processes of a local sport organization. Are the processes adequate?
4   Examine the staffing levels of a major annual event in your city/province/region. Are the staffing levels stable?
5   Should the human resource management role within sport organizations be combined with another functional division?
6   Should different human resource management strategies be applied to volunteers and paid staff?
7   Does the place of athletes in professional sport organizations make the need for effective human resource management practices more or less important?
8   Compare the orientation and induction processes of a sport organization and a non-sport organization. How and why do they differ?
9   Does the often public appraisal of employees in sport organizations diminish the integrity of the human resource management process?
10 Choose a small- to medium-sized organization without a human resource management specialist. Perform a job analysis for a new employee in the role of human resource management.

Further reading

Chelladurai, P. (2006) *Human Resource Management in Sport and Recreation*, Champaign, IL: Human Kinetics.
Cuskelly, G., Hoye, R. and Auld, C. (2006) *Working with Volunteers in Sport: Theory and Practice*, London: Routledge.
Doherty, A. (1998) 'Managing our human resources: A review of organizational behaviour in sport', *Journal of Sport Management*, 12(1): 1–24.
Robinson, L. (2004) 'Human resource management', in L Robinson, *Managing Public Sport and Leisure Services*, London: Routledge.
Taylor, T., Doherty, A. and McGraw, P. (2008) *Managing People in Sport Organizations: A Strategic Human Resource Management Perspective*, London: Elsevier Butterworth-Heinemann.

Relevant websites

The following websites are useful starting points for further information on the human resource management of sport organizations:

Australian Sports Commission Resources – www.ausport.gov.au/supporting/clubs/resource_library/people_management
Sport England's Running Sport Programme – www.runningsports.org
Sport and Recreation New Zealand Resources – www.sparc.org.nz/en-nz/communities-and-clubs/Toolkit-for Clubs

Managing student-athletes in the NCAA

The National Collegiate Athletic Association (NCAA) of America was 'founded in 1906 to protect young people from the dangerous and exploitive athletics practices of the time'. The NCAA began to have a significant impact on the conduct of college sport in the 1950s and as the extent and scope of college sport grew the NCAA took on a greater administrative role. In the early 1970s the NCAA adopted its current three division administrative structure (Divisions I, II and III). The NCAA is essentially an association that governs and organizes sport within the colleges and universities of America. The NCAA has media rights agreements with the major television networks in America to broadcast its games and national championships, as well as a range of sponsorship deals. In the 2009–2010 financial year US$643 million was received by the NCAA in television and marketing rights fees, which was equivalent to approximately 86 per cent of total revenue. NCAA revenue has grown steadily, from $558 million in 2005–2006 to $750 million in 2009–2010; the proportion of revenue associated with television and marketing rights fees has been in excess of 80 per cent in each of the five years between 2005–2006 and 2009–2010. According to the NCAA, more than 90 per cent of its revenue is returned to its member institutions in the form of direct distributions or services, however it is evident that the higher profile schools in Division I receive the lion's share; in 2009–2010 the Division I schools received 61 per cent of the total distribution, with a further 9 per cent allocated to Division I championships and programmes.

A significant component of the business of the NCAA can broadly be defined as human resource management, although as an organization its operations are special in many respects. As noted above, the Association was originally formed to protect young athletes from dangerous and exploitative practices. In essence the NCAA still exists to perform this role, monitoring the practices and performances of colleges, universities and their respective employees and students throughout the nation. However, it is clear that as an industry, college sport is manifestly more complex now than at the turn of the twentieth century and that the NCAA is now a large administrative organization. In 1950 there were 387 members of the NCAA, of which 362 were active, whereas in 2010 there were 1,315 members, of which 1,062 were active.

The NCAA provides a variety of what it refers to as 'student-athlete benefits'. First, the NCAA provides scholarships to athletes. The scholarships provided by the NCAA to athletes directly are typically special scholarships, either available to athletes via a competitive process or to particular types of athletes. The NCAA also provides a distribution to Division I colleges and universities via an academic enhancement fund. Second, the NCAA provides financial support to athletes. This financial support is provided in the form of injury, disability and medical insurance programmes, as well as Division I athlete opportunity and special assistance funds. Third, the NCAA provides health and safety programmes, which include a cheerleading safety initiative, as well as in-season and championship drug testing, particularly for Division I and II members. The NCAA also produces a variety of resources to assist their member institutions to develop policies and practices that improve the health and well-being of student-athletes. Finally, the NCAA runs a variety of other education programmes, clinics and workshops that assist student-athletes and their communities.

Through its committee structure and the employment of investigative officers, the NCAA also monitors violations of its rules and regulations, particularly the conduct of its member institutions in relation to their student-athletes. There are a raft of rules related to issues such as the recruitment of student-athletes, the training and development of student-athletes and the compensation of student-athletes. The issue of compensation is particularly noteworthy as the NCAA operates a strictly amateur competition, in which the student-athletes at colleges and universities throughout America are unable to receive any form of remuneration for their participation in sport.

The NCAA runs the NCAA Eligibility Center, which certifies the academic and amateur credentials of all students seeking to play sport at a Division I or II institution. In order to be considered eligible to participate in a Division I or II NCAA programme, a student-athlete must meet the requirements sets out by the NCAA. The student must have graduated from high school, have completed a minimum of 16 core courses, meet the required grade point average (GPA) and achieve a qualifying score on one of the standard university admission tests. The GPA and admission test scores for Division I student-athletes are calculated on a sliding scale, whereby a high score in one can offset a low score in the other. In addition, the student must complete an amateurism questionnaire and request amateurism certification. Some of the activities that may be reviewed by the NCAA include contracts with a professional team, receiving a salary for participation in sport, prize money received through sport, receiving benefits from an agent or prospective agent, the agreement to be represented by an agent or the provision of financial assistance based on sporting skill. By putting in place these academic and amateur eligibility rules the NCAA attempts to ensure that the integrity of the college and university system is maintained, and that the focus of college and university sport is student-athletes, not simply athletes.

Individual member institutions of the NCAA compete with each other to attract the best student-athletes across a wide variety of sports such as football, basketball, baseball, softball, track and field, golf, lacrosse, soccer and volleyball. Colleges and universities provide athletic scholarships, which enable the student-athletes to attend college or university at no cost, but given that many colleges and universities offer these scholarships, the individual institutions need to provide other benefits to attract the student-athletes. For some, the quality of the training and game facilities will be an important drawcard, while for others the opportunity to secure national television exposure or to play at a college or university that has a long history of success in a particular sport will be a deciding factor. As a result of the fierce competition to recruit student-athletes, the NCAA has detailed rules that govern what is and is not allowed by students and their prospective colleges and universities. For example, the NCAA has rules regarding the allowable recruiting materials, number of telephone calls, official visits, unofficial visits and contact between a coach and a prospective player, which all increase as the student progresses through high school. These rules also differ depending on the sport; a coach may contact a prospective basketball player or their parents not more than three times in their senior year, whereas a coach may contact prospective football players up to six times.

Once the student has made a decision about which college or university they will attend, they sign a national letter of intent (NLI), a nationwide system governed by the NCAA, which is essentially a binding agreement between the student and the respective institution. The NLI guarantees the student financial support for one year pending eligibility and the institution receives certainty that the student is committed to it alone. Most student-athletes within the NCAA have four-year sporting careers (freshman, sophomore, junior and senior). The very best student-athletes that participate in sports that have professional leagues, such as football, basketball and ice hockey, are selected via draft systems. Those that participate in non-professional sports, such as swimming or skiing, may represent their country at an Olympic Games.

Case study questions

1 The case refers to the operations of the NCAA as involving human resource management, but that its operations are special. What are some of the NCAA activities that make it a special human resource management business compared to a standard business, such as a sales or marketing company?

2 Which phases of the human resource management process does the NCAA focus its operations and activities on? Why might this be the case?

3 Beyond the fact that student-athletes do not get paid, how does the human resource management of a college or university sport programme (sometimes referred to as an athletic programme or athletic department) differ from a professional sport team or franchise?

4 In which phase of the human resource management process does the NCAA Eligibility Center belong? Why? How do the perspectives of the NCAA and its individual member institutions differ in respect to their focus in this phase of the process?

Source: NCAA websites at: www.ncaa.org; and www.eligibilitycenter.org.

Chapter 8

Leadership

Overview

Leadership is arguably the most researched yet least understood topic in the context of management. What we define as excellent leadership and who are great leaders remain points of serious and widespread academic debate. In the United States alone, more than 2,000 books on the topic of leadership are published every year. In this chapter we provide a broad outline of the different approaches that have been used to describe and analyse leadership. We will also use a number of examples and cases to explore leadership. Much of this discussion will take place in reference to the leadership challenges that confront sport organizations.

By the end of this chapter the reader should be able to:

- describe the need for leaders and for leadership;
- distinguish between leadership and management;
- outline the different levels (in the organization) that leaders can work at and how this impacts their approach to leadership;
- outline the specific challenges that leaders in sport organizations are confronted with; and
- provide an overview of your personal leadership development needs.

What is leadership?

It is not easy to find agreement among any group on a definition of leadership. Sometimes leadership is described as 'getting things done through people'. Others argue that leadership is about 'exercising power in order to influence others' or that true leadership is about 'envisioning a bright future and taking others by the hand towards it'. In other words, leadership can be many things to different people. Cotton Fitzsimmons, former coach of the Kansas City Kings argues that 'if you're a positive person, you're an automatic motivator. You can get people to do things you don't think they're capable of' (Westerbeek and Smith 2005: 34). Vince Lombardi, the famous coach of the Green Bay Packers of the 1950s and 1960s once said that

> leaders are made, they are not born; and they are made just like anything else has been made in this country – by hard effort. And that's the price that we all have to pay to achieve that goal, or any goal

> (ibid.: 54)

According to former US President Theodore Roosevelt 'the best executive is the one who has sense enough to pick good men to do what he wants done, and self-restraint enough to keep from meddling with them while they do it' (ibid.: 56), and Lou Holts, a former coach of the Notre Dame football team argued that 'all winning teams are goal-oriented. Teams like these win consistently because everyone connected with them concentrates on specific objectives. They go about their business with blinders on; nothing will distract them from achieving their aims' (ibid.: 80). Harvard professor and leadership expert Linda Hill (2008) argues that in today's global, fast changing, multiple stakeholder decision making business environments we may well have to 'lead from behind' in order to let others take charge as leaders when it is most needed (p. 127). According to these experienced, but very different leaders and leadership experts, leadership is:

- goal oriented;
- about influencing others;
- about empowering others;
- about seeing the big picture;
- about needing others; and
- about strength of character.

We can use these different components of leadership to construct a leadership definition. For the purposes of this book we define leadership as 'skilfully influencing and enabling others towards the attainment of aspirational goals'. We do appreciate that we may not do justice to the many aspects one can argue that need to be incorporated in a complete definition of leadership, but as an introduction to the topic in this book the above definition will serve its purpose. In the next section of this chapter we will further outline the ways that leadership can be viewed.

In Practice 8.1

Li Ning: Olympic gold leading to sporting goods dominance
Li Ning is one of China's favourite sons. He won six Olympic medals in gymnastics, including three gold at the 1984 Los Angeles Games. Li Ning has been an important role model for the Chinese people during a time of societal transformation, and has been used by the Chinese government as

an example of the 'new' Chinese. In 1990 Li Ning set up his own company, appropriately named after himself, and with that started an exciting journey of building the number one Chinese sporting goods company, and possibly the number one sporting goods company in the world in the near future.

As a result of his high visibility in Chinese society, and the ubiquitous recognition of his name among Chinese citizens, the company rapidly grew during the first few years of its existence. It seemed that the emerging 'Li Ning' brand could be used to sell anything. However, selling Li Ning perfume, amongst other things, turned out to be stopping the company in its progress and its ambition to grow quickly. Li Ning realized that his name could be used in the short term to sell lots of different products, but that in the long term people would only remember him for his sporting prowess. This made Li Ning and his board of directors decide to pursue a focus strategy for the company. Because Li Ning was inextricably related to sport it seemed logical that the company would focus its activities on sport products, in particular sporting goods. This focus on core business has led to Li Ning now being the biggest Chinese sporting goods company in the world and the number two company in China, aggressively pursuing number one Nike. At the beginning of 2010 Li Ning held 14.2 per cent of the Chinese market, Adidas 13.9 per cent and Nike 16.7 per cent.

Many would argue that it is impossible to overtake sporting goods giant Nike, who has access to enormous economies of scale advantages (due to their market leadership in the US). But it was only in 2008 when Li Ning was still trailing both Nike and Adidas when the gap to Nike was 3.5 per cent and the gap to Adidas 2.7 per cent. Li Ning's strategy to grow is surprisingly simple and logical. Their chairman, the visionary Li Ning himself, argues that their primary customers are children in the age category of 12–20. Capture their imagination and they will make sure their parents will buy them a (few) pair(s) of $120 sneakers. Then make sure that you focus on sports that now and in the future will be the ones that Chinese customers favour – football, basketball, running, tennis and fitness.

Li Ning has a tremendous advantage over Nike and Adidas in China, arguably because they are a Chinese company with a Chinese iconic chairman, and are in a better position than Nike and Adidas to understand the Chinese market. If you then realize that the Chinese market for sporting goods continues to grow with double digit figures per annum, much faster than the US and EU markets, and that the Chinese still spend four times less on footwear than US and UK consumers, it becomes clear that growing home market share over the next decade will greatly contribute to Li Ning also improving its standing globally. Business results at the end of 2010 also paint the picture. There were 7,915 brand retail stores in China, up 666 from 2009, of which 582 are Li Ning operated. The company also reported revenue growth of 13.5 per cent in China and 48.9 per cent revenue growth internationally (although this still only represents 1.4 per cent of the company's total turnover) and 15.3 per cent operating profit growth.

Li Ning has also realized that leadership in the global sporting goods business requires a leadership role in regard to engaging with local communities. This is why the company has developed a programme to educate physical education teachers to work in regional China. To date the company has provided the resources for 920 teachers to move to regional Chinese communities and assist local schools to develop physical education programmes. It will be interesting to watch Li Ning's progress over the next decade. We may well witness the birth of a global sporting goods giant, built by a Chinese leader in sport, on and off the field of play.

Sources: Interview with Frank Zhang, senior Vice President with Li Ning on 16 March 2008; Li Ning Company Limited – Annual results announcement for the year ended 31 December 2010 at: www.irasia.com/listco/hk/lining/announcement/a70015-ew02331ann.pdf; Moody, A. (2010) 'Li Ning goes head to head with sportswear giants', *China Daily*, online, available at: www.chinadaily.com.cn/business/2010-08/30/content_11223314_2.htm; and information at www.lining.com.

Theories of leadership

Northouse (2010) separates leadership theories into categories that relate to traits of leaders, their skills, their styles, the situation in which they have to lead or the contingency that they face. He also lists theories such as the path-goal theory, the leader member exchange theory, the transformational approach, the authentic approach, team leadership and the psychodynamic approach as separate categories. Because we only have one chapter in which to discuss leadership, the dominant theories have been conflated into four approaches: trait or personality approaches, the behavioural approach, the contingency approach and the transformational approach.

Trait or personality approaches

Although the personality and trait approaches to leadership stem from the earliest of leadership research times, popular leadership literature continues to stress the importance of personality and innate ability in the demonstration of leadership. Locke (1991) argues that trait theories (or great man theories as they are also called), are incomplete theories of leadership, irrespective of traits and/or personality of the leaders being important contributors to, or detractors from excellent leadership. He suggests that the possession of certain traits, such as energy and honesty, appear to be a vital for effective leadership. Basketball legend Michael Jordan, for example, has been credited with having an impressive range of innate leadership traits that will put him in good stead for being an excellent leader in many different contexts. Leaders must use their traits to develop skills, formulate a vision and implement this vision into reality. This being the case, it appears that traits only form part of the picture.

Although empirical evidence linking the personality of leaders with their success is weak, much of the popular literature still focuses on leadership traits as a way to better understand leadership. In general, the trait theories are based on the assumption that social background, physical features and personality characteristics will distinguish good leaders from poor leaders.

Behavioural approach

When it became clear that good leadership could not simply be explained on the basis of the innate characteristics of the leaders, organizational research began to focus on discovering universal behaviours of effective leaders. Behaviourists argued that anyone could be taught to become a leader by simply learning the behaviours of other effective leaders.

Behavioural strategy takes behaviours as signs of learned responses to contingencies. If research shows that to behave in a certain manner results in success for a leader, then one can learn to discharge those behaviours in particular leadership situations. The behavioural approach to leadership was also a response to early approaches to management as a whole. Frederick Taylor was an early champion of the idea that managers should use science to improve efficiency. This approach became known as Taylorism or scientific management (see Schermerhorn 2010: 31), a philosophy in which there was limited attention for the human side of the mass production movement. Rather, under Taylorism, humans were simply 'part of the larger machines' and standardization of human labour would lead to great efficiency and higher profits. Managers, according to Taylor, should begin by studying the tasks workers performed, break jobs down by analysing, measuring and timing each separate element of the job in order to determine the most efficient manner of doing the job. The most efficient method for each job became both the standard method that workers were supposed to adopt and a means for measuring worker productivity.

In response to Taylor's ideas, behaviouralists demanded a new 'human relations' approach to management of organizations involving an examination of the interaction between managers and workers. In the Hawthorne experiments, which were originally designed to study the effects of lighting upon factory workers, Elton Mayo discovered that human relations between workers, and between workers and supervisors, was most important in ensuring efficiency (see Schmermerhorn 2010: 35). In other words, to focus on interaction between humans, and by studying the best ways of interacting, managers could better lead the people that worked for the organization. Another behavioural approach to the study of leadership is the so-called Theory X and Theory Y, developed by Douglas McGregor (ibid.: 38). The theories are formulated based on the assumptions that leaders have about individuals. Managers that have Theory X assumptions argue that the typical employee dislikes work and needs direction at all times. They also think that employees need to be coerced to perform their duties. Theory Y managers believe that employees are self-motivated and committed to work and to the company. They naturally seek responsibility for the work they perform. As a result, Theory Y leaders would behave in quite different ways from Theory X leaders.

Another behaviouralist approach was formulated by Blake and Mouton. They developed the managerial grid model along two dimensions; one with a concern for people and one with a concern for production. Blake and Mouton argued that differing levels of concern along those dimensions would lead to different styles of leadership (ibid.: 317). For example, managers with low levels of concern for people and production will have an impoverished style of leadership whereas those leaders with high concern for people and production can be typified as having team-style leadership qualities. The Blake and Mouton approach has also been used to differentiate person-centred leaders from task-centred leaders. Ultimately it is important to conclude that the behaviouralist approach to leadership leads to the identification of different styles that can be described as more or less successful.

Contingency approach

It became increasingly clear to those studying leadership that traits and behaviours of leaders were often observed in relation to the situation at hand, or in other words, according to situational contingencies. Isolated behavioural and trait approaches failed to take account of how situational variables, such as task structure, the characteristics of the environment or subordinate characteristics could impact and moderate the relationship between the behaviour of a leader and the different outcomes.

In contingency theories of leadership, the core argument is that different leadership styles and approaches will apply to a range of possible management situations. This is why, for example, the on-field leadership brilliance of Diego Maradona with the Argentinean team resulted in winning the 1986 World Cup, but when Diego was required to achieve similar results with club teams in different cultures (Napoli in Italy and Barcelona in Spain) or even as the national coach of the Argentinean side at the 2010 World Cup in South Africa, he failed dismally, also resulting in the exposure of a number of personal leadership flaws. The centrality of leader behaviour and/or personality needs to be de-emphasized, and in the contingency approach we turn our attention to the leader in conjunction with circumstances that are specific to the situation at hand, including characteristics of the subordinates and the work setting. In the next section we will present three situational theories of leadership that have influenced the ways in which leadership is understood and practiced. They are:

- Fieldler's Least Preferred Co-worker Approach
- Hersey and Blanchard's Situational Leadership Theory
- Path Goal Theory

Fiedler's least preferred co-worker approach

Fiedler's (1967) model is based on the following three axioms:

1   the interaction between the leader's personal characteristics and some aspects of the situation determines the effectiveness of the leader;
2   leaders are either 'task oriented' or 'person oriented'; and
3   effectiveness of the leader is determined by the leader's control of the situation.

Fiedler comes to his classification of task- or person-oriented leadership by the use of a measurement scale called the 'Least Preferred Co-worker' (LPC) scale. The instrument asks leaders to assess co-workers on a series of bi-polar descriptors including pleasant-unpleasant, cold-warm and supportive-hostile in order to assess to what degree they think they would not work well together with that co-worker. A leader who obtains a low LPC is more motivated by task achievements and will only be concerned about relationships with subordinates if the work unit is deemed to be performing well. A leader who obtains a high LPC score will be more motivated to develop close interpersonal relations with subordinates. Task-directed behaviour is of a lesser concern, and only becomes important once sound interpersonal relations have been developed. According to Fiedler, if the least preferred co-worker still scores relatively high it indicates that the leader derives a sense of satisfaction from 'working on good relationships', indicating a person-oriented leadership style.

The model further suggests that control is dependent on three combined contingency variables:

1   the relations between the leader and the followers;
2   the degree of task structure (or the degree to which the followers' jobs can be specified clearly); and
3   the leader's position of power or amount of authority, yielding eight possible conditions presented in Figure 8.1.

| Condition | Situational favourability | | | Effective leadership |
	Leader-member relations	Task structure	Position power	
1	Good	High	Strong	Low LPC
2	Good	High	Weak	Low LPC
3	Good	Weak	Strong	Low LPC
4	Good	Weak	Weak	High LPC
5	Poor	High	Strong	High LPC
6	Poor	High	Weak	High LPC
7	Poor	Weak	Strong	High LPC
8	Poor	Weak	Weak	Low LPC

Source: adapted from Fiedler 1967: 34.

Figure 8.1: Fiedler's Situational Favourability Factors and leadership effectiveness.

Hersey and Blanchard's situational leadership theory

A theory claiming that as maturity of the group changes, leader behaviour should change as well, is known as the Situational Theory of Leadership. Hersey and Blanchard (1977) argued that as the technical skill level and psychological maturity of the group moves from low to moderate to high, the leader's behaviour would be most effective when it changes accordingly. When low levels of maturity are enacted in relation to the tasks being performed, a high task-behaviour of the leader should be exhibited, or in other words, a 'selling' and 'telling' approach to communicating with the subordinates. At medium levels of maturity, leaders need to be more focused on relationship-behaviours and at the highest levels of subordinate maturity, the leader needs to offer little direction or task-behaviour and allow the subordinate to assume responsibilities, or in other words, a 'supportive' and 'delegation' driven style of leadership communication.

According to sport organization theory researcher Trevor Slack (Slack and Parent 2006), there have been few attempts to empirically test the concepts and relationships that Hersey and Blanchard (1977) have outlined in their work, even in the management and organizational literature. Some attempts have been made to apply the theory directly in sport settings, but results have been inconsistent.

The path-goal theory

The path-goal theory (House 1971) takes a behavioural and situational approach to leadership. There are many roads that lead to Rome and therefore the path-goal theory suggests that a leader must select a style most appropriate to the particular situation. The theory in particular aims to explain how a leader's behaviour affects the motivation and satisfaction of subordinates.

House (1971) is cited in Wexley and Yukl arguing that

> the motivational function of the leaders consists of increasing personal payoffs to subordinates for work-goal attainment, and making the path to these payoffs easier to travel by clarifying it, reducing roadblocks and pitfalls, and increasing the opportunities for personal satisfaction en route
>
> (Wexley and Yukl 1984: 176)

In other words, characteristics of the subordinates and characteristics of the environment determine both the potential for increased motivation and the manner in which the leader must act to improve motivation. Subordinate preferences for a particular pattern of leadership behaviour may also depend on the actual situation in which they are placed (Wexley and Yukl 1984). Taking those different perspectives in consideration the path-goal theory proposes four styles of leadership behaviour that can be utilized to achieve goals (House and Mitchell 1974). They are:

- Directive Leadership (leader gives specific instructions, expectations and guidance);
- Supportive Leadership (leader shows concern and support for subordinates);
- Participative Leadership (subordinates participate in the decision making); and
- Achievement-oriented Leadership (leader sets challenges, emphasises excellence and shows confidence that subordinates will attain high standards of performance).

The theory is principally aimed at examining how leaders affect subordinate expectations about likely outcomes of different courses of action. Directive leadership is predicted to have a positive effect on subordinates when the task is ambiguous, and will have a negative impact when the task is clear. Supportive leadership is predicted to increase job satisfaction, particularly when conditions are adverse. Achievement-oriented leadership is predicted to encourage higher performance standards and increase expectancies that desired outcomes can be achieved. Participative leadership is predicted to promote satisfaction due to involvement (Schermerhorn *et al.* 1994).

From Transactional to Transformational Leadership

As already noted earlier in this chapter, the scientific approach to management (Taylorism) reduced the individual to performing machine-like functions. The human relations approach to management took into consideration the human part of the labour equation, appreciating that much better results can be achieved if people's individual needs are taken into consideration when leading them towards achieving certain work outputs.

One of the most recent thrusts in leadership research is that of transactional and transformational leadership. Transactional leadership encompasses much of the theories based on rational exchange between leader and subordinate, such as the theories presented above, but transformational leaders, according to Bass (1985), are charismatic and develop followers into leaders through a process that transcends the existing organizational climate and culture. The transactional leader aims to create a cost-benefit economic exchange, or in other words, to meet the needs of followers in return for 'contracted' services that are produced by the follower (Bass 1985). To influence behaviour, the transactional leader may use the following approaches:

- Contingent Reward (the leader uses rewards or incentives to achieve results).
- Active Management by Exception (the leader actively monitors the work performed and uses corrective methods to ensure the work meets accepted standards).

- Passive Management by Exception (the leader uses corrective methods as a response to unacceptable performance or deviation from the accepted standards).
- Laissez-Faire Leadership (the leader is indifferent and has a 'hands-off' approach toward the workers and their performance).

However, leadership theorists have argued that transactional leadership merely seeks to influence others by exchanging work for wages. It fails to build on the worker's need for meaningful work and it does not actively tap into their sources of creativity. A more effective and beneficial leadership behaviour to achieve long-term success and improved performance therefore is transformational leadership. Sir Alex Ferguson, the long-time Manchester United manager, can be described as a transformational leader. He envisioned a future for the club and the board repaid him with the trust of keeping him at the helm at Manchester United since 1986 for more than 1,400 games. Under his guidance and supervision the club became the most successful team in the new English Premier League and the team has also won multiple Champions League crowns. Sir Alex has prepared the likes of Eric Cantona, Ryan Giggs, Roy Keane, David Beckham, Ruud van Nistelrooy, Wayne Rooney and Cristiano Ronaldo for the world stage of football leadership.

What is transformational leadership?

It has been argued by Bass and Avolio (1994) that transformational leadership is the new leadership that must accompany good management. In contrast to transactional models, transformational leadership goes beyond the exchange process. It not only aligns and elevates the needs and values of followers, but also provides intellectual stimulation and increased follower confidence. Bass and Avolio (1994) identified four 'I's' that transformational leaders employ in order to achieve superior results. These are:

- Idealized Influence: Transformational leaders behave in ways that result in them being admired, respected and trusted, and ultimately becoming a role model. The transformational leader demonstrates high standards of ethical and moral conduct.
- Inspirational Motivation: By demonstrating enthusiasm and optimism, the transformational leader actively arouses team spirit and motivates and inspires followers to share in and work towards a common goal.
- Intellectual Stimulation: By being innovative, creative, supportive, reframing problems and questioning old assumptions the transformational leader creates an intellectually stimulating and encouraging environment.
- Individualized Consideration: Transformational leaders pay special attention to each individual's needs for achievement and growth by acting as a coach or mentor.

Looking closer at the four it can be argued that charisma (the ability to inspire enthusiasm, interest or affection in others by means of personal charm or influence) is an important component of transformational leadership. Purely charismatic leaders may be limited in their ability to achieve successful outcomes, due to their need to instil their beliefs in others which may inhibit the individual growth of followers. However, transformational leaders are more than charismatic in that they generate awareness of the mission or vision of the team and the organization, and then motivate colleagues and followers towards outcomes that benefit the team rather than merely serving the individual interest.

In Practice 8.2

Right To Play: Johan Olav Koss and bettering the world

The primary objective of Right To Play, formerly known as Olympic Aid, the legacy project of the Lillehammer Olympic Organizing Committee, is to engage leaders in sport, business and media in the betterment of living conditions and developmental opportunities for children all over the world. In March 2001, Olympic Aid became an implementing NGO (non-governmental organization) and by organizing child development programmes and engaging in research and policy development it works towards improving the chances that all children are guaranteed their right to play.

Four-time Olympic gold medallist Johann Olav Koss, the current CEO and president of the organization was the driving force behind the transition of Olympic Aid into Right To Play. Having visited the country of Eritrea during his sporting career, as an athlete ambassador, he was so affected by the living conditions of the local children in particular that he decided to donate the majority of his Olympic winnings to Olympic Aid. In the process he challenged other athletes and the public to do the same, leading to the raising of US$18 million. Between 1994 and 2000, Olympic Aid continued to raise funds for children in disadvantaged situations, building on the momentum of subsequent Olympic Games.

In early 2001, Olympic Aid evolved into Right To Play in order to meet the growing demands of programme implementation and fundraising. Building on the founding legacy of Lillehammer, this transition allowed Right To Play to include both Olympic athletes and other high profile sportsmen and women as athlete ambassadors, but also to increase relationships with non-Olympic sports, to partner with a wider variety of private sector funding agents and to deepen involvement at the grass-roots level of sport. In 2005 Right To Play was instrumental in setting up the Sport for Development and Peace International Working Group (SDP IWG). This initiative emerged from the work of the United Nations Inter-Agency Task Force on Sport for Development and Peace. United in the SDP IWG are delegates from governments, UN agencies, and international NGOs that include sport governing bodies and other development agencies. The SDP IWG is run by an executive committee and supported by a bureau and secretariat. The executive committee has as its members a number of government ministers, deputy ministers and senior UN officials who work together to secure the support of national governments and the UN to use sport for development and peace purposes. The objective of the group is to articulate and promote the adoption of policy recommendations to national governments for the integration of sport and physical activity into their national and international development strategies and programmes. At www.righttoplay.com it can be read that

> Sport for Development and Peace evolved from a growing body of evidence showing that well-designed sport-based initiatives incorporating the best values of sport can be powerful, practical and

cost-effective tools to achieve development and peace objectives. Sport is now recognized by many international experts in the fields of development, education, health, sport, economics and conflict resolution as a simple, low cost, and effective means of achieving a diverse range of development goals.

When asked what he had learned as a global leader at the occasion of the tenth anniversary of Right To Play, Johan Koss commented that it is important for a leader to stick

> to the mission and the vision of the organization, not taking anything for granted but working towards and through the challenges that surface. Being part of a leadership circle with many international organizations has certainly strengthened our credibility, but has also given me the experience and the understanding of the challenges they are overcoming, which are very similar to what we have seen on a daily basis. My goal for Right To Play over the next ten years is to put us on a sustainable path – making sure that programmes and activities in the local communities can be sustained, replicated, and are accessible to all children. This is a critical element to the areas where we are currently already working.
>
> Secondly, we need to work with governments and institutions around the world to further enhance the Sport for Development agenda, so that institutions like the United Nations recognize the benefits of sport and play in their poverty reduction strategies and their national development plans so that this becomes a priority in the future. If these two elements of programme sustainability and policy development and implementation can happen over the next ten years, we will ensure that the future generation of children will have access to sport and play.

The vision of leading athlete Johan Olav Koss has been translated into a highly successful organization that he continues to head up today as an organizational leader, developing and delivering a range of child and community development programmes that use sport and play as vehicles of communication and fund raising. To a large extent, sport leads the way as well.

Source: excerpts and information from www.righttoplay.com and from the site formerly at: http://iwg.sportanddev.org/en/index.htm (successor site: www.sportanddev.org/en/about_this_ platform); and personal communication with Johan Olav Koss in December 2010.

Leadership and management

At this stage of the chapter it will be useful to briefly consider the debate about the relationship between leadership and management, and how to distinguish between the two. Kotter (1990) has conducted extensive research work in order to find out how to differentiate managers from leaders. He concluded that management effectiveness rests in the ability to plan and budget; organize and staff; and control and solve problems. Leadership, however, is principally founded upon the ability to establish direction; align people; and to motivate and inspire. According to Kotter, leaders achieve change whilst managers succeed in maintaining the status quo. Bass (1990), however, states that 'leaders manage and managers lead, but the two activities are not synonymous' (p. 383). It goes beyond the scope of this book to further elaborate on the distinction between leadership and management. Suffice to say that in the context of discussing management principles in sport organizations, management without leadership is much less likely to be successful than a capable manager who can also provide excellent leadership. In the next section we will therefore put forward what can be described as the five key functions of leadership:

- to create a vision;
- to set out strategy;
- to set objectives and lead towards performance;
- to influence and motivate people; and
- to facilitate change and nurture culture.

To create a vision

A vision can be described as 'a state of the future that lies beyond the directly imaginable by most people'. This view of the future, in the context of an organization, is a positive and bright state of being that only the 'visionary' (one who is characterized by unusually acute foresight and imagination) can see at that time. In other words, the leader is responsible for envisioning a future for the organization that can become reality if the people working in the organization can be aligned towards achieving that 'envisioned state'. It is often said that good leaders distinguish themselves from good managers because they do have a vision whereas managers do not. How to achieve the vision through strategy is the next function of the leader.

To set out strategy

The process of strategic planning is all about the different ways that a vision can be achieved. It constitutes two principal perspectives: that of the organization and that of the individuals making up the organization. Visionary leaders are not necessarily successful leaders if they are not capable in translating the vision into action strategies. The process of strategic management is therefore concerned with carefully managing the internal organization, including considering the individual needs of workers; and the external environment in which many opportunities and threats impact the ability of the leader to achieve the vision. To be better prepared for action, the leader needs to be involved in setting measurable objectives.

To set objectives and lead towards performance

Setting objectives is the next function of the leader. Once the broad strategies have been set out (and these strategies are never set in concrete, they need constant updating), it is time to link measurable outcomes to these strategies. In other words, what do we want to achieve in the short term, in order to work towards our visionary objectives that lie ahead in the distant future? Stated differently, the leader often is involved in setting objectives at different levels of the organization, ranging from 'visionary' and strategic objectives to mostly delegating the responsibility to set more operational objectives at lower levels of the organization. Only when SMART (specific, measurable, achievable, resources available, time bound) objectives are set, the leader will be in a position to manage the performance of the organization and its employees effectively. An important part of the performance of an organization is achieved through the people management skills of the leader.

To influence and motivate people

In our overview of the different approaches to leadership, we have already commented on the different styles that leaders chose to develop (because they better fit their skill set) in order to influence groups of people and communicate with individuals or teams. Where setting objectives is important in making people aware of the targets of performance, the actual activation and application of people skills is critical when trying to steer people in a certain direction. This is where leaders with charismatic appeal will have an easier job. Their natural ability to inspire enthusiasm, interest or affection in others by means of personal charm or influence will put these leaders in a favourable position in regard to achieving the objectives that were set.

To facilitate change and nurture culture

Finally it is important to acknowledge that in this day and age, change is constant. Leaders who are incapable of assisting others to understand why 'change' is needed and how this change can be achieved with minimal disruption and maximum outcomes will have a difficult time surviving in the organizations of the twenty-first century. Most organizations are required to keep close track of the market conditions that they are working under and the impact changes in market conditions will have on their structures and strategies. Often a rapid response to changing market conditions is needed and this is where the interesting relationship with the organization's culture comes into play. Ironically, a strong and stable organizational culture can contribute to the need to constantly modify direction and changing the systems and structures of the organization. It is the leaders' responsibility to create and nurture a culture in which change is accepted as part of the natural way of organizational life. A strong culture is the backbone of any successful organization and the maintenance of culture is therefore one of the primary areas of leadership responsibility.

In Practice 8.3

Arjan Bos transforms professional speed skating

Arjan Bos is the chairman of the board and CEO of Dutch insurance company TVM. Based in the city of Hoogeveen in the northern part of Netherlands, TVM has steadily grown from a small player in the international transport insurance industry to become one of the main specialist insurers in their line of business. Starting their business in the domestic marketplace of the Netherlands, they are now also market leaders in Belgium and Luxembourg and are rapidly gaining market share in countries such as Denmark and some of the new EU members in Eastern Europe. Sport has played a significant role in their rise to dominance.

Arjan Bos was still a law student at Groningen University when his father was heading up TVM as its CEO. TVM is not a family business, it just happened that Arjan was the best candidate for the job when his father decided it was time to retire in 2001. But it was much earlier, in 1988, when Arjan took his first summer job at TVM whilst finishing his law degree. After ten years of sponsoring amateur cycling, TVM had become seriously involved as a sport sponsor in 1986 when they decided to start sponsoring a small professional cycling outfit. Arjan travelled with the professional cycling team to the big European summer events such as the Tour de France and the major classic courses, as the hospitality host of the team. TVM had decided to sponsor cycling driven by the company's desire to enter the Belgium marketplace.

Cycling, not football, is the most popular sport in Belgium and it was decided that it might be a good idea 'to do something with cycling' in order to gain exposure for TVM products in Belgium. Arjan's working at the coalface of professional cycling taught him many important lessons that were critical in the decisions that he had to take regarding the direction of the company later in life. He learned the importance of building a strong team, and what it takes to build a strong team in order to perform at the top level: a good atmosphere, what motivates people, how to inspire individuals and small teams and, last but not least, how one can build this network by entertaining people through sport.

Still a student, Arjan had the private numbers of ministers and captains of industry in his notebook. To achieve this he only had to provide them with a great hospitality experience and take them out on a day with the team at the event. TVM liked his work so much that he was promoted to PR manager of the company in 1990, although he was still a student. In 1994, upon graduation, he was offered the position of head of communication and marketing, and he further advanced in the company to become the director of sales and marketing in 1997. His exposure to the cycling team remained intense as the majority of TVM's marketing budget was poured into sport sponsoring.

Throughout the years they had found that sport did offer them a separate place in the mind of the consumer, and if quality is combined with long-term planning, customers will associate the products of the company with similar characteristics. When Arjan Bos was offered the job of chairman of the board and CEO of the company, he was the first to acknowledge the importance of his time as public face of the company through the cycling team. As spokesperson, figurehead, troubleshooter and networker he had not only gained the trust of his superiors but also built his reputation as a capable and hardworking colleague amongst the employees of the organization. In the meantime TVM had broken its relationship with cycling in 1999 after 13 years of sponsoring a professional team, and moved into sponsoring marathon speed skating.

So far the story still looks like a simple sponsor-sponsee relationship – TVM hands over significant resources to a professional skating team to prepare for and participate in competition. However, Arjan's time in professional cycling and his general understanding of 'common' sport sponsorship relations had taught him a few valuable lessons. He found that one of the critical success factors of successful sponsorship was to have unlimited access to the star athletes of the sport, because they are the ones who perform and hence communicate on behalf of the company. Another success factor was to have better control over the publicity and public relations in regard to the sponsored property. Arjan Bos's solution to deal with these issues was surprisingly simple and straightforward. Rather than to sponsor a (skating) team he made them employees of the (insurance) company and integrated them into the company's overall communication strategy. He placed the skating team in a separate structure belonging to the TVM holding company. By turning the athletes into employees, their loyalty first and foremost has to be to their employer, cutting out competition from other potential sponsors. Sub-sponsor contracts are exclusively entered into by TVM and individual sponsorships for the athletes need to be first approved by TVM.

In regard to preparing for peak performance the TVM company obtained full control over the appointment of the technical staff, and is now in a position to plan for the long-term future (success) of the team. All planning and preparation is geared towards winning multiple gold medals at the Winter Olympic Games of Sochi (2014) after a rather disappointing performance of only two gold medals at the 2010 Vancouver Olympics during which gun skater Sven Kramer took a wrong inner lane turn and lost a certain gold medal on the 10 km distance. The team continues to hold multiple world and Olympic champions, including medal-winning top coaches. However, it took a visionary sport manager who also turned out to become a highly successful corporate leader, to bring sport and business together as close as they can be, under the wings of one brand and one company.

Source: interviews with Arjan Bos, chairman of the board and CEO of TVM Insurance on 26 May and 26 June 2008 and 6 December 2010.

Leadership challenges in sport organizations

So far we have mainly been talking about generic leadership theory and principles, simply, because they apply to sport organizations in the same way as they do to non-sport organizations. We have also discussed the interrelationship between leadership and management and how leadership is largely about establishing visionary direction, then motivating and aligning people and structures towards that direction. The In Practice 8.3 has shown that sometimes, visionary direction needs to be supplied from outside. However, there will also be specific challenges for leaders (and managers) of sport organizations that are based on the unique characteristics of (some) sport organizations. In our discussion of these characteristics we will take a closer look at the leadership and management challenges sport organizations at the local, national and international levels.

Small community-based sport clubs and regionally based sport associations

Small community-based sport clubs are traditionally established and managed by the same people; those who share a passion for a particular sport and are interested in participating in some form of organized competition. Regional volunteer associations are similar in their structure and processes in that they largely coordinate the competitions that the community clubs are playing in and, as such, they represent the interests of the individual clubs. Most of these clubs and associations are run by volunteers leading to relatively low levels of professionalism and standardization of organizational processes. They operate in suburban or regional communities with little desire or incentive to expand and grow beyond their identified community base. The main challenge for the leaders of small clubs, and their representatives at the regional level is, first and foremost, to survive in an environment of decreasing levels of volunteer labour and commitment. Increasing competition for the scarce leisure time of members leads to a diminishing supply of free labour. Club and association leaders need to envision how they can transform their ways of operating into more professional and competitive ways of sport service delivery, but they have to do that without abundant volunteer resources. Most of these challenges are of a tactical or operational nature. Typical leadership questions that club and association leaders are faced with today are:

- Can small clubs survive or should they consider merging or relocating?
- How can we retain our younger members and our most valued volunteers?
- How can we attract new resources to the club in order to pay for professional services?
- How can we maintain the culture of the club?

National sporting organizations

Many national sporting organizations have already successfully negotiated and adapted to the changing community landscape of sport, and are now in a position to face the next set of challenges. In much the same way as community and regionally based sport organizations, national governing bodies are confronted with higher levels of customer expectations in combination with fewer resources to deliver those services. In a better position than community organizations to lobby for resources at the different levels of government, many of the national governing bodies have increased their levels of professionalism and standards of service delivery by employing professionally educated staff in their organizations. Leaders are now facing increased competition for paying customers to become affiliated to the sport's governing bodies. A major dilemma for national governing bodies is the fact that they only have one core product, their sport, which only offers limited strategic scope to expand into existing or new markets. The leaders of national sporting organizations (NSOs) also are confronted by commercial organizations that are only interested in the high performance end of their sport. The TVM example in this chapter shows that the Royal Dutch Skating Association is losing control over its elite skating athletes. NSOs also face the issue of the increasing gap between the 'haves' (i.e. the popular television and Olympic sports) and the 'have nots' (i.e. minority sports). In other words, do leaders want 'all sports for all' or, rather, let the market decide about the sports that will stay and grow and those that will fade into insignificance. The answer to this question also impacts where leaders of NSOs will focus much of their attention; on elite or mass participation sport. Most of these challenges are of a strategic nature. Typical leadership questions that the leaders of national sport governing bodies are faced with today are:

- Are we a national or international sport or in other words, what is our marketplace?
- What is best for our sport: a focus on elite; on mass participation; or an equal balance between the two?
- How can we better deliver our sport through the regional and local associations and clubs? (This is a systems question.)
- How can we change our systems of governance to be better prepared for radical (short term) changes in the sport market?

International federations and professional sport

Although there may be quite significant differences in size and structure between the international federations (IFs) and professional sport organizations (ranging from clubs to the governing bodies), the leaders of these organizations are largely confronted with the same leadership challenges. If NSOs were already concerned with questions about what their marketplace is, then the IFs and professional sport organizations should be able to answer those questions now. As with the lead that NSOs are taking in relation to the community and regional sport organizations below them in the hierarchy, the IFs are leading the way for NSOs in regard to their leadership challenges. Both the IFs and professional sport organizations are required to make genuinely visionary decisions in that competition is forcing them to think outside the square of previous operations. The World Wrestling Federation (now World Wrestling Entertainment – WWE) had to make a decision about operating in the sport or entertainment market, Manchester United and the New York Yankees are working on market expansion beyond football and baseball, and the world governing body for football, FIFA, is seriously considering its options beyond simply organizing football competitions (albeit a few very profitable ones). Europe's governing body for football, UEFA, has major headaches about the possibility that the strongest European clubs will create a competition of their own, which will virtually eliminate the highly lucrative Champions League that is owned and operated by the UEFA. The leaders of IFs and professional sport organizations face truly visionary leadership challenges. Typical leadership questions that these leaders are confronted with today are:

- Are we in the business of sport or are we simply competing for people's leisure time?
- How much control do we need to exercise in terms of our chain of distribution? For example, do we need to own our sporting facilities and broadcast centres rather than contracting with other owners?
- How will the market for sport, entertainment and leisure develop over the next decade? Where do we need to be placed in order to become and remain major players in those markets?
- Who will be the leaders for the sport of the future?

Summary

In this chapter we described what it takes to be a leader. We argued that irrespective of leadership type or style, leaders are goal oriented; they influence others; they empower others; they need to remain focused on the big picture; they need others to achieve their goals; and they have strong characters. Based on these components of leadership we discussed a number of theoretical approaches to leadership including the trait/personality, behavioural and contingency approaches, ultimately resulting in a discussion about transactional versus transformational leadership. Prior to looking at the future challenges for leaders in sport at the end of the chapter, we highlighted the differences between managers and leaders by outlining what are the functions of leaders. These functions were the creation of a vision; the setting out of strategy; setting objectives and measuring performance; influencing and motivating people; and, finally, to facilitate change and nurture organizational culture.

Review questions

1   Are leaders born or can they be made? Justify your answer by comparing the different leadership theories discussed in this chapter.
2   Does sport offer valuable leadership lessons to business? What are the specific characteristics of sport organizations that challenge leaders in sport organizations more than leaders in business and how can this knowledge be transferred to a non-sport context?
3   'A good manager is also a good leader'. Do you agree or disagree with this statement? Justify your answer.
4   Explain how leadership is important for the performance of a sport organization.
5   Interview the leader of a small sport organization. How would you describe their leadership style?
6   Is there any difference in the leadership skills required to be the CEO of a major professional sport franchise versus the manager of community sports club?
7   What criteria would you use to evaluate the leadership skills of a sport manager?
8   Is it possible to compare the performance of leaders of two different sport organizations? Why or why not?

Further reading

Amar, A.D., Hentrich, C. and Hlupic, V. (2009). 'To be a better leader, give up authority', *Harvard Business Review*, 87(12): 22–24.

Bass, B.M. (1990) *Bass & Stogdill's Handbook of Leadership: Theory, Research, and Managerial Applications*, 3rd edition, New York: Free Press.

Hill, L.A. (2008) 'Where will we find tomorrow's leaders?' *Harvard Business Review*, 86(1): 123–129.

Kotter, J.P. (1990) *A Force for Change: How Leadership Differs from Management*, New York: The Free Press.

Kouzes, J.M. and Posner, B.Z. (2006) *A Leader's Legacy*, Hoboken, NJ: Jossey-Bass.

Locke, E.A. (1991) *The Essence of Leadership: The Four Keys to Leading Successfully*, New York: Lexington Books.

Northouse, P.G. (2010) *Leadership: Theory and Practice*, 5th edition, Thousand Oaks, CA: Sage.

Slack, T. and Parent, M. (2006) *Understanding Sport Organizations: The Application of Organization Theory*, 2nd edition, Champaign, IL: Human Kinetics.

Thomas, R.J. (2008) *Crucibles of Leadership*, Boston, MA: Harvard Business School Publishing Corporation.

Relevant websites

Right To Play – www.righttoplay.com
Li Ning – www.lining.com
The Centre for Creative Leadership – www.ccl.org
The Test Café Leadership Test – http://leaderscafefoundation.webs.com/theleadershiptest.htm
Leadership directories – www.leadershipdirectories.com
Stephen Covey – www.stephencovey.com

Frank Lowy leads the world game down under from soccer to football

Frank Lowy was the interim chairman of the Australian Soccer Association (ASA) and became the founding chairman of the Football Federation Australia (FFA) when the ASA was renamed in 2005. At the time, football (or soccer as it had been known in Australia) was going through a period of revolutionary change.

Football in Australia has always been a sport of migrants, as opposed to the firmly established indigenous football code of Australian Rules football. Australian soccer has been riddled with problems that emanated from the very ethnic foundations of the sport – a reluctance of clubs at all levels of the game to give up their overt expressions of ethnic heritage. An independent report into the state of Australian Soccer – the Bradley Report – recommended the elimination all ethnic affiliations and symbolism in relation to clubs that played in Australia's highest level competition but to no avail.

In 2003, however, the Australian government commissioned another review of Australian soccer that became known as the Crawford Report. Crawford reported an absence of proper governance and leadership in Australian soccer. The report highlighted financial, staffing, political and leadership problems. Despite these problems it was observed that 'soccer' remained the sleeping giant of Australian sport with several things going for it such as substantial (and increasing) grass-roots participation, a reasonable talent development pathway, strong growth in female participation and passionate, albeit latent, public support.

This is where Frank Lowy enters the frame. Born in Czechoslovakia on 22 October 1930, Lowy became a self-made billionaire by establishing his Westfield shopping centre empire of around 120 malls in Britain, the US and Australia. From a Jewish background, Lowy moved to Hungary after surviving the Holocaust during his early teen years. At the age of 22 he migrated to Australia with one suitcase of belongings and without speaking a word of English.

Unsurprisingly, given his experiences as a young man, Lowy feels that life is a series of fights, struggles that one must win in order to succeed. This has made him very successful in business and he is renowned for being a tough, uncompromising leader within his businesses and a fierce opponent for his competitors. Combine this with vision, passion and a keen eye for detail and one has a leadership cocktail for success.

One of the most pertinent recommendations coming from the Crawford Report was the need for strong, uncompromising leadership and proper governance. Frank Lowy could not only bring that, he also happened to be a passionate football follower who was independently wealthy and keen to invest some of his private fortune into improving the world game in Australia. A new chairman for football was found and in 2004 he assembled the National Soccer League Task Force. The goal of the task force was to respond to the Crawford Report findings and outline a strategic vision and direction for football in Australia. One of the main considerations of the task force involved creating a governance structure for Australian soccer and a new format for the struggling National Soccer League (NSL). Frank Lowy acknowledged that without good personnel – people who have proven track records rather than the 'right' ethnic affiliations – one will not be able to achieve lofty strategic objectives. Lowy therefore sought to recruit the best possible CEO for football at the time and he appointed hugely successful rugby administrator John O'Neill (2004–2006) who was succeeded by Ben

Buckley (2006–). It was no coincidence that Buckley came from the FFA's biggest rival of them all, the Australian Football League. O'Neill's main achievements included the creation of a new-style national competition, diminishing the inherited debt of the FFA and heading up a very successful World Cup qualifying campaign leading to qualification for the first time since 1974. Australia reached the second round of the World Cup in Germany, ultimately losing (controversially) to later champions Italy.

Buckley's appointment was another stroke of brilliance. After a career as a professional AFL player Buckley held positions with Nike Japan and EA Sports from 1994 to 1999. Following this Buckley became the AFL's broadcasting and strategy general manager before being promoted to chief operating officer. He was the right man to take up the fight with the competing football codes and to develop the sport commercially so that resources could be generated to further develop the game at all levels.

Long before becoming chairman of the FFA it was clear to Lowy that without playing the game at the pinnacle event – the World Cup – football would have no chance of becoming a mainstream sport in Australia. Lowy was instrumental in bringing one of the world's best football coaches to Australia to take the country to the World Cup. This feat was achieved by Guus Hiddink, the Dutch wonder coach, taking Australia to the 2006 World Cup in Germany. However, at the time Australia was still playing in the Oceania confederation which required the winner of World Cup qualifying in the region to play off against a fourth or fifth ranked qualifier from South America or Asia. In other words, after all the hard work was done, there remained the hurdle of further qualification against much stronger opposition. Lowy and others lobbied hard with the Asian Football Confederation (AFC) and FIFA to make a move to the AFC, as this would provide 'easier' qualification for the World Cup, access to much higher level competition for the national team, and access to the Asian Champions League for the teams in the Australian A-League. The move of Australia to the AFC was unanimously endorsed by the AFC and FIFA in 2006 and Lowy could be very pleased with what had been achieved in just two short years since he started his job as chairman.

Although Lowy's focus had been on bringing the right people to football and advancing the national team to play at the World Cup, in Australia the focus had largely been on creating a viable national league. Unprecedented in the world of football the old National Soccer League and its constituent clubs had been disbanded and replaced with the A-League. For the league to be commercially successful it required sustainable in-stadium attendance and mass media spectatorship. It is common knowledge in sport business that strong spectatorship ultimately needs to be underpinned by strong participation. Football in Australia in that regard had a few things going for it, the game had youth and family appeal, was attractive to women – to watch and play it – and people were pretty much fed up with the ways of how 'old soccer' was mismanaged. Lowy and Buckley's national Football Development Plan was released in 2007 and included the following important areas of game development:

- *National Team Excellence:* Qualify for all World Cups at all age groups across both men's and women's teams and create a talented pathway programme that sustains this success for generations to come.
- *Hyundai A-League:* Manage a national competition that is commercially viable and sustainable, is highly popular and is a distinctive and innovative entertainment option in Australian sport.
- *Football Development:* Provide high quality leadership and support for member federations and the participating football community, which continually raises the overall standards of football, provides opportunities for all and fosters life-long support for the game.

- *Major Events:* Host major football and non-football events that are commercially advantageous to FFA, and raise the profits of the game in Australia and Australia's presence in international football.

Additionally, in a new age of professionalism for the sport and to drive the sport forward in the future, four areas of operational excellence were identified:

- *Financial Growth:* Generate revenue growth through broadcasting, internet and mobile communications partnerships, innovative new sponsorships, new competition formats, growth in attendances, government partnerships and new business development.
- *Engagement with Asian Football Confederation:* Our new position in Asia opens the opportunity to develop commercial partnerships, and new competition formats and to assist our development through participation on key committees, and to enhance relationships through Football Diplomacy.
- *Partnerships:* Build positive working relationships with key stakeholder groups: member federations, players and players associations, clubs, standing committees, federal and State governments, FIFA, AFC, Australian Sports Commission, AOC and other key agencies.
- *Governance and Administration:* Complete the governance and administration reforms at all levels of the game to ensure the game provides the governance infrastructure to support the games growth and potential.

In the space of seven years Frank Lowy and CEOs John O'Neill and Ben Buckley have transformed the fortunes of football in Australia. They have driven the change from a sport that was governed based on factional, ethnically influenced interests to a professionally run national organization with international ambitions. Despite obvious growing pains and in the face of strong competition in all major cities from competing football codes there is a groundswell of grass-roots support for the sport, increased spectatorship, televised games and relative success at the elite level. Irrespective of a failed bid to bring the World Cup to Australia, there is a genuine belief and excitement about the prospect that it is possible the World Cup will eventually come to Australia. So where will football be in 2030? Where would you take it if you were Frank Lowy?

Case study questions

1 Can you explain the difference in leadership roles that Frank Lowy and Ben Buckley fulfil?
2 What type of leadership skills do you believe were essential for Frank Lowy to possess to lead the FFA to a position of parity with the other football codes?
3 Lowy clearly appointed O'Neill to achieve different outcomes from Buckley. What kind of leadership skills will be required for the FFA during the next five years?
4 Compare leadership at Soccer Australia with leadership at the Football Federation of Australia. What are the main differences?
5 Looking at the national Football Development Plan, if you had to pick your priority game development objective and your priority operational excellence objective, what would they be? Explain your answer.

Chapter 9

Sport organizational culture

Overview

This chapter explores the influence organizational culture imparts upon sport organizations. It examines why organizational culture is pivotal, highlights its impact and explains how it can be diagnosed. Several cases and numerous examples will be used throughout the chapter to help explain the role of culture in a sport organization's performance.

By the end of this chapter the reader should be able to:

- define the meaning of organizational culture;
- specify why culture is important to sport organizations;
- explain how different contexts can affect an organizational culture;
- connect organizational culture and organizational identity;
- identify how sport organizational cultures can be diagnosed;
- show the dimensions across which sport organizational cultures can be measured; and
- discuss how sport organizational culture can be changed.

What is organizational culture?

Culture was originally defined by anthropologists as the values and beliefs common to a group of people. These researchers set themselves the task of investigating, interpreting and translating the behavioural and social patterns of groups of individuals by trying to understand how they relate to their environment. From an organizational perspective, although people in organizations run the technology and invent the processes, they in turn, as part of the process, have much of their behaviour determined by the systems they operate. In other words, there are underlying forces that impact upon behaviour. The concept of culture is a way of putting a name to these forces.

There is no single accepted definition of organizational culture. For example, organizational culture is viewed by some as the 'personality' of an organization, while for others it represents the things which make an organization unique. Several assumptions about organizational culture are well-accepted though. These include:

1   Culture tends to be inflexible and resistant to easy or rapid change.
2   Culture is shaped by an organization's circumstances, its history and its members.
3   Culture is learned and shared by members of an organization and is reflected in common understandings and beliefs.
4   Culture is often covert; the deep values and beliefs causing behaviour can be hidden from organizational members making them difficult to identify.
5   Culture is manifested in a variety of ways that affect the performance of an organization and its members.

Although elements of commonality exist in the way in which researchers conceive and define culture in organizations, much inconsistency and controversy can still be found. However, for the purposes of this chapter, we shall discuss organizational culture in a way consistent with the view of Schein (2010), who invokes a more psycho-dynamic view. This means that he believes culture is, in part, an unconscious phenomenon, driven by deep-level assumptions and beliefs, and where conscious views are merely artefacts and symbolic representations. For example, most sport clubs members would report that on-field winning is important. Schein's interpretation of organizational culture would lead to questions about *why* winning is important. Does it have to do with a need to belong to a successful group, the pressure of peers or some other more mysterious explanation? While many people involved in sport would think this question easy to answer, it is less easy to specify the underpinning values that drive unusual rituals, ceremonies, myths, legends, stories, beliefs, memorabilia and attitudes. In current and former nations of the British Commonwealth, cricket is played with enormous enthusiasm, but can take up to five days to complete a single match, which often ends in a draw. Similarly, to the uninitiated, American football seems quite strange with each team comprising separate players for offensive and defensive manoeuvres. Off the field can be just as odd. In Australia, many (Australian rules) football clubs have 'sausage-sizzles' (barbecues), 'pie-nights' (involving the traditional meal of a meat pie) and a host of rituals associated with drinking beer. In addition, many sport organizations are packed with memorabilia and expect their employees to work during evening training sessions and weekend games. Sport organizations are rich with strong, meaningful cultural symbols, which on the surface seem easy to interpret, but sometimes are only superficial symptoms of deeper issues.

What we are searching for is not the superficial, but rather the unconsciously held, fundamental concepts of right or wrong; what an organization might perceive as correct or incorrect values. These values, which are the foundation of an organization's culture, do not simply exist or come into being by their own volition. Instead, they are painstakingly built up by members of the organization as they gradually learn to interact and achieve their collective and individual aims. An organization's founders, together with the more influential of the organization's past and present members, are usually the most influential in determining the culture. For this reason, we prefer to examine the long-held assumptions and beliefs in an organization.

For the purposes of this chapter, we shall define sport organizational culture as follows:

> *Sport organizational culture is a collection of fundamental values, beliefs and attitudes that are common to members of a sport organization, and which consequently set the behavioural standards or norms for all members.*

This definition reflects the view that sport organizations have ways of approaching things that have evolved over time. In many ways, organizational culture holds answers to questions about solving problems. Culture is how 'things are done around here' and how 'we think about things here'.

The importance of culture to sport organizations

We can expect that different types of sport organizations will possess different kinds of cultures. For example, professional clubs and major national leagues are more likely to emphasize dispassionate business values, while smaller, not-for-profit associations are more likely to value participation and fun. Some sport organizations like Italian and Spanish football clubs are geared almost exclusively to winning and are prepared to go heavily into debt in order to do so. Others, like the company Formula One Holdings, manage the commercial rights to major events and have little other interest than to make money. While the Fédération Internationale de l'Automobile seeks to regulate motor sport, others still, like the International Olympic Committee are interested in developing sport around the world, and in so doing acquire vast sums of money and spend it liberally.

Sports organizations are increasingly compelled to join the commercial world, and are under great pressure to adopt the operational and structural characteristics of business enterprises. The influence of modern communication has been profound, with sporting results being available from almost anywhere connected to the internet. Many sporting organizations have realized that in order to remain competitive they must provide similar entertainment value to that provided by other sports on television as well as the wide array of alternative leisure options available. Subsequently, corporate boxes line major sporting venues, sport is blanketed across pay or cable and free-to-air television, high profile athletes earn extraordinary sums and politicians associate themselves with certain teams. The commercial and competitive pressures placed upon sport organizations from local football clubs, universities and colleges, to professional leagues and teams, has encouraged sport managers to embrace business tools and concepts like organizational culture. Culture is important to sport organizations because its understanding can help to bring about change. Since culture commands such a powerful influential on the performance of an organization's members, it is critical that cultural traits remain both appropriate and strong. In the case of sport, it is common to have strong cultures that have been forged by tradition and a fierce sense of history, but some cultural characteristics like excessive drinking and on-field violence may no longer suit the more professional management approach that needs to be assumed.

Commentaries on organizational culture, while as disparate as the number of researchers pursuing its investigation, generally emphasize its most superficial manifestation. Moreover, organizational business culture is frequently seen as mono-cultural; perceived at one level, and as one entity. An organization is distinguished as a giant cultural mass, constructed equivalently throughout, and with little or no internal variability. However, this way of thinking is difficult to sustain when analysing a sporting organization. Sporting club cultures possess numerous cultural themes, and can be perceived readily at several levels, or as several subcultures. For example, as an organizational or administrative unit comparable to other business organizations; as a supporter organization, whose aims, objectives and traditions may be different (such as winning matches in preference to making a financial profit); and as a player unit, where motivation may vary from glory to money. While a player may perform for a club because of loyalty or remuneration (or any number of other reasons), supporters are usually passionately attached to a clubs' colours and traditions, expecting only on-field success in return. At the same time, some sport organizations are driven by broader agendas or values that relegate both winning and profit to background issues.

In Practice 9.1

Values-driven cultures and the Special Olympics

Volunteer sport organizations sometimes struggle in finding the balance between the corporate planning model and the values-driven model. After all, in the absence of hierarchical structures and reporting relationships, co-responsibility becomes more salient than delegation. In this respect, values-driven sport organizations operate on the goodwill of their patrons and volunteers. 'Who we are' can be even more important than 'what we do'. For example, 'management by objectives' focuses on planning and strategy, or what to do. It emphasizes productivity, results-focus, top-down leadership and heavy measurement. In contrast, 'management by values' places an emphasis on how to go about achieving results. More interest resides with communication and conversations within an organization in order to enhance creativity and interactive debate. Rather than a top-down approach, a values-orientation begins with the bottom up. Accountability trumps accountancy, interpretation overrides analysis, flexibility supersedes control, improvisation surpasses planning and people are more important than facts.

The Special Olympics World Summer Games in Athens 2011 offers an excellent example of a values-driven sport organization that has to locate a balance between careful planning and cultivating relationships. From a cultural viewpoint, the Special Olympics exists because it fosters a specific belief system that permeates all the organizations that fall under its movement: people with intellectual disabilities can enjoy sport and benefit from participation. While organizations connected to the Special Olympics provide services and events to enable the intellectually disabled to train and compete in sport, in many ways what they do is subservient to how they do it. For example, Special Olympics programmes are principally organized by volunteers. At the same time, the expenses for training, events and marketing are paid by sponsorships, donations and government grants. As a result, not only does the Special Olympics movement require considerable personal sacrifice from volunteers, the limited paid administrators must carefully account for the spending of scarce resources. Imagine what cultural values such a structure demands.

Some of the values infusing the World Summer Games in Athens are exposed through the choice of imagery it employs. Consider the Games emblem, a radiant sun overlaid with a spiralling olive branch made out in a combination of red for passion, orange for optimism, blue for freedom and green for hope. A less heavy symbolism appears in the official mascot. A smiling, animated face adorns a sun with arms and legs as a warm expression of acceptance, joy and energy. In addition, the motto, 'I'm in', is designed to inspire participation and the impulse to become part of the Special Olympics 'family'. It is easy to find reflections of these symbols in the values presented by other organizations affiliated with the Special Olympics. For example, Special Olympics Europe/Eurasia urges the public to 'Be a Fan for' respect, courage, opportunity, joy, generosity, inclusion, human spirit, transformation, unity and inspiration. 'Be a Fan' reproduces a Special Olympics' key value statement, which appears in its Strategic Plan 2011–2015 as a registered trademark and signature declaration. At the same time as the Strategic Plan reinforces the cultural values pivotal to the Special Olympics' identity, it also outlines a 'strategic framework' for building the movement, advancing leadership, managing resources and delivering quality programmes and events. In a growing movement encompassing nearly 4 million athletes, the values-driven approach faces a cultural tension between its goals and its meaning.

Subcultures and sport

In sporting organizational cultures there is the additional hurdle of translating and adopting a culture directly from traditional business theory. It is dangerously simplistic to assume that a sporting organization should adopt the methods and practices of a traditional business without addressing the cultural variables. While business methods can be transferred to accommodate the organizational strategies of a sporting club, a direct transfer fails to confront the issue of what it is that makes the culture of a sporting organization differ from that of a traditional business enterprise.

Ideal business culture tends to reflect a willingness by an organization's employees to embrace a standard of performance that promotes quality in the production of goods and services, in the attempt to generate a financial profit. This cultural ideology, while cognisant of business necessities, is unable to cater for the more diverse structures that exist in a sporting organization. In any business, financial realities must be acknowledged, but in a sporting business, additional behavioural variables require recognition and respect. While different businesses have different cultures, they are less variable than the cultural differences between individual sports. It cannot be assumed, for example, that a single unified culture exists for all sports. Sport managers must be aware of the cultural nuances of their respective sports and the influence they have upon players, employees, members, fans and the general public.

Culture is not a simple matter within a single sport either. Professional players, for example, have a different cultural attitude from most amateurs and spectators. This variability of attitudes is symptomatic of a wider, more troublesome area: the clash of cultures within sports. This is illustrated best at an international level, where players from different countries have been brought up with profoundly different ideologies of the game, and how it should be played.

Football – the 'world game' – is indicative of this culture clash, in addition to the immense cultural significance inherent in the game. Like all living cultures, sport is incessantly changing, dynamic in nature and subject to constant reinterpretation by its participants and viewers. The only apparent consistency in sporting culture is the pursuit of competition, the love of winning, and the ability to summon strong emotional responses in both victory and defeat.

Clearly, there is a need to study organizational cultures, accounting for the effect of the sport itself. For example, in the same way that we might expect that accounting firms might share some cultural traits, so might we predict that bocce clubs do as well. Similarly, the tradition and discipline central to a bocce club might be expected to encourage cultural characteristics different from the youthful and eclectic philosophy found in a BMX club. Furthermore, these cultural characteristics might seep into the behaviours of executive officers and employees of the clubs. Since so many sporting organizations covet tradition and the accomplishments of the past, they also tend to be resistant to change. However, before any change can occur, an organization's culture needs to be accurately diagnosed.

In Practice 9.2

Interpreting culture at the Tony Blair Sports Foundation

As a management concept, organizational culture introduces new ways of thinking about how groups of people operate together to pursue common goals. Culture has inflamed new perspectives about old performance issues, where organizational values and identity can be used to explain everything from excellence to employee satisfaction. While some sport organizations are so well known and enduring that their cultural characteristics have become intuitive expectations, it is less easy to decipher the foundations of newer sport organizations. In fact, cultural analysis cannot escape complexity because it includes the *beliefs* held by individuals, how they *think* things work, *interpreting* their behaviour, *understanding* physical tangible outcomes like artefacts and determining what those artefacts *symbolize*.

The Tony Blair Sports Foundation (TBSF) was established in 2007 by the former British Prime Minister. His intention was to give back to the North-East of England, a region to which he felt indebted due to his personal background. The region is suffering from declining health due in part to diminishing levels of physical activity. Blair's starting premise – his underpinning belief – acknowledged that greater participation in sport can make a significant difference to physical health and well-being. In a speech he delivered in 2009 about how sport can replace enmity with friendship, Blair observed:

> As we think about how to begin to tackle regional and ethnic conflicts that with the passage of time seem only to become more deep-rooted and more insuperable, and how to stop future generations from being sucked into a spiralling conflict tragedy, sport has a role to play.
>
> (Office of Tony Blair 2009)

In the TBSF, sport presents a powerful vehicle for positively affecting people's lives. This supposition represents cultural assumptions revealing how they think about their organization and how their behaviour within it should be interpreted.

Instead of promoting sport and participation directly, the TBSF tackles coaching support as a key barrier. By recruiting and training more coaches and officials, the TBSF allows local communities to make better use of their existing sporting facilities. Participation is curtailed by the opportunity young people have for engaging in sport supervised by trained adults. As a result, the most important organizational artefacts reflect an increase in the number of new sport volunteers. In this situation, new programmes for coaches and officials symbolize a renewed opportunity for sport to influence more young people's lives. Deep beliefs about the influence sport has on health, community and individual spirit lie at the core of the TBSF and affect all of the cultural values and operational decisions radiating from its foundation.

Organizational identity

Like all social concepts, organizational identity allocates meaning to largely intangible but pivotal organizational behaviours. From a social perspective, identity describes how individuals perceive themselves, as well as how they are perceived by others. Because identity represents an individual's self-perception, it also tends to be durable, providing a long-term, stable, distinctive and enduring image. Similarly, as social entities, organizations exhibit identities established by the adoption, reinforcement and rejection of particular characteristics created by its members over time. The process operates as an extension of personal identity where individuals adopt or reinforce characteristics they perceive as advantageous while discarding the negative. For example, an organization might adopt team-based work practices if its members expect collaboration to be advantageous. An organization establishes its identity through the collective self-perceptions of insiders, which in turn accompanies how it performs (culture), the way it expresses itself and the way it is perceived by outsiders (image). However, an organization might perceive itself in a manner incompatible with outside perceptions. Change to bring the two into alignment is difficult because identity reflects long-term, stable perceptions about an organization's idiosyncratic characteristics. Such perceptions determine not only an organization's understanding of itself, but also how such statements are received and accepted (or rejected) by stakeholders.

Culture is about the way we do things and identity is about how we perceive or are perceived. Furthermore, things are done in a particular way due to culture, but also to reinforce or change perceptions. In this respect, organizational culture and identity work together in a reciprocal and dynamic manner. Culture is the more contextual, tacit and emergent side, whereas identity is the more textual, explicit and instrumental side. Another way of looking at it expresses identity as a manifestation and artefact of culture. However, like culture, identity reveals an organizational contradiction. Change is necessary in order for an organization to survive a competitive environment, but at the same time, identity has to endure enough to maintain a sense of continuity. Appropriate cultures change while strong cultures endure. Understanding the role identity plays in organizations is also essential to culture's diagnosis.

Diagnosing and managing organizational culture

The central problem remains that in order to grasp the concept of culture and its relationship to the individual, the group and the organization, an in-depth approach is required. Sport organizations create intentions and atmospheres that influence behaviour, routines, practices and the thought systems of people. These systems and processes subsequently form patterns that are acquired primarily through socialization, or learning over time from the reactions and behaviours of others. In essence, individuals within an organization are exposed to what researchers call 'culture revealing' situations, which might include the observable behaviour of other members, their organizational methods, 'artefacts' – the photos, honour boards and other memorabilia on show – and interactive communication, or the way in which individuals talk to each other. Some of these common, superficial and observable representations of organizational culture are reproduced in Table 9.1. These are important to recognize because the driving values and belief systems behind them can never be seen as anything more than observable 'symptoms'.

Although the superficial aspects of culture can be observed, the difficulty comes in their interpretation because they are merely surface representations of deeper values. Thus, a useful cultural diagnosis will always seek to understand what drives the observable behaviour. For example, what does it mean if an employee makes a mistake and is severely reprimanded by his or her boss? What does common jargon imply? Why are certain rituals typical, like the celebration of employee birthdays?

Table 9.1: Observable symptoms of sport organizational culture

Symptom	Explanation
Environment	The general surroundings of an organization, like the building it is housed in and the geographical location, like the city or in a grandstand
Artefacts	Physical objects located in the organization from its furnishings to its coffee machine
Language	The common words and phrases used by most organizational members, including gestures and body language
Documents	Any literature including reports, statements, promotional material, memos and emails produced for the purpose of communication
Logos	Any symbolic visual imagery including colours and fonts that convey meaning about the organization
Heroes	Current or former organizational members who are considered exemplars
Stories	Narratives shared by organizational members based at least partly on true events
Legends	An event with some historical basis but has been embellished with fictional details
Rituals	Standardized and repeated behaviours
Rites	Elaborate, dramatic, planned set of activities

The question remains as to how overt observations relate to deeper values. Most researchers recommend some form of classification system that describes organizational culture in the form of 'dimensions', each one a deeper, core value. These dimensions reflect on particular organizational characteristics as an aid to categorizing cultures. The summation of these characteristics may be used to describe an organization's culture, which can then allow for comparisons to be undertaken between organizations. For example, observable evidence in the form of an end of season awards night in a sporting club might be suggestive of the nature of the organization's reward/motivation values. Enough observable evidence can lead a sport manager to make some tentative conclusions about each dimension. Table 9.2 lists some common dimensions used to describe organizational culture. They can be seen as continua, an organization's position somewhere between the two extremes.

Any analysis that captures the complexity of organizational culture may have great difficulty in separating the interwoven strands of organizational history and personal relationships. As a result, concrete conclusions may be difficult to establish. It is therefore important to take advantage of the symbolism created by sport's abundant myths, rituals and ceremonies in order to gain a complete understanding of the full range of human behaviour within a complex organization. The traditions, folklore, mythologies, dramas, and successes and traumas of the past, are the threads that weave together the fabric of organizational culture.

A psychological approach is helpful in identifying and interpreting human behaviour in organizations as cultural phenomena. Psychologists, originally stimulated by the work of Carl Jung, suggest that there are different levels of behavioural awareness, from the conscious to unconscious. Organizational psychologists have appropriated this kind of thinking and transposed it to culture. The key analogy is that an organization is like a mind.

From the psychological viewpoint, the readily apparent and observable qualities of a sporting organization are the same as the conscious part of an individual mind. These include the physical environment, the public statements of officials, the way individuals interactively

Table 9.2: Cultural dimensions

Dimension	Characteristics
Stability/changeability	Disposition toward change: degree to which organization encourages alternative 'ways of doing things' or existing ways
Cooperation/conflict	Disposition toward problem resolution: degree to which organization encourages cooperation or conflict
Goal focus/orientation	Clarity and nature of objectives and performance expectations
Reward/motivation	Nature of reward orientation of organizational members: degree to which organization encourages seniority or performance
Control/authority	Nature and degree of responsibility, freedom and independence of organizational members
Time/planning	Disposition toward long-term planning: degree to which organization encourages short-term or long-term thinking

communicate, the form of language used, what clothes are worn and the memorabilia that fills the rooms and offices. Another of the most important observable qualities involves the place of sporting heroes. They represent rich and highly visible indicators of the culture being sought. Heroes offer an insight into the culture of an organization, since the members as well as power brokers select them. In addition, heroes indicate those qualities in individuals respected and admired by a wider audience. The hero is a powerful figure in a sporting organization and may be simultaneously an employee and ex-player. The hero may also be charismatic, entrepreneurial or just plain administrative, which often characterizes business enterprises. By understanding the orientation of hero figures, both past and present, it is possible to map trends in cultural change. Heroes can be both reactionary and progressive. For example, heroes that reinforce the dominant culture will not change the values and attitudes that the culture emphasizes. On the other hand, a hero that transcends and transforms the dominant culture will be a catalyst for change in the behaviours and values of a club. Often a hero is the most powerful medium for change to be successful.

Tradition is another window into the culture of an organization. Like heroes, traditions are readily observable through memorabilia. However, the underlying values and assumptions that give meaning to heroes and tradition reside in the deeper levels of a culture. Tradition may on one hand be preserved by the present cultural identity, while on the other hand the sporting organization may have developed a contemporary cultural personality. Thus, it is useful to acknowledge the importance of tradition and history to a sporting organization because it may be a cultural linchpin, or a stepping stone from which their contemporary cultural character has been launched.

In order to bypass the obstacles (in the form of stereotypical views and superficial signs) that can block an assessment of culture, it is essential to analyse and explore natural, observable outcroppings of culture; places where the cultural understandings can be exposed. By analysing these sites, it is possible to gain a practical insight into the underlying culture of the organization. This level deals with organizational rites and rituals because their performance is readily apparent, and in performing these rites, employees generally use other cultural forms of expression, such as certain customary language or jargon, gestures and artefacts. These rites, which are shared understandings, are additionally conveyed through myths, sagas, legends or other stories associated with the occasion, and in practical terms may take the form of barbecues or presentations. In order to actively assess this level of culture, not only must observational techniques be employed, but meanings must be attached to them. This requires more than a superficial level of analysis.

There are also 'unconscious' parts of organizations as well. In effect, it is the unconscious that controls the individual. This incorporates the beliefs, habits, values, behaviours and attitudes prevalent in a sporting organization. An accurate assessment of this level of culture is difficult and fraught with the danger of misrepresentation. For example, how employees say they behave and what they state they believe, has to be compared to their actual behaviour.

As a cautionary note, sport managers should be aware that multiple interpretations can be made based on the same evidence. For example, one way of looking at culture is to focus attention on consistency and congruence of policies and practices within a sport organization, as members are confronted with problems to solve. In contrast, it is also valid to consider ambiguities and inconsistencies in behaviour. These anomalies often represent the difference between espoused values and actual values. Cultural manifestations can be interpreted in multiple ways, and change over time and location. It is important to look for patterns, exceptions and values targeted for change.

Changing cultural values at the Hong Kong Jockey Club
One of the largest horse racing organizations in the world, the Hong Kong Jockey Club (HKJC) has survived and prospered through feast and famine, colonial oversight, scandals, the equine flu and now a new generation of computer-savvy, internet-dedicated gamblers. From the time when the British drained a swamp in 1841 to create a track, horse racing in Hong Kong has rarely ceased from operation. Founded in 1884, the HKJC has provided an enduring backbone for racing, albeit with an unusual business model.

While striving to be a world leader in the delivery of horse racing and sporting and betting entertainment, the HKJC also represents Hong Kong's pre-eminent charitable organization. It takes around HK$120 billion (approximately US$16 billion) in total bets each year and donates HK$1.5 billion towards charitable and community projects. As an organization more than 125 years old, a suite of traditional cultural values have become entrenched. Dominant values represent the strongest norms and are held by the majority of members. Typically, dominant values become embedded in mission statements and objectives, underpinning an organization's philosophy and core ideology. In consequence, an organization may be distinguished on the basis of its dominant cultural characteristics. Facing a proliferation of unauthorized bookmakers, both on- and offline, the HKJC had to embrace a set of emerging values, emphasizing a responsive technology-driven internet gambling service. Emergent cultural values refer to new meanings, beliefs and ways of doing things, reflecting the dynamic relationships formed by organizational members, which continually change and reform over time. Of course internet betting sites have no requirement to cover the costs of staging events or paying local taxes. As a result, they can offer better odds, cannibalizing the market share of racing clubs. To combat the situation, the HKJC launched a vigorous online campaign of its own. Presently, the HKJC takes around 35 per cent of bets through its website or mobile devices. An interesting twist was that the key to success relied upon the Club's traditional cultural features. Reputation proved decisive with gamblers uncertain about unregulated sites. In the end, the HKJC managed to change its operational priorities while maintaining its cultural strengths.

Changing organizational culture with mapping

Cultural understanding stems from successfully translating information into meaning. Every aspect of a sporting organization is symbolically representative in some way of its culture. All information is not equal, however, yet all possible data must be analysed in order to establish the most comprehensive image possible of the existing culture. In order for a culture to be created and bolstered, shared values and beliefs must in some way be reinforced and transferred to organizational members through tangible means.

A cultural map summarizes the predominant features of a sporting organization's culture, and provides a means through which raw data can be interpreted into measurable criteria. It works by providing sets of categories in which information can be collected and summarized with the intention of identifying the main themes that continually emerge. Some researchers believe that this approach can also be used in a more statistical form, the numbers attached to responses from questions derived from the dimensions and answered by organizational members.

While the range and diversity of information available for cultural analysis is profound, many cultural studies ignore all but the most apparent and accessible data. A holistic cultural analysis will utilize every available piece of information, with the more obvious elements becoming vehicles for the transmission of less tangible, more subjective facets of culture. However, the culture of any one sporting organization cannot be classified into one of just a few categories, even though there are many models offering a handful of neat classifications. In reality, there are as many organizational cultures as there are sporting organizations, and they cannot be generically categorized into one of a fixed number of groups. Sporting clubs are immersed in tradition, history, values and myths, and these should figure prominently in any diagnosis. From an accurate diagnosis change becomes far easier.

The main lesson for cultural change is that it cannot be tackled without a clear, prior understanding of an organization's chief cultural traits and how they manifest. Once an accurate diagnosis has been undertaken, through some form of formal or informal cultural map, elements of culture can be managed. Since a sport manager cannot literally change people's minds, they instead have to change people's actions. To some extent this can be imposed or encouraged, but it is a slow process. For example, new rituals can be introduced to replace older, less desirable ones, like a club dinner instead of a drinking binge. Entrenched values and beliefs can be extremely difficult to change, and even with the right introduction of new symbols, language, heroes, stories, employees and so on, genuine cultural change in an organization can take many years or even a new generation of organizational members before it takes hold.

Summary

In the world of sport management, organizational culture has gained prominence as a concept useful in assessing and managing performance. Sport organizational culture can be defined as the collection of fundamental values and attitudes that are common to members of a sport organization, and which subsequently set the behavioural standards or norms for all members. The difficultly remains, however, that the deep values common to organizational members are not easy to access. As a way of getting around this inaccessibility problem, sport managers can use cultural dimensions that suggest some of the possible values that are present. A step further, cultural maps show the variables and observable manifestations of culture that need to be investigated. These maps use the tip of the cultural iceberg (the accessible aspects of culture like symbols and artefacts) to estimate the iceberg's underwater composition (the deep values and beliefs of organizational members). Once a thorough diagnosis has been completed, sport managers can work toward adapting and replacing undesirable cultural characteristics.

Review questions

1   Why is organization culture important to sport managers?
2   Explain how organizational culture can manifest at different levels.
3   Describe the difference between superficial elements of culture and deeper elements of culture. What is the difference between organizational culture and identity?
4   What is a cultural dimension?
5   How can organizational culture be measured in a sport organization?
6   How does measuring organizational culture help in changing it?
7   Select a sport organization you belong or have belonged to. Create a list of attributes or values that you believe embodies its organizational culture. Which are the characteristics that distinguish it from other similar sport organizations?
8   Select a sport organization you belong or have belonged to. Describe ten artefacts that are on show in its premises and explain how each illuminates organizational culture.

Further reading

Frontiera, J. (2010) 'Leadership and organizational culture transformation in professional sport', *Journal of Leadership and Organizational Studies*, 17(1): 171–186.

Jung, T., Scott, T., Davies, Huw T.O., Bower, P., Whalley, D., McNally, R. and Russell, M. (2009) 'Instruments for exploring organizational culture: A review of the literature', *Public Administration Review*, 69(6): 1087–1096.

Schein, E. (2010) *Organizational Culture and Leadership*, 4th edition, San Francisco, CA: Jossey-Bass.

Schroeder, P.J. (2010) 'Changing team culture: The perspectives of ten successful head coaches', *Journal of Sport Behavior*, 33(1): 63–88.

Smith, A. and Shilbury, D. (2004) 'Mapping cultural dimensions in Australian sporting organizations', *Sport Management Review*, 7(2): 133–165.

Smith, A., Stewart, B. and Haimes, G. (2012) *Organizational Culture and Identity: Sport, Symbols and Success*, New York: Nova Science Publishers.

Relevant websites

Ultimate Fighting Championship – www.ufc.com
Tony Blair Sports Foundation – www.tonyblairsportsfoundation.org
Hong Kong Jockey Club – www.hkjc.com
Special Olympics World Summer Games 2011 – www.specialolympics.com

Making money hand over fist: cultural dynamics of the Ultimate Fighting Championship

It was never supposed to work. The Ultimate Fighting Championship, or UFC, presented violent, no-holds-barred combat, contained in an octagon-shaped steel cage, offering to answer the age-old martial arts question: which fighting style would win in a real fight? UFC gathered boxers, kick-boxers, Thai boxers, wrestlers and martial artists from judo and jiu-jitsu to karate and kung fu, to face each other with few rules. Determined illegal in most states within the US, and political dynamite from its inception, the UFC struggled to acquire venues, sponsors, television coverage and endorsements from governing athletics commissions. In short, UFC looked like it would never get off the ground until a new team transported it into the fastest-growing professional sport of all time. At the heart of the UFC beats a culture unmatched in professional sport for its aggressiveness, appetite for risk, and desire for innovation.

UFC1 debuted in 1993 featuring an eight-man single-elimination tournament including fighters from a diverse array of fighting styles and traditions. Although intended as a one-off event, the tournament generated so much interest that the UFC began to produce regular shows. However, the organization fell on hard times, banned in two-thirds of US states and stunted by unfavourable publicity decrying no-holds-barred fighting as barbaric 'cockfighting'. Today, the UFC enjoys spectacular success, due in large part to the charismatic, straight-talking UFC president, Dana White, who resurrected the sport from almost certain extinction. Confident, brash and aggressive, White's approach has shaped the UFC's culture into a dominant, fan-driven publicity machine.

It is hard to ignore the likelihood that White's approach, and his non-corporate background, has been the pivotal influence in creating an organizational culture for the UFC that no typical MBA graduate could ever duplicate. A university dropout from South Boston, White thinks his previous experiences delivered the ideal training for building the UFC. For White the key to success lies in knowing the fight business. He saw clearly what fans wanted, and convinced long-time friends, Las Vegas casino owners Lorenzo and Frank Fertitta to purchase the soon to be bankrupt organization in 2001. No strangers to the rough and tumble of business, the Fertittas' take their ownership commitment to a new level. Rumour has it that the dispute resolution clause in the contract between Lorenzo and Frank Fertitta stipulates that disagreements must be resolved by a 'sport jiu-jitsu match, where White is to referee until submission or a points decision is reached'. With an initial investment of US$2 million to buy the organization, followed by a further bankroll of US$44 million to support a growing debt, White took the helm, armed with street-smarts, a consuming passion and an undeniable insight into the psyche of the fight fan.

In a sense, White's greatest asset has been a desire to embrace the unconventional. Although UFC had been around since the early 1990s, White was able to inflame fight fans' desire to find out who would win a real contest between practitioners of different combat styles. Despite years of losses and setbacks from hostile politicians, White's strategy to get the sport sanctioned started to work. UFC made it to television and pay-per-view. In 2005, UFC introduced a reality version of the sport televised by Spike, a cable channel targeting young men. *The Ultimate Fighter* revealed the story behind fighters' lives, televising each week the latest bout in a tournament designed to culminate in an *American Idol* style of finale. White's persistence reaped dividends. A new generation of UFC fans was born, riveted by an insight into the psychology and training behind creating a fighter prepared to step inside a cage. UFC never looked back as its pay-per-view audience skyrocketed. A private company now worth more than US$1 billion, the UFC recently sold 10 per cent ownership to the United Arab Emirates government-owned Flash Entertainment.

Unlike many traditional sports, UFC has always moved at the cutting edge of publicity. Culturally, the organization commits to the relentless pursuit of fan attention. White really did understand the needs of fight fans and their insatiable desire to debate the details of fights and rate the merits of different combat styles and fighters. Perhaps more than any other emerging sport, UFC has aggressively used digital and social media to its advantage. Infused by a fearlessness few sport leagues have ever possessed, UFC has generated nearly five million Facebook Friends. Many organizations claim a high regard for a cultural identity prioritizing innovation. An exemplification of that coveted cultural feature, UFC does not fear the risks that accompany genuine innovation. For their Facebook Friends, UFC delivers live-streams of selected fights in the first exclusive content from a professional sporting event made available to a social networking site.

The demographics and psychographics of the UFC fan base reveal its markets of key appeal. Most interesting, perhaps, is the broader cultural characteristics of this consumer base, particularly when considered in the context of the well-established supporter demographics of the US big four (NFL, MLB, NBA, NHL) as well as NASCAR and MLS. UFC fans are dominated by the 18–34 male demographic, which also of course makes the sport compelling for sponsors such as beer and car manufacturers. Prominent sponsors include Anheuser-Busch, Harley-Davidson, Visa, Toyota and Burger King. Amongst professional sport in the US, UFC is second only to the NFL. Perhaps as many as a million US fans are between 12 and 17 years of age.

As of the beginning of 2011, the UFC's estimated fan base in the United States was approximately 30 million and growing in a US sporting marketplace where the only other professional leagues increasing their fan bases over the last three years have been the NHL and NBA. The Canadian and British markets presently hover around five million, while the remainder of the world accounts for an additional 20 million fans. In total, UFC enjoys a world fan base around 65–70 million. It has become America's pre-eminent combat sport, steadily surpassing boxing's declining fortunes. The future looks bright for UFC as well, having avoided the problems boxing has faced with a proliferation of fragmented and bickering governing bodies. UFC127 was staged in Sydney and televised globally in late February, 2011. Cable deals around the world allow UFC programming to be available in more than 175 countries and in 20 different languages.

Some cultural lessons are pertinent in the UFC case. Most importantly, its organizational culture aligns with the needs of the environment in which it operates. Consider, for example, the UFC's risk-taking comfort, played out through constant forays into new methods of connecting with its fans and novel approaches to generating publicity. The UFC culture also matches it target audience. Built on the interests of the 18–34 demographic, the UFC portrays its culture through a T-shirt wearing, direct, aggressive and opinionated president, former hall of fame fighters as executives, and imagery emblazoned with tattoos and bikinis, underscored by the liberal use of heavy metal and rap music. Everything about the company resonates with its target audience at a level that is difficult to fabricate without the underpinning support of strong cultural values. Dana White's video blog speaks volumes about the UFC culture. Completely uncensored, White speaks directly to the fans, offers his forthright opinions, and swears at whim. Like the company itself, White takes no prisoners and offers no apologies. He is raw, ambitious and authentic. For UFC consumers, respect comes from strength and aggression. There can be little doubt that White connects with the fans because he is one of them. Belonging and identity drive the UFC; it infuses the organization because it is run by fight fans who have never disconnected from their passion.

For UFC fans, the unique combination of risk, aggression and identity has created a cult-like allegiance. Not only has this made the events immensely successful, it has also meant that the UFC can create a vast range of auxiliary products and merchandise. T-shirts, DVDs, video games, special events, expos and mobile applications sell prolifically. While it might seem like a marketing issue, the UFC's commercial success was built on a cultural platform. Fans feel like part of the UFC organization. They connect constantly and habitually through blogs, social media, and websites. A fan focus also means that the UFC does not seem like a marketing-driven organization, unlike many in the sporting sphere, such as sport fashion manufacturers. Despite an incessant media and marketing presence, the UFC sells to the same fan base over and over. If you cannot attend an event, you can access pay-per-view, watch streaming video online, order the DVD, see the highlights on YouTube or just buy the T-shirt. Better yet, log in to hear what the president of the UFC has to say about the latest bout and post your own post-fight commentary.

Dominance and proactivity represent core values central to the UFC culture. Their compulsion is to be first: the trendsetters. They seem to do and say what they want, without seeking permission. Unapologetic and uncensored; imaginative and innovative. Most sport organizations struggle to reconcile the need for change with the heavy inertia of tradition. For the UFC, change is not a burden but a cultural necessity. Different seems right for the bad boys of professional sport. Where World Wrestling Entertainment has made a fabrication into syndication, the UFC revels in the raw, unadulterated, brutal collision of reality inside a steel cage. Spectacle and entertainment holds the foreground. White favours fighters with 'heart'. The show is sovereign over the victory. To that end, White pays significant bonuses to both winners and those who deliver the most entertaining bouts.

Every sport organization both enjoys and endures the cultural legacy of its founders and favourites. Behind Dana White's T-shirt, ripped jeans, worn Pumas and stubble-sharpened skull lies a powerhouse of cultural influence. From a banned stigma to the most successful sport organization of the last decade, the UFC owes much of its celebrated success to a suite of cultural commitments that make most professional sports seem dull. UFC is professional sport's great contender.

Case questions

1 What do you think it means for an organization to have 'core cultural values'? What are the UFC's core cultural values?
2 What does it mean to have a strong and appropriate culture? Use the case to illustrate your point.
3 How has the UFC culture assisted in connecting the organization to fans?

Chapter 10

Financial management in sport

Overview

This chapter examines the critical importance of sound financial management in ensuring effective outcomes for sport organizations. Throughout the chapter examples are used to illustrate both the theory underpinning the financial management of sport organizations and the practical things that should be done to sustain their financial viability.

After completing this chapter the reader should be able to:

- explain how sport has changed over the last 50 years and its implications for the source and use of funds;
- understand the importance of effective financial management in sport;
- identify the ways in which sport organization financial arrangements can be reported;
- explain how assets are organized and how they differ from liabilities;
- explain how profits and or surpluses are calculated for sport organizations, and the difference between operating profit and net profit; and
- explain how budgets operate and explain why they are crucial to effective financial management of sport organizations.

The financial evolution of sport

As the previous chapters have demonstrated, sport is now a sophisticated institution with an often complex legal and financial structure. It is in many respects a fusion of business and entertainment where the consumers are the fans and the players, the producers are the clubs, associations and leagues, and the distribution channels are the sport arenas and sport stadia (Carter 2011; Foster *et al.* 2006; Gómez *et al.* 2010; Quinn 2009; Shropshire and Davis 2008; Smit 2007; Stewart 2007b). Like all forms of business, sport organizations require a strong system of financial management to ensure their long-term sustainability. However, this has not always been the case, and sport around the world has gone through four phases of commercial and financial development over the last 50 years.

This metamorphosis of sport into a form of business, with its associated financial systems, begins in Phase 1 with sport as a recreational and cultural practice where sport organizations are rudimentary, their revenue streams are small, sport was played mainly for fun, and activities are organized and managed by volunteer officials. This model is often described as a kitchen-table approach to sport management, since the game is administered by a few officials making key decisions from a member's home. It has some strengths, since it not only ensures the involvement of grass-roots players and members, and provided a strong local community club focus, but it also nurtures a strong set of values that centre on playing the game for its own sake, and the concomitant ideal of amateurism. At the same time, it perpetuates a simple system of management driven by an administrative committee made up of a few elected members and self-appointed officials. There is the president who is the public face of the club or association, and a secretary who keeps things ticking over by maintaining a member-register and organizing others to manage teams, run events and maintain the clubrooms and playing facilities. There is also a treasurer who looked after the financial affairs of the organization. The treasurer is more often than not unfamiliar with the theory and principles of accounting, but makes up for a lack of expertise with a mind for detail, and a desire to ensure receipts run ahead of expenses.

The second phase is commercialization, where more revenue streams are utilized, and both staff and players are paid for their services. Whereas the kitchen-table model depends on member subscriptions, player registration fees and social activities for their financial viability, the commercialized sport model uses sports' commercial value to attract corporate and other sponsors. In this phase sports that have the capacity to draw large crowds increasingly understand that these crowds can be used to attract businesses who want to increase product awareness, secure a special and exclusive sales channel or obtain access to a market segment that will be receptive to their product. Sport is still a recreational and cultural practice, where the sport's overall development is the primary goal, but there is also an emerging or secondary strategy that focuses on elite development and the building of pathways by which players can move to the premier league or competition.

The third phase is bureaucratization, where the structures of sport organizations become more complex, administrative control are established and functional specialization increases. This phase is heavily dependent upon its antecedent phase, since an effective bureaucracy requires additional resources. In this phase club, league and association structures are transformed to so as to include a board of directors whose prime responsibility is to set the strategic direction and ensure compliance with government regulation. This then, establishes an organizational divide between the 'steerers' (the board) and the 'rowers' (the chief executive officer and operational staff) who are expected to implement the board's plans and policies. In addition a business-like set of functions and processes are created, which are built around administrative support, marketing, finance, game development, coaching player development and the like. In this phase less management space is given to the sport-as-recreation-and-cultural-practice model, and more to the sport-as-business model.

The fourth and final phase is corporatization, where sport embraces the business model by valuing brand management as much as it does player and fan relations. Revenue streams are increasingly dominated by sponsorships and broadcast rights fees, merchandise sales are deepened and managers adopt a more professional outlook where the need to secure a competitive edge overrules the desire to hold on to old traditions. This is the phase in which players become full-time employees, player associations are established to protect their interests and the sport's governing bodies take on the role of employers. A formal industrial relations system is created that leads to detailed contractual arrangements, collective bargaining agreements and codes of conduct. The marketing process also becomes increasingly sophisticated as the sport club, association or league becomes a brand, members and fans become customers, sponsors become corporate partners, and the brand name and image is used to strengthen its corporate partner arrangements and build up a merchandizing arm. This phase also features a move toward managerialism, whereby sport becomes more accountable to its stakeholders for its performance and use of resources. This is particularly evident in sport's relationship with government, where government funding becomes increasingly contingent upon sport meeting certain specific and agreed upon outcomes. This focus on managerialism also leads to greater transparency through an emphasis on performance measurement. Within this framework it is no longer appropriate to measure only player performance, but also things like internal processes and efficiency, financial performance, market performance, employee – and in particular player – behaviour, and even social responsibility. Finally, sport becomes generally more regulated, with some being defined by government-framed parameters and legislation, and others being internal. The more government-bound controls involve venue safety, anti-discrimination programmes and crowd control policies. Internal regulation is highly visible within professional sport leagues and competitions, where player recruitment is governed by drafting rules, player behaviour is constrained by a combination of collective agreements and codes of conduct, salaries are set within a total wage ceiling, revenues are redistributed from the most wealthy to the most needy clubs and associations, and games are scheduled to ensure the lowest cost and greatest revenue. While this type of corporate regulation can be problematic because of its heavy emphasis on bureaucratic control and detailed performance measurement, it also ensures a disciplined system of management by creating a common purpose, setting a clear strategic direction and securing strong leadership (Stewart 2007b). A summary of each phase in the sport-as-business evolution is provided in Table 10.1.

Funding sources for sport

It is clear that the new business-based, corporate model of sport involves a significant expansion of income. However, it is important to not throw the baby out with the bath water, and so traditional forms of revenue have been maintained, although in a slightly more sophisticated form. Member fees are still important, as too are fundraising from social activities and gate receipts. However, as was touched upon previously, new and varied revenue streams have opened up over the last 30 years that have transformed sport and the way it operates (Foster *et al.* 2006; Szymanski and Kuypers 2000). The funding of sport organizations begs a number of questions, the main ones being listed here.

1   Where does the money come from?
2   Where is the money spent?
3   How are the movements of money monitored?

Table 10.1: Sport as business: evolutionary phases and features

	Values	Revenue focus	Structural focus	Management focus
PHASE 1 Kitchen table	• Amateurism • Volunteerism	• Member funds • Social club income	• Management committee	• Sustaining operations
PHASE 2 Commercial	• Viability of sport • Member service	• Gate receipts • Sponsorship	• Management portfolios	• Marketing the club
PHASE 3 Bureaucratic	• Efficient use of sport resources • Accountability	• Corporate income • Merchandizing	• Divisions and departments	• Improving club efficiency
PHASE 4 Corporate	• Delivering outputs • Building the brand	• Brand value • Broadcast rights	• Board policymaking • Staff operations	• Increasing club value • Regulating constituents

In answering these questions it is important to distinguish between funds that are used to create infrastructure and facilities, and funds for use in managing the day-to-day activities of a sport organization. So, there are two types of basic funding uses. The first is funds for investment in capital development, and the second is funds for recurrent and operating activities.

Capital funding

Capital funding, which is money to finance investment in assets, can come from a number of sources listed here.

1   Government grants, which may be federal, state or local. The point to note is that there are differences between sports that reflect not only their scale of operation but also their likelihood of generating international success. Funding may also be subject to certain conditions being met, like adopting certain policy requirements or working within a legislative framework.
2   Loans and borrowing which could be short term (up to a year) or long term (up to 20 years). Loans and borrowings are known as debt finance. The points to note are that it provides ready cash for investment in facilities and income producing assets. On the other hand, it also incurs an interest burden and may not always generate an increase in income.
3   New share issue or a public float which is known as equity finance. The points to note are that like borrowings, it provides ready access to cash, but unlike borrowing does not impose the burden of interest payment or repayment of the principal to lenders. However, it does hand over control to shareholders and there is expectation that a dividend will be delivered.
4   Retained earnings, which is money reinvested in the sport organization. The points to note are there is no interest payment and control is retained over funds used. For nonprofit sport organizations, the retention of earnings is mandatory, since this is a legal requirement.

Recurrent funding

The recurrent funding of sport involves money to fund day-to-day operations, which comes from a variety of sources depending on the type of sport enterprise. The main revenue sources are briefly noted below, together with the strengths and weaknesses of each source:

1   Membership fees, which may be full adult, associate, family and similar categories. The points to note here are that they are usually upfront and relatively stable and therefore provide an immediate source of cash. Membership also serves a marketing function by establishing a core customer base.
2   Spectator admission charge, which includes the categories of full adult, family, special groups and premium. The points to note while there is a high degree of flexibility it is subject to significant variation because of changing attendance patterns and differences in the scheduling of games.
3   Corporate facilities including boxes and hospitality. The points to note are that a large investment is required but the strengths are that business connections are made and premium rental can be charged.
4   Player fees and charges include entry fees, facility charge and equipment hire. The points to note here are that revenue is dependent on demand and the user pays for the experience.
5   Special fundraising efforts are another source of recurrent funding and may include a dinner dance, rage-party, auction night, a trivia night and so on. The points to note are

that the burden is on staff and members to arrange and attend functions. However, these types of events can be profitable through large markups on food and drink.

6   Lotteries and gaming such as raffles, bingo and gaming machines. The points to note are that permits are often required, margins are low and there is solid competition from other venues.

7   Merchandizing such as memorabilia, scarves, T-shirts, jackets and autographed equipment. The point to note is that while it can produce is a significant short-run increase in revenue, it can plateau out with a fall in on-field success.

8   Sponsorships and endorsement are another good source and may include naming rights, partnerships, signage, product endorsements and contra deals. However the point to note is that the organization can lose control and become dependent on sponsor income and defer to their partnership demands.

9   Catering may include take away or sit down food or drink. The points to note are that it is labour intensive, but because it is delivered in a non-competitive environment higher profit margins can be sustained.

10 Broadcasting rights such as television and radio, and more recently internet and mobile phone streaming rights. The points to note are that it focuses on elite sports with a large audience base, and may be irrelevant for most sports associations and clubs. At the same time it provides the single largest revenue source for professional sport leagues.

11 Investment income such as interest earned and share dividends. However the points to note are that share prices can vary at short notice, and losses can be made which increases the level of risk. In addition, interest rates may be low.

12 Government grants, which may be federal, state or local. The points to note are that there are often marked differences between sports, they can vary from year to year and, like government capital funds, are subject to contain conditions being met.

The expenses incurred in running a sport enterprise are also varied. They include:

1   Wages and salaries such as permanent, contract or casual administration staff and players. The points to note are that it is usually the largest expense item and is subject to inflation and competitive bidding as clubs aim to secure the best playing talent.

2   Staff on-costs, which include insurance, training, leave and superannuation. The points to note here are that they are legally required, ongoing and linked to the employment contract.

3   Marketing costs include advertising, sales promotion, site visits, trade displays and giveaways. The point to note here is that it is easy to exceed budget estimates since there is always a tacit assumption that too much marketing and promotion is never enough.

4   Office maintenance includes power and light, phone and fax, postage, and stationery and printing. The points to note here are that it is ongoing and tight control is required.

5   Venue maintenance includes the playing area, the viewing area and member facilities. The point to note here is that maintenance expenditure is ongoing and frequently absorbs a significant amount of revenue.

6   Player management includes equipment, clothing and footwear, medical services, fitness and conditioning, and travel. The points to note are that while they constitute an essential investment in improved performance, they also require tight budgeting.

7   Asset depreciation includes facilities, buildings, cars and equipment. The points to note here is that assets lose value and must be replaced. Also, depreciation is a non-cash expense, and it is essential that assets be amortized as expenses over their lifetime.

Key financial management questions to ask

At the same time, it is important to note that while significant segments of sport are now big businesses, most sport organizations are relatively small, and depend on the support of club members, volunteer officials, community businesses and local government to sustain their operations. While high profile professional sport leagues turn over hundreds of millions of dollars a year, the majority of sport clubs and associations are lucky to secure any more than a million dollars to fund their operations (Quinn 2009). A majority of sport is really a form of small business. A suburban supermarket turns over more money than most sport clubs and associations.

No matter what the scale or size of sport organizations, however, they all need to be managed in a sound and responsible manner. Many sport administrators do not feel comfortable handling money or planning the financial affairs of clubs and associations, which often arises out of poor background knowledge and a lack of experience in managing complex financial issues. In practice, there are many straightforward, but essential financial questions that sport managers need to answer. They include:

1   What do we own?
2   What do we owe?
3   What did we earn?
4   What did we spend?
5   Did we make a profit?
6   Do we have enough cash to pay debts when they fall due?
7   How big is our interest bill?
8   Are we borrowing too much?
9   Did we improve upon last year?
10 How do we compare with other similar sport organizations?

Understanding financial information

There is also the problem of making sense of the vocabulary of accounting. The distinction between assets and liabilities is mostly clear, with assets amounting to all those things we own and liabilities being all those things we owe to others. However, the distinction between tangible and intangible assets and current and non-current liabilities may often be less clear. The concepts of owners' equity, shareholders' funds and net worth can also cause confusion, while further difficulties can arise when contrasting operating profit with net profit.

Consequently the effective management of any sport organization requires not only a sound knowledge of the principles of financial management, but also the support of a financial recording and reporting system that allows a quick and easy reading of the club or association's financial health (Hart 2006). It is now taken for granted that a professionally managed sport organization will produce three integrated annual financial reports. The first document is a statement of performance, or profit and loss, which reports on the revenues earned for the period and the expenses incurred. The second document is a statement of position, or balance sheet, which reports on the current level of assets, liabilities and equity. The third document is a statement of cash flows, which identifies the cash movements in and out of the organization. The cash flow statement is divided into activities related to day-to-day operations, activities that involve the sale and purchase of assets, and activities that involve the securing and borrowing of funds and their repayment. The balance sheet and profit and loss statement are discussed in more detail below.

The balance sheet

The balance sheet measures the wealth of a sport organization. Assets are placed on the left hand side of the balance sheet, while liabilities are placed on the right hand side. Proprietorship (also termed owners' equity, net worth or accumulated funds) is located on the right hand side, and represents the difference between assets and liabilities. The balance sheet gives a clear picture of a sport organization's wealth at a point in time by contrasting its assets (things it owns) with its liabilities (things it owes). The balance sheet also indicates how the assets of the organization have been funded. It can be through equity (i.e. the capital of the owner/s), or from borrowed funds from some other organization or individual.

It is important to note that not all assets are the same. They can be broken down into a number of categories (Hoggett *et al.* 2006), as can liabilities. As a result a balance sheet will be set up to provide a clear picture of the level of both current and non-current assets, and current and non-current liabilities. The level of owners' equity or shareholders' capital (or accumulated funds as it is usually called in nonprofit organization statements) will also be identified in the balance sheet since it is effectively the difference between the two. This is because assets can be accumulated through either the owners' capital, reinvested profits or borrowed funds.

Assets

As noted above, assets are all those thing owned by an organization. To put it more technically, they constitute resources owned and controlled by an entity from which future benefits are expected to flow. The assets of a balance sheet are not only broken down into their various categories, but they are listed according to their degree of liquidity, with the most liquid coming first and the less liquid coming later in the statement. The measure of an asset's liquidity is the ease with which it can be converted to cash, and all those assets which can easily converted are listed under the current assets heading. The most frequently cited currents assets are cash in the bank, accounts payable or debtors (which include those short-term invoices or bills for payment has not yet been received), investments in the share market (which can be converted to cash through quick sale) and stocks of material and merchandise (which at a pinch can be sold for cash). Items like prepaid expenses (that is, bills paid in advance) can also be included here. The level of current assets is an important indicator of the financial health of a sport organization since it is the means by which bills are paid, and creditors' demands for payment are met.

Assets are also listed as fixed or non-current. These assets include everything that cannot be easily and quickly converted to cash. Some stock and materials will be listed here when they do not have high turnover. The main items will be all those tangible or material assets that are essential for generating revenue, but are difficult to sell at an appropriate price in the short term. These items include office furniture and equipment (including all sorts of sports equipment), motor vehicles, buildings and land. Building improvements (e.g. a stadium upgrade) are also examples of fixed assets. The main categories of assets are listed in Table 10.2.

The balance sheet of a sporting organization can be complicated by a number of other factors. For example, assets can either increase in value over time (i.e. appreciate) or decrease in value over time (i.e. depreciate). Property, stocks and shares, and various scarce artefacts and memorabilia are particularly prone to increase in value. On the other hand, there are other assets that can lose value quickly, and includes those things that incur constant use

Table 10.2: Balance sheet – types of assets

Asset category	Degree of liquidity	Example
Cash in the bank	High (current)	Trading account balance
Accounts receivable	Medium (current)	Monies owed by club members
Prepaid expense	Medium (non-current)	Payment of next year's insurance
Company shares	Medium (current)	Ownership of shares
Inventory	Medium (current)	Stock of sports equipment
Office equipment	Low (non-current)	Computer system
Other equipment	Low (non-current)	Office furniture
Motor vehicle	Low (non-current)	Ownership of vehicle
Property	Low (non-current)	Ownership of office building
Building improvements	Low (non-current)	Stadium renewal

and wear and tear, or become obsolete, or both. Moreover, there are assets that, while not tangible, clearly add value to the organization, and should be accounted for. Accountants have recognized these financial facts of life for many years, and have consequently devised strategies for managing these phenomena (Atrill et al. 2006).

Depreciation

Depreciation is based on the principle that all non-current assets represent a store of service potential that the organization intends to use over the life of the asset. Assets therefore have a limited life as a result of their ongoing wear and tear and probable obsolescence. Accounting for depreciation is the process whereby the decline in the service potential of an asset, such as a motor vehicle, is progressively brought to account as a periodic charge against revenue. That is, the asset is devalued in response to its purchase price or market value, and offset against income. In order to allocate the cost of the asset to the period in which it is used, an estimate must be made of the asset's useful life. This will usually be less than its physical life. For example, in the case of a motor vehicle, it may be decided that after three years it will not be operating as efficiently and therefore will be worth less after this period, even though it is still running. If an asset has a residual, or resale value, then this amount will be subtracted from the asset cost to establish the actual amount to be depreciated.

The simplest method for depreciating an asset is the straight line or prime cost method. This method allocates an equal amount of depreciation to each full accounting period in the asset's useful life. The amount of depreciation for each period is determined by dividing the cost of the asset minus its residual value by the number of periods in the asset's useful life. Take for example, a computer system that was purchased for $11,000. It is anticipated that the system will have a resale value of $1,000 after five years. Using the straight line method of depreciation the annual depreciation will be $2,000. This figure is obtained by dividing the difference between the purchase price and the residual value ($10,000) by the five years of anticipated useful life. This annual depreciation will then be posted as an expense in the profit and loss statement for the following five years. This process of spreading the cost of an asset over a specific period of time is called amortization. The idea behind this process is that there needs to be a clear way of showing the relationship between spread of benefits from an asset's use and the costs involved in creating those benefits.

Asset valuation

Asset values can also be changed to reflect current conditions and prices. Unless otherwise stated, assets are valued at their purchase price which is known as historical cost. However, many assets, particularly land and buildings, can increase in value over time. Unless this is periodically done, the true values of assets can be seriously understated. This problem can be overcome by a revaluation of the assets by a certified valuer, with a note to this effect accompanying the annual statement of financial operations and standing.

In Practice 10.1

Making assets work for you

Around the world there are many sport stadia that have made a strategic decision to completely refurbish and redesign their facilities. Of course, we all know that this type of 'grand plan' comes at a cost. We also understand that the stadia owners and managers will be most often required to secure funds from external sources to make it all happen.

Take, for example, the internationally famous and iconic Melbourne Cricket Ground (MCG) and its occupant, the Melbourne Cricket Club (MCC). In 2002 it decided to knock down its ageing stand and start again by putting up 'state of the art' facilities. But to make all this happen it had to borrow a significant amount of money. In fact, its borrowings totalled well over AUS$300 million. In 2006, and just in time for the Commonwealth Games, it had spent all its borrowed money, but what it got in return was a scintillating bundle of world-class facilities. But, as we all know, when you borrow money you not only have to pay back the full amount you borrowed – which is commonly called the 'principal', but you also have to pay an annual interest charge. If we assume the annual interest charge is around 8 per cent, then in the first few years the total interest bill will be something in the order of AUS$20–24 million. This represents a serious drain on one's cash deposits.

This heavy repayment burden immediately raises the question as to just what benefits are going to accrue from this very big investment, and when it might be clear that the decision to borrow all this money was, in fact, a good one. And there is a risk that the repayment burden may be so severe that the ability to repay may be impossible.

But the MCC/MCG has a strong cushion against any cash flow problems. It is its 'membership'. It has many thousands of members, and is able to maintain a 20-year waiting list with virtually no promotional or marketing effort whatsoever. Moreover, it is Australia's premier sport stadium, and has no difficulty securing tenants, the main ones being the Australian Football League and the Cricket Australia. And, to top it off, it regularly attracts 50,000 to 80,000 spectators to games. This very solid attendance figure consequently enables it to: (1) negotiate big catering and hospitality contracts, (2) hire out expensive corporate suits with no difficulty and, finally, (3) secure big-brand advertisers to place signage around the ground.

The financial 'moral' to this story is short and sharp. It is that investing in expensive assets is a sound thing to do, but only if you are sure the assets can deliver the best quality services. If this eventuates then you can be confident that that these services will generate sufficient additional revenue so that not only will all loans and interest bills be paid off without fuss, but that there will be a handsome surplus with which to undertake even further investments. If, on the other hand, the newly created assets are unable to deliver these benefits, the future will look very uncertain indeed. In the case of the MCC/MCG, it took a calculated risk, and reaped the rewards.

Intangible assets

For sporting clubs there is also the issue of how intangible assets should be treated, and how they can be valued. Intangible assets are by their very nature difficult to quantify, and their definition as non-monetary assets without physical substance merely confirms their ambiguity. A good starting point is to note that there are two types of intangible assets. They are first, identifiable intangibles that include things like trademarks, brand names, mastheads, franchises, licences and patents. Some of these intangibles like franchises, licences and patents have a purchase price, and they can be amortized over their expected life. The second type of intangible assets is labelled as unidentifiable, the best example being goodwill. Goodwill arises from a combination of things like superior management, customer confidence and a favourable location. Goodwill is seen to possess value since it can produce future economic benefits that cannot be directly attributable to some other material asset. Goodwill is relevant to sport organizations, since the ability to attract fans often originates from vague, but strong historical attachments between club image and fan identity. While few clubs have attempted to identify a goodwill value, it is often visible when a privately owned team is sold to a new owner. The difference between the sale price and the asset value of the team will in large part be attributable to the goodwill factor.

Liabilities

Simply put, liabilities are those things that an organization owes others. To be more exact, they are the present obligations of an entity which, when settled, involve the outflow of economic resources (Hoggett et al. 2006). Like assets, liabilities can be categorized into current and non-current. Current liabilities included monies that are owed to people in the immediate future for services and goods they have supplied. For example a club may have purchased some sporting equipment on credit for which payment is due in 30 to 60 days. This is called accounts payable or debtors. Other current liabilities include short-term borrowings, member income received in advance and taxes payable in the short term. Income received in advance is an interesting case because it is often intuitively viewed as revenue or asset and not a liability. However, under the accrual accounting model it is clearly not relevant to the current flows of revenue and expenses. But as monies received it has to be accounted for. So, what happens is that it is debited to cash in the bank and credited as something we owe to members in the future. That is, it is a liability which is listed as income received in advance. Non-current liabilities include long-term borrowings, mortgage loans, deferred tax liabilities and long-term provisions for employees like superannuation entitlements.

The accumulation of liabilities is not of itself a problem, so long as the debt is used to build income-earning assets. However, if increasing debt is associated with losses rather than profits, then the gap between assets and liabilities will increase. It is not uncommon in sport for clubs to have liabilities that exceed the value of their assets. For example in 2005 in the Australian Football League, the net worth of the Western Bulldogs and St Kilda clubs was both negative These figures indicate a lengthy period where expenses constantly exceeded revenues, and assets were used to pay debt. In the long run these sorts of trends are unsustainable.

Balance sheets can say a lot about a sport organization's financial health. However, balance sheets do not tell us much about a sport club's earnings, profits and losses over the course of a month, quarter or year. For this information we must turn to the profit and loss statement, or as it is often called in the nonprofit sector of sport, the income statement.

Profit and loss statements

It is not just a matter of examining a sport organization's assets and liabilities at a point in time in order to diagnose its financial health, it is also crucial to shift one's attention to the financial operation of sport clubs and associations over time (Atrill *et al.* 2006). The first thing to be said about the profit and loss statement is that it can go under a number of names. It can also be called an income statement, which is the nonprofit sector terminology, and is also referred to as a financial statement of performance. The point to remember about most sport organizations is that they do not focus on profits and losses, but rather surpluses and deficits (Anthony and Young 2003). In any case, it does not alter the fact that these statements looks at the revenue earned during a period (say 3 or 12 months) and compare it with the expenses incurred in generating the revenue. Profit and loss statements are straightforward to compile and moderately easy to understand, but there are some tricky areas that need to be discussed.

The first point to make is that while profit and loss statements contain many cash movements, they do not accurately represent the total cash movements in and out of the organization, since they are essentially about earned income and incurred expenses. As a result they will include many transactions that do not include the movement of cash. In other words, revenue can be earned, while the cash may come much later. But it is still a revenue item that needs to be identified in the profit and loss statement. For example, a sport consulting business may have completed a strategic planning exercise for a large national sport association and invoiced it for $50,000. If, at the end of the accounting period, the invoice has not been paid, it will still be included in the profit and loss statement as income. The adjustment or offset in the accounts will be an equivalent (i.e. $50,000) increase (or debit) in the accounts receivable asset account. If the invoice had been immediately paid, the adjustment would have been made as an increase (or debit) of $50,000 to the cash in the bank asset account.

Revenue, or income as it is frequently called, is typically divided into operating and non-operating items. Operating items include all those revenues like member income and merchandise sales that provide the funds to support the day-to-day running of the club or association. Non-operating items include funds that are irregular, or even out of the ordinary. An asset sale, a special government grant or a large donation are examples of non-operating income. As noted in the early part of this chapter, sport organization revenues have expanded dramatically over recent years, but for the non-professional clubs the main sources are member fees, gate receipts, government grants, fundraising activities and sponsors.

Expenses should also be treated cautiously. The profit and loss statement should include all incurred expenses rather than just paid expenses. Buying something on credit or by cash is an expense. On the other hand, paying for something that will not be used until next year, for example, should not be listed as an expense for the period under consideration. It is an asset (i.e. a prepaid expense). For example, rental or insurance paid in advance involves a movement of cash out of the club or association, but does not constitute an expense incurred for the current period.

Depreciation

Depreciation is another expense issue that has to be dealt with. And, to repeat, depreciation is an estimate of the wear and tear of working assets. In an office setting, computers are quickly depreciated for two reasons. First, they are heavily used and second, they quickly become out of date and obsolete. Depreciation is therefore recognized as an expense and should be included in a profit and loss statement. Depreciation can be calculated in a number of ways, the most simple being the straight-line method. If, for example, a motor vehicle is purchased for $30,000 has an estimated life of five years, and no residual value, then the depreciation expense for the following five years will be $6,000 per annum. Some sporting club finance mangers make the mistake of listing the full cost of the motor vehicle in year one as an expense, but this is clearly misleading. The correct way to treat this transaction is to list it as an asset, and then depreciate (i.e. amortize) it over its estimated lifetime. Interest-paid and interest-earned also appear on profit and loss statements. Interest paid will be classified as an expense while interest received will be classified as revenue.

Operating versus net profits

When analysing profit and loss statements it is also important to distinguish between operating profit (or surplus) and net profit (or surplus). The differences between these two terms comprise abnormal revenue and expenses, and extraordinary revenue and expenses. A transaction will be classified as abnormal if it is a regular occurrence, but in a specific case is significantly higher than normal. In the case of a sporting club an abnormal item might be an accelerated depreciation of office equipment, or a supplementary government grant. A transaction will be classified as extraordinary if it is a significant transaction, and does not regularly occur. A sporting club example includes fines for breaching salary cap regulations (this happens frequently in the Australian Football League and the National Rugby League) and the sale of an asset (this occurs in the English Premier League, where players can be traded under certain conditions).

Operating profit does not include the abnormal and extraordinary items, and is confined to those transactions that are directly related to day-to-day activities that regularly recur over the standard accounting cycle. So, operating profit is the difference between operating income and operating expenses. Net profit is something else again, and will take into account all abnormal and extraordinary items. If the sport club happens to be part of profit-making entity, then it may be required to pay tax on its profits. This item will be subtracted from operating profit to get to a net profit figure.

Depreciation is also frequently listed as a non-operating item and can also make a significant difference to the level of profit. An operating profit can be transformed into a net loss by the inclusion of depreciation as a non-operating expense. Sometimes claims are made that depreciation can distort the real profit of a sport organization, but in fact the opposite is the case. Depreciation is a legitimate expense since it takes into account that amount of assets used up to generate revenue. In the context of the above discussion a typical profit and loss or income statement is illustrated in Table 10.3.

Table 10.3: Profit and loss statement template

Item	Amount ($)	Total ($)
Operating income		
Member fees	50,000	
Events	10,000	
Grants	30,000	
Total operating income		*90,000*
Operating expenses		
Administration	50,000	
Events	20,000	
Insurance	10,000	
Total operating expenses		*80,000*
Operating profit		10,000
Non-operating income		
Special government grant	10,000	
Non-operating expenses		
Depreciation	20,000	
Net profit		0

In Practice 10.2

The financial health of the International Cricket Council
The international governing bodies for sport, otherwise known as International Sporting Organizations (ISOs), depend for their financial viability on the revenues they can secure from major sport events. One of the most highly credentialed ISOs which recently shifted its headquarters from London to Dubai in the Middle East is the International Cricket Council (ICC).

The ICC, which has 96 member countries, has traditionally run two major competitions, the World Cup and the Champions Trophy, both 50 overs per team competitions. The World Cup was last run in 2011 and 2007, while the Champions Trophy was last run in 2009 and 2005. In recent times the ICC has conducted a twenty20 competition. The success of these events is immediately reflected in the sharp subsequent increases in the ICC's operating income. The ICC's financial indicators for 2007 and 2010 are listed in Table 10.4.

As this table starkly shows, The ICC depends for its financial strength on the revenue from its international tournaments. They generate enormous amounts of cash. This means that its revenues increases sharply just after a major event, but in the seasons between events, falls away appreciably. It is also important to note its surpluses are used to (1) fund the operations of its member nations, (2) promote the game around the world and (3) assist national governing bodies develop the game locally.

	2007 (US$ million)	2010 (US$ million)
Operating income	273	77
Event income	260	75
Operating expenses	15	28
Cricket development	3	6
Total assets	151	190
Cash assets	120	40
Total liabilities	126	161
Current liabilities	125	160

Table 10.4: Financial indicators for International Cricket Council

Source: International Cricket Council 2007, 2011.

Budgeting systems

Budgeting is a crucial part of the financial management process (Hoggett *et al.* 2006). It is one thing to construct some simple accounts and diagnose the financial health of sport clubs, associations and leagues. It is another thing to make sure resources are available for allocation to the various parts of their operations. No matter how wealthy a sport organization is, its resource base will always be limited, and decisions have to be made as not only where the resources are allocated (facility maintenance, player salaries, coaching staff, equipment upgrade), but also how much each operational activity will receive. Moreover budgets are finite, and the constraining factor will always be the amount of available funds.

Budgets are really financial plans that involve the allocation of funds to strategically important operations and activities. Budgets are essential for ensuring costs and expenses are contained, and do not exceed the planned revenue. Good budgets act as a constraint on spending and provide a clear picture of the anticipated sources of revenue. Budgets come in different shapes and forms but they all share the desire to control spending patterns and make sure the spending is grounded in an appropriate level of funding and financial backing.

Benefits of budgeting

A good system of budgeting is crucially important for sport clubs and associations. As already noted, the sport world has become increasingly complex and the need to manage money effectively is stronger than ever. In addition, a well-planned budget is the basis for efficient management and ensuring viability over the long term. The benefits of budgeting are many. They can:

1   help anticipate the future and thereby assist the strategic planning process;
2   give a clear picture of resource needs and programme priorities;
3   signal where there may be revenue shortfalls;

4   allow management to better manage and monitor spending;
5   communicate the club or association's financial plans to key stakeholders; and
6   enable precise measures of financial performance to be made.

Types of budgets

Budgets are crucial part of the financial management process since they indicate the spending limits on different activities over particular periods of time. There are two types of budgets. On one hand there is the operational budget (which is sometimes called a recurrent budget), and on the other hand there is the capital expenditure budget (which is sometimes called an investment budget). Whereas an operating expenditure budget refers to spending on the day-to-day operations of the sport club, association or league, a capital expenditure budget refers to spending on buildings, facilities and equipment, and other tangible assets. Let us take a closer look at operational budgets.

Operational budgets

An operational budget is a statement of the anticipated levels of revenue for a period of time and how the revenue will be spent. The figures are estimates only, since there will always be unforeseen circumstances that will change the financial parameters in which a club or association conducts its affairs. As a result, the financial projections that underpinned the budget figures may not be realized due to changing economic and social conditions. For example, a sponsor may want to renegotiate its agreement, membership income may fall because of poor on-field performance, and coaching and support staff costs may blow out because of an increased demand for skilled specialists.

An operational budget aims to accurately estimate the likely level of revenue that a club or association will have to play with, and the anticipated expenses associated with the earning of that income. For every sport club and association it is crucial to ensure that revenue and expenses will balance, and at best, work toward the generation of a healthy surplus. The example in Table 10.5 illustrates what an operational budget will look like, and what items might be included.

This simple budget immediately reveals a number of important things. First it identifies the main items of revenue and spending. Clearly, in this fictitious case, the Sleepy Meadows Table Tennis Club (SMTTC) is heavily dependent on the local sponsor which just so happens to be the main hotel in town. It also shows that the day-to-day administration expenses are significant, although it would be good to have a breakdown of this item, since it might reveal specific activities like marketing or office rental that need to be monitored. Second, it also shows when the revenue is earned and the expenses are being incurred. While this is a not a cash budget it does indicate possible times of cash flow problems. However, this is unlikely to be a problem here since most of the revenue is expected to arrive early in the year. The budget consequently allows the SMTTC to monitor the balance between expense commitments and revenue collections for different parts of the financial planning period.

Operational budgets can be organized in different ways as well. For example an operational budget may be structured as a line item budget which is illustrated in Table 10.5. This involves breaking down spending and income into specific categories like administration, travel, marketing and entertainment, and applying overall spending limits to each item. All of the different activities or programmes in the organization will work to these limits. The SMTTC budget uses the line-item method in setting its forecast figures. At the same time, operational budgets can be rejigged as programme budgets or performance budgets.

Table 10.5: Sleepy Meadows Table Tennis Club operating budget

	March quarter ($)	June quarter ($)	September quarter ($)	December quarter ($)	Year total ($)
Revenue					
Donations	500	–	–	1,000	1,500
Sponsor	6,000	–	–	–	6,000
Member fees	1,400	200	200	200	2,000
Gaming	1,400	1,300	1,100	700	4,500
Total	9,300	1,500	1,300	1,900	14,000
Expenses					
General administration services	2,000	2,000	2,000	2,000	8,000
Coaching	–	–	–	–	0
Event administration	–	1,000	1,000	–	2,000
Travel	–	500	500	500	1,500
Table tennis supplies	2,000	–	–	–	2,000
Total	4,000	3,500	3,500	2,500	13,500

In Practice 10.3

Customizing budgets

A budget can also be organized as a programme budget. This involves allocating a designated amount of funds to each activity or programme. Each programme area is then allowed to spend on what they want, up to, but not beyond, the designated limit. For example the SMTTC may allocate funds to each of its junior, regional and veterans' league programmes along the lines of Table 10.6.

Each programme manager can then decide how best to distribute the funds to each of its programme activities. Programme budgets can be converted into performance budgets without too much difficulty. The strength of a performance budget is that it links the budget to the club or association's strategic plan. It forces the programme manager not only to work within the budget parameters, but also to ensure that the funds are directed to the

Table 10.6: Sleepy Meadows Table Tennis Club programme budget

	Junior league programme ($)	Regional league programme ($)	Veterans league programme ($)
Budget	4,000	8,000	2,000

achievement of relevant outcomes. In the case of the SMTTC a performance budget could take the shape shown in Table 10.7.

Table 10.7: Sleepy Meadows Table Tennis Cluberformance budget

Junior league programme	Regional league programme	Veterans' league programme
Goal: to provide activities that attract young children to the club	*Goal:* to provide activities that attract quality players through access to elite competition	*Goal:* to provide activities that balance social and competition table tennis
Anticipated outcome: increase in registered juniors	*Anticipated outcome:* all teams finish in top half of league table	*Anticipated outcome:* viable competition
Budget ($) 4,000	**Budget ($)** 8,000	**Budget ($)** 2,000

Summary

The above discussion of sport finances demonstrates that sound financial management is essential for the ongoing viability of sport organizations. The importance of having a proper system of financial planning, record keeping, monitoring and evaluation becomes increasingly crucial as sport becomes more commercialized and corporatized. A basic starting point is to identify the different ways in which funds and can be raised to underwrite the operation of a sport club, association, event or league. It is also essential that sport managers be able to design detailed budgets that provide transparent information that makes it clear as to not only what an activity, programme or event will cost to mount and operate, but also where the money will be coming from. It is equally important for sport managers to be able to understand financial statements, use them to diagnose the financial health of a club association, event or league, and subsequently manage costs and revenues to ensure a regular surplus or profit. It is particularly important to be able to distinguish between the different ways of measuring surpluses and profits, and in particular, the difference between operating and net profit.

Review questions

1   Identify the different commercial stages sport has gone through in the last 50 years, and the implications it has for sport's financial operations

2   Explain the essential features of corporate sport, and what makes it increasingly challenging to manage from a structural and financial perspective.

3   Why are budgets so fundamental to the effective management of sport clubs, associations, events and leagues?

4   Distinguish between a capital expenditure budget and an operating budget.

5   Balance sheets are important tools for monitoring and measuring the financial health of a sport organization. What comprises a balance sheet, and what does it measure?

6   Identify the main asset categories of a professional sport club, and explain under what circumstances players can be treated as assets.

7   Identify the main liability categories of a professional sport club, and explain under what circumstances long-term borrowings can be seen as either a drain on resources, or alternatively a crucial means of generating revenue and profits.

8   Surpluses and profits are important to the long-term development of sport organizations clubs since they indicate that not only were all costs covered for the period under consideration, but that there are funds available for reinvestment in the club or association's future activities and programmes. What is required for profits and surpluses to be generated, and under what circumstances can an operating profit end up leading to a net loss?

9   What is the easiest way of distinguishing a wealthy sport organization from a poor sport organization?

10 What must a sport organization do if it aims to increase its wealth and financial health over the long term?

Further reading

The four-phase model of sport's economic and financial development was first developed by Bob Stewart in Stewart (2007b) *The Games are Not the Same: The Political Economy of Football In Australia*, pp. 3–22.

For an extensive discussion of the finances of North American professional sport leagues see Howard and Crompton (2004) *Financing Sport*, where they provide a chapter-by-chapter breakdown of revenue sources, with special attention to ticket sales and broadcasting rights' fees. See also Foster *et al.* (2006) *The Business of Sports: Cases and Text on Strategy and Management*.

One of the most detailed analyses of English Premier League finances is contained in Szymanski and Kuypers (2000) *Winners and Losers*. See also Carter (2011) *Money Games*, for a lot of interesting updates on the financial structure of big time commercialized sport.

For a simple introduction to the structure and function of balance sheets, profit and loss statements and cash flow statements see Hart (2006) *Accounting Demystified*. For a more detailed and technical review of financial statements and what they say, see Hoggett *et al.* (2006) *Accounting*. See also Atrill *et al.* (2006) *Accounting: An Introduction*. For a succinct discussion of financial statements of nonprofit organizations see Anthony and Young (2003) *Management Control in Nonprofit Organizations*.

For an extensive introduction to the budgeting process see Hoggett *et al.* (2006). A detailed analysis of costing and budgeting processes is also contained in Anthony and Young (2003).

Relevant websites

For details of Manchester United FC financial position and the general financial operations of the English Premier League – www.footballeconomy.com/stats2/eng_manutd.htm
For more details on the financial operation of the International Cricket Council – http://icc-cricket.yahoo.net/publications/annual_report.php
To secure a detailed evaluation of the London Olympic games budget see the National Audit Office (NAO) Report – www.nao.org.uk/publications/0607/olympics_2012_budget.aspx
For an alternative assessment of the London Olympic Games budget, with a breakdown of the costs of various venues – www.thisislondon.co.uk/standard-mayor/article-23484734-details/ Mayor+seeks+City+financial+expert+to+check+growing+cost+of+Olympics/article.do

Budgeting for the Delhi 2010 Commonwealth Games

In 2005 London won the right to host the 2012 Olympic Games. The bid was impressive, and there is little doubt that the Games, as both a spectacle and as a major sporting event, will be a raging success. By all accounts the massive urban renewal programme that is accompanying the London Games project will also provide significant commercial and social benefits. However, it is not as clear as to whether it will be a financial success. Like all bids before it, the London Bid Committee created a budget that quickly escalated in size. But, in defence of the London Games budget, the other point to note here is that the budgets for all recent Olympic Games have also escalated in the lead up to the event. Sydney 2000 and Athens 2004 both suffered from this problem. The Beijing 2008 Olympic Games was also very costly to mount and run, and when the facilities were re-examined, it appears that no expenses were spared, and that any budget blowout was silently underwritten by the State.

In the initial draft bid document of 2003, the costs of staging the London Games were estimated to be just under £2 billion, which by previous Games standards was significant, and certainly in excess of the Sydney Games. In 2006 the budget was reset at around £3.5 million. However in March 2007, the minister for the Olympics, Tessa Jowell, announced an updated budget of £9.3 billion. This was a massive increase, and it raised the questions of (1) just what capital and operational activities the budget would cover, (2) what specific costs had been identified, or not identified, and (3) why they had escalated so much in such a short space of time. While the then Mayor of London, Ken Livingstone, optimistically confirmed that the Games Organizing Committee would aim to make a profit, there was growing concern that the Games budget was spiralling out of control.

The above examples suggest that when cities are bidding for mega-sports festivals they are very cautious about what the costs will be, but when they are chosen to stage the event, then, financially speaking, all hell breaks loose. We naively thought the 2010 Delhi Commonwealth Games would have been different for the very important and proper reason that India is a developing nation, and that as result a frugal but efficient financial plan would have been front and centre. However, a similar budget blowout appears to have occurred. So what went wrong, what budget items were so difficult to control, and could anything have been done to better manage the Games' finances?

Before we tackle the details of the Delhi budget blowout, it is instructive to begin with a brief review of the history of the Commonwealth Games. Its origins were contained in a proposal by the Reverend Astley Cooper in 1891 when he wrote an article in the London *Times* newspaper suggesting a '"Pan-Britannic-Pan-Anglican Contest and Festival" be organized every four years as a means of increasing the goodwill… and understanding of the "British Empire"'. While the idea was warmly received, it lay dormant for nearly 20 years. However, in 1911 it was decided to hold a 'Festival of the Empire' in London to celebrate the coronation of King George V. As part of the festival an inter-Empire sports championship was held in which teams from Australia, Canada, South Africa and the United Kingdom competed in events such as boxing, wrestling, swimming and athletics (Dheensaw 1994).

The First World War intervened in 1918, but the idea was once again revisited, when, in 1928, Melville Marks Robinson of Canada was invited to organize the first

British Empire Games. The inaugural Games were held in 1930 in Hamilton, Ontario, Canada, and on the basis of what turned out to be worthwhile experience, it was resolved to mount something similar every four years. The Games were held in Sydney in 1938, were discontinued during the Second World War, but were resurrected in 1950 when they were staged in Auckland, New Zealand. This was the beginning of a golden period for the Games, and over the following 60 years many memorable events were witnessed (Dheensaw 1994). The 2006 Melbourne Games was a cultural and sporting highlight, and confirmed Melbourne's status as a world leader in the staging of mega-sport-events. During this period a number of name changes were also made. The name changed to British Empire and Commonwealth Games in 1954, to the British Commonwealth Games in 1970, and assumed the current name of the Commonwealth Games in 1978.

The 2010 Commonwealth Games, the twenty-fourth, succinctly known as CWG2010, were held in Delhi, India, in October 2010. It was the first time that the Commonwealth Games had been held in India and the second time it was held in Asia, with Kuala Lumpur, Malaysia's capital city, having staged the festival in in 1998. Just over 6,000 athletes from 71 nations competed in 21 sports and 272 events. It was big, and in fact was the largest international multi-sport event ever to be staged in India, eclipsing the Asian Games of 1951 and 1982.

While the opening and closing ceremonies were successfully delivered at the Jawaharlal Nehru Stadium, it was generally agreed that there were many organizational teething-troubles during the early stages of the Games. Crowds were also very thin during the first week of the Games. Despite these problems the Games were enjoyed by not only most of the people who attended, but also by the athletes themselves. The television broadcasts were professionally produced, and the events themselves were often quite memorable, with many outstanding individual results.

As is always the case with these type of events, the initial total budget estimates by the Indian Olympic Association in 2003 for hosting the Games were highly optimistic at around Rs.1,600 crore, which converted to around US$360 million. This was quite a conservative figure for such a big event – and for some critics, frighteningly low – but it was considered reasonable in view of India's world-renowned capacity to deliver solid results with meagre resources. However, by 2006, the event budget had escalated and projections at the time has touched Rs.5,200 crore, or US$1.3 billion, nearly a four-fold increase. A report of the Standing Committee on Human Resource Development provided a revised budget breakdown, and the following figures were published:

- the conduct/operation of the games would now cost Rs.900 crore, or $200 million;
- the Games Village would now cost Rs.955 crore, or $220 million;
- venue infrastructure, but without furnishing, was now set at Rs.1,700 crore, or $380 million;
- civil infrastructure came in at Rs.1,300 crore, or $294 million; and
- the Indian contingent's training programme would cost Rs.300 crore, or $70 million.

In early 2010 another review found that the Games budget was out of control, and had increased exponentially. Many explanations were given for the blowout, and included things like (1) there was a bout of steep inflation, (2) all projects have been delayed, (3) waste and inefficiencies were the rule rather than the exception, and (4) some projects had been mismanaged. It was also hinted that some additional 'shadowy' practices – that is, bribery – had occurred, but they were largely anecdotal. In a climate of high anxiety the following points were noted:

- The Commonwealth Games Village, which had an initial 2003 budget estimate of Rs.465 crore, or $100 million, was now Rs.1400 crore or about $230 million. In addition capital losses had occurred because many apartments remained unsold, and the Indian government was forced to buy them off contractors.
- The budget for 11 stadia was Rs.1,200 crore, or $280 million in 2003, but in the space of seven years had risen to Rs.5,000 crore, or $1.2 billion. Construction was also way behind deadline, which was another concern that had to be monitored.
- Works on road flyovers were altered midway, and new unplanned additions had to be made. The budget for this item came in at Rs.1,700 crore, or $380 million.
- Streetscaping was another unplanned expenditure with a budget of Rs.1,000 crore, or $250 million.
- Security, too – and not surprisingly – had been allocated additional expenditure with a revised budget of Rs.370 crore, or $80 million.
- In the light of frequent delays, event planning also suffered. What was estimated to cost Rs.920 crore, or $240 million in 2003, now had a budget estimate figure of Rs.2,307 crore, or $550 million.

As the Games approached, the official total budget – which took into account both capital and operating items – accelerated to an estimated Rs.11,500 crore, which, at the then exchange rate, weighed in at US$2.6 billion, a figure which had crucially excluded non-sports-related infrastructure development. The American publication *Business Today* reckoned this was hopelessly conservative, and claimed that the Games actually cost Rs.60,000 crore, or US$13.3 billion, when all the related urban renewal projects had been included. Whatever the precise number was, it was agreed that the 2010 Delhi Commonwealth Games were probably the most expensive ever, and reached a figure that was never envisaged. So why did things go so horribly wrong?

In the first place, the organization of CWG 2010 was beset by delays. In January 2010, the Indian Olympic Association vice-chairman Raja Randhir Singh expressed concern that Delhi was not up to speed in forming and organizing its Games committee. And, following a 2009 Indian government report showing two-thirds of venues were behind schedule, the Commonwealth Games Federation president Mike Fennell stated that the slow progress constituted a serious risk to the whole event. Singh also called for a revamp of the Games' Organizing Committees. A.K. Walia, the Indian finance minister also noted that that so many things had come at the last moment, and cited the 'street-scaping project as a case in point'. He went on to say that while the Indian government was looking at international sporting events as a chance to increase their urban infrastructure, it had actually resulted in several projects being approved which had no direct relation to the Games, but which had in fact been included in the budget allocation. In addition, all of this was framed by allegations of long delays, and chronic corruption amongst many of the event planners and organizers. It was a very bad gig indeed!

But, even more to the point, why is there a budget blowout at nearly every modern-day mega-sports-festival? Are the people drawing up the budget estimate incompetent, or are they so optimistic that they cannot face the reality of a high cost operation? Or, alternatively, do they decide that escalating costs is part of the essential nature, or, indeed, the embedded character of the mega-sport-event 'beast', and that it just cannot be controlled, whatever is done?

Case study questions

1 What exactly were the 2003 budget estimates, and what had happened to them by 2006?

2 By how much did the budget estimate figures actually rise between 2003 and 2010?

3 Were there any specifically serious cost blowouts? Do these figures surprise, and if so, why? What went wrong?

4 Is there a way out of this financial and budgeting impasse for future mega-sport-events and festivals?

5 What budgeting advice would you give to the organizers and host cities of the 2012 and 2016 Olympic Games, and the 2014 Commonwealth Games?

Chapter 11

Sport marketing

Overview

The principles and tools of sport marketing are essential knowledge for sport managers to be able to position their sport club, player, code or event in the highly competitive sport market. This chapter examines the marketing of sporting organizations, sport leagues and codes, players and athletes, sporting equipment and merchandise, and sporting events. The purpose of this chapter is to overview the key concepts of sport marketing, with special emphasis on the process of sport marketing as outlined in the Sport Marketing Framework provided.

After completing this chapter, the reader should be able to:

- explain the key concepts of sport marketing;
- describe the process of sport marketing using the steps of the Sport Marketing Framework;
- define the role of strategy, positioning and branding in sport marketing; and
- understand how to deploy the sport marketing mix.

Defining sport marketing

Marketing generally refers to the process of planning and implementing activities which are designed to meet the needs or wants of customers with particular attention on the development of a product, its pricing, promotion and distribution. Marketing seeks to create an exchange, where a customer or consumer relinquishes money for a product or service that they believe is of equal or greater value. Sport marketing is focused on satisfying the needs of sport consumers, or those people who use sport-related goods or services through playing sport, watching or listening to sport, buying merchandise, collecting memorabilia or using sporting goods. There are two dimensions to sport marketing: the marketing *of* sports and marketing *through* sports. The first dimension is the marketing *of* sport products and services directly to consumers such as sporting equipment, professional competitions, sport events and facilities, and recreational clubs. The second dimension involves the marketing of other, non-sport products and services *through* sport. Some examples include a professional athlete endorsing a food or fashion brand, a corporation sponsoring a sport event, or even a drinks manufacturer arranging to have exclusive rights to provide their products at a sport event.

In order for a sport organization to be successful, it must mean something to sport consumers. In practice, this demands that a consumer is aware of the sport organization, its brand and the products or services it offers, and has responded to them in a positive way. The process of cultivating such a response is known as branding, and when a sport brand has carved out a firm place in the market and in consumers' minds, then it is said that it is positioned. The consequence of successful branding and the acquisition of strong market positioning is an ongoing relationship between a sport brand and its users.

Sport marketing is therefore best understood as the process of planning how a sport brand is positioned, and how the delivery of its products or services are to be implemented in order to establish a relationship between a sport brand and its consumers. This may be achieved by the marketing *of* a sport brand, or marketing *through* a sport brand.

The Sport Marketing Framework

The Sport Marketing Framework puts the sport marketing definition into practice by providing an approach to meeting sport consumers' needs. The Framework outlines a step-by-step process for planning and implementing the key principles of sport marketing. The Sport Marketing Framework involves four stages:

1   identify sport marketing opportunities;
2   develop a sport marketing strategy;
3   plan the marketing mix; and
4   implement and control the strategy.

Stage 1 of the Sport Marketing Framework, identify sport marketing opportunities, involves analysing the conditions of the external marketplace, considering the conditions within the sport industry specifically and examining the activities of competitors. This stage also involves studying the internal capabilities of a sport organization by identifying its goals and limitations. Finally, in order to identify marketing opportunities, it is necessary to collect information about market circumstances with a particular emphasis on existing customers and other potential consumers.

After all of this information has been collected and analysed, Stage 2 of the Framework, develop a sport marketing strategy, may be undertaken. Stage 2 involves determining the direction of the sport marketing programme, taking into account what was learned during Stage 1. It is important at this stage to document the strategy with both objectives and performance measures in order to keep it on track, and ultimately to evaluate whether the strategy was successful.

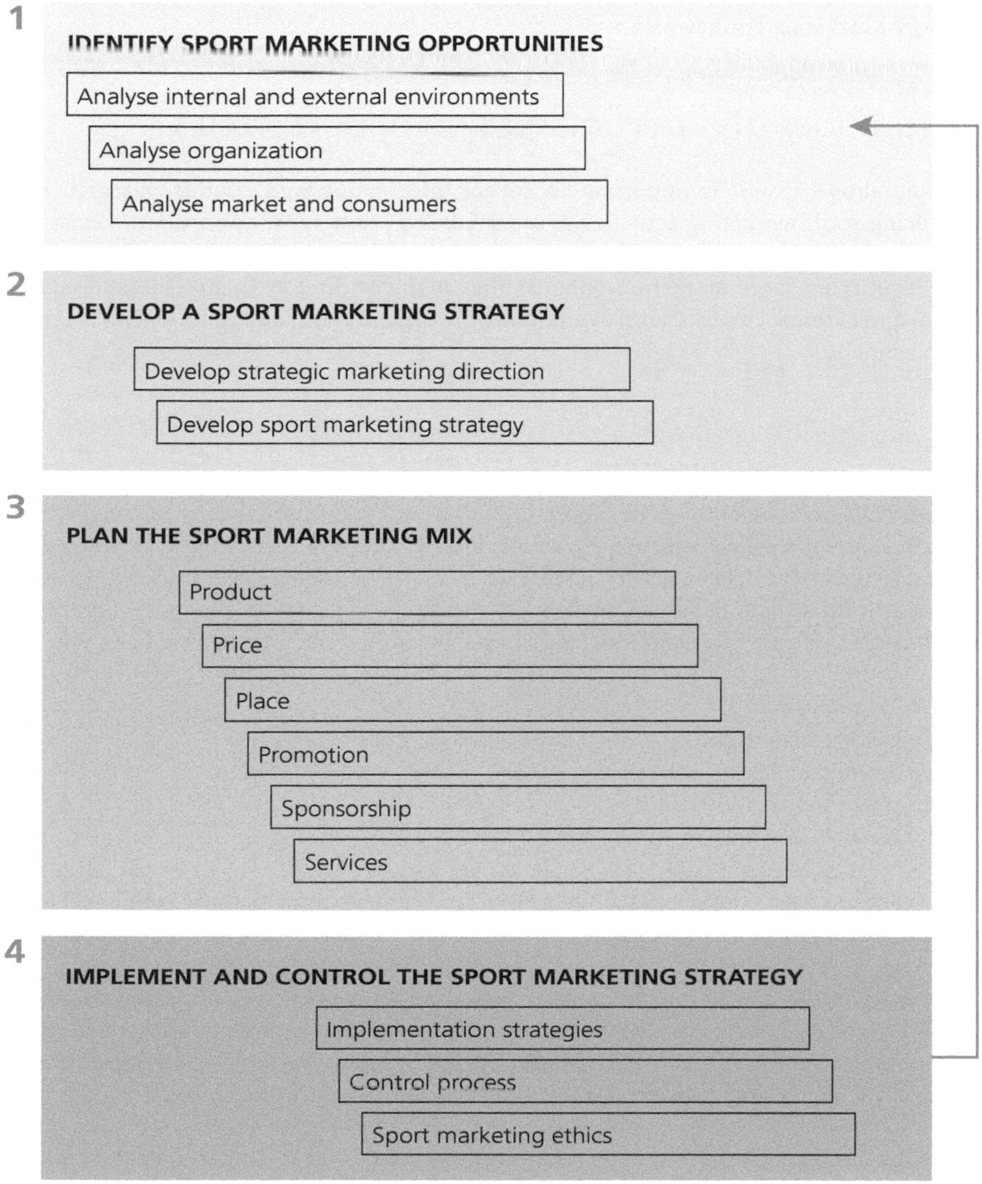

1

IDENTIFY SPORT MARKETING OPPORTUNITIES

Analyse internal and external environments

Analyse organization

Analyse market and consumers

2

DEVELOP A SPORT MARKETING STRATEGY

Develop strategic marketing direction

Develop sport marketing strategy

3

PLAN THE SPORT MARKETING MIX

Product

Price

Place

Promotion

Sponsorship

Services

4

IMPLEMENT AND CONTROL THE SPORT MARKETING STRATEGY

Implementation strategies

Control process

Sport marketing ethics

Figure 11.1: **The Sport Marketing Framework.**

Once the direction is set, the specific tactics of the strategy can be specified revolving around how to distinguish or 'differentiate' the sport organization's brand and products in the market, deciding on to whom the strategy is targeted towards to (segmentation), and what marketing mix (the product offering, pricing strategies, promotional strategies and distribution systems) will be employed. Stage 3 of the Framework involves the precise determination of the sport marketing mix and how they will combine to achieve the strategy set out. Finally, Stage 4, implement and control the strategy, involves measuring outcomes and taking remedial action so that the plan stays on target. Figure 11.1 provides an illustration of the Sport Marketing Framework.

Stage 1: Identify sport marketing opportunities

This step shows that it is important to collect information and conduct research before introducing sport marketing activities. It is essential to know what opportunities exist in the marketplace, what competitors are doing, what can be delivered and what consumers actually want. Identifying sport marketing opportunities involves three elements: (1) analysing the internal and external environment; 2) analysing the organization; and 3) analysing the market and consumers.

Analyse the internal and external environment

The first element in identifying sport marketing opportunities involves assessing the internal and external environments of the sport organization. The internal environment refers to the conditions in which a sport organization undertaking the marketing process is placed. The external environment refers to the market in which the sport organization is operating, including the broad national/global environment, the sport industry and the sport organization's competitors. There are five main tools for conducting an internal and external analysis:

1   SWOT analysis;
2   competitor analysis;
3   five forces competitor analysis;
4   organizational analysis; and
5   market and consumer research.

Given that these aspects of internal and external analysis overlap with those conducted for any strategic planning and are covered in more detail in Chapter 5, they will only be mentioned briefly here.

The term SWOT is an acronym for the words strengths, weaknesses, opportunities, threats. The SWOT analysis can be divided into two parts. The first part represents an internal analysis of an organization, which can be summarized by its strengths and weaknesses. Strengths are those things an organization does well and weaknesses are the things an organization finds difficult to do well. The second part of the SWOT technique is concerned with external factors, or opportunities and threats. Opportunities could include environmental situations which could be used to the organization's advantage. The SWOT analysis influences what a sport organization is capable of achieving in their marketing plan and highlights potential areas in which there might be an opportunity.

A competitor analysis focuses on the external environment by revealing opportunities or threats associated with other organizations in the same marketplace. A competitor analysis should examine several kinds of competitors: *direct* competitors who produce a similar product or service; *secondary* competitors who sell *substitute* products that meet similar customer needs but in a different way; and *indirect* competitors who sell different products and services altogether that might satisfy consumers' needs. A competitor analysis should consider a wide range of variables, including their strategies, strengths, vulnerabilities and resources, and as well as their next likely actions.

In addition to conducting a competitor analysis, it is possible to conduct a five forces analysis which focuses on five forces which drive competition in the sport industry. It is used to help work out whether the industry is an attractive one to conduct business in and whether there is scope for existing or new products to be developed. The five forces are described in detail in Chapter 5.

Analyse the organization

The second component of Stage 1 involves understanding the purpose, aims and goals of the sport organization developing the plan, as well as understanding the needs of its stakeholders. The first three of these elements can be determined by locating (or if necessary developing) the mission statement, vision statement and objectives of the sport organization. More about these can be found in Chapter 5.

Stakeholders are all the people and groups that have an interest in a sport organization, including, for example, its employees, players, members, the league, association or governing body, government, community, facility owners, sponsors, broadcasters and fans. A marketing strategy can be strongly influenced by the beliefs, values and expectations of the most powerful stakeholders. As a result, careful analysis of the goals and objectives of each stakeholder must be completed before a strategic direction can be set.

Conduct and examine market and consumer research

The final step in the first stage is to conduct and examine market research. Market research means gathering information about the market and the consumers it contains. It is the process of learning about the marketplace and what consumers want, listening to their desires and expectations, and determining how to satisfy them. It is also used to determine whether consumers have reacted to a marketing plan as expected.

In general there are two broad types of market research: quantitative and qualitative. Quantitative research gathers statistical information which is superficial but diverse. The most common method of gathering quantitative information is to conduct a survey or questionnaire. Qualitative research gathers non-numerical information (such as words from an interview of a person). Qualitative information is in-depth, and usually gathered from a narrow and relatively small sample of people. Common types of qualitative research in sport include focus groups, suggestion boxes and complaint analysis. This information is pivotal in deciding what kinds of products and services should be offered to sport consumers.

Stage 2: Develop a sport marketing strategy

The second stage of the Sport Marketing Framework involves two components: (1) develop strategic market direction; and (2) develop a sport marketing strategy. With the information-gathering stage completed, the direction of the sport marketing strategy can be determined and documented in the form of objectives and performance measures. These act as a guide through all the coming stages of the Sport Marketing Framework. Next, the actual sport marketing strategy can be decided in the form of a positioning approach that differentiates the sport organization's brand and product offerings from competitors and segments the market into target groups.

Develop the strategic marketing direction

A marketing objective is a goal that can realistically be achieved as the result of the marketing strategy. It can be expressed as a sentence that highlights what will occur as a result of marketing activities. There are basically four different types of marketing objectives that sport organizations might wish to pursue: (1) higher levels of participation or involvement; (2) on-field performance; (3) promotion of messages about the sport or its benefits; and (4) profit.

For each objective set it is important to add a performance measure. In this case, the term means a way of objectively estimating, calculating or assessing whether the objective has been achieved. It usually involves finding a way to quantify or put a number to the objective.

Develop a sport marketing strategy

Assuming that sport marketing objectives and performance measures have been set, the second part of Stage 2 can be undertaken by developing the actual sport marketing strategy. The process of developing a sport marketing strategy requires four steps. Steps 1 and 2 are associated with market segmentation, Step 3 is the choice of market positioning strategy, and Step 4 involves determining the marketing mix.

Market segmentation is a term that describes the process of categorizing groups of consumers together, based on their similar needs or wants. A market is the total group of potential consumers for a product and includes retailers, businesses, government, media and individuals. Market segmentation is a process of breaking this total group down into smaller groups based on a characteristic that the consumers have in common like age, gender, sporting interests or attendance levels. Once a particular segment or segments of the market have been targeted, it is possible to customize the product and marketing strategies to meet their specific needs.

The process of market segmentation involves two steps. First, the market must be divided into subgroups based on a common feature or features. This can be done with the help of market research. There are six common factors that are often used to divide a market into subgroups: (1) demographic; (2) socio-economic; (3) lifestyle (psychographic); (4) geographic; (5) product behaviour; and (6) product benefits. After the market is divided into subgroups, the segments to be targeted must be specified. The segment or segments chosen must be big enough and different enough from the others to justify the effort.

There are three approaches to segmentation: focused segmentation; multiple segmentation; and undifferentiated segmentation. Focused segmentation occurs when one segment only is chosen and one marketing mix is customized for it. Multiple segmentation involves choosing more than one segment, and then developing one marketing mix for each segment. Finally, undifferentiated segmentation involves no choice at all where the entire market is considered a legitimate and worthwhile target.

Once decisions have been made about market segmentation, the next step is to choose a market positioning strategy for each segment identified. Market positioning refers to how a sport organization would like consumers to think and feel about their brand and its product offering when compared to competitors. For example, does a sport organization want to be thought of as offering luxury, high quality, or basic, value-for-money, products? Do they see it as conservative and reliable, or exciting and changeable? There are many different positioning strategies that can be selected that may suit the segment that is being targeted. It is important that the positioning strategy reflects a form of differentiation. That is, the positioning strategy must communicate to each target segment that the sport organization's brand and product offerings are special or different in some way from others available. It may be on the basis of the components of the product offerings, the quality of the products or services delivered, the price at which they are offered or even the method by which they are delivered. If Stage 1 has been completed carefully, there should be many possibilities for capitalizing on market opportunities that align strongly with the internal capabilities of the sport organization. Like all strategic decisions, market positioning and differentiation should reflect a match between external opportunities and internal competitive advantages.

The idea of branding is closely linked with positioning. A brand is like an identifying badge (often a name or a logo) that helps consumers recognize a product or an organization. A brand becomes linked with the consumers' opinions and views of the sport organization. Because branding and positioning are linked, it is important to keep branding, segmentation and positioning strategies closely related.

In Practice 11.1

The real brand: only on Twitter
Athletes and clubs must to do more than perform on-field. They also need to develop and maintain an effective social media presence. In the past few years, hundreds of teams and individual athletes have recognized the potential in social media platforms to build brand equity, and have begun to use Twitter, Facebook and blog sites to communicate with fans. Twitter is one of the more recent additions in the social media toolkit for many teams and athletes who have begun to tweet small bites of information to interested consumers on a daily basis. It offers a platform where almost anything goes, from commentary on player drafts, injury updates, game reviews, post-game quotes, statistics and even locker-room rifts. Chad OchoCinco, the NFL wide receiver from the Cincinnati Bengals, has tweeted about everything from his dinner plans to taunts directed at opponents in upcoming games. Orlando Magic, a team that has never won an NBA Championship, is the second most followed sport team in the world on Twitter where it offers links to game highlights, in-game updates, fixture forecasts and courtside seat giveaways. The incentives for following Orlando Magic are sometimes breathtaking, as was the case when star player Dwight Howard paid to have his one millionth Twitter follower flown over to Orlando to see a game.

Shaquille O'Neil, the recently retired Boston Celtics centre, was among the first to realize the potential of the Twitter medium and tweets to over 3.5 million followers. Shaq began tweeting in November 2008 when he discovered an imposter had been using the platform for months to send messages to hundreds of unsuspecting fans. Shaq's first tweet read 'This is the real SHAQUILLE O'NEAL', and his followers have listened to him ever since at @SHAQ (formerly @THE_REAL_SHAQ) to read his comments on topics ranging from the game itself to Oprah, fettuccini and cancer research. Like Shaq's original account name suggests, Twitter is a tool to build the idea of more 'real' relationships with customers and fans; it is a medium for promoting brand awareness and building strong brand loyalty. In fact, Twitter involves much more than providing dry information like the text found in media releases, because it allows sporting identities and teams to connect directly with fans, who receive and respond to messages in real time via their computers and mobile phones. Followers on Twitter want to experience a consistent connection with their teams and sporting heroes. Fans want to feel like they are part of the organization through constant content and 'insider' information. Moreover, fans want to believe they have access to the 'real' people in the team. This means that Twitter presents an avenue to build ideas in the minds of consumers about what a sport brand stands for. Through Twitter, a consumer will create a picture of the ideas and symbols that are connected to that person or team, such as where they eat, what they think about, what charities they support and how they perform on-field. However, it is important not to overlook the fact that Twitter is also a two-way communication tool, and that sport organizations can invite real-time feedback, gather market intelligence and nurture the growth of fan-networks.

The top ten athletes on Twitter
(According to www.tweeting-athletes.com on March 1 2011.)

1 Shaquille O'Neil, Boston Celtics – centre: 3,562,192 followers
2 Kaká, Real Madrid (Spain) – midfielder: 2,891,613 followers
3 Lance Armstrong, professional cyclist: 2,752,998 followers
4 Tony Hawk, professional skateboarder: 2,314,600 followers
5 Serena Williams, professional tennis player: 1,929,561 followers
6 Cristiano Ronaldo, Real Madrid (Spain) – winger: 1,907,886 followers
7 Dwight Howard, Orlando Magic – centre: 1,861,318 followers
8 Ryan Sheckler, professional skateboarder: 1,758,696 followers
9 Paul Pierce, Boston Celtics – forward: 1,744,228 followers
10 Chad OchoCinco Johnson, Cincinnati Bengals – wide receiver: 1,738,927 followers

Stage 3: Plan the sport marketing mix

The marketing mix is a set of strategies that cover product, price, promotions and place (distribution) and are commonly referred to as the 'four Ps'. They are collectively identified as a 'mix' because they should be combined and coordinated together in order to deploy the market positioning strategy. To the traditional four Ps it is necessary to add an additional two elements of the marketing mix: sponsorship and services. Both are already part of the marketing mix; sponsorship is part of 'promotions' and services are considered through 'product'. However, both are of central importance to sport marketing and are therefore given elevated status here.

Product

A product can include: (1) a good (physical item being sold); (2) a service being delivered; (3) an idea; and/or (4) a combination of any of these. A sport product can be defined as the complete package of benefits that a sport organization presents to sport consumers through offering goods, services and/or ideas. Sport goods are physical items that can be touched. Sport shoes, tennis rackets, memorabilia, golf balls and skateboards are examples. These goods are all tangible, meaning that they exist as physical objects. Sporting goods usually have a high degree of reliability, meaning that their quality does not change much from one product to the next. They can also be stored after they are made, because they are not perishable. Sport services will be considered independently in a forthcoming section.

A sporting product can be made up of a mixture of both goods and services. One important principle in sport marketing is to try to design products to have a mixture of tangible and intangible elements in order to help it stand out from competitors. To do this sport marketers think of the sport product as having three important variables: (1) the core benefit; (2) the actual product; and (3) the augmented product. Figure 11.2 shows that the core benefit represents the main advantage that consumers receive from buying the product. The actual product refers to the features of the product itself. As long as the core benefit of the product is wanted by consumers then developing the right features can help to make it fit their needs perfectly. The augmented product refers to any extras or extensions that are added to the features of the product. These may be additional benefits, bonus extras, or even the image of a product and how people see it.

Branding

Branding is one of the key strategies that sport marketers use to augment their products by associating them with certain ideas. The added value that a product has because of its brand name is called brand equity. Branding is much more than choosing a good name, or having

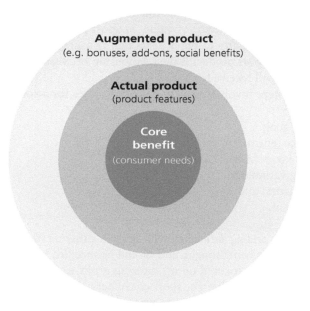

Figure 11.2: **Sport product features.**

a good logo designed; it revolves around building the brand. Once potential consumers are aware of a sport brand, it is important to help them connect certain ideas about what it stands for that reflect an intended positioning strategy. Sport marketers achieve this by manipulating the brand image, which encompasses all of the symbols and ideas that influence the image of a brand such as its name, logo, product features, product quality/performance, packaging, price, advertising, promotion, customer service and distribution channels. The ultimate goal of branding is consumer loyalty. Brand loyalty is improved through high levels of product quality, convenience of distribution, keeping up regular contact with customers and customer loyalty programmes.

Related to the idea of branding is licensing. Licensing occurs when a sport organization allows another organization to use their brand name or logo for a fee. The company who buys the right to use the brand (called the licensee) will then produce a good, service or promotion, and will give a percentage of the money they make back to the real owner of the brand (called the licensor). Licensing is a common product strategy in sport and each year it generates billions of dollars in sales internationally. It is particularly popular with merchandizing (toys, collectible cards, games, school supplies, videos, DVDs and magazines) and apparel. Sport clubs and leagues do not have the resources to make all of these products by themselves. Instead, they may make an agreement with another company to make the merchandise for them, and agree to share a percentage of profits.

Price

The way that a sport product is priced not only influences it financial impact, but also has a powerful effect on the way that consumers perceive it. The price of a sport product represents what a consumer gives up in exchange for using or owning it. Price is usually thought of in financial terms, but may include other things that a customer has to give up in order to obtain the product, such as time (e.g. waiting in a queue) or social costs (e.g. being in an aerobics class with others instead of one-on-one instruction). A useful way to think about pricing decisions is to consider them in terms of value. In sport marketing, the value of a product is a factor of how its price relates to the benefits that consumers believe they will receive in exchange. The value of a sport product is the relationship between its price and the benefits a consumer believes they will receive from it.

There are six main steps involved in setting the right price for a sport product:

1 setting a pricing goal;
2 determining price sensitivity;
3 conducting a break-even analysis;
4 assessing pricing variables;
5 selecting price tactics; and
6 setting a price point.

First, because different pricing strategies will achieve different things, it is important to determine what outcome is being sought, and should be specified in the form of pricing goals. These may range from those focused on maximizing profit to those designed to provide the product or service to as many different sport consumers as possible. Second, it is necessary to determine how sensitive consumers are to price changes. Consumers are sensitive to price if they do not buy a product when the price is high, or if they buy more of it when the price is lowered. The more sensitive they are, the more they will change their buying habits when the price changes. Third, a break-even analysis should be conducted to ascertain how many sales are needed in order to recover the costs of producing the product. Fourth, other variables that might affect price should be considered including the pricing strategies of competitors, legal or regulatory limitations that may be relevant and the impact of the other marketing mix variables. Fifth, a pricing strategy should be selected that underscores the overall market positioning strategy. There are many different types of pricing strategies that sport organizations might use including those designed to maximize profit, following competitors, setting a low introductory price, adding a flat margin to costs, using market demand as a guide and pricing according to the segment of consumers being targeted. Sixth, and finally, a price point is selected. It is important to realize that price needs to be reconsidered constantly and should always remain consistent with a market positioning strategy.

Promotion

Promotion is concerned with communicating with consumers, providing them with information about product offerings and trying to persuade them to buy. Ultimately, promotion is pivotal in shaping and cultivating brand image. Sport promotion can be defined as the way that sport marketers communicate with potential consumers to inform, persuade and remind them about their product offerings.

There are four main promotional activities known together as the promotions mix because they are typically used in concert to create an integrated promotional strategy. The promotion mix elements are: (1) advertising; (2) personal selling; (3) sales promotion; and (4) public relations. Advertising is a form of one-way communication where a sport marketer pays someone else to have their product or company identified. Common examples include television commercials, magazine and newspaper advertisements, radio spots, internet pop-ups, posters, billboards and advertisements on public transport. Personal selling involves one-to-one communication between a consumer and a salesperson such as talking to a customer on the phone, talking face-to-face or even telemarketing. Endorsements and sponsorships are two forms of personal selling that are common in the sport industry. Sales promotions are short-term programmes that aim to stimulate an increase in sales. They give consumers an incentive (or a bonus) to use the sport product. Common examples include 'two-for-one' offers, prize giveaways, competitions and free trials or samples. Public relations programmes try to build a favourable image for a sport organization, its brand and product offerings in the community. It is not paid for by the sport organization and usually involves publicity in the media in the form of a news item.

In Practice 11.2

Three cheers for merchandise sales by the Dallas Cowboys cheerleaders
The first sports licensing deal was likely to have been about an ashtray. A Chicago ceramics manufacturer reportedly approached the Chicago Cubs baseball team for permission to produce ashtrays in the shape of their home ground Wrigley Field. Philip Wrigley, then owner of the Cubs, agreed on the proviso that a royalty would be paid for each item sold. The Chicago Cubs went on to license team T-shirts, bobble-head dolls and hats.

Sports merchandizing has since become a multibillion dollar business and logos are now slapped onto almost any surface imaginable. Over the decades it has become more difficult for teams to grow merchandizing efforts as the market has become saturated with a complex array of products made available through increasingly diverse outlets. These days almost anything can be purchased from car licence plates to cookie jars and dog sweaters.

It has become more important than ever for sport organizations to understand consumer preferences in order to access new merchandizing markets. Some teams have risen to this challenge by reinventing retro-classics, trading on nostalgia for athletes of bygone eras through vintage inspired apparel. The Dallas Cowboys, which licenses some of the best-selling NFL merchandise, took a different approach when they discovered that it is not only their on-field players who can inspire merchandise sales. Promoted as 'all-American' girls, the Cowboys cheerleading squad has become a franchise in itself. Fans can purchase Mini Poms, cheerleading uniforms, necklaces, mouse mats and women's jackets. Some products readily appeal to male fans, such as the annual swimsuit calendar and the travel mug emblazoned with a blonde cheerleader. Other goods are targeted directly towards female fans including the Body Slimming Yoga DVD, which promises a 'Power Squad bod'.

The Dallas Cowboys have successfully used their cheerleading squad as a tool to boost merchandizing by reaching new market segments in an already cluttered marketplace. Licensing programmes do not work only because of promotional exposure or profit generated from sales, they can also enhance fan-affinity and increase market penetration. In the end, licensing works because of *fan identification*. It allows fans to connect with their team, and to express their emotional involvement through something as simple as stadium cushion or a sexy calendar.

Place

Place refers to the location where a sport product or service is delivered or the method of distributing a product. As a result, the terms 'place' and 'distribution' are interchangeable. Both describe how a sport product or service gets from the producer to the final consumer. The process of distribution can be explained through the concept of a sport distribution channel, which comprises a series of organizations or individuals through which a sport product must pass. There are both direct and indirect distribution channels. A direct distribution channel is short where the producer sells the product directly to the consumer. Examples include internet sales of sporting merchandise and sport services like live matches and coaching lessons. An indirect distribution channel is longer where there are a number of organizations or people (called intermediaries) involved along the way. Examples include sporting goods products like athletic shoes and equipment.

Ticket sales are one of the most important sources of revenue for sport organizations that run competitions or events. Ticket distribution is therefore an extremely important issue for sport marketers that relates to the 'place' element of the sport marketing mix. When consumers contact a ticket distributor to buy a ticket for a sport event, they are often looking for more than just a ticket. They want convenience, fast and friendly service, questions answered and a reasonable price. If a consumer becomes unhappy with the service or price they receive from a ticket distributor, they can feel dissatisfied about the sport event or club as well. It is essential that sport organizations carefully control their contracts with ticket distributors.

The sport facility is perhaps the most important distribution channel in the sport industry. There are numerous features of sport facilities that affect their success as a distribution vehicle for sport products. The important features of a sport facility can be summarized into four main areas: (1) location and accessibility; (2) design and layout; (3) facilities; and (4) customer service. Table 11.1 summarizes the variables influencing distribution in sport facilities.

Sport marketers do not always have control over the features of sporting facilities and may be able to do little to enact change without substantial resources. For this reason it is important that sport marketers attempt to bolster the distribution of sport by managing a number of other aspects of the venue. First, seating selection influences sport consumers' experience and can be used to enhance their viewing comfort as well as the marketing messages they are exposed to. Second, scoreboards and signage are an essential method of communicating marketing messages irrespective of the size of a venue, and can enhance sport consumers' experience of the event. Third, lighting and sound systems can be used to attract sport consumers at attractive times and can also improve the atmosphere of a venue and event. Fourth, transport can be used to assist sport consumers in accessing a facility and can be marketed as a special customer service. Fifth, media facilities can encourage broadcasting and general media interest in events that occur in a sport facility. Sixth, the provision of childcare facilities can be important in attracting sport consumers during non-peak periods or to special events. Seventh, selling merchandise in sport facilities is a powerful marketing tool because it provides sport consumers with a convenient way of spending more money on items that emphasize the sport product's brand image. Finally, the supply of food and beverages is amongst the most lucrative of all services that can be offered at a sport facility.

Sponsorship

Although sponsorships and endorsements are part of the promotional mix, they are so important to sport that they deserve special treatment. Sport sponsorship is a business agreement where an organization or individual provides financial or in-kind assistance to a sport property (the sport organization or person being sponsored such as an athlete, team, event, association or competition), in exchange for the right to associate itself with the sport property. Sponsorship is an example of marketing through sport. The objectives of sponsorship can vary greatly, depending on the size of the partners, the type of sponsorship, and the type of sport property being supported. Some common objectives for the sponsor are to promote the public image of their organization, to increase customer awareness, to manage their brand image and to build business relationships. In general, sponsorship helps to generate goodwill amongst consumers. The amount of goodwill generated can vary depending on the kind of sport property being sponsored, the degree of involvement that consumers have in the sport property, the time at which the sponsor becomes involved, and when/how the sponsor ceases the sponsorship.

Sponsorship works through an image transfer from the sport property to the sponsor. This image transfer works best when there is a strong sponsorship affinity, or a good fit or match between the sponsor and the sport property. Two things are particularly important for ensuring a good match: an overlap of target markets; and an overlap of brand positioning strategies. As a result, sponsorship works best when the two partners are linked to the same group of consumers and have a similar kind of message. Most sponsors support their sport sponsorship programmes by leveraging them with additional marketing activities. For a sponsor to make the most of a sponsorship they usually need to undertake other promotional activities drawing attention to it. Sometimes sponsorship leveraging can cost several times the amount that is spent on the sponsorship itself. Sponsors also have to be careful about ambush marketing, where another company (other than an official sponsor, and often a competitor

Table 11.1: Distribution variables of sport facilities

Location and accessibility	Attractive location
	Convenient to get to
	Good signage and directions
	Enough parking
	Accessible by public transport
	Accessible by different forms of public transport
	Easy to enter and exit facility
	Disabled access (ramps, lifts, washroom facilities)
Design and layout	Fits in with local area
	Attractive design (size, colour, shape, light)
	Ambience and atmosphere
	Easy to get from one area to another
	Good direction signs
	Seating arrangements with good viewing
	Weather protection
	Control of noise levels
	Areas for non-smokers and non-drinkers
	Lighting of playing area
	Protection from heat and cold
	Air circulation
	Adequate storage
	Safety issues (emergency procedures, fire detection, stand-by power, emergency communication, exits)
	Security (surveillance, control room, entrance security)
	Spectator control (zones, safe barriers, security, police)
Facility infrastructure	Variety of food and drink outlets
	Overall seating quality
	Premium seating available
	Corporate boxes and special services
	Toilets – number and location for convenient access
	Childcare facilities
	Scoreboards and screens
	Message centres and sound systems
	Emergency medical services
	Merchandise areas
	Broadcasting and media requirements
	Wireless internet connectivity and network infrastructure
Customer service	Queuing and waiting times
	Prominent information stands/booths
	Efficient, friendly and helpful staff
	Sufficient security and emergency staff
	Entrance staff, ushers
	Services for elderly, disabled and children
	Telephone enquiry service

to the official sponsor) creates marketing communications that give the impression that they are associated with the sport property. Whilst evaluating sponsorships can be difficult, it is important that a careful evaluation strategy is implemented. Being able to demonstrate that sponsorship has a positive outcome for corporations is the best way to legitimize it as a marketing technique, and to attract and retain sponsors.

In Practice 11.3

Usain Bolt and fast cash

Nicknamed 'Lightning Bolt', Jamaican sprinter Usain Bolt is a three-time World and Olympic gold medallist. He is known as the fastest man in the world and holds the Olympic records for the 100 and 200 metre sprints, in addition to the 4 × 100 metre relay record, which he holds with his Jamaican teammates. Bolt rose to prominence on the world stage at the 2002 Junior World Championships, and by 2009 he was the first man to hold both the 100 and 200 m World and Olympic titles at the same time.

After winning the 200 m title as a 16-year-old boy at the 2002 World Junior Championships, Bolt entered into a sponsorship agreement with Puma. It has proved to be an enduring relationship. At the 2008 Beijing Olympics, Bolt flashed down the 100 m track in 9.69 seconds, improving his personal best by 0.03 seconds in what Michael Johnson described as the greatest performance in the history of the 100 m event. After the race Bolt removed his Puma Complete Theseus shoes to show off for the cameras the custom made, golden sprint spikes. In a carefully orchestrated strategic marketing move, the same shoes were already available at retail, minus the personalized gold upper and the inscription Beijing 100 m Gold. The athletic shoes, just like the Usain Bolt YugoRun product currently being aggressively marketed, were designed in collaboration with Usain Bolt himself, and promised to help competitive sprinters 'maximize their talent' and 'knock those tenths off' as a result of the fastest spike used by the fastest man in the world.

Today the Puma website boasts Usain Bolt apparel (such as the long sleeve T-shirt featuring Bolt's iconic victory pose), Chasing Bolt videos, an interactive game that asks if you are 'ready to take Bolt on' and options to subscribe to Usain Bolt-only news. Puma chairman Jochen Zeitz has described Bolt as a 'revelation' who has shone a spotlight on the sport with his personality and talent. In late 2010 Bolt re-signed with Puma to the end of 2013 in what the sporting goods company described as the largest ever endorsement to be given to a track and field athlete. The deal almost certainly places Bolt among the top earners across all sports. Numerous press reports have speculated that the value of the deal is comparable to Nike's US$32 million dollar sponsorship of footballer Cristiano Ronaldo.

Puma recognizes that Usain Bolt offers more than exposure, although since the deal encompasses the 2012 London Olympics, they are likely to enjoy significant market penetration through the endorsement. However, unlike more traditional sponsorship relationships, the association between Puma and Bolt utilizes the sprinter as more than a promotional asset. Usain Bolt is also involved in product development, offering a unique perspective on performance requirements and product testing, whilst also adding valuable cachet to positioning strategies which emphasize the elite science of shoe design. Furthermore, Bolt's identity functions as an online hub for Puma, through which consumers can engage with the manufacturer and meet their needs for content, entertainment and product information.

Services

Sport services cannot be seen, felt or tasted; they are intangible because they exist only as an experience, inconsistent in terms of quality, and perishable in that they can only be offered and experienced once at any point in time. Sport services are inseparable because they are consumed at the same time as they are produced. Sport organizations offer services where their staff, team or athletes provide an experience to consumers. For example, services are offered through fitness centres, local participation-based competitions, professional sport matches and support services like sport physiotherapists.

It is a common view that when it comes to marketing a service, there are three additional Ps that should be added to the standard four. These are participants, physical evidence and process. Participants are those individuals who are involved in delivering and receiving a service. Physical evidence refers to the tangible or visual elements of a service such as a sporting facility. Process is concerned with the steps involved in delivering a service. All three of these new Ps revolve around service quality and customer satisfaction. Sport consumers are more likely to be loyal users of a service if they perceive it to be of high quality with consistent levels of delivery, leading to satisfaction.

Service quality may be seen as the degree to which a service meets the needs and expectations of customers. For example, if a customer expects a level of service that is higher than they feel they actually receive, they are likely to believe that the service is lower quality, and will tend to be dissatisfied. One key method of focusing on service quality is to work hard on ensuring that five aspects of its delivery are present. These five areas are: reliability; assurance; empathy; responsiveness; and tangibles. Reliability refers to the ability to offer a service in a consistent and dependable way. Responsiveness refers to a willingness to help customers and to provide them with the service on time. Assurance refers to the level of confidence and trust that a customer has in the service. Empathy refers to the ability to get to know customers and their needs, and to deliver a personalized service. Tangibles refer to the physical features of the service such as information booklets, equipment, appearance of staff, facilities and characteristics of a sport venue. If these aspects of service quality are emphasized, then customer satisfaction is likely to be maximized.

Stage 4: Implement and control the sport marketing strategy

The final stage of the Sport Marketing Framework is to implement and control the sport marketing strategy. Implementing a sport marketing strategy means putting the plans into action. Many sport organizations discover that it is harder to implement a marketing strategy than it sounds. There are, however, two important actions that sport marketers can perform in order to help them to implement a marketing strategy more effectively. These are to use implementation strategies and to use a control process.

A sport marketing plan is more likely to be successful if there is a clear leader or group of leaders who take responsibility for its implementation. In addition, it is important that all members of the sport marketing team have a good understanding of the marketing plan and, where possible, have all made a contribution according to their unique skills and knowledge. This demands a team comprising a combination of staff and volunteers who have the right mix of skills, experience and attitudes in the first place. Whether the implementation of the marketing strategy will be successful depends on the individual and team efforts of staff and volunteers. The final part of implementing a marketing strategy is to review and evaluate its outcomes on a regular basis. It is vital to keep track of how well the plan is going, and to make changes if things are not going as intended. A control process provides the structure to this feedback.

The sport marketing control process has five main steps. The first step involves setting performance measures. These should already be in place in accordance with Stage 2 of the Sport Marketing Framework. The second step is to put the performance measure into action by evaluating performance before and after the marketing strategy has been implemented, leading to the third step, a comparison of results to determine gaps, shortfall and performance successes. With these variations in the fore, the fourth step is to determine whether the variance is favourable or not, and whether intervention needs to occur. The final step is to make remedial changes to the marketing strategy and mix in order to bring it back in line with marketing objectives.

While the implementation of a sport marketing plan should align with a sport organization's objectives, it should also fit within the broader boundaries of ethical behaviour. Ethics in sport marketing typically refers to whether the traditional four Ps of the marketing mix are deployed within a moral and professional code. Mostly these include issues associated with unsafe or poor quality products, deceptive or predatory pricing, misleading or dishonest promotions and exploitative or collusive distribution. In the sporting world, other major marketing issues are concerned with publicizing the private lives of athletes, exploiting passionate fans and children who idolize sport stars through athlete endorsements of commercial products, the use of venues with unsafe facilities, unrealistic promises associated with health, fitness and weight-loss products, the use of performance-enhancing drugs and the over-pricing of high profile matches and special sport events. In short, informed, autonomous consumer decisions based on the faithful representation of the product features and its price lie at the core of responsible and ethical sport marketing.

Summary

This chapter was structured around the Sport Marketing Framework. Stage 1 is to identify sport marketing opportunities which involves undertaking several kinds of assessments: a SWOT analysis, a competitor analysis, a five forces competitor analysis, an organizational analysis, and market and consumer research. All of these analyses allow sport marketers to better understand market circumstances, consumer preferences, the sport industry, competitors' activities and the internal organization context.

Stage 2 of the Sport Marketing Framework is to develop a sport marketing strategy. This stage begins with decisions about the direction of the marketing programme, which is subsequently documented using marketing objectives and performance measures. Stage 2 also involves deciding on the basic theme of the marketing strategy. To that end, it requires the identification of the target market/s (segmentation), the positioning strategy (differentiation) and the composition of the marketing mix to deploy the strategy.

Stage 3 of the Sport Marketing Framework requires planning the sport marketing mix in detail. Here, decisions about the four Ps of marketing, the product, price, promotions and distribution (place) are determined, along with specific approaches to sponsorship and the management of sport services.

Finally, Stage 4 is to implement and control the plan. Plans are put into action, facilitated by implementation strategies. It is also essential to keep the plan on track by using a control process that emphasizes the comparison of the results from marketing activities with the performance indicators and objectives set in Stage 2. Remedial action is then taken to correct the plan where it has been unsuccessful, has strayed off course, or needs supplementation in order to capitalize on some unexpected opportunity.

Sport marketing revolves around the premise of satisfying the needs of sport consumers, in so doing cultivating a relationship with them that leads to a strong brand loyalty. Sport marketing lies at the intersection of strategy, where sport organizations focus on what they are good at, and market opportunities, where sport consumers are offered what they want. The best way of finding this intersection is to use a systematic approach like that outlined in the Sport Marketing Framework.

Review questions

1 Explain the difference between the marketing of sport, and marketing through sport.
2 What are the steps in the Sport Marketing Framework?
3 What is the relationship between sport marketing objectives and performance measures? How are these relevant to controlling the marketing plan?
4 What is the purpose of market positioning?
5 What is the difference between a sport product and a sport service?
6 What effect does pricing have on positioning? Provide an example of how price can influence a consumer's perception of a product.
7 What are the four tools of the promotions mix? Provide an example of each.
8 Provide a good example of a sponsor and sport property relationship that enjoys a high level of affinity.
9 What is the relationship between service quality and customer satisfaction?

Further reading

Ferrand, A. and Stotlar, D. (2010) 'Introduction: New perspectives in sport event marketing', *International Journal of Sport Management and Marketing*, 7(3/4): 145–155.

Kahle, L. and Close, A. (eds) (2011) *Consumer Behavior Knowledge for Effective Sports and Event Marketing*, New York: Taylor & Francis.

Pitt, L., Parent, M., Berthon, P. and Steyn, P. (2010) 'Event sponsorship and ambush marketing: Lessons from the Beijing Olympics', *Business Horizons*, 53(3): 281–290.

Rowe, D. and G. Callum (2010) 'Sport, media, and consumption in Asia: A merchandised milieu', *American Behavioral Scientist*, 53(10): 1530–1548.

Shilbury, D., Westerbeek, H., Quick, S. and Funk, D. (2009) *Strategic Sport Marketing*, 3rd edition, Sydney: Allen & Unwin.

Smith, A. (2008) *Introduction to Sport Marketing*, Oxford: Elsevier Butterworth-Heinemann.

Relevant websites

www.twitter.com
www.dallascowboyscheerleaders.com
www.puma.com/running/athletes/usain-bolt
www.london2012.com

> ### CASE STUDY

Will the real sponsor please stand up? Ambush marketing and the International Olympic Committee

The 2012 London Olympics is set to become one of the top three most expensive sporting events in history. The cost of the event will likely reach £9.3 billion, awarding it the 'bronze medal' after the 2008 and 2004 Games, which ran up bills of £25 and £10 billion respectively. As a result the London Games, like all international sporting events, would not be feasible without the support of corporate sponsors. Sponsors will not only provide cash to help bankroll proceedings, but they will also contribute technology, services, products and personnel to help the Games run smoothly.

Although modern forms of Olympic Games sponsorship began in the 1960s, it was not until the Los Angeles Games in 1984 that organizers began to maximize the potential for sponsorship dollars. Up until that time the number of sponsors sought for the event had been steadily increasing, although very few companies were able to secure global rights since they had to negotiate separately with the International Olympic Committee (IOC) and the relevant national organizing committee (Coca-Cola being a prominent exception).

Rather than attempting to boost sponsor numbers further, organizers for the 1984 Games decided to do the opposite, emphasizing exclusivity. The number of sponsors was limited to 35 whilst the amount to be paid by each one increased substantially. All contract negotiations were centralized through the IOC, opening up the opportunity for genuinely global exposure. In addition, the IOC drew up a list of commercial sectors and allowed only one corporate representative from each sector to become a partner.

As a direct result of these innovations, sponsors including Kodak, VISA and Panasonic were lured by the promise of exclusivity. They, along with others including 3M, Federal Express and Coca-Cola, were willing to pay large amounts for the promise of unparalleled exposure on the world stage. Association with the Games not only delivered international brand recognition, but sponsors were also able to align themselves with an event that conjured ideas of prestige, excellence, determination, celebration and cross-cultural tolerance.

On the back of the success of the Los Angeles experience, the TOP (The Olympic Partners) sponsorship programme was launched at the 1988 Calgary Winter Games, offering the right to use the Olympic symbols worldwide for a fee. Since that time the Games has continued to pose a unique sponsorship proposition to global corporations. However sponsorship of the games represents an opportunity incorporating some risks. Above and beyond the significant sums required to buy in, sponsors are also limited by the IOC's Clean Venue policy. In addition, they must operate under the ever-present threat of ambush marketing from their competitors.

Unlike most large-scale sporting events, the Olympic Games maintain a Clean Venue policy. This means competition occurs in space that is free of advertising and where athletes are forbidden from exhibiting sponsorship or commercial identification other than a modest trademark on apparel. The policy also limits advertising outside, around and above venues as far as possible.

The IOC claims that the Clean Venue approach protects the field of play from commercial concerns and maintains the focus on sport. It serves to protect what the

Olympic brand stands for, to defend the idea that sport belongs to everyone, and that humanity can 'build a better world through sport' with the three Olympic values of excellence, respect and friendship.

The corporate conglomerate the MARS group has tested the limits of the Clean Venue policy on more than one occasion when the IOC has clamped down on their marketing activities. This occurred, for example, when MARS dressed staff in M&M character suits and asked them to line up along the marathon route. Staff members were instructed to jump forward and wave at TV cameras as the runners flashed by. MARS argued that it was generating fun and cheering the runners on, by the IOC held firm to the idea that venues would remain free of advertising and forced MARS to abandon its strategy.

The Clean Venue concept differentiates the Games from all other sporting events and has undoubtedly increased the brand's equity. However, the provisions have also increased pressure on the IOC to ensure that sponsors get value for their investment. Since official sponsors pay a premium for an exclusive association, but must tolerate significant restrictions on their marketing efforts, TOP partners demand assurance that their competitors will not ambush the event and steal valuable exposure.

Ambush marketing occurs when a brand with no official sponsor status uses marketing strategies to imply that an association exists. It occurs when a business attempts to attach itself to a major sporting event without paying sponsorship fees. Since only one corporation from each industry sector is permitted to enjoy official status, a constant threat exists that the lure of global brand exposure will fuel the ambush marketing efforts of competitors. As a result, a key factor in being able to offer value to sponsors lies in the capacity of the IOC to reassure corporations that their investment is protected, and will not be undermined by an unexpected marketing campaign launched by a competitor.

Over the history of the Olympics numerous examples can be cited of corporations attempting to benefit from the goodwill of the Games gratis. In the 1984 Los Angeles Games, for example, Fujifilm was the official sponsor but confusion was created when Kodak sponsored the television broadcasts. Ironically, their roles were reversed at the 1988 Seoul Games.

Since the early 1980s, regulations have prevented such obvious marketing opportunities from being exploited. However, rather than eliminate ambush marketing altogether, the IOC's efforts have prompted companies to ambush in more creative ways. In a particularly blatant campaign during the 1996 Atlanta Games, Nike undermined official sponsor Reebok by dominating billboards around the host city. Reebok were dealt another blow when Linford Christie wore contact lenses embossed with the Puma logo at a press conference prior to the 100 metre final.

The IOC characterizes ambush marketing as 'cheating', and regular sponsors like Coca-Cola also take a dim view of what they call 'stealing' through ambush campaigns. In their attempts to control these threats, the IOC has begun to exert pressure on the host city to control ambush marketing. As a result, during the bidding for the 2012 Games, Queen Elizabeth II promised that Britain would deliver new legislation to protect the Olympic Charter.

Less than two weeks after London was awarded the 2012 Games, the London Olympic Bill was given its first reading in Parliament. Since then, laws have been passed aiming to protect the rights of official sponsors for the 2012 Olympic and Paralympic events, giving the London Organizing Committee the right to pursue legal action against businesses which falsely suggest an association. Amongst other restrictions, the legislation prohibits companies from using a combination of words like Olympics, London, 2012, or gold. London Olympic Games patrons will also be banned from wearing apparel with advertising logos, or carrying any promotional material from non-TOP sponsors.

The IOC has become increasingly aggressive in its protection of marketing rights and it now has a team of lawyers prosecuting organizations for any minor breaches. Most brands would normally protect their intellectual property rights through regulations related to trademarks, design rights and copyright, but the London Organizing Committee of the Olympic Games (LOCOG) now has unparalleled powers to prevent ambush marketing in 2012. Similar legal powers were set in place for the 2010 FIFA World Cup, and their experience may yield important lessons for the upcoming London Games experience.

In 2006, the South African government passed the Merchandise Marks Act to help prevent ambush marketing at their globally exposed sporting events like the World Cup of Football. Unlike the Olympics, FIFA venues allow sponsorship advertising, although ambush marketing still presents a threat. Despite the threat of litigation at the 2010 World Cup during the Holland versus Denmark match, 36 attractive young women removed their Dutch team apparel to reveal matching orange mini-dresses. The event was sponsored by Budweiser, but the dresses revealed a small logo for Dutch brewer Bavaria. The company claimed they were innocent of ambushing because the clothing had been given away with packs of beer. Regardless, FIFA filed charges against Bavaria claiming it was not sanctioned to use the World Cup brand. Two women were also charged separately by South African authorities under the Merchandise Marks Act in 2006.

The charges against the female spectators were later dropped after FIFA and Bavaria reached an out-of-court settlement. However, Bavaria undoubtedly benefited from the enormous publicity that resulted. It was not the first strike against Bavaria in the FIFA books. At the 2007 Germany World Cup, scores of Dutch men watched the match in their underwear after venue stewards ordered them to remove their orange plastic lederhosen emblazoned with the Bavaria name. We can be thankful, perhaps, that the spectators were not wearing Bavaria underwear. Given the publicity that Bavaria generated through these two events, one cannot help but wonder whether the score is Bavaria 2, Budweiser 0. Olympic Games organizers might be wise to generate alternative, more flexible strategies for responding to breaches in legislation at the 2012 event.

Case study questions

1 What is the real problem with ambush marketing?
2 What could the IOC, and other global event organizers, learn from the way that Bavaria ambush stunts at the FIFA World Cups were handled?
3 What lessons could official sponsors learn from their ambushing competitors?

Chapter 12

Sport governance

Overview

This chapter reviews the core concepts of organizational governance, explores the unique features of how sport organizations are governed and summarizes the key research findings on the governance of sport organizations. The chapter also provides a summary of principles for governance within community, state, national and professional sport organizations.

After completing this chapter the reader should be able to:

- identify the unique characteristics of organizational governance for corporate and nonprofit sport organizations;
- differentiate the various models and theories of governance relevant to sport organizations;
- understand and explain the role of boards, staff, volunteers, members and stakeholder groups in governing sport organizations;
- understand some of the challenges facing managers and volunteers involved in the governance of sport organizations; and
- identify and understand the drivers of change in governance systems within sport organizations.

What is governance?

Organizational governance is concerned with the exercise of power within organizations and provides the system by which the elements of organizations are controlled and directed. Governance is necessary for all groups – nation states, corporate entities, societies, associations and sport organizations – to function properly and effectively. An organizational governance system not only provides a framework within which the business of organizations are directed and controlled but also 'helps to provide a degree of confidence that is necessary for the proper functioning of a market economy' (OECD 2004: 11). Governance deals with issues of policy and direction for the enhancement of organizational performance rather than day to day operational management decision-making.

The importance of governance and its implied influence on organizational performance was highlighted by Tricker (1984) when he noted 'if management is about running business, governance is about seeing that it is run properly' (p. 7). The Australian Sports Commission (ASC) defines governance as 'the structures and processes used by an organization to develop its strategic goals and direction, monitor its performance against these goals and ensure that its board acts in the best interests of the members' (ASC 2004). Good organizational governance should ensure that the board and management seek to deliver outcomes for the benefit of the organization and its members and that the means used to attain these outcomes are effectively monitored.

A 1997 report to the Australian Standing Committee on Recreation and Sport (SCORS) identified a major concern amongst the sporting community, which was the 'perceived lack of effectiveness at board and council level in national and state sporting organizations' (SCORS Working Party on Management Improvement 1997: 10). Major sport agencies in the UK, New Zealand and Canada have also identified improving governance of sport organizations as a strategic priority. Failures in the governance of national sport organizations such as the Australian Soccer Association (2003), Athletics Australia (2004), Basketball Australia (2007) and Cricket Australia (2011), together with reviews of professional sport governance such as those conducted by the Football Governance Research Centre at the University of London, continue to highlight the importance of developing, implementing and regulating sound governance practices in both amateur and professional sport organizations.

Corporate and nonprofit governance

The literature on organizational governance can be divided into two broad areas: (1) corporate governance that deals with the governance of profit-seeking companies and corporations that focus on protecting and enhancing shareholder value; and (2) nonprofit governance that is concerned with the governance of voluntary-based organizations that seek to provide a community service or facilitate the involvement of individuals in social, artistic or sporting activities.

Studies of corporate governance have covered 'concepts, theories and practices of boards and their directors, and the relationships between boards and shareholders, top management, regulators and auditors, and other stakeholders (Tricker 1993: 2). The literature in this field focuses on the two primary roles of the board in first, ensuring conformance by management and, second, enhancing organizational performance. Conformance deals with the processes of supervision and monitoring of the work of managers by the board and ensuring that adequate accountability measures are in place to protect the interests of shareholders. Enhancing organizational performance focuses on the development of strategy and policy to create the direction and context within which managers will work.

The unique characteristics of nonprofit organizations demand a governance framework different from that of the corporate firm. Nonprofit organizations exist for different reasons from profit-seeking entities, and generally involve a greater number of stakeholders in their decision-making structures and processes. The relationships between decision-makers – the governance framework – will therefore be different from those found in the corporate world. The management processes employed to carry out the tasks of the organizations might well be similar, but a fundamental difference between nonprofit and corporate organizations is found in their governance frameworks.

While many sports organizations such as major sporting goods manufacturers, athlete management companies, retail companies and venues can be classed as profit seeking, the majority of sport organizations that provide participation and competition opportunities are nonprofit. These organizations include large clubs, regional associations or leagues, state or provincial governing bodies and national sport organizations.

Is there a theory of sport governance?

Clarke (2004) provides a unique overview of the development of theories of corporate governance. Some of the important theories applied to the study of organizational governance include agency theory, stewardship theory, institutional theory, resource dependence theory, network theory and stakeholder theory. In this section we shall examine each of them in turn and assess how relevant they are to understanding the governance of sport organizations.

Agency theory proposes that shareholders' interests should prevail in decisions concerning the operation of an organization. Managers (agents) who have been appointed to run the organization should be subject to extensive checks and balances to reduce the potential for mismanagement or misconduct that threatens shareholders' interests. This has been the predominant theoretical approach to the study of corporate governance and has focused on exploring the best ways to maximize corporate control of managerial actions, information for shareholders and labour in order to provide some assurance that managers will seek outcomes that maximize shareholder wealth and reduce risk. In relation to corporations operating in the sport industry that have individual, institutional and government shareholders, this theory helps explain how governance systems work. For the majority of nonprofit sport organizations, which have diverse stakeholders who do not have a financial share in the organization (aside from annual membership fees), agency theory has limited application.

Stewardship theory takes the opposite view to agency theory and proposes that rather than assume managers seek to act as individual agents to maximize their own interests over those of shareholders, managers are motivated by other concepts such as a need for achievement, responsibility, recognition and respect for authority. Thus, stewardship theory argues that managers' and shareholders' interests are actually aligned and that managers (agents) will act in the best interests of shareholders. This theoretical view can also be applied to sport corporations such as Nike, FoxSports or a listed professional football club franchise. The application of either agency or stewardship theory is dependent on the actions of the managers (who choose to act as agents or stewards) and the view of shareholders (who create either an agent or stewardship relationship through their conscious choice of governance framework). Stewardship theory is arguably more applicable than agency theory to the study of nonprofit sport organizations where managers may have a connection to the sport as an ex-player, coach or club official and therefore have a deeper sense of commitment to the organization and are more likely to act as stewards.

Agency and stewardship theories focus on the internal monitoring issues of governance. Three theories that seek to explain how organizations relate to external organizations and acquire scarce resources are institutional theory, resource dependence theory and network theory. *Institutional theory* argues that the governance frameworks adopted by organizations are the result of adhering to external pressures of what is deemed acceptable business practice, including legal requirements for incorporation. Such pressures reflect wider societal concerns for proper governance systems to be employed. Further, if all organizations of a similar type and size seek to conform to these pressures they are likely to adopt very similar governance frameworks, a situation know as institutional isomorphism. Evidence of this is apparent throughout club-based sporting systems such as in Canada, Australia, New Zealand and the UK where most national and state or provincial sporting organizations operate under remarkably similar governance frameworks.

Resource dependence theory proposes that in order to understand the behaviour of organizations, we must understand how organizations relate to their environment. Organizations paradoxically seek stability and certainty in their resource exchanges by entering into interorganizational arrangements which require some loss of flexibility and autonomy in exchange for gaining control over other organizations. These interorganizational arrangements take the form of mergers, joint ventures, co-optation (the inclusion of outsiders in the leadership and decision-making processes of an organization), growth, political involvement or restricting the distribution of information (Pfeffer and Salancik 1978). Such arrangements have an impact on the governance structure adopted, the degree to which stakeholders are involved in decision-making, and the transparency of decision-making.

A final theory that attempts to explain elements of governance based on how organizations relate to external organizations is *network theory*. Network theory posits that organizations enter into socially binding contracts to deliver services in addition to purely legal contracts. Such arrangements create a degree of interdependency between organizations, and facilitate the development of informal communication and the flow of resources between organizations. This is particularly true of sport organizations that, for example, rely on personal contacts to facilitate the success of major events by securing support from high-profile athletes, using volunteers in large numbers from other sports organizations and depending on government support for stadia development of event bidding. Network theory can help explain how governance structures and processes, particularly concerning the board of sports organizations, evolve to facilitate such informal arrangements.

These three theories emphasize the need to examine governance in terms of the external pressures that organizations face and the strategies, structures and processes they put in place to manage them. Such an approach offers a more realistic view of how and why organizations have a particular governance framework than agency and stewardship theories.

Stakeholder theory provides another perspective for examining the relationship between organizations and their stakeholders. It argues for conceptualizing a corporation as a series of relationships and responsibilities which the governance framework must account for. This has important implications for corporations acting as good corporate citizens and particularly for sport organizations that need to manage a myriad of relationships with sponsors, funding agencies, members, affiliated organizations, staff, board members, venues, government agencies and suppliers.

Much of the writing and research on organizational governance has been based on corporations rather than nonprofit entities. Applying a particular theory to the study of sport organizations must be done with regard to the type and industry context of the sport organization being studied. Sport organizations and their governance frameworks have diverse elements that prevent the development of an overarching theory of sport governance.

The value of the theories presented here is that each of them can be used to illuminate the governance assumptions, processes, structures and outcomes for sport organizations.

Governance structural elements

The governance elements of a corporate or profit-seeking sport organization are the same for any general business operation. These elements can include paid staff, including a CEO who may or may not have voting rights on a board, a board of directors representing the interests of many shareholders (in the case of publicly listed company), or directors who are direct partners in the business. The real differences in governance elements can be found in volunteer sport organizations (VSOs).

A simple governance structure of VSOs is depicted in Figure 12.1 and comprises five elements: members, volunteers, salaried staff, a council and a board. Normally, members meet as a council (usually once per year at an annual general meeting) to elect or appoint individuals to a board. If the organization is large enough, the board may choose to employ an executive and other paid staff to carry out the tasks of the organization. Together with a pool of volunteers, these employees deliver services to organizational members. The board acts as the main decision-making body for the organization and therefore the quality of its activities is vital to the success of the organization.

Members of a VSO can be individual players or athletes, or in some cases, members are classified as other affiliated organizations such as a club that competes in a league provided by a regional sports association. Members can also be commercial facility providers such as basketball, squash or indoor soccer stadiums. The membership council comprises those people or organizations that are registered members and may be allocated voting rights according to membership status. The board comprises individuals who have been elected, appointed or invited to represent the interests of various membership categories, geographic regions or sporting disciplines in decision-making. The senior paid staff member, often designated the

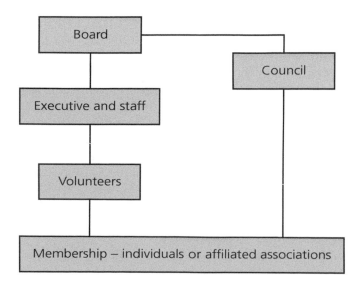

Figure 12.1: Typical governance structure of a volunteer sport organization.

Sport governance

CEO, is employed by and reports directly to the board. Other paid staff are appointed by the CEO to assist in performing various organizational tasks. These staff must work with a variety of volunteers in sport to deliver essential services such as coaching, player and official development, marketing, sport development and event delivery. Finally, a wide range of stakeholders such as sponsors, funding agencies, members, affiliated organizations, staff, board members, venues, government agencies and suppliers must be consulted and managed in order for the organization to operate optimally.

The majority of national and state or provincial sport organizations that provide participation and competition opportunities in club-based sporting systems are governed voluntarily by elected office bearers, who fill positions on either committees or boards. Most of these VSOs operate under a federated delegate system with club representatives forming regional boards, regional representatives forming state or provincial boards and state or provincial representatives forming national boards.

This traditional governance structure has been criticized for being unwieldy and cumbersome, slow to react to changes in market conditions, subject to potentially damaging politics or power plays between delegates and imposing significant constraints on organizations wishing to change. On the other hand, the majority of sports organizations still use this model today and value its ability to ensure members have a say in decision-making, the transparency of decisions and the autonomy granted to organizations at every level of the system. In Practice 12.1 explains a typical governance structure of a professional sports league.

In Practice 12.1

British Basketball League
The top men's professional basketball league in the UK is the British Basketball League (BBL). The BBL is an independent company owned by its 12 member franchises, each with an equal shareholding in BBL. In season 2011–2012 the franchises were the Cheshire Jets, Essex Pirates, Glasgow Rocks, Guildford Heat, Jelson Homes DMU Leicester Riders, Marshall MK Lions, Mersey Tigers, Newcastle Eagles, UCP Marjon Plymouth Raiders, Sheffield Sharks, Worcester Wolves, and the Worthing Thunder. Each franchise has a representative on the BBL board of directors who oversee the operation of a central BBL office in Leicester, UK, which manages administration, marketing and media functions. The interesting aspect of the governance structure of the BBL is that each club operates as a franchise in designated areas across the UK in order to maximize commercial and media value within their local community.

Unlike other sports where second division champions are promoted to replace the bottom ranked team in the top league, the BBL operates independently of the second tier competition, the English Basketball League (EBL). There is no promotion and relegation between the BBL and the EBL, and EBL clubs cannot join the BBL based on their performances in official competition alone. However, EBL clubs and any other organizations can apply for a franchise from the BBL.

Prospective licensees can apply to join the BBL by submitting a detailed business plan to the BBL franchise committee that specifies venue details, proof of an acceptable level of financial backing and an explanation of how the franchise will be sustainable. Because government funding for basketball goes to England Basketball, the BBL receives no government financial support. Instead, it derives its income from sponsorship, media partnerships, merchandizing and ticket sales. Commercial and media rights generate the largest portion of income for the league and clubs.

The challenge of organizing a viable professional basketball league in a country dominated by football, rugby and cricket is significant. Competition for sponsorship pounds, access to appropriate venues, securing media rights and maintaining market share in a crowded professional sport market are all challenges for the directors of the BBL and the managers of their member clubs. The simple organizational structure adopted by the BBL in using the US-style franchise system is an attempt to combat these challenges. The governance structure allows the league and clubs to plan for future expansion, manage income and costs across all elements of the organization, and ensure equitable decision-making amongst the member clubs.

Source: British Basketball League website at www.bbl.org.uk

Governance models

There are three generic governance models that can be applied to nonprofit sport organizations: the traditional model outlined by Houle (1960, 1997); the Carver policy governance model (1997); and the executive led model (after Block 1998; Drucker 1990; Herman and Heimovics 1990, 1994). A governance model can be defined as a set of policies and practices that outline the responsibilities of the various governance elements and the processes used to carry out the governance function. All of the following models relate to organizations that are governed by boards that employ a paid executive and staff as opposed to more informal organizations that maintain a collective and informal structure. The models are more relevant to these organizations because boards that carry out the 'hands on' work of the organization, such as a small community club, are 'usually so strongly influenced by personalities and special circumstances that few generalizations can be made about their general nature or how they may be improved' (Houle 1997: 3).

Traditional model

Houle (1960, 1997) outlined a 'traditional model' for governance of nonprofit organizations that is based on five elements. The first of these is the human potential of the board where the board ensures a systematic recruitment process is in place accompanied with ongoing board member development. Second, the work of the board is structured according to a set of by-laws, policies are clearly defined and minutes of the board and committee meetings are consistently reported. Third, the roles of and relationships between the board, executive and staff should be well defined and developed enabling clear decision-making to occur. Fourth, the operation of the board should be undertaken in a positive group culture and based on an annual work plan, regular meetings with well-managed agendas and ongoing evaluation of the board and its work. Finally, the board has a focus on maintaining external relationships through formal and informal representation of the organization to the community. The model advocates that 'the work is done by the staff, the administration by management and the policy making by the board; in this traditional model, the board is truly in charge of the organization' (Fletcher 1999: 435).

This model has been widely used amongst nonprofit organizations and is probably the most widely used by nonprofit sport organizations. It clearly separates the tasks of staff and volunteers and highlights volunteer board members as being accountable for the organization. The model has been criticized for the idealistic view that the board alone has ultimate responsibility for the organization (Heimovics and Herman 1990), and the rather simplistic notion of the board making policy while the staff do the work (Herman and Heimovics 1990) which does not reflect the reality of the working relationships that occur in most nonprofit organizations.

Policy governance model

Carver (1997) outlines five elements of a 'policy governance' model for the effective governing board. The first of these is determining the mission and strategic direction of the organization, with a focus on the desired outcomes, rather than becoming immersed in the detail of the means to achieve them. Second, setting executive limitations or constraints for the work practices and the means that staff employ to achieve the mission set by the board. Third, establishing clear board and executive roles and relationships. Fourth, ensuring governance processes are clearly defined in areas such as board member selection and succession, the reporting of activities of the board and staff, and ensuring the board focuses on the policies of the organization rather than cases or specific issues. Finally, the board's role should be more than simply ensuring conformance to financial procedures and ethical management practice; it should also develop clear performance measures related to strategic outcomes.

Like the traditional model, Carver's model has been criticized for its 'idealized view of the board, operating above the messiness of the board-executive relationship as it really exists in nonprofit organizations' (Fletcher 1999: 436). The model also does not address the important role of the board in managing external relationships and it 'clearly subordinates the CEO to the board and expects the board alone to set the parameters of the relationship' (ibid.).

Executive led model

The executive led model, in contrast to the previous models, advocates the executive as central to the success of nonprofit organizations. Drucker (1990) argued that the ultimate responsibility for the performance of a nonprofit organization, including its governance, should rest with the executive. His views were supported by Herman and Heimovics' (1990) research that found that the reality of most boards was that they depended on their executive for information almost exclusively and looked to them to provide leadership. Hoye and Cuskelly (2003) also found this was the case in VSOs. Block (1998) argued that because the executive is working in an organization much more than the average board member, they have better access to information and therefore they must also 'be at the core of leadership and decision-making activities' (p. 107).

Board-staff relationships

The gradual introduction of professional staff into VSOs over the last 20 years has created the need for volunteers and paid staff to work together at all levels, including at the board table. This has led to some degree of uncertainty about what roles should be performed by each group and the extent to which staff and volunteers should be involved in strategic planning, policy development, performance evaluation and resource acquisition. The potential for tension between these groups as they negotiate their respective roles has been well established, as has the ongoing desire of volunteers to maintain a degree of involvement in decision-making while at the same time utilizing the expertise of paid staff to assist them in running their organizations. This then is the crux of board-staff relationships: what areas do volunteers maintain control over and which do paid staff control?

Hoye and Cuskelly (2003) found that VSO boards perform better if a degree of trust exists between the board and staff and that board leadership was shared amongst a dominant coalition of the board chair, executive and a small group of senior board members. As mentioned earlier, the executive controls the flow of information to board members and so the quality, frequency and accuracy of this information are vital to their ability to make decisions. Ensuring the board and executive work together effectively enhances this information flow and therefore the performance of the board.

Principles of good organizational governance

The notion of good organizational governance extends beyond ideas of monitoring to ensure conformance and developing to improve performance discussed earlier in this chapter. Henry and Lee (2004) provide a list of seven key principles for good organizational governance in sport organizations:

1   Transparency – ensuring the organization has clear procedures for resource allocation, reporting and decision-making.
2   Accountability – sports organizations need to be accountable to all their stakeholders.
3   Democracy – all stakeholder groups should be able to be represented in the governance structure.
4   Responsibility – the board has to be responsible for the organization and demonstrate ethical stewardship in carrying out that responsibility.
5   Equity – all stakeholder groups should be treated equitably.
6   Efficiency – process improvements should be undertaken to ensure the organization is making the best use of its resources.
7   Effectiveness – the board should establish and monitor measures of performance in a strategic manner.

This list of principles is not exhaustive but it does give us a clear indication of the philosophical approach organizations should adopt in designing and implementing an appropriate governance framework. It may be somewhat surprising to find that even some of the more high-profile sport organizations in the world struggle to implement good governance standards. Corporate governance of English Premier League football clubs has come under increasing scrutiny in recent years, due in part to the annual reviews of corporate governance undertaken by the former Football Governance Research Centre (FGRC) based at Birkbeck College in the University of London. The Premier League (PL) is the flagship of the game's governing body in England, the Football Association (FA). The FA is in turn under the control of a European governing body, the Union of European Football Associations (UEFA), which in turn is a member of the world's governing body, the Federation of International Football Associations (FIFA).

The regulatory system for Premier League clubs comprises of four elements: (1) regulation by the football authorities; (2) regulation through the legal system in terms of company law, consumer law, labour law and competition law; (3) regulation by a code of corporate governance developed by the Premier League; and (4) shareholder activism and stakeholder participation. The football authorities (namely FA and UEFA) have developed criteria such as a 'fit and proper person' test aimed at improving the quality of individuals appointed or elected to govern Premier League clubs, and the development of a code of corporate governance that provides guidelines for good governance. These actions are largely designed to ameliorate the effects of poor financial management within the Premier League clubs (since 1992 50 per cent of PL clubs have been in hands of administrators or insolvent) and to improve the sustainability of clubs that are promoted or relegated between the FA leagues. The FGRC noted that the PL clubs that regularly compete in the UEFA Champions' League hold a distinct financial advantage over other PL clubs. As a consequence the governing body of the PL must be cognizant of the more powerful clubs and their potential to influence decision-making at the board table.

The English legal system requires PL clubs to fulfil a number of obligations for communicating with shareholders, consultation with fans, the use of customer charters and dialogue with Supporters' Trusts. The FGRC noted that while the majority of PL clubs do an adequate job in this area, there was room for improvement. In addition, PL clubs that are listed public companies must follow a Combined Code that sets out principles for the activities of directors, director's remuneration, accountability and audit requirements, relations with shareholders, and institutional shareholders. The FGRC found that while PL clubs are moving towards having more independent directors, they fall short compared to other listed companies.

There are now more than 70 Supporters' Trusts for clubs in the FA, and about 60 per cent of PL clubs have a Supporter's Trust. The trusts fulfil an important governance role, with 25 per cent of PL clubs having a trust representative on their board. This representation means that committed fans have the chance to participate in decision-making at the highest level in regard to the future of their club, and in return support the club in sport development, marketing and fundraising activities.

While there are signs that PL clubs have generally accepted good governance practices and abide with the majority of codes of conduct and principles for good governance, they do fall down in certain areas of governance practice. These include the lack of performance evaluation of individual directors or the overall board in a small number of clubs, and a significant portion of clubs failing to adopt standard strategic planning practices. While the English PL enjoys enormous global profile as a leading football competition, the governance of the member clubs does not reach such exalted heights. The importance of good governance for a sport is highlighted via In Practice 12.2.

In Practice 12.2

Amateur Swimming Association

The Amateur Swimming Association (ASA) was the first governing body of swimming to be established in the world (1869) and has evolved to become the English national governing body for swimming, diving, water polo, open water and synchronized swimming. The ASA supports over 1,200 affiliated swimming clubs through a national/regional/and sub-regional structure. It endeavours to ensure every athlete – whatever their age or level of experience – belongs to a club that provides the best possible support and environment through schemes such as swim21, the ASA's 'Quality Mark' for clubs (similar to the Sport England Clubmark programme discussed in Chapter 3). It organizes competitions throughout England, from grass-roots to elite level, including the highly successful Age Group and Youth Championships that attract more than 1,600 young swimmers aged 11–17, and the ASA Nationals.

The ASA website (www.swimming.org/asa) states that the English talent programme is a world-leading, seamless pathway that puts in place performance opportunities for swimmers to develop their skills and potential. The ASA operates a Learn to Swim award scheme based on the National Plan for Teaching Swimming. In 2010, close to 2 million certificates and badges were issued to children all over the world under this scheme. Swimming is the number one participation sport, with over 20 million people swimming every year, and the ASA is dedicated to giving more people more opportunities to swim for health and for fun.

It should be noted that the ASA is not a provider of swimming facilities, therefore it acts as a catalyst and facilitator to ensure that suitable facilities, with appropriate access and programmes, are provided to meet the needs of the community and aquatic clubs. The ASA operates comprehensive certification and education programmes for teachers, coaches and officials. It has pioneered work on the UK Coaching Framework and is developing e-learning programmes, all of which are helping to drive up quality and 'raise the bar' to ensure the ASA has an appropriately skilled workforce for the whole swimming industry.

The ASA's Strategy 2009–2013 sets out four objectives.

1   Ensure everyone has the opportunity to learn to swim.
2   Offer everyone the opportunity to enjoy swimming or water-based fitness activities for health and fun throughout their lifetime.
3   Ensure everyone achieves their different personal health goals throughout their lifetime.
4   Ensure the nation achieves gold medal success on the world stage.

Source: the ASA website at www.swimming.org/asa.

Board performance

Board performance has been found to be related to the use of appropriate structures, processes and strategic planning; the role of the paid executive; whether the board undertakes training or development work; personal motivations of board members; and the influence of a cyclical pattern in the life cycle of boards. How to measure board performance, however, is a subject of ongoing debate. Herman and Renz (1997, 1998, 2000) support the use of a social constructionist approach to measure board performance based on the work of Berger and Luckmann (1967). Their view is that the collective judgements of those individuals directly involved with the board can provide the best idea of its performance. A widely used scale, the Self-Assessment for Nonprofit Governing Boards Scale (Slesinger 1991), uses this approach and provides sporting and other nonprofit organizations with an effective way to gauge board performance.

Aspects of board activity that are evaluated using a scale of this type include: the working relationship between board and CEO; working relationships between board and staff' CEO selection and review processes; financial management; conduct of board and committee meetings; board mission statement and review of the mission; strategic planning; matching operational programmes to the mission and monitoring programme performance; risk management; new board member selection and training; and marketing and public relations. The performance of the board in undertaking these activities is then rated by board members, executives and the chair of the board. While this approach is open to criticisms of self-reporting bias, the fact that the whole group makes judgements on performance and then compares perceptions is an aid to board development and improvement.

The evaluation of individual board member performance is more problematic. Research into the human resource management practices related to board members shows that smaller sports organizations may struggle to find board members, while larger sports have an element of prestige attached to them so the problem is the opposite – how to engage in succession planning within a democratic electoral process. Very few board members are inducted, trained, provided with professional development opportunities and evaluated at all in regards to their role and the role of the board, a potentially serious problem for nonprofit sport organizations given the significant responsibilities with which board members and board chairs are charged.

Drivers of change in governance

VSOs are increasingly under pressure from funding agencies to improve the delivery of their core programmes and services. Funding agencies recognize that sport's capacity for this delivery depends to a large extent on sport organizations being appropriately governed and as a result have implemented a range of measures to improve the governance of VSOs. For example, the Australian Sports Commission has a dedicated programme of management improvement for national sport organizations (NSOs) that provides advice on governance issues, funding to undertake reviews of governance structures and provides information on governance principles and processes. Sport England has negotiated detailed strategic plans with NSOs to improve the delivery and coordination between regional sport organizations.

The threat of litigation against sport organizations, their members or board members has forced sport organizations to address issues such as risk management, fiduciary compliance, incorporation, directors' liability insurance, and board training and evaluation. The heightened awareness of the implications of governance failure due to several much-publicized corporate cases of impropriety worldwide has also forced sport organizations to improve their governance systems. Legislative changes to address issues of equity and diversity are additional pressures sports organizations must face and their governance systems, particularly membership criteria, voting rights and provision of information must change accordingly.

The threat of competition in the marketplace also has forced sports organizations to become more commercial and business focused, primarily through employing paid staff. Large clubs and regional sports associations that in the mid-1990s were exclusively run by volunteers are increasingly investing in paid staff to manage the increased compliance demands from government and their members and customers. As discussed earlier, the employment of paid staff changes the governance structures, the decision-making processes and the level of control exerted by volunteers. Maintaining governance structures devised decades ago creates many problems for sports organizations. In Practice 12.3 highlights some of the problems that result from poor governance and how one organization has been forced to change.

In Practice 12.3

The trouble with Scottish football
In the executive summary of Henry McLeish's exhaustive report of his 2010 Review of Scottish Football he said:

> The governance of the game may have been appropriate and effective in another era but is totally inappropriate for the modern era. The representative and participative structure of the Scottish Football Association (SFA), the traditions, procedures and decision-making and the inherently defensive and insular approach of the organisation all present a serious obstacle to the modernisation of football in Scotland. Modernising the governance of the game is the central challenge of this review.

In other words, the governance system could not have been worse. The failure of the national team to qualify for any major international tournament since the 1996 European Championships and the 1998 World Cup, the inconsistent performance of the top Scottish clubs in European competitions, and the lack of sustainable growth in both the quantity and quality of players emerging from the Scottish football system were the catalysts for the review. McLeish went on to detail a litany of problems with the governance of football in Scotland:

> The governance is inappropriate for the current and future context of football:

- There is a lack of effective formal consultation between the major stake-holders in the game and a serious lack of respect, confidence and trust.
- The game is very fragmented and at times lacks any overall sense of purpose.
- There is a great deal of insularity, exclusiveness and isolationism.
- Decision making is slow and delivery does not match the urgency and complexity of the issues involved.
- There is a great deal of sectional and vested interest at work at the expense of the health and well-being of the overall game. Openness, transparency and accountability are lacking.
- The game overall generates a great deal of indiscipline and a lack of respect for the rules and regulations of the game.
- Roles and responsibilities are confused and unproductive with the elected officials too involved in what is essentially the work of the Chief Executive and his management team.
- The committee structure may function for the benefit of the existing representatives but is ill-equipped and outdated and is not able to deal with the modern world of football and the speed with which events and issues emerge and have to be dealt with.

- There is no sense of modernisation and while there is some excellent work taking place within the SFA it is hard to see the current organisational structure allowing this to flourish.
- There seems little concept of public value or return on investment permeating the SFA and once again the failure to reform decision making, policy and planning procedures and structure means that the full potential of the organisation is not being realized and incentives to change are simply not there.
- There is no performance culture within the SFA and for all intents and purposes the work is isolated in silos. It is constantly worth repeating that much of the weakness of the SFA is based on legacy and history and a traditional mind-set that surrounds the work of the institution.
- The shape and structure of the organisation has largely remained intact despite the changes in personnel and the passing of time.
- There is also a lack of outside involvement in the work and deliberations of the SFA.
- Non-football people are thin on the ground and with the exception of some committees, independent experts and informed outsiders are currently excluded from the different parts of the structure.

Having said that, McLeish did identify that most people involved in Scottish football wanted things to improve:

There is little dispute as to the importance of the SFA and what it should strive to achieve as a governing body:

- Governance with integrity.
- Performance of Scotland's national teams.
- Effective working relationships with the two other bodies, the SPL and the SFL and the myriad of organisations that make up the game.
- Effective oversight of the implementation of the laws of football.
- Promotion of participation, standards, and financial well-being of the game.
- Fostering of development at all levels.
- Constructive dialogue with government and other sports.
- Effective representation of the game in Scotland and internationally.

However, the governance system in the SFA was preventing these very things being achieved.

The work of the SFA has become progressively less suitable and less effective in the light of these limited objectives to carry out its role in the modern game especially at a time when the scale of economic, social and life style change continues to dominate and have such a direct impact on football and the conditions in which it operates. The review has also pinpointed a number of challenging but less tangible issues to address including:

- The lack of trust, respect and confidence in the governance of football.
- The lack of a coherent and comprehensive narrative for the future of the game overcoming the informality of the workings of the structures.
- The game is not served well by the general perception of many outside Hampden that the SFA is defensive and where narrow sectional or constituency interests often seem more important that the national interest and the national game.

This example highlights the impact that poor governance can have on a sport organization. It remains to be seen if the SFA can reform itself, develop effective governance systems, and transform its performance in the next few years.

Source: McLeish, H. (2010) Review of Scottish Football, Part 2 Governance, Leadership, Structures. Edinburgh: Scottish Football Association.

Summary

Organizational governance has been described as the exercise of power within organizations and provides the system by which the elements of organizations are controlled and directed. Good organizational governance should ensure that the board and management seek to deliver outcomes for the benefit of the organization and its members and that the means used to attain these outcomes are effectively monitored.

A distinction is made between corporate governance that deals with the governance of profit-seeking companies and corporations that focus on protecting and enhancing shareholder value, and nonprofit governance that is concerned with the governance of voluntary-based organizations that seek to provide a community service or facilitate the involvement of individuals in social, artistic or sporting activities.

Sport organizations and their governance frameworks have diverse elements that prevent the development of an overarching theory of sport governance. A number of theoretical perspectives, namely agency theory, stewardship theory, institutional theory, resource dependence theory, network theory and stakeholder theory can be used to illuminate parts of the governance assumptions, processes, structures and outcomes for sport organizations.

The traditional governance structure for VSOs outlined earlier has been criticized for being unwieldy and cumbersome, slow to react to changes in market conditions, subject to potentially damaging politics or power plays between delegates and imposing significant constraints on organizations wishing to change. On the other hand, the majority of sports organizations still use this model today and value its ability to ensure members have a say in decision-making, the transparency of decisions and the autonomy granted to organizations at every level of the system.

A number of models for sport governance exist, each emphasizing different levels of responsibility for the chair of the board and paid executive. VSO boards perform better if a degree of trust exists between the board and staff and that board leadership is shared amongst a dominant coalition of the board chair, executive and a small group of senior board members. While evaluation systems for board performance are still relatively simplistic, they do cover a wide range of board activities. Evaluation of individual board member performance is more problematic and is the subject of ongoing research.

Finally, VSOs are increasingly under pressure from funding agencies to improve the delivery of their core programmes and services. The threat of litigation against sport organizations, their members or board members, has forced sport organizations to address issues such as risk management, fiduciary compliance, incorporation, directors' liability insurance, and board training and evaluation. The heightened awareness of the implications of governance failure due to high profile corporate cases worldwide has also forced sport organizations to improve their governance systems.

Review questions

1 Explain the difference between corporate and nonprofit governance.
2 What theory would you apply to the study of negligence on the part of a board of directors of a sport organization?
3 Explain the role played by boards, staff, volunteers, members and stakeholder groups in governing sport organizations.
4 What criteria would you apply to gauge the performance of a nonprofit VSO? How would these criteria differ for a professional sport club?
5 What are the important elements in developing good relationships between boards and paid staff in VSOs?
6 Compare the governance structures of a multidisciplinary sport (e.g. gymnastics, canoeing, athletics) with a single discipline sport (e.g. field hockey, netball, rugby league). How do they differ? What impact does this have on volunteers involved in governance roles?
7 Review the governance performance of a VSO of your choice using Henry and Lee's (2004) seven principles of governance presented in this chapter.
8 What issues does a potential amalgamation present for a VSO?
9 How are board performance and organizational performance linked?
10 Interview the CEO and the board chair of small VSO. Who do they perceive to be the leader of the organization?

Further reading

Carver, J. (1997) *Boards that Make a Difference: A New Design for Leadership in Nonprofit and Public Organizations*, 2nd edition, San Francisco, CA: Jossey-Bass.
Clarke, T. (ed.) (2004) *Theories of Corporate Governance*, Abingdon: Routledge.

Football Governance Research Centre (2004) *The State of the Game: The Corporate Governance of Football Clubs 2004*, Research paper 2004 No. 3, London: Football Governance Research Centre, Birkbeck, University of London.

Henry, I. and Lee, P.C. (2004) 'Governance and ethics in sport', in J. Beech and S. Chadwick (eds), *The Business of Sport Management*, Harlow: Prentice Hall.

Hindley, D. (2003) *Resource Guide in Governance and Sport*, Learning and Teaching Support Network in Hospitality, Leisure, Sport and Tourism, online, available at: www.heacademy. ac.uk/assets/hlst/documents/resource_guides/governance_and_sport.pdf.

Houle, C.O. (1997) *Governing Boards: Their Nature and Nurture*, San Francisco, CA: Jossey-Bass.

Hoye, R. and Cuskelly, G. (2007) *Sport Governance*, Oxford: Elsevier Butterworth-Heinemann.

Hoye, R. and Doherty, A. (2011) 'Nonprofit sport board performance: A review and directions for future research', *Journal of Sport Management*, 25(3): 272–285.

Organisation for Economic Co-operation and Development (2004) *Principles of Corporate Governance*, Paris: OECD.

Relevant websites

The following websites are useful starting points for further information on the governance of sport organizations:

Australian Sports Commission – www.ausport.gov.au
Sport and Recreation New Zealand – www.sparc.org.nz
Sport Canada – www.pch.gc.ca/progs/sc/index_e.cfm
Sport England – www.sportengland.org
Sport Scotland – www.sportscotland.org.uk

Governance reform in Australian football: A perennial challenge?

In August 2002, the then Australian Federal Minister for the Arts and Sport, Senator Rod Kemp, announced that Soccer Australia (SA) had agreed to a major structural review of soccer in Australia to be managed by the Australian Sports Commission. The review was undertaken after almost two decades of crises in the sport with the result that in mid-2002, SA was AUS$2.6 million in debt, had reduced staffing levels at the national office, was racked by political infighting, had a lack of strategic direction and had enjoyed mixed results in the international arena. The review examined the structure, governance and management of soccer at all levels across Australia.

During the course of the review it was found that many of the constituent bodies at state and regional levels suffered from similar financial difficulties, political infighting and inappropriate governance systems. These created problems of mistrust and disharmony, a lack of strategic direction, inappropriate behaviour and factionalism that hampered national decision-making. While the sport enjoyed a large grass roots participation base, a good talent pool for national teams, good training programmes, strong growth in female participation and passionate public support, its governance system was preventing it capitalizing on these strengths.

The review found that the governance system needed to change in four key areas:

1 ensure independence of the governing bodies;
2 separate governance from day-to-day management;
3 change the membership and voting structures for the national and state organizations; and
4 the relationship between SA and the National Soccer League.

In all, the review made 53 recommendations aimed at improving the structure, governance and management of SA. The first three recommendations in the report illustrate the parlous state of affairs that existed in the organization in 2002. The review recommended that (1) the membership of SA be changed to recognize key interest groups and reduce the power of larger states and the NSL; (2) a new constitution be developed; and (3) that each state affiliate adopt a model constitution and membership agreements. These recommendations alone represent wholesale change in the governance system, but the review went on to recommend a further 50 changes to governance processes and structures throughout the sport.

The sweeping changes made to the governance systems of Soccer Australia as a result of the review, and the subsequent appointment as Chief Executive Officer of John O'Neill (ex-CEO of the Australian Rugby Union who has subsequently returned to the ARU) ushered in a new era for the sport. On 1 January 2005, Soccer Australia changed its name to Football Federation Australia (FFA) as part of the ongoing process of repositioning the sport. These changes in governance enabled the sport to:

● successfully relaunch a national league – the Hyundai A-League with eight new teams (now ten) and a lucrative pay-TV rights deals that has enabled it to attract some of the top European-based Australians back to play in Australia including Harry Kewell and Brett Emerton;

- have the financial capacity to employ a supercoach in Guss Hiddink who managed to get the Socceroos to the second round of the 2006 World Cup before being cruelly beaten by the eventual champions Italy; and
- be in a position to bid for the future rights to host the World Cup.

Despite these reforms, football in Australia was still subject to some systemic failures. First, after the dramatic ride to secure entry to the 2006 World Cup, Australia secured a place to the 2010 World Cup after it managed to move from the Oceania to the Asian Federation which had more team slots allocated for the final 32 World Cup teams. Alas, under new coach Pim Verbeek, Australia was bundled out after the first round – the hopes of a nation dashed once again. Second, after five years, the new A-League suffered its first casualty with the North Queensland Fury having its licence withdrawn for its inability to meet its licence obligations with FFA. Third, and most importantly, Australia's bid to win the right to host the 2022 World Cup failed to secure more than a single vote – the AUS$50 million investment by the federal government to support the FFA led bid had amounted to nothing.

After the dust has settled, the federal government announced a second review in eight years into the governance, management and structure of football in Australia, this time to be conducted by the chairman of the Australian Sports Commission. The press release from FFA in April 2011 stated:

> Former Federal Sports Minister and current Chairman of the Australian Sports Commission, the Hon. Warwick Smith, AM, has been appointed to head a review of football in Australia in partnership with Football Federation Australia (FFA). The Federal Sports Minister, Senator the Hon. Mark Arbib, announced the joint review as a first step towards ensuring Australian football is in a position to deliver the best possible AFC Asian Cup in Australia in 2015.
>
> The AFC Asian Cup is Asia's premier sporting event and will draw an expected television audience of more than one billion. Over the course of the 23 day tournament in January 2015, up to 500,000 fans are expected to attend the 32 matches, which will be played in New South Wales, Victoria, Queensland and the Australian Capital Territory.
>
> FFA CEO Ben Buckley confirmed that while the Smith Review would primarily focus on the AFC Asian Cup 2015, it would also examine the structures and resources required to continue football's development in Australia. Football in Australia has many needs, from the kids playing at the community level through to the Qantas Socceroos on the international stage and now the responsibility of hosting Asia's biggest football event, said Ben Buckley. 'FFA welcomes the collaborative approach from the Federal Government and their continuing support to ensure the game is positioned to reach its enormous potential across the nation.' 'The review provides the opportunity to look at the efficiencies in our current structure and how the various levels of the game can better work together. We all want to make football the best it can be.'
>
> FFA is well advanced in setting strategic priorities for the next World Cup cycle. There are three pillars around which our strategy is built:
>
> 1 Continuing national team excellence, in particular with qualification of the Qantas Socceroos for the 2014 FIFA World Cup
> 2 Growth and sustainability of the Hyundai A-League model
> 3 Connecting with the 1.7 million Australians who make up the football community to create greater engagement and productive partnerships

'In this context, the Smith Review is a timely and positive step towards ensuring FFA can implement its strategic plans and make the most of the exciting opportunities ahead,' concluded Buckley.

Source: Australian Sports Commission (2003) *Independent Soccer Review: Report of the Independent Soccer Review Committee into the Structure, Governance and Management of Soccer in Australia,* Canberra: Australian Sports Commission. Football Federation Australia, (2011) 'AFC Asian Cup focus of football review', news release 27 April 2011. Sydney: Football Federation Australia.

Case questions

1 Why did the Australian federal government initiate the 2003 Review into the governance of football in Australia?
2 What were some of the reasons the FFA is now subject to a further review?
3 Compare the Crawford Review of 2003 with the 2011 report into the review of the Scottish Football Association. What similarities and differences are there in the governance and structural issues of these two football governing bodies?
4 Why do governing bodies of sport seem to be in a perpetual state of review, in particular in the areas of governance and structure?

Chapter 13

Performance management

Overview

This chapter examines the ways in which sport organizations manage their operations and evaluate their performance. Particular attention is given to the special features of sport organizations, and how these features create the need for a customized performance management model. The imperative of using a multi-dimensional model of performance management is highlighted, together with the need to accommodate the conflicting demands that arise from the claims of multiple stakeholders. Throughout the chapter cases and incidents are used to illustrate the concepts and principles that underpin effective performance in sport organizations.

After completing this chapter the reader should be able to:

- explain the concept of performance management;
- describe how the special features of sport necessitate the formulation of a customized performance management model;
- identify the stakeholders that that need to be taken into account when building a performance management model for sport organizations;

- construct a multi-dimensional model of performance management that accommodates sport's special features, and gives appropriate weight to financial factors, internal processes, market awareness and penetration, and social responsibility; and
- apply the model to a variety of sport situations and contexts.

Sport and performance

From a management perspective sport is a very interesting institution to study since it is both similar to and different from traditional business organizations (Smith and Stewart 1999; Smith and Stewart 2010). Its similarities have arisen out of its relentless drive over the last 30 years to become more professionally structured and managed. Large segments of sport have consequently copied the values and practices of the business world, and as a result players and administrators are paid employees, and strategic plans are designed. In addition, games and activities become branded sport products, fans become customers to be satisfied and surveyed, and alliances with corporate supporters are developed (Carter 2011; Slack 1997).

At the same time, sport is also different from business (Smith and Stewart 1999; Smith and Stewart 2010). First, it has a symbolic significance and emotional intensity that is rarely found in an insurance company, bank or even a betting shop. While businesses seek employee compliance and attachment, their primary concern is efficiency, productivity and responding to changing market conditions. Sport, on the other hand, is consumed by strong emotional attachments that are linked to the past through nostalgia and tradition. Romantic visions, emotion and passion can override commercial logic and economic rationality (Foster *et al.* 2006; Quinn 2009). Second, predictability and certainty, which are goals to be aimed for in the commercial world, particularly with respect to product quality, are not always valued in the sporting world. Sport fans are attracted to games where the outcome is uncertain and chaos is just around the corner (Fort 2011; Sandy *et al.* 2004, Szymanski 2009; Zimbalist 2006). Third, sport is not driven by the need to optimize profit in the ways that large commercial businesses are. In practice, sport organizations face two conflicting models of organizational behaviour when deciding upon their underlying mission and goals. The first is the profit maximization model, which assumes that a club is simply a firm in a perfectly competitive product market and that profit is the single driving motivational force. The second is the utility maximization model, which emphasizes the rivalry between clubs, and their desire to win as many matches as possible (Downward and Dawson 2000; Fort 2011). The utility view assumes that sporting organizations are by nature highly competitive and that the single most important performance yardstick is competitive success. These differences therefore beg the question of where to begin when setting up a performance management system for sport organizations.

Where to begin?

In many respects sport is always subject to intense scrutiny. For example, in elite competitive sport, players and teams are rated and ranked continuously. In cricket, for example, an ever-expanding array of statistics are used to calculate not only batter scoring rates and bowling strike rates, but also patterns of scoring and fielding efficiency. Moreover, everyone has an opinion on the performance of coaches in various professional sport leagues which range from win-loss ratios to how the game strategies impact on scoring efficiency and player movements. At the same time, many sporting clubs do not take the time to undertake a comprehensive evaluation of their off-field performance. And, if they do, they limit their analysis to just a couple of issues like operating profits and membership levels. We argue here that it is better to use an evaluation model that covers a range of performance dimensions and embraces a variety of measures.

A systematic approach to performance management is an essential tool for identifying strengths and weaknesses and revealing the ways in which overall organizational performance can be improved. It is also important for deciding where scarce resources should be allocated in order to achieve the best possible outcome. It can also give a picture of how one organization, club or league is doing in relation to other organizations, clubs or leagues. This performance snapshot can be used to identify weaknesses and design strategies than improve critical result areas in the next season or annual sporting cycle. In short, the use of some sort of performance management model is crucial to the long-term success of sport organizations. However, the question remains as to how best to go about implementing an appropriate model of performance management, and where to begin?

A good starting point is to look at performance management from a strategic perspective. That is, we should initially focus our attention on what the organization wants to achieve. In other words, a performance management system should be linked to an organization's vision, goals and objectives (Hums and Maclean 2009; Robbins and Barnwell 2002). These objectives can be used to identify what it needs to do well to improve its performance. It is at this point that the primary goals of sport organizations become quite different from those of business organizations. While commercial leisure centres and most American professional sport teams seem to be focused on maximizing profits, most other sports clubs, even with a large revenue base, are more concerned with priorities like winning more games than their rivals and servicing the needs of members. However it is not always clear just what the primary goal of a sport organization is, or what is the best measure for deciding how well the organization has performed. In commercial terms the most successful association football (or soccer) club is Manchester United, closely followed by Real Madrid, Barcelona and the two Milan teams, whose capacity to secure revenue is unrivalled in European football. However, neither Manchester United nor Real Madrid got to the Champions League final in 2003, which was won by Porto, a relative pauper. This situation was reversed in 2008 when Manchester won the Champions League competition when it defeated its English Premier League rival, Chelsea. Between 2009 and 2011 though, the richest teams dominated the Champions League, which suggests that commercial and on-field success are in fact related.

In the USA National Football League (NFL), the Cincinatti Bengals rarely got to the end of season play-offs during the late 1990s and early part of the twenty-first century but, because of its frugal spending and the NFL's income equalization strategy, made a greater profit than some of the better-known teams. In this case it was never clear just what the primary performance goal was, but in the end the Bengals were probably best known for their ability to make a profit rather than their capacity for winning.

On balance though, it has to be said that there is a close correlation between revenue and success in most professional sport leagues. In other words, clubs that have a large resource base and the capacity to secure the best facilities, the best coaches and the best players, will on balance have the best win-loss ratio. But this also begs the question as to whether there may be other ways of measuring performance and estimating the success and failures of a sport organization. In some instances it may be important to consider what are called process factors, which includes things like staff retention, player development and the overall level of morale and job satisfaction. However, despite these additional complexities and anomalies, it is clear that any performance management system must take into account and, indeed, should reflect the primary goals of the relevant club, team, facility, event or league

In Practice 13.1

Evaluating the performance of sport coaches

At first glance, the problem of working out how to best to judge the performance of a sport coach is quite simple. The intuitive response to any question about coaching performance is to examine the sport team's performance by referring to its win-loss ratio. It would follow then, that a team with a win-loss ratio of 0.80 or 80 per cent has outperformed a team whose win-loss ratio was 0.60 or 60 per cent. Alternatively, a current season win-loss ratio of 0.70 or 70 per cent, when contrasted with a previous season win-loss ratio of 0.50, or 50 per cent, would also suggest an improved level of performance. Not only would the coach be happy with this sort of result, but so too would the club officials and the fans.

It is fair to say that coaches are responsible for securing the best outcomes from their team. However, it is also reasonable to propose that coaches can only work within the limits set by the resources and playing talent at their disposal. There is a theory of strategic management called the resource-based view (RBV), which says that the key to getting a competitive edge is all to do with the quality of resources at your disposal (Stewart 2007a). This competitive edge can be best secured by assembling resources that are (1) valuable, and can consequently generate greater efficiencies; (2) scarce, which means they are difficult secure; and (3) inimitable, and therefore not easy to replicate. In short, superior performance will result from a strong endowment of resources that cannot be matched by competitors.

This model very quickly brings into question the idea that a coach's performance can be measured solely against a series of win-loss ratios. Under the assumptions of the RBV model, team performance has as much to do with playing talent and support service quality as it has to do with the leadership style and technical capacities of the coach. In other words, any rating of coaching performance should take into account the quality and scale of resources that the coaches have at their disposal.

Building a performance management model from a stakeholder perspective

Performance management should also be linked to an organization's key stakeholders (Atkinson *et al.* 1997; Bryson 2004; Carter 2011). If stakeholders are satisfied with the organization's performance, then clearly it is doing well. In a publicly owned sports retail business for example, a large profit and dividend will be good for management and shareholders alike.

However in a member-based sport club, success will be more about on-field performance and member services than massive profits. On the other hand, for a sport's governing body the interests of its registered players may take the highest priority. In other words, different types of sport organizations will have their own unique goals and priorities, which will in turn reflect the ways in which they rank their stakeholders (Friedman *et al.* 2004).

Stakeholders may also have conflicting needs. Sponsors may want maximum media exposure and access to players, but the clubs have a primary interest in improving player performance, which may mean less, not more player involvement in sponsor activities. In the case of a national sporting body, the national government may want international success to justify its investment in elite training and coaching programmes, whereas the rank and-file players who make up the bulk of the membership may want more local facilities. Sport organizations are therefore required to balance the often-conflicting needs and 'contradictory interests' of the various stakeholders (Chappelet and Bayle 2005: 43). The major sport organization stakeholders and their expectations are summarized in Table 13.1.

Table 13.1: **Stakeholder expectations of sport organizations**

Stakeholder type	Expectations of sport organization
Players	• On field success • Appropriate pay and benefits • Low injury rates
Employees	• Appropriate pay and benefits • Job security • Professional development
Equipment suppliers	• Reliability of demand • Player endorsement • Brand awareness
Members	• Services and benefits • Overall satisfaction
Owners/shareholders	• Return on investment • Public recognition of club or association
Sponsors	• Positive reputation of club or association • Brand awareness and recognition
Player agents	• High player morale • Payment of market rates
Fans	• Game quality and excitement • High win-loss ratio
Community/society	• Civic pride • Provides role models for young adults
Media	• Mass market • High level of public interest

The key point to note here is that a sport organization will have multiple stakeholders and their interests will have to be integrated into its evaluation processes.

An input-output approach to performance management

In developing a model for evaluating a sport organization's performance, a number of additional principles should be utilized. A second approach is to focus on inputs and outputs. This involves looking at things like quality, quantity, efficiency, cost-benefit ratios and employee productivity (Anthony and Young 2003; Bouckaert 1995). This approach provides a checklist of essential performance dimensions that need to be addressed. It ensures that no one measure is dominant, and provides for measures that not only focus on internal processes, but also look at the organization's relationships with key suppliers and customers. A summary of the ways in which input-output analysis can be applied to sport organizations is illustrated in Table 13.2.

Table 13.2: **An input-output approach to performance management in sport**

Dimension	Measure
Output: quantity	• premierships • attendance • membership • participation
Output: quality	• standard of play • features of venue/facility • standard of service • overall customer experience
Output: cost/benefit	• operating profit • costs of operation • net economic benefit • social benefit
Input: efficiency	• cost of providing service • administrative support cost • waiting time
Input: staff performance	• customer/member/fan satisfaction ratings • staff skills and experience • staff achievements

A balanced and multi-dimensional approach to performance management

A third approach is to avoid the often obsessive emphasis that shareholders place on financial measures by balancing it against the benefits that might accrue to customers, suppliers and employees (Harvard Business Review 1998). This approach is exemplified in the Balanced Scorecard (BSC) model designed by Kaplan and Norton (Kaplan and Norton 1992, 1996). The BSC has four dimensions which are reviewed below

One of the first things Kaplan and Norton (1996) note is that a good performance measurement tool should not be a 'controlling system' obsessed with keeping 'individuals, and organizational units in compliance with a pre-established plan' (p. 25). Rather it should be primarily a 'learning system' concerned with 'communication and informing (ibid.). To this end Kaplan and Norton aimed to design a performance measurement system that balanced external and easily quantifiable measures like market share and return on investment against internal and more ephemeral factors like administrative processes and staff development.

Kaplan and Norton's first dimension is 'Financial Perspective'. Although they argue that too much emphasis has traditionally been given to the so called bottom-line result, financial measures are nevertheless a fundamental starting point for evaluating the economic sustainability of an organization. They can range from total sales, operating income and net cash flow, to return on assets, debt to equity ratio and net profit. This dimension answers the question 'How do we look to shareholders?'

The second dimension is 'Customer Perspective'. In this instance the emphasis is on identifying the 'customer and market segments in which the business will compete', and to develop measures that will indicate how well the organization competes in these segments (ibid.: 26). These measures will include total sales in each segment, market share, customer acquisition, customer retention and customer satisfaction. Kaplan and Norton also suggest that for this performance dimension attention should be given to the factors like short lead times and on-time delivery that actually underpin the levels of customer satisfaction and retention. This dimension addresses the question 'How do customers see us?'

The third dimension is the 'Internal-Business-Process Perspective'. This perspective requires management to identify the 'critical internal processes in which the organization must excel' in order to secure a competitive advantage (ibid.: 26). Kaplan and Norton note that it is not just a matter of ensuring that current value-adding processes are efficient and streamlined, but that there are also systems in place to improve and re-engineer existing processes and products. This dimension addresses the question 'What must we excel at?'

The fourth dimension is the 'Learning and Growth Perspective'. Kaplan and Norton see this perspective as crucial to the long-term success of organizations. In a turbulent business environment there is an ever-increasing likelihood that the technologies and processes required to sustain a market advantage and competitive edge may race ahead of the technical and managerial skills of the staff who are responsible for managing those technologies and processes. In order to close this gap organizations will 'have to invest in re-skilling employees, enhancing information technology and systems, and aligning organizational procedures and routines' (ibid.: 27). This dimension addresses the question 'Can we continue to improve and create value?'

Finally, Kaplan and Norton suggest that each of the above perspectives should be linked to a common overarching objective that ensures consistency and mutually reinforcing conduct. In other words, the BSC is more than a 'dashboard' of 'critical indicators or key success factors' (ibid.: 29). In order to be effective it must reflect the organization's mission and goals.

Costs and benefits of a performance management system

Planning and implementing a performance management system can be costly, since it involves a lot of time-intensive analysis of an organization's processes and activities. It can also become a bureaucratic nightmare since it can produce hundreds of microscopic statements about the ways thing should be done, and how they must be measured. It should be remembered that the concept of performance management arose out of the mechanistic time-and-motion studies of Frederick Winslow Taylor in the early part of the twentieth century. According to Taylor the key to increasing productivity was to systematically analyse work practices in order to identify the most efficient process, which could then become a best-practice template (Anthony and Young 2003; Stewart 1989). Taylorism also underpinned the development of Management by Objectives (MBO) and Total Quality Management (TQM) which were later refined into a broader model of performance management (Bouckaert and van Doren 2003). As a result, a rigidly structured performance management system can stifle initiative and creativity by setting narrowly defined work standards and strict standards of workplace behaviour.

At the same time, a well-thought-out performance management system can provide a number of long term benefits (Anthony and Young 2003; Williams 1998). First, it makes sure that the core activities of an organization are directly linked to its primary aims and goals. Second, it can motivate employees by setting targets that are rewarded when they are attained. Third, it ensures greater accountability by clearly identifying not only what is to be achieved, but also who is responsible for making it happen. Fourth, it completes the management cycle by making sure processes are monitored, and outcomes are measured against some sort of minimum performance standard. Finally it forces management to come up with a quantifiable measure of its key outputs, and eliminate ambiguous aims and nebulous objectives (Anthony and Young 2003).

In Practice 13.2

Measuring the performance of football leagues in Australia
The Australian Football League is the showcase competition for Australia's only indigenous game of any significance, Australian rules football. Australian rules football was invented in Melbourne in 1858, and went on become one the nation's most popular sports (Hess and Stewart 1998; Hess *et al.* 2008). In 2010 it generated revenues of more than AUS$360 million, and drew a total season attendance of more than 7 million fans (AFL 2011). Its average game attendance just over 38,000 compares favourably with the major European football leagues.

Historically, and in contrast to cricket and tennis, Australian rules football failed to fully embrace the nation as a whole. Whereas it captured the hearts and minds of people living in the states of Victoria, South Australia, Western Australia and Tasmania, its presence in the states of New South Wales and Queensland was for the most part marginal. In these two states, rugby league was the most popular football code, with rugby union being the second most popular code. Interestingly, and unlike most footballing nations around the world, association football, or soccer as it is more commonly identified in Australia, was very much a minor code in every state. During the 1950s and 1960s in particular, European migrants, who had been immersed in the soccer culture at home, were amazed that the world game had been relegated to the periphery of Australia's sporting landscape (Hess *et al.* 2008).

However, at the beginning of the twenty-first century, things had changed quite dramatically. The rapid commercialization of sport during the 1980s and 1990s produced a number of national sport leagues, the most powerful being the football codes. The National Soccer League – or NSL as it was often called – had the earliest beginnings, having been established in 1978. This was quite surprising given its relatively low level of nationwide support. However, it went through many traumatic changes, clubs were constantly having to deal with inter-ethnic tensions, and as a result they were rarely able to trade profitably. In 2003 the National Soccer League was abandoned while the national governing body was reformed, and new eight-team league was set up. It was completely rebadged and clubs were stripped of their ethnic origins. The A-League, as it is now called, commenced in 2006. The National Rugby League competition (NRL) is far more robust. Although the competition was fractured with the establishment of a rival Super League in 1995, it is now solidly entrenched in New South Wales and Queensland, and to a lesser extent in Victoria. However, the competition no longer has teams in either South Australian or Western Australia, although this structural problem is slightly compensated for by having a team playing in Auckland in New Zealand. Rugby union is an interesting case because like League, it has only moderate support in Australia's southern states, but is a major code in New South Wales and Queensland. Union's Super-12 competition initially comprised five New Zealand teams, three Australian teams and four South African teams. However, in 2007 another two teams were added to the competition, namely Perth in Western Australia and a fifth South African team, thereby making it a Super-14 competition. A Melbourne team was admitted for the 2011 season, and now there are 15 teams in the competition which has been divided into a New Zealand division, an Australian division and a South African division. Finally, there is the Australian Football League (AFL), which arose out of the Victorian Football League in 1986. In 2011 the AFL became a 17-club competition, having admitted a team from the Queensland Gold Coast. A second New South Wales team was admitted in 2012, making it an 18-team competition. When this happened, the AFL had a minimum of two teams in every state. This indicates that the AFL has made significant inroads in the so-called 'hostile' rugby territory of New South Wales and Queensland.

Each of the above football codes has their own unique history and culture, but it is also the case that they are serious rivals in a highly competitive sporting marketplace. There are many arguments about the relative strengths of each code, and which national competition is the most successful (Stewart 2007b). In performance management terms, this is an interesting issue to address. Neither is it immediately clear as to how one should best go about doing a comparative evaluation of the performance of the leagues. This is because there are many different ways of undertaking the performance management task.

The management team of each national competition is very sensitive to developments in the rival leagues. They are also eager to trumpet and promote their successes, particularly if it means they have secured some strategic advantage over their competitors. At the same time, there are a number of

Table 13.3: **Performance measures for Australian national sport leagues**

Item	Descriptor/measure	Examples
Financial stability	• League turnover • Net assets	AFL turnover is more than AUS$360 million. NRL turnover is around AUS$200 million
Corporate support	• Sponsorship income • Stadium suites	AFL supported by more national brands (e.g. Vodafone, Air Emirates, Toyota), than NRL
Broadcasting rights fees	• Fees from TV stations • Fees from radio stations	AFL TV rights fee currently AUS$150 million p.a.; NRL TV rights fee currently AUS$900 around million p.a.
Media exposure	• Television rating • Print media coverage	AFL grand final draws 2.9 million TV audience; NRL grand final draws 2.3 million TV audience
Public interest	• Brand awareness • Match attendance	AFL average match attendance 38,000; NRL average match attendance 18,000
Spread/coverage	• Media coverage • Spread of teams and venues	AFL teams spread around five of six states; NRL teams spread around three of six states plus New Zealand
Competitive balance	• Win-loss ratios for each team • Premierships won by each team	NRL teams have slightly more closely aligned win-loss ratios (i.e. smaller standard deviation)
Game development	• Junior development programmes • Regional development programmes	AFL spends AUS$40 million a year on community development; NRL spends AUS$18 million on community development

Source: AFL (2011) and Stewart (2007b: Ch. 8).

critical success factors that are commonly used to rank the performance of the national leagues. These factors are first, total season attendance; second, total club membership; third, aggregate league revenue; fourth, income from television broadcast rights; and finally, weekly television audiences. The five somewhat crude measures give a very good indication of just how well each league performs. However, over recent times some additional measures have been incorporated into their performance management models. First there is the issue of the viability of teams, and the ability to balance their budgets. Second, there is the competitive balance of the league, and the extent to which it can guarantee fans a close and exciting contest. Third, there is the reputation of the league and the extent to which it is seen as a responsible sporting citizen. To this end the leagues are eager to promote equal opportunity for players and administrators, put in place anti-harassment rules, and have a strong anti-doping policy. In general the leagues are very sensitive to criticism about player misconduct, particularly when it involves some sort of sexual assault. A sample of key indicators for measuring the performance of Australian national football leagues is listed in Table 13.3.

Designing a performance management model appropriate for sport

The Balanced Scorecard (BSC) has many strengths, but it also requires significant adjustment to make it better fit the special requirements of sport organizations. One approach is to maintain the four basis dimensions that underpin the BSC and use it to design a customized performance model that reflects the special features of sport organizations. To this end the following '9 point' model of performance management has been designed.

The first performance dimension focuses on wins, awards and successes. This dimension recognizes the fact that most sport associations and clubs want be seen to be doing well and producing winning players and teams. In other words, faced with the choice of winning a championship or increasing profits, most clubs would prefer the winner's pennant or medal.

However, like all organizations, sport leagues, associations and clubs need ongoing funding to ensure their long-term viability, to pay their debts when they fall due and cover their operating costs from year to year. Therefore the second dimension is concerned with financial sustainability. In this respect, measures of revenue growth will not be enough, and more specific measures of profit, liquidity, long-term indebtedness, return on investment and net asset growth are all useful indicators.

The third dimension is market distribution, or the extent to which a sport league, association or club is able to facilitate the consumption of its particular sporting practice. If its major concern is with participation, then it needs to be aware of how many facilities it provides, their location and spread, and the experiential quality they offer. If the major concern is the potential audience that can be attracted, then it needs to be aware of the number of spectator seats it can provide, the radio exposure it will receive and the scale and breadth of any television broadcast.

The fourth dimension is market size and share. It is one thing to have a broad range and spread of facilities and venues, and a large number of television-broadcast hours, but it is another thing to attract a consistently large number of participants, spectators and viewers. It is also important to compare the numbers for these indicators with the numbers for other related sports that are seen to be competitors.

The fifth dimension is customer satisfaction, which is really a measure of how strongly participants, fans and members approve of the performance of the league, association or club. Sport organizations usually engender very passionate connections with their customer and member base, but there are also many instances when they attend games or activities less frequently, or more seriously downgrade their involvement. Surveys of participants, members and fans can reveal early signs of dissatisfaction, or alternatively indicate what is sustaining the relationship.

The sixth dimension is internal procedures and processes. Like Kaplan and Norton's similarly labelled dimension, it aims to highlight the key links in the value chain and how each stage is performing relative to the others. For sporting organizations it often begins with how well players are recruited, their numbers and overall quality. The recruitment and retention of members is also an important consideration and the question often arises as to the capacity of members to contribute time, expertise and money to the association and club's activities. The ability of players to improve their skill and overall performance is also a function of the support system, and in particular the skill and abilities of the coaching staff. This leads to the capacity of the organization to ensure a safe environment where the management of risk is taken seriously, and the incidence of litigation is slight. All the above processes are of course linked to administrative functions that can either enhance the player and member experience as poor training or sloppy systems can make the experience both unpleasant and costly. Many of the above factors can be difficult to quantify, but they nevertheless need serious consideration.

The seventh dimension is product improvement. In this respect sport is no different from business in that it operates in a very competitive marketplace, and constant innovation and product improvement is essential to attract new customers and retain the old. Some sports have been very successful in modifying their games to suit the needs of special groups, while others have been unable to move beyond their traditional practices. In some spectator sports there have been very slow improvements in venue quality, while in others there has been a virtual revolution in terms of stadium design and spectator comfort. Progressive changes in the design of sporting equipment have also improved product quality. In tennis, for example, the use of carbon fibre racket frames and the creation of larger 'sweet spots' have enabled average club-players to improve their standard of play and overall skill levels.

The eighth dimension is staff development and learning. Sport is a very person-centred, time-absorbing activity and therefore requires staff who have highly refined people management skills and the capacity to create an organizational culture that retains players and members. The growing technical sophistication of sport also means that traditional administrative, officiating and coaching skills are no longer adequate and therefore large-scale retraining and education are necessary to ensure a proper fit between the staff competencies and the new technologies and infrastructure that underpin contemporary sport.

The ninth dimension covers the economic, social and environmental impact that a sport league, association or club has on its surrounding community. Increasingly the level of support a government will provide to a sport organization is contingent upon the organization's ability to produce a positive economic, social or environmental impact. This trend has been exaggerated by the growing popularity of the triple-bottom-line accounting concept, which highlights the importance of going beyond profitability and wealth creation as the sole measure of an organization's contribution to society to include environmental and social impacts (Hums and Maclean 2009; Norman and MacDonald 2004). In this case sport organizations also have a responsibility to carefully manage and sustain their environment, and establish an organizational culture that values things like diversity, equal opportunity and the fair treatment of gays, lesbians and religious minorities.

This nine-dimensional model has the advantage of being broad and inclusive, and geared to the needs of sport in general. But, it needs to be customized to fit different sporting organizations. As we indicated before, an organization's strategic intent, and stakeholder interests, will shape the design of a performance evaluation model (Anthony and Young 2003; Atkinson *et al.* 1997; Robbins and Barnwell 2002; Williams 1998). For example the evaluation model for a national sporting body should be different from the model used to evaluate a professional sport club. The national sporting body will be more interested in participation rates, club development and the provision of quality local facilities. On the other hand, a professional sport club will be more concerned with its win-loss ratio, sponsor income, television ratings and membership levels.

Performance measures

Once a model is in place, it is then crucial to design performance measures. These measures should be able to precisely identify and quantify specific indicators of success or failure. Sometimes it is difficult to put a number on a measure. Customer and fan satisfaction readily comes to mind in this respect, but there are often ways of converting a subjective opinion into a measurable indicator.

It is one thing to identify some key performance indicators, and to collect some data under each heading. However it is another thing to make sense of the data. It is therefore important to develop some sort of benchmark or standard by which to measure the performance of a sport organization. There are two ways of doing this. The first is to undertake a longitudinal study that examines the progress of a sport organization over time. Take for example the performance of Athletics Australia (AA), the national governing body for athletics in Australia. A ten-year analysis of its financial performance would show it was often unable to balance its books. In 2003 it had accumulated a seriously worrying level of debt which brought on an organizational crisis. The crisis was addressed, and over the following eight years it expanded its revenue base substantially, and in preparing for the London 2012 Olympics, was relatively resource-rich. At the same time it was still reliant on government funds to balance its books. By any financial measure, AA's performance had improved dramatically over this period, although it was starting off from a low base. The same sort of longitudinal analysis could be applied to its participation levels and elite international performance. In each the data indicated small but significant improvement.

Another way of looking at AA's performance would be to compare it with other national sport bodies to see how it ranks. That is, it will also be important to undertake a comparative study by which the performance of AA is stacked up against a number of other national sport organizations. There are two ways of doing this. The first way would be compare it with similarly funded Australian national sport bodies like Swimming Australia or Rowing Australia. In this case, AA has not performed well, since both swimming and rowing have achieved regular gold medal winning performances at both World Championships and Olympic Games over the last ten years. The second way is to compare AA's performance with an equivalent national athletic association from another country. An appropriate point of comparison here might be the Canadian Athletics Federation since both countries have similar populations and the national athletic associations have a similar resource base. In this case the comparison would yield an elite performance outcome inferior to Swimming Australia, which by international standards performs just below the level of the USA national swim governing body, which makes it number two in the world.

The lesson to be learnt here is that the performance of a sport organization cannot be measured in a vacuum, or without some yardstick and point of comparison. At the minimum, either some form of longitudinal or comparative analysis should be undertaken. Ideally, a mixture of both methods would provide the best set of results.

In Practice 13.3

Measuring performance in a community leisure centre

As we indicated in the early part of this chapter, performance management systems have infiltrated their way into every nook and cranny of the business environment and public sector (Robbins and Barnwell 2002; Bouckaert and van Doren 2003). Moreover, they are not only applied to corporate performance, but also to many of the so-called micro activities that comprise the day-to-day operations of business enterprises. Community leisure centres in particular lend themselves to micro measurement. In the first place, they provide an array of person-centred activities that are subject to strong user responses and perceptions. Second, their services are not only rated on the scale, range and quality of its tangible facilities, but also on the quality of the service provided by the staff. Third, many community leisure centres are funded and subsidized through local government rates and taxes, and therefore need to ensure that scarce community resources are utilized as efficiently as possible (van der Graaf 1994).

It is useful to examine the performance of community leisure centres from two perspectives. The first perspective focuses on the efficient use of funds, staff and space. To get some idea of how funds are being used it is always good to start with some idea of the relationship between operating costs and income. This will generate an operating profit indicator and an expense recovery rate. And where more detail is needed, something like fees (admission charges) per visit or fees per unit of space can be calculated. It is also very important to identify not only the gross subsidy that may apply but also the subsidy per visit. There are also a number of sales and marketing related measures that can be used to indicate how well funds are being used in attracting visitors. They include things like total visits per space used and promotion cost per visitor. It is also important to measure facility usage. In this instance measures include visits per metre of space, maintenance cost per unit of centre expenditure and energy cost per metre of space. Finally, there are a number of measures that provide an indication of how well staff are being utilized. They include staff cost as a percentage of total income, staff costs as percentage of total centre expenditure and the ratio of desk staff to programming staff. A sample of performance indicators for community leisure centres is listed in Table 13.4.

The second perspective focuses on the level of service quality. In this instance it is a matter of finding out what visitors think of their experiences in the centre (Beech and Chadwick 2004). Their experiences are usually divided into five categories. They are: first, the quality of the tangible product or

Table 13.4: Sample of efficiency indicators for a community leisure centre

Indicator	Description	Examples
Expense recovery rate	Ratio of total centre income to total centre expenses	Income of $5 million, expenses of $4.5 million, expense recovery rate is 1.11
Admission fees per visit	Total fees divided by number of visits	1,000 visits per week, $6,000 in fees, admission fee per visit is $6
Visits per space available	Visits divided by amount of space	1,000 visits per week, 50 square metres of space, visit per metre-space is 200
Promotion costs per visitor	Promotion costs divided by number of visitors	1,000 visits per week, $1,000 of promotion per week, promotion cost per visit is $1
Maintenance costs rate	Ratio of total centre maintenance costs to total centre income	Maintenance costs are $1.5 million, centre income is $5 million, maintenance cost rate is 0.30 or 30%
Staff costs per unit of space	Staff costs divided by space	Staff costs are $3 million, space is 50 square metres, staff cost per unit of space is $6,000

Source: AFL (2011) and Stewart (2007b: Ch. 8).

service itself; second, the reliability and dependability of the service; third, the responsiveness of staff and their willingness to assist; fourth, an assurance that staff will be trustworthy and courteous; and finally, the degree to which staff are empathetic and provide individual attention. There are many models to choose from and many rating tools. Some of the more sophisticated tools aim to calculate a service delivery gap, which is nothing more than the difference between what customers expected, and what they experienced (van der Graaf 1994). In the end, all they are doing is providing a customer rating of the facilities and personal service provided. Typically this will be done by a survey or questionnaire that asks visitors to score the specific services on a rating scale of 1–5. Ratings of 1 usually indicate low levels of satisfaction, while ratings of 5 will indicate high levels of satisfaction.

Summary

The above discussion suggests that while the introduction of performance management systems into sport organizations can be costly, and sometimes create an administrative straightjacket for its staff, officials, volunteers and members, it can also bring substantial benefits (Anthony and Young 2003). In fact a sport organization that does not provide a systematic evaluation of its performance would be derelict in its duty to stakeholders. The question is really one of what form and shape the performance management system should take. At this point it is important to say that there is no one best performance management system. It all depends on the particular sport organization being studied, its primary strategic goals and the environment in which it operates. A good starting point is to use Kaplan and Norton's BSC as the foundation, and customize it to fit the sport organization's specific needs. The 9-point model described above gives a number of possibilities, but at all times the measures should be quantifiable, linked to the sport organization's primary goals and consistent with stakeholder expectations.

Review questions

1 What does a performance management system aim to do?
2 What are the origins of performance management and what do these origins tell us about its possible strengths and weaknesses?
3 What might prevent a sport organization from implementing a system of performance management?
4 What are the benefits that will follow from the implementation of a performance management system?
5 What are the key components of Kaplan and Norton's BSC?
6 How might you go about modifying the BSC to make it better fit the special features of sport organizations?
7 What specific measures can best reveal the financial performance of a sport organization?
8 How can the intrinsically vague concept of customer satisfaction be 'hardened-up' to provide a quantitative, concrete measure of the service quality in a community leisure centre?
9 What would you advise a sport club or association to do in order to ensure it was delivering its sport services in a fair, equitable and environmentally friendly way?

Further reading

To get a more detailed picture of the fundamentals of performance management, and how it has been used in both private and public sectors, see Anthony and Young (2003); Bryson (2004); Bouckaert and van Dooren (2003); and Williams (1978). In order to obtain a fuller appreciation of the theoretical foundations of performance management, its relation to organizational effectiveness, and problems of implementation, refer to Chapter 3 of Robbins and Barnwell (2002), and Bouckaert (1995).

To secure more details on what makes sport both similar to and different from the world of business go to Smith and Stewart (2010).

For a detailed account of how to set up performance management systems for Olympic sport organizations see Chappelet and Bayle (2005: 39–110).

A comprehensive comparative evaluation of the four professional football leagues operating in Australia can be found in Chapter 8 of Stewart (2007b).

Relevant websites

For an update on the balanced scorecard approach to performance management – www.balancedscorecard.org

Japan's professional soccer (i.e. association football) league, the J-League is one of Japan's most popular sport competitions. To obtain a general picture of its overall level of performance – www.j-league.or.jp

For a detailed discussion of the Global Reporting Initiative (GRI) and related indicators – www.cisco.com/web/about/ac227/ac333/cisco-and-citizenship/global-reporting.html

Nike has developed a strong corporate social responsibility programme in recent years. For a detailed discussion of their programme – www.socialfunds.com/csr/reports/Nike_FY05-06_Corporate_Responsibility_Report.pdf

Formula One Grand Prix Circuit

Ever since the first motor cars rolled of the assembly plants in the USA in the early part of the twentieth century, people around the world have had an often obsessive fascination with them. The idea that cars could be used to create a new form of sport was quickly converted into practice, and by the 1930s many types of race meeting were established, where stock-standard touring cars were competing with customized race cars for the hearts and minds of car-racing enthusiasts.

An international governing body for motor sports was also established at this time, and having been headquartered in Paris, was given the name of the Fédération Internationale de l'Automobile, or FIA for short (Hums and Maclean 2009). It was, and still is, a non-profit-making association that now brings together more than 200 national motoring and sporting organizations from just over 130 countries on five continents.

FIA has a multifaceted role. First, it represents the rights of motoring organizations and motor car users throughout the world. It has campaigned on such things as such as safety, mobility, the environment and consumer law. FIA also promotes the interests of motorists at the United Nations, within the European Union, and through other international bodies. FIA is also the governing body for motor sport worldwide. It administers the rules and regulations for all international four-wheel motor sport including the FIA Formula One World Championship, FIA World Rally Championship and FIA World Touring Car Championship (www.fia.com).

However, plans for an elite level, high performance 'Formula One' drivers' championship were not formulated until the late 1930s. The plans were shelved with the onset of the Second World War, but in 1946 the idea was rekindled, races were held and the following year a decision was made to launch a drivers' championship (Hums and Maclean 2009). The first FIA endorsed world championship race was held at the Silverstone in England, in 1950, and while only seven of the 20 Formula One races that season counted towards the title, the championship was nevertheless up and running (ibid.).

There was no shortage of so-called 'privateers', who were drivers that operated on their own, and who bought and raced their own cars. Nevertheless, the formula was very quickly dominated by major pre-war manufactures such as Alfa Romeo, Ferrari, Maserati and Mercedes Benz. Although Giuseppe ('Nino') Farina won the inaugural title in 1950, the dominant driver over the decade was Juan Manuel Fangio from Argentina, who won five drivers' championships. The 1960s was a also a period of growth, with the Stirling Moss, an Englishman, and Jack Brabham, an Australian, being the best-known racers.

In the early 1970s Bernie Ecclestone, the English motor-sports entrepreneur, rearranged the management of Formula One's commercial rights, and turned the sport into a billion-dollar global business. In 1971 he bought the Brabham team and subsequently gained a seat on Council of the Formula One Constructors' Association (FOCA). In 1978 he became its president. Before the Ecclestone era, FIA and circuit owners controlled many aspects of the sport, but Ecclestone changed all this when he convinced the teams that their net worth would be enhanced by bypassing FIA and negotiating direct with manufacturers and circuit managers as a coordinated unit. In 1979 FIA not surprisingly clashed with FOCA over revenues and regulations, and matters deteriorated to such an extent that FOCA threatened to boycott races and even form a breakaway global circuit. But in the end it was understood that FOCA and FIA had to work together to achieve the best outcome for the sport, with Ecclestone front and centre.

Further tensions arose in the early 2000s when manufacturer-owned teams – which included Renault, BMW, Toyota, Honda and Ferrari – dominated the championship. They also used the commercial muscle of their Grand Prix Manufacturers Association (GPMA) to negotiate not only a larger share of Formula One's rapidly increasing revenues, but also a greater say in the sport's planning and management processes.

Under the ever-opportunistic eye of Ecclestone, the global expansion of Formula One continued, with new races being located in lucrative markets in east Asia and the Middle East. Whereas the inaugural 1950 world championship season comprised only seven races, the schedule expanded rapidly over the following 60 years. The number of races plateaued between 16 and 17 during the 1980s and 1990s, but has recently risen to 20. Going into 2012 the circuit was structured as follows:

1	BAHRAIN GRAND PRIX	Venue: Sakhir, Manama – Date: early March
2	AUSTRALIAN GRAND PRIX	Venue: Albert Park, Melbourne – Date: late March
3	MALAYSIAN GRAND PRIX	Venue: Sepang, Kuala Lumpur – Date: early April
4	CHINESE GRAND PRIX	Venue: Shanghai International Circuit – Date: late April
5	TURKISH GRAND PRIX	Venue: Istanbul Park – Date: early May
6	SPANISH GRAND PRIX	Venue: Circuit de Catalunya, Montmelo – Date: mid-May
7	MONACO GRAND PRIX	Venue: Circuit de Monaco, Monte Carlo – Date: late May
8	CANADIAN GRAND PRIX	Venue: Circuit Gilles Villeneuve, Montreal – Date: mid-June
9	EUROPEAN GRAND PRIX	Venue: Valencia, Spain – Date: late June
10	BRITISH GRAND PRIX	Venue: Silverstone, Northamptonshire — Date: early July
11	GERMAN GRAND PRIX	Venue: Nurburgring – Date: mid-July
12	HUNGARIAN GRAND PRIX	Venue: Hungaroring, Budapest – Date: late July
13	BELGIAN GRAND PRIX	Venue: Spa-Francorchamps – Date: late August
14	ITALIAN GRAND PRIX	Venue: Monza – Date: mid-September
15	SINGAPORE GRAND PRIX	Venue: Marina Bay – Date: late September
16	JAPANESE GRAND PRIX	Venue: Suzuka – Date: early October
17	SOUTH KOREA GRAND PRIX	Venue: Yeongam – Date: mid-October
18	INDIAN GRAND PRIX	Venue: New Delhi – Date: late October
19	ABU DHABI GRAND PRIX	Venue: Yas Marina, United Arab Emirates – Date: mid-November
20	BRAZILIAN GRAND PRIX	Venue: Interlagos, São Paulo – Date: late November

The current global circuit arrangements for Formula One are very impressive, and take in every continent except for Africa. But Formula One has also been surrounded by controversies, and allegations of greedy, anti-social and sometime even corrupt behaviour, which, according to the sport's critics, have taken the following forms.

● It assaults the environment by occupying public space, making an enormous amount of noise.

- It has an embedded dependence on fossil fuel products which makes it totally at odds with current global policies aimed at controlling greenhouse gases by reducing carbon emissions and consequently softening so-called carbon footprints.
- There are regular governance and management battles between FOCA, FIA and GPMA.
- Teams often seem to be on the verge of breaking away from Formula One and creating rival circuits.
- There are frequent accusations of race result manipulation. These allegations were confirmed in 2009 when it was revealed that Nelson Piquet Jnr had been ordered to crash his car at the 2008 Singapore Grand Prix for the benefit of his team-mate. Renault boss Flavio Briatore was subsequently banned from the sport.
- In some cities, and in Melbourne in particular, there is growing concern that the costs of mounting the race are increasing at such a rate that the costs of conducting an event will eventually outweigh the benefits. The Melbourne event, for example, is suffering from a fall in live attendance and has had extreme difficulty securing sufficient heavyweight sponsors. There is also resentment over the management fee that has to be paid to Ecclestone to retain the event. At last count it nearly $25 million, an amount which led some critics to suggest that there was no longer any point in conducting the race in Melbourne, since it was nothing more than a burden on local taxpayers.

Controversies aside, Formula One is a highly profitable enterprise, and it has enormous global reach through its international circuit, its high profile global sponsors and its lucrative television broadcast contact arrangements. Its total viewing figure is now in excess of 350 million and it regularly attracts 100,000–150,000 fans to its race meets (Hums and Maclean 2009). It is the archetypal hyper-commercial hyper-modern sporting enterprise. According to an analysis undertaken by Deloitte International, one of the world largest accounting firms, Formula One now boasts the world's highest revenue-generating annual sporting events. Each of its top eight Grand Prix events in 2008 had an average revenue of just under $220 million. This compares favourably with the per-game/event values of $25 million in the American National Football league (NFL), $8 million in the English FA Premier League and $2 million in the American Major League Baseball (MLB) (Carter 2011; Zimbalist 2006).

Formula One's 2008 global revenues of just over $4 billion make it the third most commercialized sport competition in the world. Only the NFL ($7 billion) and MLB ($6 billion) earn more revenue, but they do it by running substantially more so-called events. The Premier League clubs' combined revenue was just under $4 billion for the same period. The $4 billion is comprised of (1) central revenues, which come from broadcasting rights fees, race sponsorship and corporate hospitality; (2) team revenues, which include sponsorship and contributions from commercial partners and owners; and (3) circuit revenues, which come from ticketing and additional sponsorships (Carter 2011; Hums and Maclean 2009; Zimbalist 2006).

However, when compared with many other major sports, Formula One attracts a much lower proportion of its revenues from event day attendees. Ticket receipts and other attendee secondary spending currently represent only around 10 per cent of total revenue and this is a weakness that organizers are hoping to address in the near future.

So, how should we go about measuring the performance of the Formula One Grand Prix Circuit? Well, the short answer is 'with great difficulty'. The fundamental problem is to actually sort out what it is we aim to measure. In a global enterprise of this type there are not just the financial performance issues to consider, but also its economic, social, cultural and environmental impacts. One approach is to build a model of performance evaluation that takes into account all of these factors to some extent or other. A multi-factorial approach is gaining more credence as governments around the world are trying to secure the best outcomes from these mega-sport events. The fact of the matter is that commercial businesses are often criticized for thinking only of the profits they make, and ignoring the social consequences of their strategic decisions and the outputs they deliver. This dilemma is particularly striking in the case of tobacco companies, which have always had a close commercial link to motor racing. On one hand there are profits to be made, but on the other hand there is evidence that links smoking cigarettes to lung cancer and heart disease. Sport, and motor racing in particular, has for many years had a close relationship with tobacco producers, who have provided millions of dollars of sponsor funds to both community and professional sport (www.thelancet.com).

There is now growing pressure from both government and the public in general for businesses to move beyond the bottom line and take into account the effect their decisions have on the wider community. This idea has given rise to the concept of triple-bottom-line accounting, which gets business to consider their contribution to not just economic prosperity, but also to social justice and environmental quality. While the measurement of social justice and environmental quality is fraught with danger, the overall aim is to see that profits and net worth are just one measure of the performance of an organization. Triple-bottom-line accounting consequently provides for three measures of how a business contributes to society, with each measure being geared around the value-added concept. These measures are:

1 economic value-added;
2 social value-added; and
3 environmental value-added.

This way of measuring performance presents many challenges for sport organizations. It has already been noted that sport organizations are motivated by more than money. For a national sporting body the growth of the sport may be equally important, and for a professional sports club the dominant goal may be on-field success. However, despite the primacy of these goals, sport organizations can equally make decisions and produce outputs that have negative consequences for society in general. The heavy use of tobacco companies as sponsors may have secured a valuable source of funds, but the subsequent association of tobacco products with glamorous sport stars was instrumental in convincing young people that smoking was socially desirable, even if it might kill them in the long run. In some sports heavy drinking of alcohol products is part of the club culture, and in these cases no success is seen as complete without a long binge-drinking session. Similarly, in professional sport leagues, where neo-tribalism is strong, groups of rival supporters will often resolve their antagonism with a wild brawl. Football hooliganism in Britain is the archetypal model in this respect. All of these outputs have negative social consequences, and it therefore makes senses to encourage sport clubs, associations and leagues to measure their overall performance in terms of their social and environmental impact as well as their participation impact, win-loss impact or revenue raising impact.

Recently, a number of global businesses with the support of the United Nations developed a corporate social responsibility (CSR) programme called the Global Reporting Initiative (GRI). The mission of GRI is to design and promulgate sustainability reporting guidelines for each of the economic, social and environmental outputs identified above. Organizations that sign up to GRI are expected to enact reporting systems that are transparent and accessible, provide quality and reliable information, and include information that is relevant and complete. GRI has also compiled a list of factors under each of the economic, social and environmental headings that indicate specific issues that require addressing. A sample of factors particularly relevant to sport organizations is provided in Table 13.5.

Table 13.5: GRI performance indicators

Performance category	Performance measures
Direct economic impacts	• Sales to satisfied customers • Purchases from suppliers • Employees hired • Taxes paid • Dividend and interest paid
Product responsibility	• Safety and durability • Truth in advertising and product labelling
Work practices	• Health, safety and security • Training, education and consultation • Appropriate wages and conditions
Social practices	• No bribery and corruption • Transparent lobbying • Free from collusion and coercion
Human rights	• Non-discriminatory hiring practices • Free from forced labour
Environmental impacts	• Efficient energy use • Appropriate water recycling • Controlled carbon and other emissions • Waste management • Maintenance of biodiversity

While the GRI model of performance management is complex, it will encourage sport organizations to be more systematic in the way they build their stakeholder relations. It will also enable them to go beyond revenue growth and on-field success and evaluate the contribution they are making to the wider society, and monitor their impact on the physical environment. This can only be a 'good thing to do'. Yet when applied to the Formula One Grand Prix, it is also a 'hard thing to do'. But is not impossible, and there is great advantage in taking a more holistic approach to measuring its performance.

Case study questions

1 How does the Formula One circuit perform from a financial perspective?
2 How does it perform from a social perspective? That is, are people in the host venue better off for having the race in their backyard, so to speak?
3 Is there any political benefit from having a global circuit that covers much international territory, and brings the world together, if only for a couple of hours every fortnight?
4 Is there any unethical or, indeed, corrupt behaviour to be concerned about, and even more interestingly how might we measure it?
5 How does Formula One perform in terms of its global citizenship, and its symbolic relevance to the climate change problem and carbon emission issue?
6 Finally, on balance, how would you rate the overall performance of the Formula One Grand Prix circuit?

References

Allison, M. (2002) *Sports Clubs in Scotland Summary: Research Digest no. 59*, Edinburgh: Sports Scotland.

Amar, A.D., Hentrich, C. and Hlupic, V. (2009) 'To be a Better Leader, Give up Authority', *Harvard Business Review*, 87(12): 22–24.

AFL (2011) *Annual Report 2010*, Melbourne: Australian Football League.

Amis, J. and Slack, T. (1996) 'The size-structure relationship in voluntary sport organizations', *Journal of Sport Management*, 10(1): 76–86.

Anthony, R. and Young, D. (2003) *Management Control in Nonprofit Organizations*, 7th edition, New York: McGraw Hill.

Atkinson, A., Waterhouse, J.H. and Wells, R. (1997) 'A stakeholder approach to strategic performance measurement', *Sloan Management Review*, Spring: 25–37.

Atrill, P., McLaney, E., Harvey, D. and Jenner, M. (2006) *Accounting: An Introduction*, Frenchs Forest, NSW: Pearson Education Australia.

ASC (Australian Sports Commission) (2000) *Committee Management, Active Australia Club/ Association Management Program*, Canberra: Australian Sports Commission.

ASC (Australian Sports Commission) (2003) *Independent Soccer Review: Report of the Independent Soccer Review Committee into the Structure, Governance and Management of Soccer in Australia*, Canberra: Australian Sports Commission.

ASC (Australian Sports Commission) (2004) *Sport Innovation and Best Practice: Governance*, Canberra: Australian Sports Commission.

Australian Bureau of Statistics (2005) *Involvement in Organised Sport and Physical Activity, Australia, Cat. No. 6285.0*, Canberra: Australian Bureau of Statistics.

Baldwin, R. and Cave, M. (1999) *Understanding Regulation: Theory, Strategy and Practice*, Oxford: Oxford University Press.

Bass, B.M. (1985) *Leadership and Performance Beyond Expectations*, New York: The Free Press.

Bass, B.M. (1990) *Bass & Stogdill's Handbook of Leadership: Theory, Research, and Managerial Applications*, 3rd edition, New York: Free Press.

Bass, B.M. and Avolio, B.J. (1994) *Improving Organisational Effectiveness Through Transformational Leadership*, London: Sage Publications.

Beech, J. and Chadwick, S. (eds) (2004) *The Business of Sport Management*, Harlow: Prentice Hall.

Bellamy, R. (1998) 'The evolving television sports marketplace', in L. Wenner (ed.), *MediaSport*, London: Routledge, pp. 73–87.

Berger, P. and Luckmann, T. (1967) *The Social Construction of Reality: A Treatise on the Sociology of Knowledge*, London: Penguin.

Block, S.R. (1998) *Perfect Nonprofit Boards: Myths, Paradoxes and Paradigms*, Needham Heights, MA: Simon & Schuster.

References

Bloomfield, J. (2003) *Australia's Sporting Success: The Inside Story*. Sydney: University of New South Wales Press.

Bouckaert, G. (1995) 'Improving performance management', in A. Halachmi and G. Bouckaert (eds), *The Enduring Challenges in Public Management*, San Francisco, CA: Jossey-Bass.

Bouckaert, G. and van Doren, W. (2003) 'Performance measurement and management in public sector organisations', in T. Bovaird and E. Lofler (eds), *Public Management and Governance*, London: Routledge.

Boyle, R. and Haynes, R. (2000) *Power Play: Sport, the Media and Popular Culture*, Sydney: Longman.

Braithwaite, J. (2008) *Regulatory Capitalism: How it Works, Ideas for Making it Work Better*, Cheltenham: Edward Elgar.

Braithwaite J. and Drahos, P. (2000) *Global Business Regulation*, Cambridge: Cambridge University Press.

Bryson, J. (2004) *Strategic Planning for Public and Nonprofit Organisations: A guide to Strengthening and Sustaining Organizational Achievement*, San Francisco, CA: Jossey-Bass/Wiley.

Carter, D. (2011) *Money Games: Profiting from the Convergence of Sport and Entertainment*, Princeton, NJ: Princeton University Press.

Carver, J. (1997) *Boards that Make a Difference: A New Design for Leadership in Nonprofit and Public Organizations*, 2nd edition, San Francisco, CA: Jossey-Bass.

Cashman, R. (1995) *Paradise of Sport*, Melbourne: Oxford University Press.

Chalip, L., Johnson, A. and Stachura, L. (eds) (1996) *National Sports Policies: An International Handbook*, Westport, CT: Greenwood Press.

Chappelet, J. and Bayle, E. (2005) *Strategic and Performance Management of Olympic Sport Organisations*, Champaign, IL: Human Kinetics.

Chelladurai, P. (2006) *Human Resource Management in Sport and Recreation*, Champaign, IL: Human Kinetics.

Clarke, T. (ed.) (2004) *Theories of Corporate Governance,* London: Routledge.

Coakley, J. and Pike, E. (2009) *Sport in Society*, Sydney: McGraw Hill.

Cousens, L. and Slack, T. (2005) 'Field-level change: The case of North American major league professional sport', *Journal of Sport Management*, 19(1): 13–42.

Cuskelly, G. (2004) 'Volunteer retention in community sport organisations', *European Sport Management Quarterly*, 4(2): 59–76.

Cuskelly, G., Hoye, R. and Auld, C. (2006) *Working with Volunteers in Sport: Theory and Practice*, London: Routledge.

Deming, W. (1993) *The New Economics for Industry, Government, Education*, Cambridge, MA: MIT.

Dheensaw, C. (1994) *The Commonwealth Games: The First 60 Years, 1930–1990*, Sydney: ABC/Orca Publishing.

Doherty, A. (1998) 'Managing our human resources: A review of organizational behaviour in sport', *Journal of Sport Management*, 12(1): 1–24.

Downward, P. and Dawson, A. (2000) *The Economics of Professional Team Sports*, London: Routledge.

Dressler, G. (2003) *Human Resource Management*, Upper Saddle River, NJ: Prentice Hall.

Drucker, P.F. (1990) 'Lessons for successful nonprofit governance', *Nonprofit Management and Leadership*, 1(1): 7–14.

Euchner, C. (1993) *Playing the Field: Why Sports Teams Move and Cities Fight to Keep Them*, Baltimore, MD: John Hopkins University Press.

Ferkins, L., Shilbury, D. and McDonald, G. (2009) 'Board involvement in strategy: Advancing the governance of sport irganizations', *Journal of Sport Management*, 23(3): 245–277.

Ferrand, A. and Stotlar, D. (2010) 'Introduction: New perspectives in sport event marketing', *International Journal of Sport Management and Marketing*, 7(3/4): 145–155.

Fiedler, F.E. (1967) *A Theory of Leadership Effectiveness*, New York: McGraw-Hill.

Fielding, L, Miller, L. and Brown, J. (1999) 'Harlem Globetrotters International, Inc.', *Journal of Sport Management*, 13(1): 45–77.

Fletcher, K. (1999) 'Four books on nonprofit boards and governance', *Nonprofit Management and Leadership*, 9(4): 435–441.

Football Federation Australia (2011) 'AFC Asian Cup focus of football review', news release 27 April, Sydney: Football Federation Australia.

Football Governance Research Centre (2004) *The State of the Game: The Corporate Governance of Football Clubs 2004*, Research paper 2004 No. 3, Football Governance Research Centre, Birkbeck, University of London.

Fort, R. (2010) *Sports Economics*, 2nd edition, Upper Saddle River, NJ: Pearson Prentice Hall.

Fort, R. (2011) *Sport Economics*, 3rd edition, Upper Saddle River, NJ: Prentice Hall/Pearson.

Foster, G., Greyser, A. and Walsh, B. (2006) *The Business of Sports: Cases and Text on Strategy and Management*, Mason, OH: Thompson South-Western.

Friedman, M., Parent, M. and Mason, D. (2004) 'Building a framework for issues management in sport through stakeholder theory', *European Sport Management Quarterly*, 4(3): 170–190.

Frisby, W. (1986) 'The organizational structure and effectiveness of voluntary organizations: The case of Canadian national sport governing bodies', *Journal of Park and Recreation Administration*, 4(3): 61–74.

Frontiera, J. (2010) 'Leadership and organizational culture transformation in professional sport', *Journal of Leadership and Organizational Studies*, 17(1): 171–186.

Frosdick, S. and Walley, L. (eds) (1997) *Sport and Safety Management*, Oxford: Butterworth Heinemann.

Gardiner, S., Parrish, R. and Siekman, R. (2009) *EU, Sport, Law and Policy*, The Hague: Asser Press.

Gómez, S., Kase, K. and Urruria, I. (2010) *Value Creation and Sport Management*, Cambridge: Cambridge University Press.

Gratton, C. and Taylor, P. (1991) *Government and the Economics of Sport*, London: Longman.

Grattton, C. and Taylor, P. (2000) Economics of Sport and recreation, Abingdon: Taylor and Francis.

Green, M. (2006) 'From "sport for all" to not about "sport" at all: Interrogating sport policy interventions in the United Kingdom', *European Sport Management Quarterly*, 6(3): 217–238.

Green, M. and Houlihan, B. (2005) *Elite Sport Development*, London: Routledge.

Greenfield, S. and Osborn, G. (2001) *Regulating Football: Commodification, Consumption and the Law*, London: Pluto Press.

Hanlon, C. and Cuskelly, G. (2002) 'Pulsating major sport event organizations: A framework for inducting managerial personnel', *Event Management: An International Journal*, 7(4): 231–243.

Hart, L. (2006) *Accounting Demystified: A Self Teaching Guide*, New York: McGraw Hill.

Harvard Business Review (1998) *On Measuring Corporate Performance*, Boston, MA: Harvard Business Review Press.

Heimovics, R.D. and Herman, R.D. (1990) 'Responsibility for critical events in nonprofit organizations', *Nonprofit and Voluntary Sector Quarterly*, 19(1): 59–72.

Henry, I. and Lee, P.C. (2004) 'Governance and ethics in sport', in J. Beech and S. Chadwick (eds), *The Business of Sport Management*, Harlow: Prentice Hall.

Herman, R.D. and Heimovics, R. (1990) 'The effective nonprofit executive: Leader of the board', *Nonprofit Management and Leadership*, 1(2): 167–180.

Herman, R.D. and Heimovics, R. (1994) 'Executive leadership', in R.D. Herman and Associates (eds), *The Jossey-Bass Handbook of Nonprofit Leadership and Management*, San Francisco, CA: Jossey-Bass, pp. 137–153.

References

Herman, R.D. and Renz, D.O. (1997) 'Multiple constituencies and the social construction of nonprofit organizational effectiveness', *Nonprofit and Voluntary Sector Quarterly*, 26(2): 185–206.

Herman, R.D. and Renz, D.O. (1998) 'Nonprofit organizational effectiveness: Contrasts between especially effective and less effective organizations', *Nonprofit Management and Leadership*, 9(1): 23–38.

Herman, R.D. and Renz, D.O. (2000) 'Board practices of especially effective and less effective local nonprofit organizations', *American Review of Public Administration*, 30(2): 146–160.

Hersey, P. and Blanchard, K. (1977) *Management of Organizational Behaviour: Utilizing Human Resources*, Englewood Cliffs, NJ: Prentice-Hall.

Hess, R. and Stewart, R. (eds) (1998) *More than a Game: An Unauthorised History of Australian Football*, Melbourne: Melbourne University Press.

Hess, R., Nicholson, M., Stewart, B. and de Moore, G. (2008) *A National Game: The History of Australian Rules Football*, Melbourne: Viking/Penguin.

Hill, L.A. (2008) 'Where will we find tomorrow's leaders?' *Harvard Business Review*, 86(1): 123–129.

Hillary Commission (2000) *The Growing Business of Sport and Leisure: The Impact of the Physical Leisure Industry in New Zealand*, Wellington: Hillary Commission.

Hindley, D. (2003) *Resource Guide in Governance and Sport*, Learning and Teaching Support Network in Hospitality, Leisure, Sport and Tourism, inline, available at: www.heacademy. ac.uk/assets/hlst/documents/resource_guides/governance_and_sport.pdf.

Hockey Canada (2007) *Annual Report 2007*, Calgary: Hockey Canada.

Hockey Canada (2010) *Annual Report 2010*, Calgary: Hockey Canada.

Hoggett, J., Edwards, L. and Medlin, J. (2006) *Accounting*, 6th edition, Milton, Qld: Wiley.

Horne, D. (1964) *The Lucky Country*, Ringwood: Penguin Books.

Houle, C.O. (1960) *The Effective Board*, New York: Association Press.

Houle, C.O. (1997) *Governing Boards: Their Nature and Nurture*, San Francisco, CA: Jossey-Bass.

Houlihan, B. (1997) *Sport Policy and Politics: A Comparative Analysis*, London: Routledge.

Houlihan, B. and Green, M. (2007) *Comparative Elite Sport Development: Systems, Structures and Public Policy*, London: Elsevier.

Houlihan, B. and White, A. (2002) *The Politics of Sport Development: Development of Sport or Development through Sport?* London: Routledge.

House, R.J. (1971) 'A path-goal theory of leader effectiveness', *Administrative Science Quarterly*, 16(3): 321–338

House, R.J. and Mitchell, T.R. (1974) 'Path-goal theory of leadership', *Contemporary Business*, 3(Fall): 81–91.

Howard, D. and Crompton, J. (2004) *Financing Sport*, 2nd edition, Morgantown, WV: Fitness Information Technology.

Hoye, R. and Cuskelly, G. (2003) 'Board-executive relationships within voluntary sport organisations', *Sport Management Review*, 6(1): 53–73.

Hoye, R. and Cuskelly, G. (2007) *Sport Governance*, Oxford: Elsevier Butterworth-Heinemann.

Hoye, R. and Doherty, A. (2011) 'Nonprofit sport board performance: A review and directions for future research', *Journal of Sport Management*, 25(3): 272–285.

Hoye, R., Nicholson, M. and Houlihan, B. (2010) *Sport and Policy: Issues and Analysis*, Jordon Hill: Elsevier/Butterworth Heinemann.

Hoye, R., Nicholson, M. and Smith, A. (2008) 'Unique aspects of managing sport organizations', in C. Wankel (ed.), *21st Century Management: A Reference Handbook*, Thousand Oaks, CA: Sage, pp. 499–507.

Human Kinetics National Intelligence Council (2000) *Global Trends 2015: A Dialogue about the Future with Nongovernment Experts*, Washington, DC: National Foreign Intelligence Board.

Hums, M. and Maclean, J. (2009) *Governance and Policy in Sport Organisations*, 2nd edition, Scottsdale, AZ: Holcomb Hathaway.

Hylton, K. and Bramham, P. (eds) (2008) *Sports Development: Policy, Processes and Practice*, 2nd edition London: Routledge.

Hylton, K., Bramham, P., Jackson, D. and Nesti, M. (eds) (2001) *Sport Development*, London: Routledge.

Institute for Volunteering Research (2008) *Management Matters: A National Survey of Volunteer Management Capacity*, London: Institute for Volunteering Research.

Institute for Volunteering Research and Volunteering England (2008) *A Winning Team? The Impacts of Volunteers in Sport*, London: Institute for Volunteering Research.

International Cricket Council (20007) *Financial Statements 2007*, online, available at: http://icc-cricket.yahoo.net/publications/annual_report.php.

International Cricket Council (2011) *Financial Statements 2011*, online, available at: http://icc-cricket.yahoo.net/publications/annual_report.php

Jaggard, E. (2006) *Between the Flags: One Hundred Summers of Australian Surf Lifesaving*, Sydney: UNSW Press.

Jarzabkowski, P. and Spee, P.A. (2009) 'Strategy-as-practice: A review and future directions for the field', *International Journal of Management Reviews*, 11(1): 69–95.

John, G. and Sheard, R. (1997) *Stadia: A Design and Development Guide*, Oxford: Architectural Press.

Johnson, G., Langley, A., Melin, L. and Whittington, R. (2007) *Strategy as Practice: Research Directions and Resources*, New York: Cambridge University Press.

Johnson, G., Scholes, K. and Whittington, R. (2008) *Exploring Corporate Strategy*, 8th edition, London: Prentice-Hall.

Jung, T., Scott, T., Davies, Huw T.O., Bower, P., Whalley, D., McNally, R. and Russell, M. (2009) 'Instruments for exploring organizational culture: A review of the literature', *Public Administration Review*, 69(6): 1087–1096.

Kahle, L. and Close, A. (eds) (2011) *Consumer Behavior Knowledge for Effective Sports and Event Marketing*, New York: Taylor & Francis.

Kaplan, R. and Norton, D. (1992) 'The balanced scorecard: Measures that drive performance', *Harvard Business Review*, January/February: 71–79.

Kaplan, R. and Norton, D. (1996) *The Balanced Scorecard*, Boston, MA: Harvard University Press.

Kikulis, L.M., Slack, T. and Hinings, B. (1992) 'Institutionally specific design archetypes: A framework for understanding change in national sport organizations', *International Review for the Sociology of Sport*, 27(4): 343–368.

Kikulis, L.M., Slack, T. and Hinings, B. (1995) 'Toward an understanding of the role of agency and choice in the changing structure of Canada's national sport organizations', *Journal of Sport Management*, 9(2): 135–154.

Kikulis, L.M., Slack, T., Hinings, B. and Zimmermann, A. (1989) 'A structural taxonomy of amateur sport organizations', *Journal of Sport Management*, 3(2): 129–150.

Kotter, J. P. (1990) *A Force for Change: How Leadership Differs from Management*, New York: The Free Press.

Kouzes, J.M. and Posner, B.Z. (2006) *A Leader's Legacy*, Hoboken, NJ: Jossey-Bass.

Leisure Industries Research Centre (2003) *Sports Volunteering in England 2002: A Report for Sport England*, Sheffield: Leisure Industries Research Centre.

Li, M., Hofacre, S. and Mahony, D. (2001) *Economics of Sport*. Morgantown: Fitness Information Technology.

Lipsky, R. (1981) *How We Play The Game: Why Sports Dominate American Life*, Boston, MA: Beacon Press.

References

Locke, E.A. (1991) *The Essence of Leadership: The Four Keys to Leading Successfully*, New York: Lexington Books.

Lyons, M. (2001) *Third Sector: The Contribution of Nonprofit and Cooperative Enterprises in Australia*, Crows Nest, NSW: Allen & Unwin.

MacLean, J. (2009) 'Auditing performance management practices: A comparison of Canadian sport organisations', *International Journal of Sport Management and Marketing*, 5(3): 295–309.

McLeish, H. (2010) *Review of Scottish Football, Part 2 Governance, Leadership, Structures*. Edinburgh: Scottish Football Association.

Mechikoff, R. and Estes, S. (1993) *A History and Philosophy of Sport and Physical Education*, Madison, WI: Brown and Benchmark.

Nicholson, M. (2007) *Sport and the Media: Managing the Nexus*, London: Elsevier Butterworth-Heinemann.

Norman, W. and MacDonald, C. (2004) 'Getting to the bottom of "triple bottom-line accounting"', *Business Ethics Quarterly*, 14(2): 243–262.

Northouse, P.G. (2010) *Leadership: Theory and Practice*, 5th edition, Thousand Oaks, CA: Sage.

O'Brien, D. and Slack, T. (2003) 'An analysis of change in an organizational field: The professionalization of English Rugby Union', *Journal of Sport Management*, 17(4): 417–448.

Office of Tony Blair (2009) 'Tony Blair and Beyond Sport working to show how sport can replace enmity with friendship', 27 March, Office of Tony Blair, Sports Foundation, Speeches, online, available at: www.tonyblairoffice.org/speeches/entry/tony-blair-and-beyond-sport-working-to-show-how-sport-can-replace-enmity-wi.

OECD (Organisation for Economic Co-operation and Development) (2004) *Principles of Corporate Governance*, Paris: OECD.

Pattavino, P. and Pye, G. (1994) *Sport in Cuba: The Diamond in the Rough*, Pittsburgh, PA: University of Pittsburgh Press.

Pfeffer, J. and Salancik, G. (1978) *The External Control of Organizations: A Resource Dependence Perspective*, New York: Harper & Row.

Pitt, L., Parent, M., Berthon, P. and Steyn, P. (2010) 'Event sponsorship and ambush marketing: Lessons from the Beijing Olympics', *Business Horizons*, 53(3): 281–290.

Porter, M. (1980) *Competitive Strategy*, New York: The Free Press.

Porter, M. (1985) *Competitive Strategy: Creating and Sustaining Superior Performance*, New York: Simon & Schuster.

Productivity Commission (2003) *Social Capital: Reviewing the Concept and its Policy Implications*, Canberra: Commonwealth of Australia.

Productivity Commission (2010) *Contribution of the Not-for-Profit sector*, Canberra: Commonwealth of Australia.

Putnam, R. (2000) *Bowling Alone: The Collapse and Revival of American Community*, New York: Simon & Schuster.

Quinn, K. (2009) *Sports and their Fans: The History, Economics and Culture of the Relationship between Spectator and Sport*, Jefferson, NC: McFarland and Co.

Quirk, J. and Fort, R. (1992) *Pay Dirt: The Business of Professional Team Sports*, Princeton, NJ: Princeton University Press.

Racing Victoria (2009) *Racing to 2020: Racing Victoria's Vision for the Victorian Thoroughbred racing industry*, Melbourne: Racing Victoria Limited.

Rigauer, B. (1981) *Sport and Work*, New York: Columbia University Press.

Riordan, J. (1977) *Sport in Soviet Society*, Cambridge: Cambridge University Press.

Robbins, S. and Barnwell, N. (2002) *Organisation Theory*, Frenchs Forest: Pearson Education Australia.

Robbins, S.P., Millett, B. and Waters-Marsh, T. (2004) *Organizational Behaviour*, 4th edition, Sydney: Pearson Education.

Robinson, L. (2004) 'Human resource management', in L. Robinson, *Managing Public Sport and Leisure Services*, London: Routledge.

Rowe, D. (1999) *Sport, Culture and the Media: The Unruly Trinity*, Buckingham, PA: Open University Press.

Rowe, D. and G. Callum (2010) 'Sport, media, and consumption in Asia: A merchandised milieu', *American Behavioral Scientist, 53*(10): 1530–1548.

Sandy, R., Sloane, P.J. and Rosentraub, M. (2004) *The Economics of Sport: An International Perspective*, Basingstoke: Palgrave Macmillan.

Schein, E. (2010) *Organizational Culture and Leadership*, 4th edition, San Francisco, CA: Jossey-Bass.

Schermerhorn, J.R. (2010) *Management*, 11th edition, Hoboken, NJ: Wiley and Sons.

Schermerhorn, J.R., Hunt, J.G. and Osborne, R.N. (1994) *Managing Organizational Behaviour*, 5th edition, Brisbane: John Wiley & Sons, Inc.

Schroeder, P.J. (2010) 'Changing team culture: The perspectives of ten successful head coaches', *Journal of Sport Behavior, 33*(1): 63–88.

SCORS (Standing Committee on Recreation and Sport) Working Party on Management Improvement (1997) *Report to the Standing Committee on Recreation and Sport July 1997*, Canberra: SCORS Working Party on Management Improvement.

Senge, P. (1990) *The Fifth Discipline*, New York: Currency Doubleday.

Shilbury, D., Westerbeek, H., Quick, S. ad Funk, D. (2009) *Strategic Sport Marketing*, 3rd edition, Sydney: Allen & Unwin.

Shropshire, K. (1995) *The Sports Franchise Game*, Philadelphia, PA: University of Pennsylvania Press.

Shropshire, K. and Davis, T. (2008) *The Business of Sports Agents*, 2nd edition, Philadelphia PA : University of Pennsylvania Press.

Slack, T. (1997) *Understanding Sport Organizations: The Application of Organization Theory*, Champaign, IL: Human Kinetics.

Slack, T. and Parent, M. (2006) *Understanding Sport Organizations: The Application of Organization Theory*, 2nd edition, Champaign, IL: Human Kinetics.

Slesinger, L.H. (1991) *Self-assessment for Nonprofit Governing Boards*, Washington, DC: National Centre for Nonprofit Boards.

SLSA (Surf Life Saving Australia) (2010) *Annual Report: 2009–2010*, Sydney: SLSA.

Smit, B. (2007) *Pitch Invasion: Adidas, Puma, and the Making of Modern Sport*, London: Penguin Books.

Smith, A. (2008) *Introduction to Sport Marketing*, Oxford: Elsevier Butterworth-Heinemann.

Smith, A. and Shilbury, D. (2004) 'Mapping cultural dimensions in Australian sporting organizations', *Sport Management Review, 7*(2): 133–165.

Smith, A. and Stewart, B. (1999) *Sports Management: A Guide to Professional Practice*, Sydney: Allen & Unwin.

Smith, A. and Stewart, B. (2010) 'The special features of sport revisited', *Sport Management Review*, 10(1): 1–11.

Smith, A., Stewart, B. and Haimes, G. (2012) *Organizational Culture and Identity: Sport, Symbols and Success*, New York: Nova Science Publishers.

Soares, J. and Correia, A. (2009) 'Factors and focuses in the strategic decisions of sporting organisations: Empirical evidence in sports associations', *International Journal of Sport Management and Marketing, 5*(3): 338–354.

Sport England (2011a) *Clubmark Factsheet*, London: Sport England.

References

Sport England (2011b) *Sport Makers Fact Sheet*, London: Sport England.

Statistics Canada (2004) *Cornerstones of Community: Highlights of the National Survey of Nonprofit and Voluntary Organizations*, Ottowa: Statistics Canada.

Stebbins, R. (2007) *Serious Leisure*, New Brunswick, NJ: Transactions Publications.

Stevens, J. (2006) 'The Canadian Hockey Association merger and the emergence of the Amateur Sport Enterprise', *Journal of Sport Management*, 20(1): 74–101.

Stewart, B. (2007a) *Sport Funding and Finance*, Oxford: Elsevier Butterworth-Heinemann.

Stewart, B. (ed.) (2007b) *The Games Are Not the Same: The Political Economy of Football in Australia*, Carlton: Melbourne University Press.

Stewart, R. (1989) 'The nature of sport under capitalism and its relationship to the capitalist labour process', *Sporting Traditions*, 6(1): 43–61.

Stewart, R., Nicholson, M., Smith, A. and Westerbeek, H. (2004) *Australian Sport: Better by Design? The Evolution of Australian Sport Policy*, London: Routledge.

Szymanksi, S. (2009) *Playbooks and Chequebooks: An Introduction to the Economics of Modern Sport*, Princeton, NJ: Princeton University Press.

Szymanski, S. and Kuypers, T. (2000) *Winners and Losers: The Business Strategy of Football*, London: Penguin.

Taylor, T., Doherty, A. and McGraw, P. (2008) *Managing People in Sport Organizations: A Strategic Human Resource Management Perspective*, London: Elsevier Butterworth-Heinemann.

Theodoraki, E.I. and Henry, I.P. (1994) 'Organizational structures and contexts in British national governing bodies of sport', *International Review for the Sociology of Sport*, 29(3): 243–263.

Thibault, L., Slack, T. and Hinings, B. (1991) 'Professionalism, structures and systems: The impact of professional staff on voluntary sport organizations', *International Review for the Sociology of Sport*, 26(2): 83–98.

Thomas, R.J. (2008) *Crucibles of Leadership*, Boston, MA: Harvard Business School.

Tricker, R.I. (1984) *Corporate Governance*, London: Gower.

Tricker, R.I. (1993) 'Corporate governance: The new focus of interest', *Corporate Governance*, 1(1): 1–3.

van der Graaf, A. (1994) 'Service quality and sport centres', *European Journal for Sport Management*, 1(1): 42–57.

Volunteering Australia (2004) *Snapshot 2004: Volunteering Report Card*, Melbourne: Volunteering Australia.

Westerbeek, H. and Smith, A. (2005) *Business Leadership and the Lessons from Sport*, London: Palgrave Macmillan.

Wexley, K.N. and Yukl, G.A. (1984) *Organizational Behavior and Personnel Psychology*, revised edition, Homewood, IL: Richard D. Irwin, Inc.

Whitson, D. (1998) 'Circuits of promotion: Media, marketing and the globalization of sport', in L. Wenner (ed.) *MediaSport*, London: Routledge, pp. 57–72.

Williams, R. (1998) *Performance Management: Perspectives on Employee Performance*, London: Thomson Business Press.

Zimbalist, A. (2006) *The Bottom Line: Observations and Arguments on the Sports Business*, Philadelphia, PA: Temple University Press.

Index

Index